THE IRISH ESTABLISHMENT

The Irish Establishment
1879–1914

FERGUS CAMPBELL

OXFORD
UNIVERSITY PRESS

OXFORD

UNIVERSITY PRESS

Great Clarendon Street, Oxford OX2 6DP

Oxford University Press is a department of the University of Oxford.
It furthers the University's objective of excellence in research, scholarship,
and education by publishing worldwide in

Oxford New York

Auckland Cape Town Dar es Salaam Hong Kong Karachi
Kuala Lumpur Madrid Melbourne Mexico City Nairobi
New Delhi Shanghai Taipei Toronto

With offices in

Argentina Austria Brazil Chile Czech Republic France Greece
Guatemala Hungary Italy Japan Poland Portugal Singapore
South Korea Switzerland Thailand Turkey Ukraine Vietnam

Oxford is a registered trade mark of Oxford University Press
in the UK and in certain other countries

Published in the United States
by Oxford University Press Inc., New York

© Fergus Campbell 2009

British Library Cataloguing in Publication Data

Data available

Library of Congress Cataloging in Publication Data

Campbell, Fergus J. M.
The Irish establishment, 1879–1914 / Fergus Campbell.
p. cm.
Includes index.
ISBN 978–0–19–923322–9 (hbk.)
1. Elite (Social sciences)—Ireland—History—19th century. 2. Gentry—Ireland—
History—19th century. 3. Social classes—Ireland—History—19th century. 4. Power
(Social sciences)—Ireland—History—19th century. I. Title.
HN400.3.Z9E433 2009
305.5′20941509034—dc22   2009019290

Typeset by Laserwords Private Limited, Chennai, India
Printed in Great Britain
on acid-free paper by the
MPG Books Group, Bodmin and King's Lynn

ISBN 978–0–19–923322–9

3 5 7 9 10 8 6 4 2

For Padraic

Preface

On the morning of 7 December 1921, according to Breandán O hEithir's imaginary alternative history of twentieth-century Ireland, the priest of a small west Cork parish discussed the signing of the Anglo-Irish Treaty (that took place the previous evening) with the local blacksmith:

'Good morning, Con. A great day for Ireland, thank God!'

'Good morning, Father,' muttered the blacksmith, without any enthusiasm whatever. 'I suppose it's a great day for some.'

'Oh, come, come, my good man! Cheer up and celebrate Ireland's freedom. The best days are yet to come.'

'Not for me they aren't, Father. It was the gentry kept me going and what's left of them are going to leave the country now. Ireland may be free but I'm ruined.'

'Now Con, my dear man, will you listen to your parish priest. Everything will be all right. We're going to have our own gentry now. Believe you me.'

And with these honeyed words of hope the parish priest sailed off to his breakfast. The blacksmith shook his head slowly and silently, but as he turned to go he was clearly heard to mutter,

'Our own gentry! We will in our arse have our own gentry.'[1]

This book explores the nature and composition of the 'gentry' and wider 'establishment' that ruled Ireland during the final years of the Act of Union (1801–1921) and considers why they lost power during the revolutionary events that resulted in the signing of the Anglo-Irish Treaty. There were many different sections of society who, like the Cork blacksmith, felt that they would lose out as a result of the end of British rule in Ireland, but there were many more who felt that they would gain from the end of the old regime and the beginning of the new one, and this book will attempt to explain why this was so. Indeed, from the vantage point of the beginning of the twenty-first century, it is clear that the blacksmith was mistaken in his belief that Ireland would not create its own native gentry, and the priest's remarks now seem remarkably prescient. The Irish countryside is currently being transformed by the building of new 'Big Houses', many of which are furnished with paintings and furniture that once graced the houses of the old Anglo-Irish gentry; and it may be that the values, manners, and culture of the old establishment have—in some cases—been appropriated by the new millionaires that have been created by the 'Celtic Tiger' economy of the last decade. Perhaps the experience of the old establishment which ruled

---

[1] Breandán O hEithir, *The Begrudger's Guide to Irish Politics* (Dublin, 1986), 1–2.

Ireland between the Land War (1879–81) and the Great War (1914–18) and is discussed in this book resonates still in independent Ireland almost a century after its demise.

Although this book was completed while I worked as a lecturer at Newcastle University, most of the writing was done during one semester of leave from teaching (in the winter of 2005) and four long summers (2005, 2006, 2007, and 2008) spent in my grandparents' old house at Colmanstown in county Galway. Indeed, this book has been influenced by what might be called a Galway school of Irish history-writing and I have been variously encouraged, inspired, and supported by a group of scholars who are either natives of the county or academics and visiting academics at the National University of Ireland, Galway: Andrew Shields, Tony Varley, John Cunningham, Eugene Hynes, Gearoid Ó Tuathaigh, Nicholas Canny, James Donnelly, Charlie Maguire, Caitriona Clear, and Gerard Moran. Irish history is usually written in the 'high politics' style, but the members of this school have been more interested in writing the social and cultural history of Ireland, and in exploring the lives and beliefs of all of the people who lived on the island in the past.

Another Galway native has influenced this book more than any other person: my uncle, Padraic Jordan, has taught me a great deal about the nature of power, about Irish history, and about life in general, and this book really would not have been completed without his support and encouragement over the last five years. I dedicate this book to him with love, respect, and gratitude. All of the Jordans of Colmanstown have been enormously supportive of me over the last five years, and I am also grateful to my aunt, Catherine, for many acts of kindness and to Paul, Marie, Martina, and Michael for discussion, friendship and making great rock 'n' roll music. The rest of my family have also been a source of continued love and support. My mother, Margaret, has been extremely supportive of me during the writing of this book and I am grateful to both her and my late father, Sean, for teaching me the importance of history and for first inspiring my interest in Ireland. My brother, Sean, discussed this book with me at length and made important conceptual suggestions at key points, and I am grateful to him for a lifetime of friendship. My sister-in-law, Leah Loughnane, has also always been extremely encouraging and understanding and I am grateful to her for her support. Alison Stenning lights up my life with love and laughter and I am deeply grateful to her for making everything I do—including the writing of this book—better and easier. I am grateful to the Gallery Press for permission to reproduce Michael Hartnett's 'A Visit to Castletown House', and I am grateful to the National Gallery of Ireland for permission to reproduce Rose Barton's 'Going to the levee at Dublin Castle' on the cover.

Some of the research for this book was conducted while I was Leverhulme Research Fellow in the Department of Economic and Social History at The Queen's University, Belfast between 1997 and 2000 working on the project

'Irish Society on the Eve of the Great War'. I am grateful to the Leverhulme Trust for their support and also to Ken Brown and the late David Johnson for their guidance and encouragement. I am grateful to Newcastle University for one semester of research leave, and for a small grant from the Arts and Humanities Research Fund, and to my colleagues in the School of Historical Studies for providing a happy and stimulating environment in which to teach and write history. In particular, I have learned a great deal about elites in Britain, Ireland, and elsewhere, from discussions with my colleagues Joan Allen, Scott Ashley, Martin Farr, Tim Kirk, Matt Perry, Matt Rendle, and David Saunders. In the School office, I am particularly grateful to Liz Bell, Janice Cummin, Sandra Fletcher, Pat Harrison, and Rachel Nesbitt for their generous support and assistance. Lorna Scammell at Newcastle schooled me in the art of database construction and I am grateful to her for designing the database on which much of the statistical material in this book rests, and for asking interesting questions along the way. I have been lucky to have taught some excellent students at both the National University of Ireland, Maynooth (in both Maynooth and Kilkenny) and Newcastle University, and I have learned much from their questions and insights. In particular, I am grateful to my dissertation students who have worked on subjects related to this book: Philip Sheppard, John McCrory, Ben Neumark, and Michael Dennis. The staff of the Robinson Library at Newcastle University have been enormously helpful and I am especially grateful to the inter library loans team.

At Oxford University Press I am grateful to Rupert Cousens and Seth Cayley for commissioning the book and for guiding it towards publication. The anonymous readers' reports were also extremely valuable and helpful and I am grateful to each of the four readers for them. Melanie Johnstone, Paul Smith, and Francesca Warren oversaw the final publication of the book and Javier Kalhat compiled the index.

I am grateful to many historians of Ireland who have helped me in innumerable ways during the completion of this book and in particular I would like to thank Stephen Ball, Andy Bielenberg, Penny Bonsall, Bernard Canning, Vincent Comerford, Colin Coulter, John Cunningham, Paul Dillon, Kieran Flanagan, Roy Foster, Brian Griffin, Peter Hart, Jim Herlihy, Eugene Hynes, Alvin Jackson, Ewan Knox, Emmet Larkin, Stephen Lee, William Lowe, Charlie Maguire, Patrick Maume, David Miller, Philip Ollerenshaw, Chris Reid, Willie Smyth, W. A. Thomas, William Vaughan, and Kathleen Villiers-Tuthill. My greatest intellectual debts are to my friends Tony Varley and Andrew Shields, both of whom discussed the book with me at length, read drafts of every chapter, and encouraged me and inspired me throughout the writing of this book. Put simply, I could not have written the book without their generous support. Three fine historians of Ireland—Tony Hepburn, Dave Johnson, and Larry McBride—did not live to see this book completed and I owe them all thanks for their friendship, generosity, and scholarship. In particular, Larry went well beyond the call of duty by giving me his notes on the obituaries of Irish civil servants and discussing this project with me in an extensive email correspondence between 1999 and 2001. I gave a number of papers to conferences and seminars based on some of my preliminary findings for this book at Belfast, Maynooth, Newcastle upon Tyne, New York City, Oxford, and Sunderland and I would like to thank the participants at those sessions for their comments and questions. Finally, I would like to salute three teachers who inspired me while I was a schoolboy at the Newman comprehensive school in Carlisle: Jim Arnold, Barrie Day, and Richard Reardon were all extraordinary teachers—among the best I have ever had—and I am deeply grateful to them for their kindness, for their genius as educators, and for setting me on the right track.

F.C.
Newcastle upon Tyne
15 December 2008

Contents

List of Tables

List of Abbreviations

ACIS	American Conference of Irish Studies
BL	British Library
BMH	Bureau of Military History
CBS	Christian Brothers' School
CDB	Congested Districts Board
CO	Colonial Office
DATI	Department of Agriculture and Technical Instruction
DNB	Oxford Dictionary of National Biography
GPO	General Post Office
INWR	Irish North Western Railway
IPP	Irish Parliamentary Party
IRB	Irish Republican Brotherhood
ITGWU	Irish Transport and General Workers' Union
LNWR	London and North Western Railway
NAL	National Archives, London
RIC	Royal Irish Constabulary
RM	Resident Magistrate
UIL	United Irish League
UVF	Ulster Volunteer Force

A Visit to Castletown House
for Nora Graham

The avenue was green and long, and green
light pooled under the fernheads; a jade screen
could not let such liquid light in, a sea
at its greenest self could not pretend to be
so emerald. Men had made this landscape
from a mere secreting wood: knuckles bled
and bones broke to make this awning drape
a fitting silk upon its owner's head.

The house was lifted by two pillared wings
out of its bulk of solid chisellings
and flashed across the chestnut-marshalled lawn
a few lit windows on a bullock bawn.
The one-way windows of the empty rooms
reflected meadows, now the haunt
of waterbirds: where hawtrees were in bloom,
and belladonna, a poisonous plant.

A newer gentry in their quaint attire
looked at maps depicting alien shire
and city, town and fort: they were his seed,
that native who had taken coloured beads
disguised as chandeliers of vulgar glass
and made a room to suit a tasteless man
—a graceful art come to a sorry pass—
painted like some demented tinker's van.

But the music that was played in there—
that had grace, a nervous grace laid bare,
Tortelier unravelling sonatas
pummelling the instrument that has
the deep luxurious sensual sound,
allowing it no richness, making stars
where moons would be, choosing to expound
music as passionate as guitars.

I went into the calmer, gentler hall
in the wineglassed, chattering interval:
there was the smell of rose and woodsmoke there.
I stepped into the gentler evening air

and saw black figures dancing on the lawn,
Eviction, Droit de Seigneur, Broken Bones:
and heard the crack of ligaments being torn
and smelled the clinging blood upon the stones.

Michael Hartnett, *Collected Poems* (Oldcastle: The Gallery Press, 2001).

Introduction

I first had the idea for this book a decade ago in November 1998 when the *Observer* newspaper included a supplement on 'The Power 300'. This list examined the social background of the 300 people whom a panel of experts had decided were the most powerful and influential people in British society in 1998. As the newspaper explained:

There are 300 people who, more than any others, exert daily influence on the lives of people in Britain. They're not necessarily rich or famous. They may not even be the best in their field. What they do share—as they are brought together today in the first definitive list of its kind, published exclusively by the *Observer*—is something far more important. Power.

The 'Power 300' included lots of well-known people—the British Prime Minister (ranked number 1) and the Queen (30), for instance—but also lots of less-well-known power brokers, including Sir Richard Greenbury, the chairman and chief executive of Marks and Spencer (18), David Yelland, the editor of the *Sun* (73), Andrew Turnbull, the permanent secretary at the Treasury (151), and Thomas Bingham, the Lord Chief Justice (166).[1] At that time, I was writing a book about the ordinary men and women involved in popular political activity in the west of Ireland between the death of Parnell (in 1891) and the signing of the Anglo-Irish Treaty (in 1921), but it struck me that the most powerful individuals in late nineteenth- and early twentieth-century Ireland were almost as unknown as the labourers and small farmers who were involved in agrarian and nationalist agitations, and I began to wonder who the equivalents of Greenbury, Yelland, Turnbull, and Bingham were in Victorian and Edwardian Ireland.[2] The result of those ruminations is this book, which examines the social background of the 1,200 or so most powerful people who—arguably—'ruled' Ireland during the three decades before 1914, and considers how and why the composition of Ireland's 'establishment' changed between the end of the Land War (1879–81) and the beginning of the Great War (1914–18).

In adopting this approach to modern Irish history I have been influenced by some important developments in the writing of British social history since the

---

[1] 'The Power 300', *Observer*, 1 Nov. 1998.

[2] My first book was later published as *Land and Revolution: Nationalist Politics in the West of Ireland, 1891–1921* (Oxford, 2005).

1960s. Although Eric Hobsbawm and E. P. Thompson are more often identified with writing the history of the oppressed, they have both also emphasized the importance of a social history of the powerful.[3] Famously, E. P. Thompson reminded us that: 'we cannot have love without lovers, nor deference without squires and labourers', nor class without classes, so that we must investigate the nature of, and the relationship between, different classes.[4] Similarly, Hobsbawm explained that a history of the working class must also aspire to be 'the history of society as a whole . . . Research on class must . . . involve the rest of society of which it is a part. Slave-owners cannot be understood without slaves, and without the non-slave sectors of society'.[5] More recent historians of elites—among them W. D. Rubinstein and Richard Trainor—have built on the earlier work of Thompson and Hobsbawm by looking in more detail at the nature of the powerful in nineteenth- and twentieth-century Britain.[6] Indeed, since the early 1980s—and perhaps inspired by the impact of Thatcherism on British society—a largely sympathetic social history of the powerful in modern Britain has been written. However, the writing of social history in Ireland is not in as advanced a state as that in Britain, continental Europe, or the United States, and there are—as yet—relatively few studies of either the powerful or the powerless in Ireland. This book is an attempt to rectify that state of affairs by exploring the composition, ideas, and activities of the powerful in late nineteenth- and early twentieth-century Ireland, and—in that respect—this book complements my earlier attempt to write the history of the Irish Revolution (1916–23) from below.[7] I have been influenced in the writing of this book, therefore, by a number of important works on elites in Britain, and notably the studies conducted by Cannadine, Perkin, Rubinstein, and Stanworth and Giddens.[8] Using these (and other) works I have also considered the extent to which the experience and composition of elite groups in Ireland was similar to or different from that in Britain.

Having outlined these gaps in Irish historical writing, it also needs to be emphasized that there are a number of important historical works on elites in Ireland upon which this study builds. Indeed, I have identified four strands of historical writing in Ireland that have influenced the writing of this book. First,

---

[3] Prior to these developments in social history, historians often examined the experience of individual members of elite groups but not the composition and nature of elite groups as a whole.

[4] E. P. Thompson, *The Making of the English Working Class* (London, 1963), 8.

[5] Eric Hobsbawm, *On History* (London, 1997), 115.

[6] W. D. Rubinstein, *Elites and the Wealthy in Modern British History: Essays in Social and Economic History* (Brighton, 1987), 11–12; Richard Trainor, *Black Country Elites: The Exercise of Authority in an Industrialized Area, 1830–1900* (Oxford, 1993), 8.

[7] Campbell, *Land and Revolution.*

[8] David Cannadine, *The Decline and Fall of the British Aristocracy* (New Haven, Conn. and London, 1990); Harold Perkin, *The Rise of Professional Society: England since 1880* (London, 1989); Rubinstein, *Elites and the Wealthy in Modern British History*; and Philip Stanworth and Anthony Giddens, *Elites and Power in British Society* (Cambridge, 1974).

there are a number of important studies of Irish political parties during the late nineteenth and early twentieth centuries. These works have been influenced by Lewis Namier whose *Structure of Politics at the Accession of George III* (London, 1929) pioneered what has become known as the prosopographical approach to the study of political history. Put simply, Namier collected systematic biographical information about MPs in order to establish a collective biography of the political elite. He then used these data to explore the social and economic motivations that may have underpinned individual and collective political behaviour.[9] This approach to political history subsequently became one of the dominant approaches adopted by British political and social historians to a variety of historical problems, and it is no surprise that it was imported into Ireland in the early 1950s. F. S. L. Lyons examined the social composition of the Irish Parliamentary Party in a Namierite fashion, and he was later emulated in this approach by studies of the Irish Parliamentary Party and other parties conducted by Conor Cruise O'Brien, Alan O'Day, John H. Whyte, Alvin Jackson, Paul Bew, Patrick Maume, and Andrew Shields.[10] My study of the political elite in Ireland between 1879 and 1914 (in Chapter 4) builds on the work of these historians.

A later but equally critical development in the evolution of the study of elites in Ireland was the publication of three seminal articles by Emmet Larkin in the late 1960s and the early 1970s.[11] These articles explored the expansion of the Irish Catholic Church in the nineteenth century and—perhaps more importantly—the development of the Catholic middle class as a social and political force in Ireland. Larkin later published a series of studies of the 'high politics' of the Catholic church in Ireland between the 1750s and the 1890s, and his work has influenced other studies of religious elites in Ireland by Connolly, Miller, and Yates.[12] Moreover, one of the questions which Larkin investigated in his early articles was the extent to which there was Catholic social mobility in nineteenth-century Ireland, and this issue was later taken up by one of his most talented students, Lawrence McBride.[13] In *The Greening of Dublin Castle*,

---

[9] Lawrence Stone, *The Past and the Present Revisited* (London, 1987), Ch. 2.

[10] F. S. L. Lyons, *The Irish Parliamentary Party, 1890–1910* (London, 1951); Conor Cruise O'Brien, *Parnell and his Party, 1880–90* (Oxford, 1957); Alan O'Day, *The English Face of Irish Nationalism* (Dublin, 1977); John H. Whyte, *The Independent Irish Party, 1850–9* (Oxford, 1958); Alvin Jackson, *The Ulster Party: Irish Unionists in the House of Commons, 1884–1911* (Oxford, 1989); Paul Bew, *Ideology and the Irish Question: Ulster Unionism and Irish Nationalism, 1912–1916* (Oxford, 1994); Patrick Maume, *The Long Gestation: Irish Nationalist Life, 1891–1918* (Dublin, 1999); and Andrew Shields, *The Irish Conservative Party, 1852–1868: Land, Politics and Religion* (Dublin, 2007).

[11] These articles were later published together in Emmet Larkin, *The Historical Dimensions of Irish Catholicism* (Dublin, 1997).

[12] Sean Connolly, *Religion and Society in Nineteenth-century Ireland* (Dundalk, 1985); David Miller, *Church, State and Nation in Ireland, 1898–1921* (Dublin, 1973); and Nigel Yates, *The Religious Condition of Ireland, 1770–1850* (Oxford, 2006).

[13] See Emmet Larkin, 'Economic Growth, Capital Investment, and the Roman Catholic Church in Nineteenth-century Ireland', *American Historical Review*, 72 (1967), 870–3.

McBride claimed that there was a 'greening' process taking place at the higher levels of the Irish Civil Service between 1891 and 1921 such that there was an increased representation of Irish-born Catholics gaining influential positions in the Irish administration. McBride's research—conducted in the mid-1970s but not published until 1991—has influenced a number of other administrative historians including O'Halpin and Maguire, as well as historians of the Royal Irish Constabulary (Griffin, Lowe, and Malcolm) and of the Resident Magistracy (Bonsall).[14] In addition, the work of R. B. McDowell on both the Church of Ireland and the Irish administration has also provided a valuable structural analysis of Irish Protestantism and the Irish Civil Service.[15] This strand of religious and administrative history-writing provides the starting point for my discussion of religious and administrative elites in Ireland discussed in Chapters 2, 3, and 6.

The influential work of Lyons and Larkin can be described as emerging from what might be termed the 'high politics' approach to history writing but the other two strands of historical writing upon which this study builds are more influenced by developments in sociology and the wider social sciences. Kieran Flanagan's doctoral dissertation was a critical contribution to the development of the study of elites in Ireland because it explored for the first time the relationship between educational provision and social mobility in nineteenth-century Ireland, particularly with regard to recruiting to the Indian Civil Service.[16] Flanagan's regrettably unpublished study was completed in the Department of Sociology at Sussex University in 1978, and it influenced a number of subsequent works (by Hutchinson, Garvin, and Paseta) which further developed his discussion of educational provision, social mobility, and the way in which blocks on Catholic social mobility may have been one of the causes of the Irish Revolution (1916–23).[17] Garvin's work also provided an analysis of the social composition and world view of the republican elite that took power in Ireland after the Easter

---

[14] Lawrence McBride, *The Greening of Dublin Castle: The Transformation of Bureaucratic and Judicial Personnel in Ireland, 1892–1922* (Washington, DC, 1991); Eunan O'Halpin, *The Decline of the Union: British Government in Ireland, 1892–1920* (Dublin, 1988); Martin Maguire, *The Civil Service and the Revolution in Ireland, 1912–1938* (Manchester, 2008); Penny Bonsall, *The Irish RMs: The Resident Magistrates in the British Administration of Ireland* (Dublin, 1997); Elizabeth Malcolm, *The Irish Policeman, 1822–1922: A Life* (Dublin, 2006); William Lowe, 'Irish Constabulary Officers, 1837–1922: Profile of a Profession', *Irish Economic and Social History*, 22 (2005), 19–46; William J. Lowe and Elizabeth L. Malcolm, 'The Domestication of the Royal Irish Constabulary, 1836–1922', *Irish Economic and Social History*, 19 (1992), 27–48; and Brian Griffin, 'The Irish Police, 1836–1914: A Social History', PhD thesis (Loyola University, Chicago, 1990).

[15] R. B. McDowell, *The Irish Administration, 1801–1914* (London, 1964); id., *The Church of Ireland, 1869–1969* (London, 1975). See also Donald Harman Akenson, *The Church of Ireland: Ecclesiastical Reform and Revolution, 1800–1885* (New Haven, Conn. and London, 1971).

[16] Kieran Flanagan, 'The Rise and Fall of the Celtic Ineligible: Competitive Examinations for the Irish and Indian Civil Services in Relation to the Educational and Occupational Structure of Ireland, 1853–1921', DPhil (University of Sussex, 1978).

[17] John Hutchinson, *The Dynamics of Cultural Nationalism: The Gaelic Revival and the Creation of the Irish Nation State* (London, 1987); Tom Garvin, *Nationalist Revolutionaries in Ireland,*

Rising, while Paseta reconstructed the behaviour and beliefs of the university-educated Catholic Home Rule elite that the new republican elite allegedly replaced.[18] Finally, this study has been influenced by developments in Irish social and economic history dating from the 1970s. In particular, revisionist work on the Irish landlord class (by Donnelly, Dooley, Solow, and Vaughan)—discussed in detail in Chapter 1—provides the basis for my study of the landed elite; and pioneering studies of Irish economic and business history (by Bielenberg, Ó Gráda, and Ollerenshaw)—discussed in Chapter 5—have influenced my investigations of the Irish business elite.[19]

This book constitutes a departure from the existing literature, however, by providing for the first time a survey of what might be described as 'the Irish establishment' as a whole. By combining a synthesis of the existing literature on each of the elite groups under review with a systematic analysis of the composition of the Irish establishment in 1881 and 1911, this book provides the first examination of who the individuals were who held power in Ireland and how the composition of the establishment changed over time. I have also used a wide range of private papers, memoirs, autobiographies, and biographies to explore—in an ethnographic manner—how members of the Irish establishment acted, thought, and felt. The members of the Irish establishment have been defined as those individuals who wielded a great deal of power on the basis of their control of or access to critical resources (economic, political, religious, and bureaucratic) which meant that their decisions often affected many peoples' lives.[20] This book is largely a study of six elite groups who are examined in separate chapters: landlords (who owned estates of more than 10,000 acres), administrators (members of the Irish office and senior civil servants), upholders of 'law and order' (senior Royal Irish Constabulary officers), members of parliament, religious leaders (bishops of the Church of Ireland and the Catholic church and Presbyterian moderators), and businessmen (the directors of firms valued at more than £200,000). While there are other elite groups that could have been included, this study does include the most influential wielders of economic, political, religious, and bureaucratic power in Irish society

---

1858–1928 (Oxford, 1987); and Senia Paseta, *Before the Revolution: Nationalism, Social Change and Ireland's Catholic Elite* (Cork, 1999).

[18] The hypotheses advanced by Hutchinson, Garvin, and Paseta will be discussed in detail in Conclusion.

[19] James Donnelly, *The Land and the People of Nineteenth-century Cork: The Rural Economy and the Land Question* (London, 1975); Terence Dooley, *The Decline of the Big House in Ireland: A Study of Irish Landed Families* (Dublin, 2001); Barbara L. Solow, *The Land Question and the Irish Economy, 1870–1903* (Cambridge, Mass., 1971); W. E. Vaughan, *Landlords and Tenants in Mid-Victorian Ireland* (Oxford, 1994); Andrew Bielenberg, *Cork's Industrial Revolution, 1780–1880: Development or Decline?* (Cork, 1991); Cormac Ó Gráda, *Ireland: A New Economic History, 1780–1939* (Oxford, 1994); and Philip Ollerenshaw, *Banking in Ireland: The Belfast Banks, 1825–1914* (Manchester, 1987).

[20] Eva Etzioni-Halevy, *The Elite Connection: Problems and Potential of Western Democracy* (Cambridge, 1993), 94.

during the period under review. It might be objected that the personnel of the cultural elite (novelists, playwrights, poets, educationists, and newspaper editors) are not systematically examined in this book, but the influence of their ideas on the way that other members of the elite thought about themselves is considered. The absence of the officers of the British army in Ireland might also be considered a serious omission but the officer commanding the forces in Ireland is included in this study since he was a senior member of the Irish administration. The most serious omission from this book—it could be argued—is an extended discussion of Irish women's role in the establishment. Put simply, there were very few women in any of the elite groups under review—a state of affairs that tells its own story—and in most cases women were formally excluded from positions of power (this was the case among the political, religious, and policing elites). However, there were a small number of women involved in some of the elite groups under review, notably the landed elite and the Irish administration, and they are discussed in detail in Chapters 1 and 2; and—where the evidence allows—I consider the ways in which women were involved in the establishment as well as their observations about it.

My definition of the Irish establishment is based on a positional analysis: in other words, it includes those individuals who by virtue of the formal position which they held—be that political, economic, religious, or administrative—were able to influence critically important decision-making in Irish society during this period. An alternative method of defining who held power would be by a so-called 'decisional analysis' or an examination of how specific decisions were reached, and of who initiated and who vetoed critically important proposals.[21] Broadly speaking, those who held positional power probably also held decisional power but a systematic analysis of how power and decision-making worked in practice would require a different book from the one I have written. I have been more concerned with establishing what kinds of people occupied positions of power rather than with describing the way in which their power worked in practice. I have also largely ignored those individuals who held what might be termed 'informal' power. According to Putnam: 'History is replete with *éminences grises*—men and women of power whispering instructions from the shadows behind the throne.'[22] There were many voices—many of them undoubtedly women's voices—whispering instructions into the ears of the members of the Irish establishment, but this book does not pay much attention to them. Analyses of informal power or of specific decision-making in Ireland during this period must await another book, and another historian.

Can the elite groups discussed in this book be described as an 'Irish estab-lishment'? The term 'establishment' is generally used in Britain to refer to the

---

[21] Robert D. Putnam, *The Comparative Study of Political Elites* (New Jersey, 1976), 15–17.
[22] Ibid. 16.

constellation of elite groups—political, landed, entrepreneurial, religious, and administrative—that join together to become a ruling class composed of individuals who intermarry, socialize, share the same values and beliefs, and run the country more or less as they please.[23] This definition of an 'establishment' fits a little awkwardly on the Irish elite groups included in this study, but it fits none the less. Certainly, many of the landlords, politicians, businessmen, civil servants, senior police officers, and Church of Ireland bishops included in this study routinely met each other both formally and informally at Dublin Castle offices, at vice regal balls, at the House of Commons or the House of Lords, at gentlemen's clubs, at private balls and dinners held in London and Dublin, at county clubs and provincial Big Houses, and on the committees of the various charities and universities and schools which many of them also ran. Lady Augusta Gregory, the wife of a Galway landlord, as well as a playwright, folklore collector, and director of the Abbey theatre, was at the centre of one of the many social networks of which the Irish establishment was composed.[24] When prominent members of British and Irish society visited her Big House at Coole Park she insisted that they sign one of her fans, and they demonstrate that her visitors included Prime Ministers (Gladstone and Asquith), Chief Secretaries (George Otto Trevelyan), landlords (the Marquess of Dufferin and Ava), politicians (Lord Randolph Churchill), visiting artists (Henry James and Mark Twain), as well as home-grown talent (J. M. Synge and W. B. Yeats).[25] It is likely that many other landlords, politicians, and senior professionals hosted similar dinner parties and social events that also gathered together the members of the Irish establishment. All of this official and social interaction undoubtedly created a sense of 'establishment' consciousness, and suggests that there was a socially unified Irish establishment that was largely responsible for ruling Ireland during this period. But—in many respects—this was largely a Protestant establishment because Irish society at the end of the nineteenth-century was profoundly divided along sectarian lines. Even so, some Catholic civil servants, police officers, and businessmen were also the members of gentlemen's clubs in Dublin and they would have met their Protestant colleagues at the Royal St George Yacht club at Kingstown or at the vice regal balls and Dublin Castle social events to which they were invited.[26]

[23] 'The Power 300', *Observer*, 1 Nov. 1998.

[24] Lady Augusta Gregory was the youngest daughter of Dudley Persse, who owned an estate of 12,785 acres in Galway, and married Sir William Gregory, who owned an estate of 4,893 acres in Galway in 1881.

[25] Colin Smythe, *A Guide to Coole Park, Co. Galway: Home of Lady Gregory* (London, 2003), 57.

[26] The St Patrick's Ball held at Dublin Castle on 17 Mar. 1887, for instance, was attended by a large number of peers and titled gentry, local office holders (lord lieutenants and deputy lieutenants), landowners, senior civil servants, senior police officers, army officers, judges, doctors, and businessmen (see *Irish Times*, 18 Mar. 1887). A valentine's dinner hosted by the Lord Lieutenant at Dublin Castle in 1905 was also attended by peers and titled gentry, landowners, senior civil servants, former MPs, businessmen, and educationists (see ibid. 15 Feb. 1905). It is worth pointing out that the members of the establishment were recruited from different social classes, but real

Yet it might be objected that the Home Rule MPs and Catholic bishops—also included in this study—cannot be considered as part of an Irish establishment. They did not socialize in the same gentlemen's clubs as the landlords, business-men, and civil servants; they did not generally attend the social gatherings at Dublin Castle; some of them were not even prepared to set foot in Dublin Castle for formal meetings with the Irish administration; and they were constitutional nationalists (rather than Unionists). But the leaders of the Irish Parliamentary Party were involved in advising the government on senior appointments to the police and the Civil Service; they were prepared to meet senior civil servants at private houses in Dublin; and they were asked and agreed to advise the government on its Irish policy. Senior Home Rule MPs might have kept 'the establishment' at arm's length in public, but there is no doubt they were part of the same networks and circles as the senior civil servants and the British political elite. Similarly, the Catholic bishops might not have usually attended social events at Dublin Castle (although Cardinal Paul Cullen did) or joined a yachting club but they were closely allied with the leadership of the Irish Parliamentary Party from at least the 1880s onwards, and prominently involved in advising the government on the provision of education in Ireland from the 1860s.[27] Of course, from one vantage-point even Home Rule was not the prelude to full independence but a way for Ireland to remain a part of the British empire, and, if this definition is accepted, Home Rulers can be regarded as a part of the establishment, rather than as its enemies. The Irish establishment, then, might not have been quite as unified and coherent as its British counterpart—and it might be more useful to think of it is a series of overlapping social networks rather than as a single whole—but all of the elite groups included in this study can be considered as composing an 'establishment'.

To what extent was this 'establishment' Irish? All of the individuals discussed in this book held power in Ireland and to that extent can be regarded as part of an Irish establishment. In addition, the vast majority of power-holders in late nineteenth- and early twentieth-century Ireland had also been born in Ireland and could claim Irishness as their birthright. Of course, there were also some extremely powerful individuals in Ireland who had been born elsewhere: in England, Scotland, and Wales; in continental Europe; in Canada, the United States, and Australia; and even in Latin America. Indeed, the fact that a substantial minority of powerful individuals were British born raises the question of whether parts of the Irish establishment were a colonial or post-colonial (rather than

power remained in the hands of the dominant class, which was—by the end of the nineteenth century—the middle class and especially the business class.

[27] On Cullen at Dublin Castle, see W. E. Vaughan, 'Ireland *c.* 1870' in id. (ed.), *A New History of Ireland*, v *Ireland under the Union*, i *1801–1870* (Oxford, 1989), 737–8. John Healy, Bishop of Clonfert, 1884–1903 and Archbishop of Tuam, 1903–18, attended Summerhill college at Athlone at the same time as Sir Antony MacDonnell, who was under secretary for Ireland, 1902–8. See P. J. Joyce, *John Healy: Archbishop of Tuam* (Dublin, 1931), 6.

native) establishment, and this point will be discussed in the conclusion. It is certainly the case, however, that most of the landlords, businessmen, civil servants, police officers, bishops, and politicians who dominated Irish society during this period were its native-born sons and daughters.

This book is largely based on a study of almost 1,200 biographies of prominent men and women in Irish society between the end of the Land War (in 1881) and the eve of the Great War (in 1911). I have used censal dates at which to take snapshots of the composition of the Irish establishment to enable the use of manuscript census returns (for 1901 and 1911) in the collection of data, and also to facilitate the comparison of my data with the more general data on social structure contained in the decennial census reports. For all of the 1,200 individuals included in this study, I have compiled information on their birth and death, marriage and family, social origins and inherited economic position, place of residence, education, personal wealth, occupation, religion, and experience of holding office of various kinds. This biographical information was then placed into a historical database containing more than 25,000 separate pieces of information so that the social characteristics of each of the elite groups under review could be analysed and examined in a variety of different ways. I then examined the changing composition of the Irish establishment by examining the social composition of each elite group at two key dates—usually 1881 and 1911—in order to assess the extent to which the composition of the Irish establishment was transformed between these dates.[28] In order to ensure accuracy and to assist with my conceptual and analytical thinking about the data, I alone have been responsible for collecting all of the data, for inputting it into the database, for analysing the data, for developing a conceptual framework, and for writing up my findings in this book. The difficulties of compiling such an extensive research base have—I hope—earned me a few days off in purgatory and I have tried to write the book in a manner that will not leave the reader feeling too overwhelmed by the weight of statistical evidence.

Broadly speaking, 1879 and 1914 have been adopted as the start- and end-dates for this book because this period arguably witnessed a final attempt by the British state to integrate Catholic and nationalist Ireland into the United Kingdom, or at least into the wider British Empire.[29] The Land War of 1879–81 marks the critical starting point for this book because it led to the development of a popular mass movement in Ireland in favour of Home Rule. This mobilization forced the British state to respond to Irish demands with the Liberal Party offering limited Home Rule within the Empire after 1886 and the Conservatives introducing a series of political and social reforms after 1891 with the intention

[28] See Appendix for a discussion of the methodology and sources used in this book.
[29] A similar point is made by R. V. Comerford who argues that the disestablishment of the Church of Ireland in 1869–91 could be seen 'as a new beginning for the [Act of] union'. R. V. Comerford, 'Gladstone's First Irish enterprise, 1864–70', in Vaughan, *A New History of Ireland*, v. 443.

of 'killing Home Rule with kindness'. Both of these initiatives were likely to have an impact on the composition of the Irish establishment partly because one of the strategies adopted by both Liberal and Conservative governments was to appoint Catholics to senior positions in the administration in an attempt to win the support of the Catholic middle class for British rule in Ireland. One of the central questions which this book addresses, then, is the extent to which the progressive policies introduced by the British government during this period transformed the composition of the Irish establishment between 1879 and 1914. By 1914, the Indian summer of British rule in Ireland was over as the Great War set in train a series of revolutionary events that led to the obliteration of Home Rule, the end of the Irish establishment as it was then constructed, and the end of British rule in Ireland.

The central question which this study seeks to answer is: was the Irish establishment between 1879 and 1914 'open' and representative of Irish society or 'closed' and unrepresentative of Irish society? Was a 'greening' of Irish society taking place during this period whereby Irish-born Catholics were becoming more influential and gaining greater power in Irish society? In order to answer these questions, an attempt will be made to quantify the extent to which Irish-born Catholics were able to join the Irish establishment which was still dominated by British and Irish-born Protestants in the post-Famine period. It is worth pointing out that in nineteenth-century Ireland 'Protestant' and 'Catholic' denoted ethnic or ethno-religious affiliations as much as religious identifications. After the Reformation, the British state was distinctively Protestant in character, and after the victory of William of Orange at the Boyne and Aughrim in 1690–1, the British state in Ireland alienated the Catholic majority of the population. During the period of the operation of the penal laws (1690–1829) Irish Catholics were the oppressed majority of the population who were viewed by the state as disloyal while British and Irish-born Protestants were the dominant and ruling group in Irish society. In nineteenth-century Ireland, then, Protestants were regarded as either British or pro-British and they tended to occupy positions of power, while Catholics were regarded by the state as disloyal and were largely excluded from positions of economic, political, or bureaucratic power.[30] During the period under review, then, the terms 'Irish Catholic' and 'Irish Protestant' denoted cultural, ethnic, and often political affiliations as much as they signified religious identifications.

In general terms, all the chapters in this book are organized in the same way. Each chapter begins with a discussion of the history and structure of the particular elite group and the way in which they were recruited. In the next section of each chapter I discuss the composition of that elite group as a whole, and examine the social characteristics of all of the members of that elite group in both 1881

---

[30] Brian Girvin, *From Union to Union: Nationalism, Democracy and Religion in Ireland—Act of Union to EU* (Dublin, 2002), 3–4.

and 1911. In the following section of each chapter, I examine the ways in which the composition of the elite group in question did or did not change between 1881 and 1911. And in the final section of each chapter I try to explain why the composition of the elite group either did or did not change over this period, and consider whether it can be described as an 'open' or 'closed' elite group.

This book also attempts to identify the nature and composition of the Irish establishment in terms of the theoretical literature on elites. Broadly speaking, there are two dominant bodies of theory relating to elites. On the one hand, there are the ideas of the classical elite theorists, Roberto Michels, Gaetano Mosca, and Vilfredo Pareto.[31] These political theorists, who developed their ideas at the same time as the rise of Fascism in Italy, suggest the following five propositions regarding the nature of elites in society. First, that power is always distributed unequally; second, that all societies can be divided into two main groups—the elite and the non-elite; third, that elites are homogenous, unified, self conscious, and share the same values and interests; fourth, that elites are self-recruiting, and tend to be drawn from privileged and exclusive sections of society; and fifth, that the elite is autonomous, all-powerful, and answerable only to itself.[32] In general terms, the classical elite theorists suggest that elites are homogenous, self-perpetuating, and that recruitment is not 'open' to all members of society. By this definition, the members of the elite hold great power over a society which they are not representative of (in terms of their class, ethnicity, and so on), and from which they are largely detached.

An alternative theory of elites—known as democratic elite theory—was developed later in the twentieth century with its origins in the liberal thought of the seventeenth, eighteenth, and nineteenth centuries. In particular, democratic elite theory was informed by the idea that the maintenance of democracy was dependent upon the separation of powers in the state.[33] The democratic elite theorists largely agree with the classical elite theorists that power is distributed unequally in any society, but they counter the classical elite view with the following four propositions. First, that rather than dividing society in a dichotomous manner, it is more useful to propose a three-tier division of elites, sub-elites, and the public. This approach takes into consideration the influence of middle-ranking members of elite groups (sub-elites) on the leadership, and also recognizes the potential influence of the public on elite decision-making. Second, that the elite, far from being homogenous and unified, is actually diverse in its composition, and contains individuals from different social backgrounds, with different belief-systems, who can disagree with one another. Third, that recruiting to the elite is not 'closed' but 'open' to society at large on a meritocratic basis,

[31] Robert Michels, *Political Parties* (London, 1915); Gaetano Mosca, *The Ruling Class* (New York, 1939); and Vilfredo Pareto, *The Mind and Society* (New York, 1935).

[32] Putnam, *Comparative Study of Political Elites*, 2–4.

[33] Etzioni-Halevy, *Elite Connection*, 53–4.

so that the members of the elite are representative of society as a whole. And fourth, that the power of the elite is not unlimited but constrained by pressure from the public, and by checks on elite-power from within the elite itself with one elite group restraining another, for instance.[34] The final aim of this book is to consider which of these models of elite behaviour—that of the classical elite theorists or that of the democratic elite theorists—best fits the data on elites in Ireland between 1879 and 1914.

The classical elite theorists propose that a 'closed' elite that is not representative of the society over which it rules will eventually be overthrown by revolution. Mosca argued that: 'A ruling class is the more prone to fall into errors . . . the more closed it is, actually if not legally, to elements rising from the lower classes.'[35] And he further elaborated that:

When the aptitude to command and to exercise political control is no longer the sole possession of the legal rulers but has become common enough among the people; when outside the ruling class another class has formed which finds itself deprived of power though it does have the capacity to share in the responsibilities of government—then that [regime] has become an obstacle in the path of an elemental force and must, by one way or another, go.[36]

Given that we know that some sections of the Irish establishment as constituted between 1879 and 1914 were destroyed by the revolution, we might assume that the Irish establishment did exclude a newly educated Catholic middle class from positions of power and influence, and that this was one of the causal factors of the Irish Revolution. However, many Irish historians have argued that most members of Irish society were relatively happy with their lives by 1914, and that it was the onset of the Great War that set in motion a turbulent domino effect leading to insurrection, revolution, and the end of the old world order. Most historians of elite groups in Ireland have argued that the Irish establishment was becoming increasingly representative of Catholic and Home Rule opinion by the beginning of the twentieth century. This is the dominant argument advanced in work by McBride, Lowe, Malcolm, Bonsall, and Paseta, and it is a proposition that will be discussed in detail in the final section of this book.[37]

On the evening of 25 May 1914, the six-year-old son of a Catholic police sergeant, and his younger brother, were woken up by their father and taken on an adventure through the streets of Athlone. Patrick Shea, who would later become a senior civil servant in Northern Ireland, wrote in 1981:

I remember being wakened by my father in a dark bedroom, being brought into the brightly-lit kitchen and told to hurry and get dressed for going out . . . As we hurried

---

[34] The definition of democratic elite theory presented here is that of Eva Etzioni-Halevy as outlined in her book, *Elite Connection*, 94–108.

[35] Quot. Putnam, *Comparative Study of Political Elites*, 44.   [36] Quot. ibid. 193.

[37] See McBride, *Greening of Dublin Castle*; Bonsall, *The Irish RMs*; Malcolm, *The Irish Policeman*; Lowe, 'Irish Constabulary Officers: Profile of a Profession'; and Paseta, *Before the Revolution*.

along empty streets, dimly lit by flickering gas lamps, past silent, shuttered shops and dark doorways, Jack and I had to run to keep up with Father's long strides . . . At the top of Connaught Street, where the gas lamps ended, we turned into the Batteries, a sort of town common . . . We clung closer to Father as he led us across the dewy ground . . . As we went up the far slope, leaning forward into the hard, rising ground, we began to hear the dull beating of a drum and the murmuring sound of many voices. Then quite suddenly we were at the top, out of breath and at the end of our journey. In the centre of the wide, grassy arena an enormous fire was burning and around it a great crowd of people was gathered; a boisterous, cheering, talking, laughing assembly of all ages and conditions. Somewhere a brass band was playing an Irish air . . . As we watched, exhilarated and a little frightened, the discordant noises of the crowd began to respond to the rhythm of the band buried somewhere amongst them and suddenly everyone was singing; singing with fervour and passion and joy . . .

A nation once again.

A nation once again.

And Ireland, long a province, be

A nation once again.

This great fire at Athlone was held to celebrate the passing of the third Home Rule Bill in the House of Commons, and the next morning Patrick and Jack told their younger brother Tim about what they had seen the night before and took him to where they had seen the crowds and heard the singing. When they got there they found that the field was now 'silent and deserted. Where the great fire had been there was only a ring of blackened stones . . . of the sights and sounds which had excited and thrilled us, nothing remained'.[38] In Shea's dream-like memory, this celebration of Home Rule almost becomes a kind of apparition—after all, Home Rule would never become a reality—and in a wider sense the possibility of Home Rule haunted the Irish establishment between 1879 and 1914 just as it haunted the imagination of Patrick Shea throughout his life. This book will explore how the phantom of Irish nationalism—both as object of fear and object of desire—shaped the thoughts and actions of the Irish establishment during these years when it still had the potential to become either a nightmare vision or a future reality.

[38] Patrick Shea, *Voices and the Sound of Drums: An Irish Autobiography* (Belfast, 1981), 4–6.

1

Land

In 1930, Elizabeth Bowen inherited the small county Cork estate where she had spent part of her childhood, and *Bowen's Court*, her history and personal memoir of the Bowen family and their estate, was published in 1942. *Bowen's Court* is, at one level, a eulogy for the Big House and family estate that she loved so deeply. At another level, however, the book can be read as an epitaph for the whole system of landholding that vanished from Ireland during the first two decades of the twentieth century. Although Bowen's Court was much smaller than the landed estates owned by the men and women studied in this chapter—and for that reason the landlord–tenant relationship appears to have been more intimate than it was on the great estates—the decline of landlordism in Ireland as a whole is evoked by Bowen's microhistorical account. In one prescient passage, for instance, she describes the mark that silence left on the house during the long periods at the beginning of the twentieth century when the house was empty while she and her parents lived in Dublin:

nobody lived at Bowen's Court, no one at all. For a grander house . . . these periodic desertions would be in the general plan. But Bowen's Court was, in essence, a family home: since 1776 it had been a symbolic hearth, a magnetic idea, the focus of generations of intense living. Now, the caretaker . . . unshuttered the windows in the morning only to let light fall on to sheeted furniture. Fires were lit, but to warm nothing but air. No voices were heard in the surprised rooms, and, when the windows were left open, birds began to fly unalarmedly in and out. It may be said that Bowen's Court met and conquered the challenge of emptiness—but on the house the conquest has left its mark.[1]

The silence and emptiness of Bowen's Court suggests the broader fate of the Big House in Ireland which was conquered by land purchase and, in some cases, by fire, between 1903 and 1923. During this period, the Irish landlord class was

[1] Elizabeth Bowen, *Bowen's Court and Seven Winters* (London, 1984), 403. Bowen's father was pursuing a career as a barrister in Dublin which is why the family left Bowen's Court empty for long periods and lived instead in Dublin. The Bowen estate consisted of 1,680 acres, valued at £1,221 in 1876. The acreage and valuation of every estate in Ireland was calculated by the British government in 1876 and where the acreage and valuation of an estate are noted in this book the information has been obtained from this source. *Copy of a return of the names of proprietors and the area and valuation of all properties in the several counties of Ireland*, HC 1876 (412), lxxx. 395 [hereafter referred to as *Return of Landowners of One Acre and Upwards*]. The acreage occupied by tenant farmers has been identified in Griffith's valuation unless otherwise stated.

expropriated by a series of Land Acts that caused two-thirds of the land of Ireland to be sold by the landlord to the tenant, leaving many Big Houses derelict, ruined, silenced, and empty by the early 1920s; and the ruins of Big Houses are scattered around the Irish countryside today. However, in the late 1870s, at the beginning of the period examined in this book, the Irish landlord class had a great deal of 'intense living' still to do in their Big Houses. On the eve of the Land War that began in 1879, the Irish landlords were still the dominant class in Irish society and possessed enormous political and economic power.

In nineteenth-century Ireland, land was the chief source of wealth and power. The Irish economy was dominated by the agricultural sector, with agricultural production constituting a substantial proportion of gross national income. In addition, land ownership conferred political and social power. Irish local government was controlled by landlords through the Grand Jury system until 1898; and the majority of Irish MPs—at least until the 1870s—were from landed backgrounds.[2] In fact, the landlord class in Victorian Ireland was able to exercise considerable power in a variety of spheres. They evicted 70,000 tenants between 1846 and 1853 (and a further 30,000 during the Land War); they pressured their tenants into voting for their candidates at elections; they convicted men and women who were tried at petty sessions in their capacity as magistrates; they sat in the House of Commons and the House of Lords; they were often responsible for governing Ireland and sometimes occupied senior positions in the administration; and they largely controlled the lives of their tenants.[3] Some tenants were even expected to comply with 'estate rules' that went well beyond the generally accepted contractual obligations of lessees. 'These rules included obtaining permission from the landlord to marry, forbidding the exercise of overnight hospitality, encouraging the attendance of children at Protestant schools, fines for setting snares and traps, and maintaining the secrecy of landlord/tenant dealings.'[4] The extent of the Irish landlords' power was such that Lord Leitrim could order a tenant who had ploughed up some of his pasture land to put back each piece of land—sod by sod—by hand.[5]

  [2] R. F. Foster, *Modern Ireland, 1600–1972* (London, 1988), 377. In 1859, for instance, 87 of the 105 Irish MPs at Westminster were from landed families.

  [3] W. E. Vaughan, *Landlords and Tenants in Mid-Victorian Ireland* (Oxford, 1994), 23; K. Theodore Hoppen, *Elections, Politics, and Society, 1832–1885* (Oxford, 1984), 147–8; the Duke of Abercorn, who owned 63,557 acres in counties Donegal and Tyrone, was Lord Lieutenant of Ireland twice: between 1866 and 1868 and between 1874 and 1876. For further discussion of the number of evictions, see below.

  [4] Eamonn Slater and Terence McDonough, 'Bulwark of Landlordism and Capitalism: the Dynamics of Feudalism in Nineteenth-century Ireland', *Research in Political Economy*, 14 (1994), 74. Lyne has shown that tenants on the Lansdowne estate in the 1850s had to ask permission from the Land Agent to get married and if they did not do so they were liable to be forced to emigrate while their parents were evicted. Gerard J. Lyne, *The Lansdowne Estate in Kerry under the Agency of William Steuart Trench, 1849–1872* (Dublin, 2001), 238.

  [5] Vaughan, *Landlords and Tenants in Mid-Victorian Ireland*, 104.

In 1870, there were about 6,500 landlords in Ireland.[6] The majority of these were the descendants of the new landlords who had gained their estates following the Tudor, Jacobean, Cromwellian, and Williamite confiscations of the sixteenth and seventeenth centuries.[7] These confiscations had largely dispossessed the Catholic Gaelic and Old English landowners, and subsequent legislation—the penal laws—forbade Catholics from owning land. However, some Catholic landowners did survive the dispossession of the plantations and the penal laws of the eighteenth century generally by holding their estates in trust to Protestant neighbours and relations.[8] Indeed, the 1861 census shows that the Irish landlord class was more or less evenly divided between Protestant Episcopalians (48 per cent) and Catholics (43 per cent).[9] Even so, as we shall see, the bigger Irish estates were generally owned by Protestants, with Catholic landowners tending to own smaller estates of between 500 and 2,000 acres. A small number of the great landowners bought into land during the eighteenth century. The 2nd Lord Ormathwaite who owned more than 11,000 acres in Cork and Kerry 1881, for instance, was the descendant of John Walsh who had invested in Irish land in 1764 with the profits of a successful career in the East India Company.[10]

There was, therefore, considerable differentiation within the Irish landlord class *c*.1870. Hoppen has usefully divided the Irish landlord class into five different categories: those with between 500 and 1,000 acres (2,683); those with between 1,000 and 2,000 acres (1,788); those with between 2,000 and 5,000 acres (1,225); those with between 5,000 and 10,000 acres (438); and those with estates of more than 10,000 acres (303).[11] What is striking about these figures is that 741 landlords (who owned estates of more than 5,000 acres) owned almost half of the land of Ireland (48.8 per cent or approximately ten million acres). Some of these landlords owned extremely large estates: Richard Berridge owned 171,117 acres in county Galway, while the Marquis of Downshire owned 115,000 acres in Antrim, Down, Kildare, King's county, and Wicklow. A significant number owned estates of about 30,000 acres (Lords Ashtown, Clonbrock, and Dunsandle) and an even larger number owned estates of between 10 and 20,000 acres (Ebenezer Bustard, Conway Richard Dobbs, Caroline Goold, and so on). The members of the Irish landlord class at the beginning of the twentieth century were extremely conscious of the gradations

---

[6] Ibid. 6. A landlord is defined as the owner of an estate of more than 500 acres who rents some of his estate to tenants.

[7] Cormac Ó Gráda, 'Irish Agriculture after the Land War', in Stanley Engerman and Jacob Metzer (eds.), *Land Rights, Ethno-nationality and Sovereignty in History* (London, 2006).

[8] Patrick Melvin, 'The Composition of the Galway Gentry', *Irish Genealogist*, (1986), 81–8.

[9] Vaughan, *Landlords and Tenants in Mid-Victorian Ireland*, 11. Presbyterians accounted for 7% of landlords.

[10] James Donnelly, 'The Journals of Sir John Benn-Walsh Relating to the Management of his Irish Estates, 1823–64', *Journal of Cork Historical Society*, 79 (1974), 88.

[11] Hoppen, *Elections*, 107, Table 25.

based on status, wealth, and position within the Irish landlord class. Indeed, Nora Robertson, whose father was a Protestant army officer based at Cork during the 1890s, observed that there was a very clear hierarchy in the minds of Irish landowners at that time as she recalled in 1960:

The top social rows were then too well-known and accepted to be written down but, because a new generation may be interested and amused, I will have a shot at defining an order so unreal and preposterous as to be like theatricals in fancy dress . . . *Row A*. Peers who were Lord or Deputy Lieutenants, High Sheriffs and Knights of St. Patrick . . . *Row B*. Other peers with smaller seats, ditto baronets, solvent country gentry and young sons of Row A . . . *Row C*. Less solvent country gentry, who could only allow their sons about £100 a year . . . They were recognised and respected by A and B and belonged to Kildare St. Club. *Row D*. Loyal professional people, gentlemen professional farmers, trade, large retail or small wholesale . . . Such rarely cohabited with Rows A and B but formed useful cannon-fodder at Protestant Bazaars and could, if they were really liked, achieve Kildare St.[12]

This chapter will examine in detail the social characteristics of the wealthiest members of the Irish landlord class, those landowners who owned more than 10,000 acres in Ireland 1881, and who probably occupied most of the places in rows A and B in Robertson's schema.

In 1881, there were 304 landowners in this category, but eleven of these were companies or institutions, one could not be identified, and two (those of Grattan Bellew in county Galway) were rationalized into one estate. This chapter focuses on the remaining 291 landowners, and explores their background, their family life, their education, and their careers as army officers, MPs, and estate managers. It may be objected that this study examines only the top tier of the landed elite since it does not examine the social background and characteristics of the small and medium-sized Irish landlords who occupied row C. On the other hand, it was these men and women who were responsible for leading their class through the Land War (1879–81) and beyond, and in whose hands the fate of Irish landlordism rested during the turbulent years of the late nineteenth century.

I

Who were the great landowners in Ireland in 1881? The 291 landlords included in this study were among the wealthiest individuals in the United Kingdom. They owned 7,213,310 acres or about one-third of the land of Ireland. Collectively, their gross income from the rents of their Irish estates was approximately

---

[12] Nora Robertson, *Crowned Harp: Memories of the Last Years of the Crown in Ireland* (Dublin, 1960), 74. The Kildare Street Club was a gentlemen's club in Dublin that catered for the Irish landlord class, and it will be discussed in detail later in the chapter.

£4,295,340 per annum.[13] The average annual income from rent was £14,761 per annum, which was a great deal more than the annual income of many other elite groups in Irish society.[14] The Lord Chancellor earned £6,000 annually; a high court judge earned £3,500; a Church of Ireland bishop earned £1,500; the head of a Government Department earned between £1,200 and £1,800; the Inspector General of the Royal Irish Constabulary earned £1,800; a Resident Magistrate earned £675; a senior fellow at Trinity College Dublin earned between £1,300 and £1,600 and a junior fellow just £800; the Jesuit fellows at University College Dublin earned £400; a barrister earned between £800 and £1,000; the directors of Boland's Dublin bakers earned £1,400 and a retired major earned £400.[15] At the other end of the social spectrum, a small tenant farmer on the Clanricarde estate at Woodford, county Galway, had an annual income of less than £40,[16] a white collar worker in Eason's department store in Dublin earned between 7s. and £4. 10s. per week; and a rural or an urban unskilled labourer earned between 5s. and 15s. per week.[17] The Irish landlord class and particularly the great landowners who owned estates of more than 10,000 acres were, therefore, among the wealthiest men and women in Ireland but during the period under review they were being superseded in the ranks of the super-rich by the directors of the big railway companies, and the owners of the breweries, tramways, and shipbuilding companies. Even so, Vaughan has estimated that the Irish landlord class as a whole received £340 million as rental income between 1850 and 1879 making them 'one of the best-paid vested interests in the British empire'.[18]

It would be wrong to consider these landlords as exclusively Irish. The data on their place of birth are patchy but figures in the 1861 census suggest that the vast majority of the Irish landlord class (97 per cent) were Irish born.[19] Even so, not all of them lived and owned land exclusively in Ireland. Of the

[13] According to John Ball Greene, 33% should be added to Griffith's valuation to get the letting value of Irish land in the 1870s. Vaughan, *Landlords and Tenants in Mid-Victorian Ireland*, 51. Griffith's valuation of the 291 landlords' land (quot. John Bateman's *Great Landowners of Great Britain and Ireland* (1883; 4th edn, Leicester, 1971)), was £3,229,579. It should be noted that the relationship between Griffith's valuation and the actual rental value in the 1870s varied enormously between estates, but this figure provides a rough guide to these landlords' likely income from rent on the eve of the Land War (1879–81). This figure does not include the likely rent that Irish landlords would gain from their land elsewhere in the United Kingdom.

[14] Some of the individual Irish landlords earned a great deal more than this each year from their estates: Lord Clanricarde, for instance, probably had a gross rental income each year of about £27,712 (based on the valuation of his estate in 1876).

[15] R. B. McDowell, *Land and Learning: Two Irish Clubs* (Dublin, 1993), 33; Tony Farmar, *Ordinary Lives: The Private Worlds of Three Generations of Ireland's Professional Classes* (Dublin, 1991), 20–2.

[16] Fergus Campbell, *Land and Revolution: Nationalist Politics in the West of Ireland, 1891–1921* (Oxford, 2005), 10.

[17] Farmar, *Ordinary Lives*, 22; Paul Dillon, 'Labour and Politics in Kerry, 1879–1916', PhD (University College Dublin, 2003).

[18] Vaughan, *Landlords and Tenants in Mid-Victorian Ireland*, 218, 6.   [19] Ibid. 4.

291 under review, 76 (26 per cent) also owned land in England, Scotland, or Wales. While the vast majority (89 per cent) did have at least one residence in Ireland, 117 of them (40 per cent) also had at least one residence in England. This may have been a residence on part of their English estates or a town house in London where they perhaps stayed during the London season or when they were sitting in the House of Commons or the House of Lords. However, slightly more than half of the 'great' Irish landowners (58 per cent) lived on at least part of their Irish estates all the time, with about one-quarter (24 per cent) living permanently on their Irish estate. In general, it was the better-off landlords in this study (those who owned tens of thousands of acres) who resided in both Britain and Ireland, while those who owned between 10 and 20,000 acres tended to reside permanently in Ireland.[20] Those who resided permanently in England usually visited Ireland regularly: the Mitchell brothers, for instance, lived at Bradford 'but they visit[ed] the Lodge [at Tourmakeady] once or twice a year'.[21] And Sir John Benn-Walsh visited his Cork and Kerry estates in twenty different years between 1821 and 1864 usually in late summer for a fortnight.[22] The vast majority of the 291, like their colleagues in other parts of the United Kingdom, were Protestant: 92 per cent were Episcopalians, 7.5 per cent were Catholic, and just one (or 0.5 per cent) was Presbyterian.[23] Indeed, Robertson observed that there were very few Catholics in rows A, B, C, or D: 'There were perhaps a dozen (also very loyal) Roman Catholic families who qualified for the first two Rows; many more, equally loyal but less distinguished, moved freely with the last two.'[24] This suggests that the survival of the Catholic landowners at the top level of the Irish landlord class was minimal, and that most of the 'great' landowners did not share a common ethnic background with their tenants, most of whom were Catholics.

The upper tier of the Irish landlord class was a largely 'closed' elite group. Almost all of the landlords under review (83 per cent) succeeded to their position as landowners of more than 10,000 acres in 1881. In other words, the overwhelming majority were born into the landed elite, and inherited their estates from their fathers or other close relations. Moreover, it is likely that most of the remaining 17 per cent of landowners in this study also succeeded to their estates (as the evidence is inconclusive regarding their succession). However, a significant proportion of the great landowners in 1881 were not the descendants of the planters of the sixteenth and seventeenth centuries. During the Great Famine (1845–9), many landlords became severely indebted and were forced to sell their estates under the Encumbered Estates Act of 1849. Under the terms

---

[20] It is likely, then, that those landlords not included in this study who owned estates of between 500 and 10,000 acres probably spent most of their time living on their Irish estates.

[21] *Irish Times*, 18 Nov. 1905.   [22] Donnelly, 'The Journals of Sir John Benn-Walsh', 87.

[23] The religious beliefs of 266 landlords could be identified.

[24] Robertson, *Crowned Harp*, 75.

of this Act, a creditor could petition for a sale when encumbrances exceeded half of the estate's net rent (defined as the gross rent less taxes and fixed charges).[25] Consequently, the ownership of about one-quarter of agricultural land was transferred during the thirty years after 1849, most of it in the 1850s.[26] The losers tended to be the owners of smaller estates, while the beneficiaries were investors and the wealthier landlords who took the opportunity to further amalgamate their estates.

In order to assess how many of the great landowners in 1881 may have joined the landed elite via the Encumbered Estates Court, a search was made for each of the great landowner families in a list of local office holders in Ireland in 1848 (contained in Thom's *Official Directory* in 1848 and therefore before the introduction of the Encumbered Estates Act introduced the following year). If a landowner family was an office holder (lord lieutenant, deputy lieutenant, high sheriff, or magistrate) in 1848 then the likelihood is that they owned their estate before the Encumbered Estates Act was introduced, and that they were the descendants of the sixteenth- and seventeenth-century planters. Of the 291 great landowners in 1881, 86 (30 per cent) could not be identified in Thom's *Official Directory* for 1848. This suggests that more than two-thirds of the great landowners in 1881 were the descendants of the men and women who had colonized Ireland in the early modern period.[27] However, slightly less than one-third were not office holders in 1848, and at least some of these can be proven to have purchased their estates through the Encumbered Estates Court.[28] At least eight (3 per cent) of the great landowners in 1881 were businessmen who probably purchased their Irish land in the post-Famine period. Nathaniel Buckley, for instance, was a cotton manufacturer at Ashton under Lyne who purchased an estate in county Cork; Thomas Arthur Hope was a Liverpool merchant who purchased land in Tyrone; and Abraham Joseph Mitchell was a Bradford manufacturer who purchased land in county Mayo. Broadly speaking, however, entry to the 'great' landowner class in post-Famine Ireland was 'closed'. The members of this elite group were generally 'born' rather than 'made'.

The inheritance of Irish estates operated according to the principle of primogeniture. In 1881, the vast majority of landlords (75 per cent) were the first born sons in their families, with 6 per cent being second sons (many of whom eventually inherited from their elder brothers) and 19 per cent 'other' sons (who may have inherited from uncles or even grandfathers). In most cases, the landlords

---

[25] Vaughan, *Landlords and Tenants in Mid-Victorian Ireland*, 133.

[26] Hoppen, *Elections*, 106, n. 1.

[27] Of course, there were also a small number of descendants of the Gaelic or Old English landowners in 1881 including, for instance, Lord Clanricarde.

[28] Henry Hodgson of Merlin Park, Galway, for instance, purchased his 17,064 acre estate (valued at £1,121) from the Blakes of Galway in the 1870s, through the Encumbered Estates Court.

under review succeeded their fathers as landed proprietors.[29] Technically, the heirs of estates were tenants for life rather than landowners. When the eldest son of a landed family married or reached his majority, a settlement was drawn up entailing the estate on the eldest grandson (often not yet born). This strategy was adopted to ensure that the estate was passed intact from one generation to the next. However, such arrangements were reasonably flexible, allowing the owner to sell outlying properties or to mortgage part of the estate to pay trustees. These settlements also contained contingency plans to allow for the eventuality of no grandson being born, in which case priority was to be given to male over female heirs, and to direct rather than lateral descent or ascent.[30]

Marriage arrangements were an important aspect of maintaining the power and wealth of landed families. When an heir became engaged to marry, negotiations were entered into by both families to agree a marriage settlement. Usually, the bride received an annual allowance from her husband's estate (known as pin money) and she also brought with her a dowry, which might be used to alleviate some of the debts of the estate. These marriage settlements were arranged in a businesslike fashion. For instance, when Alice Dillon (Lord Clonbrock's daughter) became engaged to Ambrose Congreve in 1866, the solicitors of both parties met at the Sackville Street Club in Dublin in June to arrange a settlement, and several other meetings were required before final terms were agreed in July.[31]

A significant number of the landlords under review did not marry (13 per cent), possibly because they inherited their estates late in life.[32] Of those who did marry, the vast majority (69 per cent) formed alliances with other landed families, thereby consolidating their status and wealth.[33] Among those landlords who were peers (in this study), more than half (51 per cent) married the daughters of peers.[34] The landlord class, then, did not generally marry outside of itself. To do so was to incur the wrath of landed society as Geoffrey Taylour (the 4th Marquis of Headfort) found out in 1901 when he married a dancer, and was forced to resign his commission in the Irish Guards.[35] It is possible that the 7th Earl of Orkney's decision to marry Connie Gilchrist 'the well-known burlesque actress' also met

[29] Of 220 individuals who inherited their estates: 172 (78%) succeeded their fathers; 22 (10%) succeeded their brothers; 13 (6%) succeeded their uncles; 7 (3%) succeeded their grandfathers; 2 (1%) succeeded their cousins; 2 (1%) succeeded their husbands; 1 (0.5%) succeeded his 'kinsman'; and 1 (0.5%) succeeded her aunt.

[30] Terence Dooley, *The Decline of the Big House in Ireland: A Study of Irish Landed Families* (Dublin, 2001), 69.

[31] Ibid. 69–70.

[32] The marriage details are known for 280 landlords in my sample, of which 243 (87%) married and 37 (13%) did not.

[33] Information is available on who 202 landlords in my sample married, and 139 (69%) married the daughters of families listed in *Walford's County Families* (1879), suggesting that they were also the members of landed families.

[34] Information is available on who 101 peers in my sample married, and 52 married the daughters of peers.   [35] Dooley, *Decline of the Big House in Ireland*, 67.

with the frowns of his fellow landlords in 1892.[36] As in other sections of Irish society, landlords' marriage patterns tended to consolidate class position, rather than risk the possibility of marrying 'beneath' oneself. In many cases, landlords married into neighbouring families, as Edith Somerville suggested in 1925: 'to love your neighbour—or, at all events to marry her—was almost inevitable when matches were a matter of mileage, and marriages might have been said to have been made by the map.'[37] When landlords strayed from this 'map', they were regarded as transgressors of this code. Sir Randolph Churchill married Jennie Jerome, an American, at a time 'when such an alliance was considered as experimental as mating with a Martian'.[38] Ill-advised marital or extramarital relationships were probably also avoided because they could cause serious legal problem with estate inheritance. Francis Lorenzo Comyn, for instance, owned substantial estates in Clare, Galway, and Mayo in 1881 but these had been threatened by legal action in 1862 when his dead brother's will was contested by what the *Irish Times* described as 'a loose woman'. Apparently, his brother John, who had died falling out of a cab in London in 1834, had had a relationship with a beautiful widow who subsequently contested—unsuccessfully—John's will, which left his property to his younger brother.[39] In general, landlords married when they were comparatively young and the average age at marriage of the great landowners was 30, which was slightly earlier than that for the rest of Irish society.[40]

In comparison to other sections of Irish society, landlords' marriages were not particularly fertile.[41] On average, landlord marriages—according to this study—produced 2.2 children, which was considerably less than the average number of children of tenant farmers at the same time. This may have been caused by cultural factors—most landlords (in this sample) were Protestant, while most tenant farmers were Catholic—but it also suggests the possibility that landlords may have made use of contraception. Indeed, what is striking about landlord marriages is the extremely high proportion in this study (29 per cent)

---

[36] The 7th earl was the nephew of the 6th earl who owned the 10,958 acre estate (valued at £5,031) in Tipperary, Queen's county, Kerry, and Buckingham in 1881 (*Irish Times*, 23 July 1892).
[37] Edith Somerville and Martin Ross, *Irish Memories* (London, 1925), 71.
[38] Dooley, *Decline of the Big House in Ireland*, 45.   [39] *Irish Times*, 12, 13, and 17 June 1862.
[40] Of the generation born between 1896 and 1905, the mean age at marriage was 33 for men and 27 for women. D. Rottman and P. O'Connell, 'The Changing Social Structure of Ireland', in Frank Litton (ed.), *Unequal Achievement: The Irish Experience, 1957–1982* (Dublin, 1982). Of 223 of the great Irish landowners about whom information on age at marriage is available, 0.4% were married before the age of 21; 59% were married aged between 21 and 30; 29.5% were married aged between 31 and 40; 8.5% were married aged between 41 and 50; and 2.6% were married aged between 51 and 60. It should also be emphasized that Rottman and O'Connell's survey is of individuals born in the 1890s and early 1900s whereas most of the landlords in this study were born during the first half of the nineteenth century.
[41] Of 89 of the great landowners who were married and about whom information on their fertility is available, 26 (29%) had no children; 13 (15%) had one child; 5 (6%) had two children; 13 (15%) had three children; 9 (10%) had four children; 7 (8%) had five children; 3 (3%) had six children; 3 (3%) had seven children; 4 (4%) had nine children; 2 (2%) had ten children; 2 (2%) had twelve children; and 2 (2%) had fourteen children.

who did not have any children whatsoever, despite the necessity of producing a male heir. It is impossible to say whether this was because marriages arranged in a businesslike way were loveless, or because the landlord class experienced greater difficulty with conception than other sections of Irish society. Consequently, more than one-third (37 per cent) of the landlords in my sample failed to produce a son to inherit their estates. It is also possible that the tendency for many landowners to marry their cousins may have resulted in a higher incidence of infertility. In the absence of a direct heir, in most cases (13 per cent) the estate passed to the landlord's brother, but also to daughters (4 per cent), nephews (3 per cent), cousins (1 per cent), uncles (1 per cent), and sisters (0.5 per cent). In about one in eight cases, there was no heir to the estates in my sample. The absence of sons and heirs may be one factor in explaining the long-term decline of the landlord class in Ireland from the mid-nineteenth century onwards. Of course, the figures presented here are of the legitimate children of the Irish landlords and it is possible that there were other children born to these landlords outside marriage. Indeed, some tenants on Lord Leitrim's estate alleged that he had demanded sexual favours from his tenants' daughters if they wanted his permission to marry, and local folklore suggests that droit de seigneur may have been practised on estates in county Galway during the nineteenth century, although it is impossible to verify these claims.[42]

A small proportion (ten or 3 per cent) of the great landowners in 1881 were women. Women only inherited estates when there was no male heir. Sophia Isabel Butler of Castle Crine inherited an estate in counties Clare and Tipperary—along with her two sisters Anna and Henrietta—when their father died in 1857 leaving no son.[43] Women also occasionally inherited from their husbands if they died without leaving a male heir. When the Venerable Frederic Falkiner Goold, Archdeacon of Raphoe, died in 1877 leaving four daughters, his wife Caroline inherited the Limerick estate.[44] In some instances, there was a male heir who was deemed too young to be able to inherit, and so the mother inherited the estate until he reached his majority. Alice Emily Bagot took over the running of her husband's estate at Ballygar, county Galway, when her husband died in 1877 leaving only a two-year-old son.[45] One of the landowners in this study, Lady Louisa Isabella Georgina Fitzgibbon, inherited an estate in counties Limerick and Tipperary from her aunt in 1873. The lives of these women would have been very different from their male counterparts: they did not attend public schools or universities; they did not join the army or take up politics; they did not sit on the bench at Petty Sessions; and they probably handed over the management of

---

[42] Droit de seigneur was the practice whereby the landlord demanded to spend the first night with his tenants' wives. Lyne, *Lansdowne Estate in Kerry*, 283, n. 42. Interview conducted by the author with P. J. Ruane of Colmanstown, county Galway, 16 Sept. 2008.

[43] The estate consisted of 11,854 acres (valued at £4,044).

[44] The estate consisted of 10,966 acres (valued at £3,090).

[45] The Bagot estate in Galway consisted of 12,396 acres (valued at £4,400).

the estate to a paid Land Agent (as many male heirs would also have done). In general terms, however, the female members of landed families had much greater freedom than women in other sections of Irish society. They were usually the mistresses of their households but with a substantial personal allowance they were in a position to pursue their own interests and perhaps philanthropic pursuits.

The career of the Irish landlords began with private education in the Big House. A schoolroom was normally set aside for tuition, either on the top storey of the house or on the bedroom corridor. Nannies and governesses were responsible for the early stages of education, with governesses often recruited from either England or Europe. While daughters usually remained at home under the tuition of governesses, many of the sons then went on to public school: half of the landowners in this study had attended public school. It was possible to identify the secondary schools attended by 144 of the landlords (it is likely that the other 147 who did not list their secondary education in directories were educated privately at home). The most popular destinations for the future 'great' landowners of Ireland were the Clarendon schools: Eton (57 per cent), Harrow (21 per cent), Rugby (6 per cent), Winchester (2 per cent), and Charterhouse (1 per cent).[46] A handful attended other slightly less-prestigious English Public Schools: Westminster (2 per cent), Radley (1 per cent), and Cheltenham (1 per cent). The sons of Catholic landowners tended to attend prominent English Catholic schools: Oscott (2 per cent), Downside (1 per cent), the Oratory School, Edgbaston (1 per cent), and Stoneyhurst (1 per cent), although one of the Catholic landlords (the Earl of Granard) attended Eton.[47]

An English public school education—whether Protestant or Catholic—was regarded as the appropriate training for a future landlord with its emphasis on 'independence, stoicism, courage, honour, loyalty and manliness'.[48] However, some of the Irish landlords hated Eton where 'The food was wretched and tasteless . . . the thrashings . . . were excessive . . . [and the] Irish boys were ridiculed . . . especially on St Patrick's Day'.[49] Even so, the advantages of attending an English public school were widely acknowledged. Lord Dunraven, who was instead sent to St Columba's in Dublin, later regretted that he had 'lost . . . the education, the discipline and the wholesome training of Eton, or any other great public school, and the intimate friendships that spring from public school life'.[50] Nora Robertson confirmed that attendance at an English public school was regarded as essential by the members of the great landowner class in Ireland:

It had become obligatory to look and speak like an English public school man and, therefore, anyone who could scrape together the necessary cash sent his son to an English

---

[46] The Clarendon schools are Eton, Harrow, Winchester, Rugby, St Paul's, Merchant Taylors, Charterhouse, and Shrewsbury. They are so called from being the subject of a parliamentary investigation by Lord Clarendon's commission in 1861.

[47] For a full discussion of the provision of education in nineteenth-century Ireland, see Ch. 2.

[48] Jessica Gerard, *Country House Life: Families and Servants, 1815–1914* (Oxford, 1994), 84–5.

[49] Dooley, *Decline of the Big House in Ireland*, 50–1.   [50] Ibid. 71.

public school. Even if he could not afford a renowned one yet anything was better than Ireland. The one Southern Irish public school, St. Columba's College at Rathfarnham, sister school to Radley, at first seemed a reasonable and cheaper substitute but, with the advent of quick railway travel, those who had the money preferred the certainty of their sons getting rid of an Irish brogue and meeting people who might be more useful afterwards . . . Moreover since, as we have reluctantly observed, it was essential for anyone with a place to keep up to marry money, a young man educated at an expensive English public school and a good college at Oxford or Cambridge was more likely to meet eligible sisters. After all, people truly believed that they were doing the best for their sons and, the world being as it is, they probably were.[51]

Undoubtedly, public schools provided access to a network of young men who would grow up to become the leading political, administrative, and judicial figures of their generation, and this provided many useful contacts and opportunities for the heir to an Irish estate. The English public school system also cemented contacts between Irish landlords and the wider British landed elite, and nurtured a common culture among landlords in the United Kingdom.

Although some Irish landlords may have had what Hoppen described as 'a contempt for mere intelligence', almost half of those included in this study (47 per cent) had gained a university education.[52] The vast majority of these (68 per cent) attended Oxford or Cambridge, with slightly less than one-third (30 per cent) attending Trinity College Dublin.[53] Nora Robertson observed that 'Trinity [had] ceased to be the right thing for the larger county families. It was considered provincial'.[54] Certain Oxbridge colleges were particularly popular with the future Irish landlords—thirty-six attended Christ Church, Oxford, and twenty attended Trinity College, Cambridge—because these colleges were where the sons of the great landowners in the United Kingdom tended to congregate. Indeed, Oxbridge provided a forum for valuable contacts and networks to be established. Frederick Wrench, for instance, who went on to become a prominent figure in the Irish Land Commission, became friends with Henry Bellingham, one of the great Irish landowners, while at Exeter College, Oxford, and eventually married Bellingham's sister. The possibility of establishing potentially useful future contacts might explain the Irish landlords' preference for the 'social delights' of Oxbridge, over the 'late-Victorian brilliance' of Trinity College Dublin.[55] The preference for English universities also suggests that the landlords saw themselves as part of a wider British landowning class, and that their sense of Irishness was perhaps less important to them.[56]

Oxbridge also conferred greater social status than Trinity College Dublin. Consequently, the better-off landlords in my sample (those whose estates were

[51] Robertson, *Crowned Harp*, 101.   [52] Hoppen, *Elections*, 116.
[53] Of the 137 who attended university, 65 attended Oxford, 28 Cambridge, 41 Trinity College Dublin, 1 Durham, and 1 Edinburgh. One attended both Trinity College Dublin and Oxford.
[54] Robertson, *Crowned Harp*, 101.   [55] Hoppen, *Elections*, 116.
[56] Vaughan, *Landlords and Tenants in Mid-Victorian Ireland*, 11.

valued at more than £5,000) were more likely to go to Oxford (80 per cent) than to Trinity College Dublin (20 per cent), while the less-well-off (those with estates valued at less than £5,000) were more inclined to attend Trinity College Dublin (66 per cent) than Oxbridge (34 per cent). Perhaps those landlords with a larger income could afford to pay for their sons to go to Oxbridge, while those with tighter budgets sent their sons to Trinity. After all, as one of the characters in Shane Leslie's novel *Doomsland* recalled: 'the difference between Trinity and Oxford was the difference between sampling beer and champagne.'[57]

Rather than attending university, many of the Irish landlords pursued a military career between completing their secondary education and taking over the family estate.[58] Nora Robertson explained that

Better off Anglo-Irishmen were less University-minded than their contemporaries in England. Most younger sons, and eldest sons until they inherited their patrimony, joined the fighting services... Before 1914 in Ireland... one might say that some military service in India took the place of a University in Irish county family life.[59]

Indeed, the army was regarded as an important training ground for landlords, providing them with experience of leadership and self-sacrifice. The presence of children's army uniforms in the play room at Strokestown House suggests that the male children were being groomed for the military during their childhoods.[60] More than one-third (37 per cent) of the great Irish landowners in 1881 had been officers in the army or the navy. The most popular regiments for the Irish landlords were the Life Guards, the Coldstream Guards, and the Royal Irish Fusiliers, and many of the landlords in this study saw active service.[61] The earls of Annesley, Dorchester, Listowel, Longford, Lucan, Orkney, and Roden all served in the Crimean War, while the Earl of Caledon served in the Egyptian campaign, Lord Athlumney in the Boer war, and Viscount Gormanston in the Indian mutiny. Neither did they take a back seat in these campaigns: the 5th Earl of Annesley was wounded in the Kafir or Cape Frontier wars, and the 3rd Earl of Listowel was severely wounded at the Alma during the Crimean war.

During the nineteenth century, the majority of British army officers were recruited from the landed class because a private income was the essential precondition for becoming an army officer. From 1870, admission to the military academies at Sandhurst and Woolwich was by competitive examination, but the cost of being an army officer could be as high as £700 per year in excess

[57] Shane Leslie, *Doomsland* (London, 1923), 143.
[58] Of 103 landlords who pursued military careers, only 32 of these also attended university.
[59] Robertson, *Crowned Harp*, 101, 102.
[60] I visited Strokestown House—which has been preserved in its shabby Victorian grandeur—in September 2008. On Mahon, see Patrick Vesey, *The Murder of Major Mahon* (Dublin, 2008). In 1881, Henry Sandford Pakenham-Mahon owned Strokestown House and the 28,123 acre estate (valued at £15,080) in counties Roscommon and Westmeath.
[61] Dooley, *Decline of the Big House in Ireland*, 73.

of salary.[62] In effect, this restricted access to the officer class of the British army to members of the landed elite, and the younger sons of Irish landlord families were especially prominent in the army.[63] However, the proportion of officers in the British army who were drawn from landed backgrounds did decline during the nineteenth century from 53 per cent in 1830 to 40 per cent by 1912; and these men were replaced by officers drawn from middle-class backgrounds (who increased from 47 per cent to 59 per cent over the same period).[64] At the end of the nineteenth century, the British army consisted of some 165,000 men including 6,670 officers. During the nineteenth century, between 20,000 and 30,000 soldiers were usually stationed in Ireland.[65] A significant proportion of the officers and men in the British army were Irish born: in 1893, the Irish Chief Secretary, John Morley estimated that 13.5 per cent of the British forces were Irishmen.[66] The Irish-born men who were officers in the British army were generally recruited from landed backgrounds: of twenty-eight officers of the 5th Royal Irish Lancers in 1914, for instance, five (18 per cent) had Irish connections and this included three men who were from aristocratic and landed backgrounds.[67] Undoubtedly, the Irish landlords' service in the army further integrated them into the wider British landed elite, and ensured that they were perceived as an integral component of the British state in Ireland. Even so, Nora Robertson suggested that a stint in the army may not have been as intellectually beneficial as a university education:

Intrinsically there is no reason why active soldiers should not be as well educated and objectively minded as civilians with a University training. But are they? Does life in Cantonment India or in an officers' mess make for a speculative critical mind? Pleasant as the pre-First War soldier was, he was community trained. He was not expected or encouraged to be original and know better than his company commander.[68]

A career as a political representative was regarded as a natural extension of the great landowners' leading position in Irish society. In 1857, C. W. Cooper described himself as the 'just and legitimate claimant of the votes and support of his tenantry', and the House of Commons was seen as a useful training ground for estate management.[69] Consequently, fifty-one of the landlords under review were members of parliament for Irish constituencies, and eighteen for English

[62] David Cannadine, *The Decline and Fall of the British Aristocracy* (New Haven, Conn. and London, 1990), 270.

[63] Three-quarters of the younger sons in a study carried out by Dooley became army or navy officers (Dooley, *Decline of the Big House in Ireland*, 74).

[64] Elizabeth A. Muenger, *The British Military Dilemma in Ireland: Occupation Politics, 1886–1914* (Dublin, 1991), 13.

[65] Ibid. 209, n. 3. By the end of the nineteenth century, there were nearer 30,000 troops in Ireland, and the increased number was required—presumably—to help the policing of the crisis generated by the Land War (1879–81).

[66] This represented a decline from 23.7% in 1873 (ibid. 12, 13, 18).   [67] Ibid. 16, 18.

[68] Robertson, *Crowned Harp*, 102.   [69] Hoppen, *Elections*, 117.

constituencies (with four holding both Irish and English seats). Altogether, a total of sixty-five (22 per cent) of the great landowners in this study were MPs at some point in their careers. However, most of them were MPs well before 1881. The earliest date at which one of them was elected was 1826, when the Earl of Lucan became the Conservative representative for county Mayo, and the last date was 1900, when Count Arthur John Moore stood down as the nationalist representative for Derry city. The vast majority of Irish landlord-MPs did not survive beyond the 1874 general election (the first to be held after the introduction of the secret ballot in 1872). Indeed, only six (9 per cent) of this sample continued to sit as MPs after 1874, and only three after 1880 (all of which were in Ulster constituencies).[70] Colonel Edward Saunderson's membership of the Orange Order enabled him to win support from middle- and working-class Protestants, which probably played a part in his election as the Unionist representative for North Armagh between 1885 and 1906.

Most (about two-thirds) of the Irish landlord-MPs were Conservatives, although a significant minority were Liberals. Only one, the Catholic Arthur John Moore, was a member of the Irish Parliamentary Party, and support for Irish nationalism was extremely unusual among the 'great' Irish landowners (although the leader of the Irish Parliamentary Party in the 1880s was the Wicklow landlord Charles Stewart Parnell).[71] Using club membership as a guide, it is possible to estimate the political viewpoint of 151 of the landlords in my sample, which reveals that three-quarters were Conservatives (74 per cent), almost one-quarter were Liberals (24 per cent), and one (1 per cent) was a nationalist.[72] There does appear to be some differentiation between the political behaviour of Catholic and Episcopalian landlords. When Catholic landlords were politically active, they usually supported the Liberals or the Home Rulers rather than the Conservatives.[73]

The Irish landlords were closely integrated into the British political system as MPs, but also as members of the House of Lords and as government officials. Irish landlords sat in the House of Lords as both representative peers for Ireland (there were twenty-eight of these elected at any one time) and as the holders of peerages.[74] Almost one-quarter (22 per cent) of the great Irish landlords sat in the

---

[70] Edward James Saunderson was Liberal MP for Cavan, 1868–74 and Unionist MP for north Armagh, 1885–1906; Richard William Ker was Unionist MP for Down between 1884 and 1890; and Arthur John Moore was nationalist MP for Derry City between 1899 and 1900.

[71] Parnell owned an estate of 4,678 acres (valued at £1,245).

[72] It was assumed that landlords who were members of the Carlton club were Conservatives, while members of the Reform or Brooks's club were presumed to be Liberals. See Vaughan, *Landlords and Tenants in Mid-Victorian Ireland*, 13.

[73] Two of the 34 Liberals in my sample were Catholics, while none of the politically active Catholics was Conservative.

[74] Irish peers did not automatically sit in the House of Lords, as did English/British peers.

House of Lords, and this cemented their contacts with the wider British landed elite. This position also provided them with enormous power and influence, at least until the passage of the Parliament Act in 1911 that removed the House of Lords' power to veto legislation passed by the House of Commons. Gladstone's second Home Rule Bill was passed in the House of Commons, but defeated by the House of Lords in 1893, and—if the Parliament Act had not been passed in 1911—the Lords would undoubtedly have blocked the third Home Rule Bill that eventually became law in 1914.

It is also worth noting that a number of Irish landlords participated in government at a senior level. The Duke of Abercorn, who owned 63,557 acres in counties Donegal and Tyrone, was Viceroy (Lord Lieutenant) of Ireland on two occasions: first between 1866 and 1868, and second between 1874 and 1876. Similarly, the 6th Marquess of Londonderry was Lord Lieutenant between 1886 and 1889. Eleven (4 per cent) of the other landlords in my sample also held senior positions as, for example, Administrator General of Bengal (Maurice Fitzgerald Sandes); Governor General of Canada (held by 4th Viscount Monck, the Earl of Dufferin, and Lord Lansdowne); Governor General of India (Lord Lansdowne); Governor of New South Wales (Lord Belmore); Under Secretary of State for War (held by the Earl of Dufferin, Lord Lansdowne, and Lord Longford); and Under Secretary of State for the Home Department (George Clive). Perhaps because their social background gave them experience of associating with members of the aristocracy, and their participation in 'grand tours' conferred some linguistic proficiency, a number of them (2 per cent) were employed as diplomats: the 2nd Marquis of Clanricarde, for instance, was attaché at Turin, while the Catholic 7th Earl of Granard was attaché at Dresden. However, what is striking about these figures is just how few of them were selected to participate in the highest levels of British government. We might have expected more of them to have been appointed as Viceroy of Ireland, for instance; and the absence of Irish landlords among the senior administrators in Ireland certainly meant that their influence on British policy in Ireland was increasingly reduced as the nineteenth century progressed.

The Irish landlord class were also prominent in local government and virtually controlled the local administration of their counties until 1898. Many landlords were firmly embedded in the administration of their counties. Almost half (41 per cent) of the landlords in my sample acted as the High Sheriffs of their counties, and all of these men would have qualified for 'Row A' of Irish society as outlined by Nora Robertson. The High Sheriff was the principal representative of central government in the county (appointed by the Lord Lieutenant), and played an important role in the upholding of law and order. His main duties included the selection of the Grand Jury, and the supervising of the conduct of parliamentary elections.[75] One in ten of the landlords under review also acted as

---

[75] Virginia Crossman, *Local Government in Nineteenth-century Ireland* (Belfast, 1994), 7.

Lord Lieutenants of their counties. These individuals played an important role in the appointment of local magistrates, and conveyed to the Lord Chancellor their opinion of the conduct of the magistracy in their counties.[76] Almost two-thirds (65 per cent) of the great landowners acted as magistrates in their counties: this gave the Irish landlords important judicial power to convict those tried for ordinary crimes at petty sessions. However, the British government increasingly felt that the Irish landlords—as a whole—were unreliable magistrates because of absenteeism, perceived idleness, and failure to attend regularly; and in 1836 the Constabulary (Ireland) Act empowered the Lord Lieutenant to appoint magistrates to reside in localities that were disturbed by political and agrarian conflict as he saw fit.[77]

Landlords also dominated the Grand Juries which were responsible for raising money by means of county rates for a variety of purposes ranging from the construction and repair of roads to the upkeep of hospitals and lunatic asylums.[78] During the second half of the nineteenth century, the Grand Juries were gradually displaced by the Boards of Poor Law Guardians as the most important local bodies. These boards were composed of both elected members and local magistrates sitting *ex officio*.[79] Since the majority of magistrates were landowners, this gave them substantial influence over the Boards of Poor Law Guardians until at least the Land War (1879–81), when landlord influence on such Boards fell into decline.[80] Even so, landowners maintained a firm grip over local administration until the Local Government Act of 1898 established new local bodies (county councils and urban or rural district councils) which were democratically elected on the same basis as the parliamentary franchise. Although some landlords were elected to the new county councils, the majority of county councillors elected at the first elections in 1899 were nationalists and not drawn from the landlord class. In terms of local political power, landlord influence in Ireland was almost completely destroyed by the 1898 local government act. This was particularly the case in the three southern provinces of Connacht, Munster, and Leinster where nationalists won 456 (92 per cent) of the available positions on county councils and Unionists won only thirty-nine (8 per cent).[81] Given that landowners were much more likely to be Unionists than nationalists, this suggests that landlord influence in local government in Ireland—outside Ulster—virtually ceased after 1898.

---

[76] Ibid. 17–18.

[77] This was the origin of the Resident Magistracy; see Penny Bonsall, *The Irish RMs: The Resident Magistrates in the British Administration of Ireland* (Dublin, 1997), 11–12.

[78] Crossman, *Local Government*, 25.   [79] Ibid. 39.

[80] William L. Feingold, 'Land League Power: The Tralee Poor Law Election of 1881', in Samuel Clark and James Donnelly (eds.), *Irish Peasants: Violence and Political Unrest, 1780–1914* (Manchester, 1983).   [81] Cannadine, *Decline and Fall*, 173.

Many of the Irish landlords were also the members of London and Dublin clubs. Gentlemen's clubs played an important role in binding the landed elite together, and also in providing a context where landlords could associate with the members of other elite groups, many of which were also members of London, Dublin, and Belfast club-land. By the 1840s, there were about twenty clubs in London, reflecting the fact that clubs now catered for large sections of the professional and business classes, as well as for the famous political and social figures in Victorian London society.[82] The different clubs catered for those with different opinions and tastes: the Carlton was a centre for Conservatives, the Reform a gathering point for Liberals, the Garrick a meeting place for artists, and so on.[83] However, what united all clubs was that they provided the necessities and comforts of life—food, wine, newspapers, books, cards, billiards—at a reasonable cost.[84]

Irish club life developed along similar lines to that in London. At the end of the seventeenth century, there were many taverns and coffee houses in Dublin. Early in George III's reign, a group of gentlemen who met in Daly's coffee house constituted themselves Daly's club and in the 1780s they built a purpose-designed clubhouse on the north side of College Green (between Foster Place and Anglesea Street).[85] Daly's became 'a fast place where high play and heavy drinking were indulged in where many a reckless challenge to a duel was thrown down'.[86] As a result of a schism in Daly's Club—when a popular candidate was blackballed—the Kildare Street Club was established in 1782.[87] By the mid-1850s, this club had become the most popular in the city and its members purchased numbers one, two, and three Kildare Street, where a new club house was built.[88] In 1860, the club had 700 members; in 1894, 630; and in 1914, 688. The drop in membership was probably caused by the agricultural depression of the 1870s and the Land War.[89] Even so, by the 1880s the Kildare Street Club was the centre of landlord life in Dublin with the majority of its members coming from landed families.[90] According to Nora Robertson:

The Kildare Street Club in Dublin was the Unionist focus. It appeared then [at the beginning of the twentieth century] as the symbol of what was unchangeable and absolute. It dates from the end of the 18th century and was at first more social than political. During the Home Rule struggle it became wholly political.[91]

---

[82] McDowell, *Land and Learning*, 3–4.   [83] Dooley, *Decline of the Big House in Ireland*, 63.
[84] McDowell, *Land and Learning*, 4–5.   [85] Ibid. 9, 14.
[86] Dooley, *Decline of the Big House in Ireland*, 62.   [87] McDowell, *Land and Learning*, 16.
[88] Dooley, *Decline of the Big House in Ireland*, 62.   [89] McDowell, *Land and Learning*, 53.
[90] Dooley estimates that 90% of the 800 members of the Kildare Street Club in the 1880s were from landed families. According to McDowell, the membership of the club at this time was probably about 600 and only about one-half of the members were from landed families (*Decline of the Big House in Ireland*, 62; McDowell, *Land and Learning*, 53–4).
[91] Robertson, *Crowned Harp*, 76.

Of the membership of the Kildare Street Club in 1860, half were landowners, about a quarter were regular army officers, about one in eight was a legal man (judge, barrister, and so on), and a small proportion (2 per cent to 3 per cent) were Church of Ireland clergymen, including Bishop Plunkett of Tuam. The club also attracted some members of the emerging business elite, including two Bank of Ireland directors and Benjamin Lee Guinness.[92] The club was becoming a focal point for a variety of different elite groups, and this probably fostered the development of a common culture and ethos among the Irish establishment as a whole.

According to Sir Shane Leslie, who was born into a great estate in county Monaghan, 'A gentleman's standing in his world was signalled by his list of clubs and it was worth paying hundreds of pounds in subs'.[93] Clubs—like schools and the hunting field—enabled members of the landlord class to net-work with one another. As well as twenty or so clubs in London, there were a further eleven in Dublin, and as many as thirteen scattered throughout the provinces: usually in provincial towns like Belfast, Cork, Limerick, Galway, Tralee, and Waterford.[94] In Cork city, there were two clubs: the County, which catered for the Protestant businessmen, professionals, and landowners, and the City club which provided a home for those who were not eligi-ble to join the County ('mostly Roman Catholic business folks, or anyone whose loyalty was suspect').[95] Gentlemen's clubs tended to cater for specif-ic groups and appear to have been divided between essentially Unionist and nationalist establishments which served to keep even middle- and upper-class Catholics and Protestants apart. However, even clubs that were dominated by Protestant businessmen and landowners were occasionally disrupted by inter-nal conflicts. When Nora Robertson and her family arrived in Cork they found that

the County Club was still divided between those who had sided with the Committee or with the Plaintiff, in a recent law suit connected with cards. Before we issued invitations to a party, I had to consult a list showing the personnel of the two sides. Feeling was too strong for it to be tactful to ask opposite sides to the same party . . . The plaintiff was a rich young man, married to one of the most beautiful women in Ireland. They were very much taken up by Row A and this caused some jealousy in the B ranks. Moreover it cannot be disputed that he was an ungracious loser at games, which made him unpopular. Play for high stakes began at the Club and it soon became clear that something crooked was going on. Because he was unpopular and because he was winning, suspicion fell on the young man.[96]

---

[92] McDowell, *Land and Learning*, 53–7.   [93] Dooley, *Decline of the Big House in Ireland*, 61.
[94] Hoppen, *Elections*, 119; McDowell, *Land and Learning*, 4. Landowners sometimes were the members of reading rooms in provincial towns like Loughrea. See Bernadette Lally, *Print Culture in Loughrea, 1850–1900: Reading, Writing and Printing in an Irish Provincial Town* (Dublin, 2008), 57.
[95] Robertson, *Crowned Harp*, 76.   [96] Ibid. 77.

Joseph Pike, one of the directors of the Bandon and South Coast Railway Co. and a prominent Quaker businessmen in Cork (who was married to Frances Annie Critchley), initiated a case against the committee of the county club when he was accused of cheating at cards. In the event, Pike won his case, and it seems clear that he was not guilty, but the case divided the members of the Irish establishment at Cork city for a considerable period of time.[97] Indeed, it is important to bear in mind that the Irish establishment was not an entirely united or coherent elite group and that there were important disputes and conflicts within it.

Even so, the membership of gentlemen's clubs undoubtedly held the Irish establishment together. Of the landlords under review, more than two-thirds (70 per cent) were the members of at least one club (in London, Dublin, or the Irish provinces).[98] On average, each of these individuals was the member of three clubs. The minimum number of clubs of which an individual was a member was one, while the maximum was an extraordinary twelve. The Earl of Dunraven, for instance, combined membership of political and social clubs like the Carlton and the Kildare Street, with that of sporting clubs like the Turf, Jockey, and the Royal Yacht Squadron, Cowes. Indeed, yachting became a popular pastime for the Irish landlords: seventeen of them (8 per cent of the clubbable landlords) were members of the Royal Club at Kingstown or the Royal Yacht Squadron at Cowes. The number of Irish landlords who took up yachting was probably even higher than this figure suggests: apparently 80 per cent of members of the Royal St George Yacht Club in Kingstown were also members of the Kildare Street.[99] The most popular clubs were those in London—more than half (52 per cent) of the Irish landlords who joined clubs were members of the Carlton—while more than one-third were the members of Dublin clubs (see Table 1.1).

Of course, many were members of both London and Dublin clubs—thirty-eight (19 per cent) were members of the Carlton and the Kildare Street—and this further cemented contacts between the Irish landlords and the wider British landed elite. As well as the Kildare Street Club in Dublin, the Sackville Street Club on the north side of the city was also popular among the Irish landlords, although it was reputed to be less amenable to Catholic landlords.[100]

---

[97] On the Cork card case, see the *Irish Times*, 26 Jan. 1894; 10 Mar. 1894; 9 May 1894; 10 May 1894; 16 May 1894; 18 May 1894; 22 May 1894; and 23 May 1894. A micro-historical study of the Cork card case might reveal a good deal about the world view of members of the Irish establishment.

[98] It is likely that those landlords who were not the members of gentlemen's clubs owned smaller estates on which they were resident and were probably not involved in political life.

[99] McDowell, *Land and Learning*, 75.

[100] The Sackville Street Club was occupied by the anti-Treaty forces during the Irish Civil War and destroyed by fire in 1922. McDowell, *Land and Learning*, 38.

Table 1.1. Landlords' Club
Membership

London	
Carlton	107 (52%)
Reform	8 (4%)
Travellers	45 (22%)
Whites	35 (17%)
Garrick	7 (3%)
United Service	14 (7%)
Brooks	24 (12%)
Turf	9 (4%)
Athenæum	12 (6%)
Marlborough	9 (4%)
Boodles	11 (5%)
Devonshire	3 (1%)
Dublin	
Kildare Street	71 (35%)
Sackville Street	39 (19%)
Number	204

According to Maurice Headlam, a senior member of the Irish Civil Service, the Sackville Street Club: 'was formed of those who seceded when Kildare Street decided to admit Roman Catholics.'[101] The Kildare Street may have been more tolerant of Catholics, but after 1880 it was not possible to be a Home Ruler and a member of the club, and when Sir Thomas Esmonde, a Catholic landowner, was elected as a nationalist MP he withdrew from the club.[102] Catholic nationalists were probably more inclined to join either the Catholic Commercial Club (the president of which was the Archbishop of Dublin) or, following the Parnell split of 1890–1, the National Club, which was under the leadership of John Redmond, who was chairman of the Irish Parliamentary Party, 1900–18.[103] The Protestant members of the Irish landlord class may also have been bound together in the Freemasons: the Duke of Abercorn was the grand master of Freemasons in Ireland, and many of the other landlords were undoubtedly Freemasons too.[104] This may also have bound the Irish landlord class together with businessmen, professionals, civil servants, and police officers.

[101] Maurice Headlam, *Irish Reminiscences* (London, 1947), 43. However, one of the Catholic landowners in my study (Lord Gormanston) was a member of the Sackville Street Club.

[102] McDowell, *Land and Learning.*   [103] Ibid. 26.

[104] Catholics were and are prohibited from joining the Freemasons under threat of excommunication by the Catholic hierarchy because the Masons were regarded as anti-clerical and anti-Catholic.

II

To what extent did the composition of the Irish landed elite change between 1881 and 1918? In order to assess the social characteristics of the 'great' landowners in the early twentieth century a search was made for 10 per cent of these landowner families in *Walford's County Families* (1918 edn). Altogether thirty landowners in 1881 were randomly sampled (10 per cent of the total), and a search was made for the descendants of these families in *Walford's County Families* in 1918. Of the thirty families, nine were based in Leinster, eight in Ulster, seven in Connacht, and six in Munster. This study revealed that there was a certain amount of continuity between 1881 and 1918, with three of the great landowners being the same person in both years (the Marquis of Lansdowne; the Earl of Norbury; and Richard William Blackwood Ker). There were also discontinuities: most notably four (13 per cent) of the thirty landowner families could not be identified in *Walford's County Families* in 1918. This was probably because these families had either sold their land and were no longer identified as county families or because they had failed to produce an heir to succeed to the family estate. Two of the landowners in 1918 were women—Mrs Julia Elizabeth Mary Talbot and Lady Gertrude Millicent Palmer—both of whom were the widows of two of the great landowners in 1881 (William John Talbot and Sir Roger William Henry Palmer respectively). And most of the landowners in 1918 were Episcopalian with the exception being the Catholic Sir Henry Christopher Grattan Bellew.

Broadly speaking, the social characteristics of the descendants of the great landowners in 1918 were very similar to those of their predecessors in 1881. Some of the descendants of the great landowning families of the 1880s continued to be involved in political life: five (19 per cent of the random sample) were members of the House of Lords but only three (12 per cent) had been members of the House of Commons (one of whom was an MP for an Irish constituency (Richard William Blackwood Ker)), revealing the steep decline in the proportion of landlord-MPs. More than half of them (sixteen or 62 per cent) were army officers while only one (4 per cent) had been trained as a barrister. Most of the landowners in 1918 lived at least some of the time on their Irish estates: eleven (42 per cent) of them lived exclusively on their Irish estates; a further eleven (42 per cent) lived in both England and Ireland; and only a minority (four or 16 per cent) lived exclusively in England. Although this evidence is impressionistic, it does suggest that the Irish landlord class were more likely to be permanently resident in Ireland than their forebears in the 1880s. In part, this was because some of the great English landowners who had also owned estates in Ireland, Scotland, or Wales tended to sell them off following the agricultural depression of the late 1870s and retained only their estates in England. By 1918, then, most landowners in Ireland were probably permanently resident and did not own estates elsewhere.[105]

In terms of education, more than half of them (fourteen or 54 per cent) had received a secondary education, with the vast majority of these (twelve or 86 per cent) attending English public schools (Eton, Harrow, Rugby, and Cheltenham) and one other attending English Catholic public schools (Beaumont and Downside). One (7 per cent) of the landowners in 1918 who had received a secondary education had been educated at an English Protestant school (Colchester Grammar) which suggests the declining wealth and social standing of the Irish landlord class between 1881 and 1918. About one-quarter (seven or 27 per cent) of the landowners in 1918 had also attended university, with most of these (six or 86 per cent) attending Oxbridge and one (14 per cent) attending London University. None of the landowners in 1918 had attended Trinity College Dublin, which suggests the Irish landed class were in retreat from their Irishness. A handful of landowners in 1918 had received a vocational education, with three attending the military academies at Gosport and Sandhurst, one attending the Royal Agricultural College, and another who had trained as a barrister. Like their predecessors in 1881, a significant proportion of the landowners in 1918 (ten or 38 per cent) were the members of London and Dublin clubland. The London clubs were the most popular, especially the Carlton (four or 40 per cent); the Turf (four or 40 per cent); the Marlborough (three or 30 per cent); and Brooks's (two or 20 per cent). Of the Dublin clubs, the Kildare Street was the most popular (two or 20 per cent), and one of the landowners in 1918 (10 per cent) was a member of the Royal St George Yacht Club at Kingstown. There was some decline, then, in the proportion of landowners in 1918 who were the members of clubs with membership of the Carlton down from 52 per cent to 40 per cent (between 1881 and 1918), and membership of the Kildare Street Club down from 35 per cent to 20 per cent over the same period.

It may be that the descendants of the 'great' landowners in 1918 had less money than their predecessors to enable them to join clubs, and perhaps also less inclination to attempt to influence the political process through the membership of elite networks in London or Dublin. The period between 1881 and 1918 witnessed a steep decline in the Irish landlords' power and wealth. Indeed, in most cases, the descendants of the great landowners in 1918 were no longer the owners of substantial estates. By 1918, almost two-thirds of the land of Ireland had been sold by the landlords to their tenants, and even those diehard landowners who had refused to sell at first had been forced to sell their estates

---

[105] Cannadine, *Decline and Fall*, 137. The Devonshires and Fitzwilliams, for instance, sold their land in Ireland but they remained important landowners in Derbyshire and Yorkshire.

by the end of the Great War.[106] The descendants of the 'great' landowners in 1918, then, may have retained home farms or demesne land (usually of several hundred acres) but they no longer derived the bulk of their incomes from the ownership of substantial estates in 1918. A series of Land Acts introduced by the British government between 1870 and 1909 gradually undermined the economic power of the Irish landlord class, and compelled them to sell their estates to their tenants; and the next section of the chapter will examine the changing relationship between the Irish landlords and the British state after 1879.

III

Why did the British state effectively force the Irish landlord class to sell their land to the Irish tenant farmers? Historically, British rule in Ireland had been based on an alliance with the Irish landlord class (which was largely Protestant) and the Irish Protestant middle class. The relationship between the British state and the Irish landlords was, however, not an easy one, and from the beginning of the nineteenth century the cracks in this relationship were evident. Indeed, the Act of Union itself constituted an attack by the British state on the power of the Irish landlords and the Protestant middle class who had dominated Grattan's parliament between 1782 and 1801. In short, the British state believed that the United Irishmen's insurrection of 1798 revealed that the Irish 'Ascendancy' was incapable of governing Ireland effectively and so—from 1801 onwards—the British state and not the Irish landlord class governed Ireland.[107] Furthermore, the British state appears to have expected Irish landowners to behave like the English landowners who—it was believed—presided over their localities in a benevolent manner, and were responsible for upholding law and order in a consensual manner. In England, landlords were regarded as governing their localities with affection and paternal care so that they won the loyalty and support of their tenants. However, as a number of nineteenth-century commentators explained, Irish landlords did not behave in a like manner. Fintan Lalor, the Young Irelander, for instance, observed that:

The feelings that exist in England between landlord and tenant, coming down from old times, and handed on as an heirloom from generation to generation—the feeling of family pride, the feeling of family attachment, the habit of the house, the fashion of the land, the custom of the country, all those things that stand for laws, and are stronger than laws, are here unknown.[108]

---

[106] By 1918, 64% of tenanted land had been purchased in Ireland. See Campbell, *Land and Revolution*, 91.

[107] The United Irishmen's insurrection attempted to create a democratic Irish republic but it was suppressed and defeated by the British military forces in 1798.

[108] Quot. Terry Eagleton, *Heathcliff and the Great Hunger* (London, 1995), 54. Young Ireland was a romantic nationalist group that was active between 1842 and 1848.

Similarly, Gustave de Beaumont, who visited Ireland twice in the 1830s, observed that:

The Irish aristocracy, for the most part, does not govern at all, and when it governs, it governs badly. It wants the first condition necessary to the existence of a beneficent government, which is, to feel sympathy instead of contempt for its subjects. It is detested when absent; it is cursed when present; it possesses all the land in a country where the people have nothing but the land for their support, and immense revenues of which it never returns one farthing to the wretches from whom those revenues are raised. It possesses immense civil powers, and it makes such use of these powers, that neither government nor subjects recognise any proceeding but force, the one to impose the law, and the other to evade it. It has great religious privileges, which it has so strangely abused, that it has rendered its creed hateful among a thousand other objects of hate. Here are vices so great and enormous, that it may be said to possess nothing of aristocracy but name.[109]

For various reasons, Irish landlords were unable to replicate the informal rule of their English, Scottish, and Welsh colleagues and, therefore, failed to win the support of their tenants. For this reason, the control of law and order was gradually taken away from them and instead vested in the state. The formation of the Resident Magistracy in the 1820s, for instance, placed the control of law and order in the hands of state-appointed officials rather than those of the landed elite in the Irish countryside. In terms of this process, the Great Famine (1845–9) constituted a critical turning point. The British state had expected Irish landowners to take responsibility for relief measures during the crisis, and their failure to do so appears to have irrevocably transformed the British view of the Irish landed elite.[110]

From about 1870 onwards, it is clear that the British state in Ireland was now attempting to build an alliance with the Catholic middle class. After the failed Fenian insurrection of 1867, Gladstone was determined to 'pacify Ireland' and he began to dismantle the basis of Protestant power in Ireland. In 1869–70, the Church of Ireland was disestablished; in 1870, a Land Act was introduced that gave Irish tenants compensation for improvements; and in 1872 the secret ballot was introduced. Each of these measures undermined the power of the Irish Protestant landlord class: the privileged status and financial support for their Church was removed; they were no longer the exclusive and sole owners of their estates since their tenants now had certain limited rights to their landholdings; and their ability to control the way in which their tenants voted at elections was taken away. For the members of the Irish landlord class, as Elizabeth Bowen recalled,

this abrogation of their power . . . was felt as a bitter blow. It was '*Et tu, Brute!*' One felt injured in spirit, if not in purse . . . the landlords were, or felt themselves, sacrificed to the

---

[109] Gustave de Beaumont, *Ireland: Social, Political and Religious* (Cambridge, Mass., 2006), 203.
[110] Hoppen, *Elections*, 167–8.

hopes of successful continuance of that very Union to which they had looked to maintain their authority.[111]

However, the critical episode in transforming the position of the Irish landlord class was the Land War of 1879–81, which ultimately forced the British state to expropriate the Irish landlords. The world agricultural depression of the late 1870s caused the prices of agricultural produce in Ireland to drop to such an extent that many Irish small tenant farmers could no longer afford to pay their rents: the value of agricultural produce dropped by 36 per cent; the value of crops by 50 per cent; and the value of livestock by 36 per cent.[112] Many tenants were therefore forced to petition their landlords for rent reductions to tide them over the crisis. In this context, the Land League was established in April 1879 to campaign for rent reductions and quickly gained mass support. During the resulting conflict, 863 'agrarian outrages' were committed in 1879 (rising to 2,585 in 1880, 4,439 in 1881, and 3,433 in 1882) and about 30,000 tenants were evicted between 1879 and 1882.[113]

Broadly speaking, the Land War removed any remaining popular support for landlordism and also seriously threatened the legitimacy of the British state in Ireland. In response to the crisis, and in an attempt to shore up the legitimacy of the British state in Ireland, Gladstone introduced his second Land Act in 1881. The Act established 'fair rent' courts to which tenants were entitled to apply for judicial revisions of their rents every fifteen years. The first wave of judicial revisions in 1881–2 reduced tenants' rents across Ireland by an average of 20 per cent and the second wave, in 1896–7 reduced first-term judicial rents by a further 22 per cent.[114] Most importantly, the 1881 Land Act effectively put an end to the Irish landlords' absolute ownership of their land, and created a system of dual ownership. After 1881, the State, and not the individual landlord, had the power to determine rents. Furthermore, the legislation restricted landlords' powers to evict to cases where the tenant had not paid her rent. After 1881, then, it was inevitable that the whole landlord system in Ireland would unravel. The system of dual ownership was unworkable in the long term because the third revision of rent (which tenants could avail themselves of in 1911–12) would result in a reduction of the Irish landlords' income from rent by about 60 per cent on the pre-1881 levels. The logic of the 1881 Land Act was, therefore, for the landlords to sell. In 1885, the Ashbourne Act first introduced a small scheme of government-subsidized land purchase, and in 1903, Wyndham's famous Land Act invested £180 million in land purchase. Under the terms of the Act, the government bought the land from the landowner and the purchasing tenant paid an annuity to the British government over a 68½-year period. Landlords

---

[111] Bowen, *Bowen's Court*, 396.   [112] Dooley, *Decline of the Big House in Ireland*, 91.
[113] Charles Townshend, *Political Violence in Ireland: Government and Resistance since 1848* (Oxford, 1983), 151; Vaughan, *Landlords and Tenants in Mid-Victorian Ireland*, 23.
[114] Fair rent figures in Campbell, *Land and Revolution*, Ch. 2.

were offered a 12 per cent bonus to persuade them to sell, and by 1918 two-thirds of the land of Ireland had been transferred from the landlord to the tenant.

The Land War was, therefore, the critical point at which expropriation of the Irish landlord class by the British state became inevitable. But, what were the underlying causes of the Land War? There are—in broad terms—two main explanations of the origins of the conflict. The first—largely nationalist—accounts of the Irish Land War suggest that the catalyst for the war may have been the agricultural depression of the 1870s, but that the real cause of the conflict was the cruel and predatory behaviour of the Irish landlord class. Pomfret, for instance, advanced the following three general propositions about landlord–tenant relations in nineteenth-century Ireland: first, that evictions were endemic and persistent; second, that rent levels were 'out of proportion to the yield'; and third, that landlords did not invest in the improvement of their properties.[115] According to this interpretation, then, the Land War was caused by the widespread popular hostility of the tenant farmer class to the behaviour of the landed elite which found expression in the agitations of the Land League.

Over the last thirty years, however, revisionist historians have provided a new interpretation of the nature of landlordism in nineteenth-century Ireland. While acknowledging that some landlords did behave in a ruthless manner, it has been suggested that landlords in general ran their estates in a fairer and more equitable manner than the nationalist interpretation suggested. Although technically landlords were able to evict tenants and to increase rent levels each year, in practice this tended not to happen. There were about 500,000 tenant farmers in Ireland in the 1860s, ranging from poor small farmers to comparatively well-off large farmers or graziers. The vast majority of them had a yearly tenancy, although about one-fifth held leases on their land. Technically, the yearly tenant could be evicted with only six months' notice to quit; rents could be increased each year; and evicted tenants had no rights to compensation for improvements they had made to their holdings. However, in practice this did not happen. The law presumed that a yearly tenancy continued unchanged from year to year, unless it was given up by the tenant. If the landlord wanted to change it, therefore, he could do so only by going into court. While this did not prevent landlords from evicting their tenants or increasing their rents, it did make such practices more difficult and it was easier to let custom run its course and to leave yearly tenancies unchanged.[116]

Furthermore, evictions were not as common as nationalist interpretations of the origins of the Land War suggested. Admittedly, there were 70,000 families

[115] These assertions are made in J. E. Pomfret, *The Struggle for Land in Ireland, 1800–1923* (Princeton, NJ, 1930). See the discussion of Pomfret in Vaughan, *Landlords and Tenants in Mid-Victorian Ireland*, pp. v–x.

[116] Vaughan, *Landlords and Tenants in Mid-Victorian Ireland*, 7.

evicted during the Great Famine and its immediate aftermath (1846–53) mainly due to tenants' inability to pay their rents, as well as the widespread starvation and emigration of tenant farmers (one million died of disease and hunger and a further million emigrated). According to Donnelly, 65,412 families were evicted between 1849 and 1854 but of this number 16,672 were readmitted either as legal tenants or caretakers so that a minimum of 48,740 families were permanently dispossessed during this period. Given that each of these families probably included an average of five people, about a quarter of a million people were affected by this wave of evictions.[117] Between the end of the Famine (1853) and the beginning of the Land War (1878), however, evictions were comparatively infrequent. Eviction rates were low between 1853 and 1861, when they began to increase; they fell away again after 1864, and only increased after 1878, reaching a peak during the Land War in 1882 (in that year there were 5,000 evictions). Even so, it is worth noting that the number of evictions during the Land War (about 30,000) was less than half that during the Great Famine (about 70,000).[118] What these figures suggest is that evictions took place on a large scale only when arrears were high and output low, particularly during the agricultural depressions of the early 1860s and the late 1870s and early 1880s. The Irish landlords did not generally evict their tenants for political or personal reasons but tended to evict only in cases of non-payment of rent. According to Vaughan, 'a majority of those evicted were insolvent'.[119]

However, even if the actual number of evictions was not as high as Pomfret suggested, there was still widespread fear of eviction among the Irish tenant farmer class. This was partly because those evictions that did take place tended to be on a large scale as part of more general clearances which gained great publicity and great popular sympathy for the evicted men, women, and children.[120] In 1851, 267 houses were levelled on the Martin estate in county Galway; 164 houses were levelled on the Lucan estate in Mayo; and there were over fifty other incidences of similar clearances in the same year.[121] Although the number of clearances was much less frequent in the post-Famine period, there were some serious mass evictions later in the century. In April 1861, for instance, forty-seven families (including eighty-five adults and 159 children) were evicted from their houses (which were unroofed and levelled) at Derryveagh, near Letterkenny, in county Donegal by John George Adair.[122] Although Adair had only purchased the Derryveagh lands in 1859 he quickly entered into a conflict with his tenants over shooting rights and trespassing sheep, and consequently his Scottish steward James Murray was shot dead in November 1860. The evictions were carried out

---

[117] Donnelly, 'Landlords and Tenants', in Vaughan, *A New History of Ireland*, v. 337.
[118] Vaughan, *Landlords and Tenants in Mid-Victorian Ireland*, 23.   [119] Ibid. 23, 25.
[120] Ibid. 25–8.   [121] W. E. Vaughan, *Sin, Sheep and Scotsmen* (Belfast, 1983), 28.
[122] Adair is one of the landowners reviewed in this chapter and he owned 52,173 acres in Donegal, Queen's county and Kilkenny.

the following year because Adair believed all of the Derryveagh tenants were implicated in the murder.[123]

Of course, even if mass evictions were not an annual event, the experience of eviction constituted an absolute disaster for the families involved. Nine of the evicted Derryveagh families were allowed to remain on the estate as caretakers but only three of these were permanently reinstated, with the rest being gradually removed during 1861; some found work on the neighbouring estate; thirteen families went to the workhouse in Letterkenny; six found shelter with friends; and fourteen other families were unaccounted for or were found still wandering through the ruins of their cottages a month later. Conditions in the workhouse were appalling: John Doherty of Castletown died there. Others took the emigrant ship to Australia. For some, the mental torment of eviction was too much and Michael Bradley tried to drown himself and was then committed to an asylum.[124] Mass evictions might not have been an annual event but the 100,000 evictions during the Famine and the Land War alone must have led to similar economic and mental traumas for upwards of half a million people. The trauma of eviction—and particularly mass eviction—was such that it was remembered for a long time in the localities where it occurred. In east Galway, for instance, evictions carried out by Lord Dunsandle during the Great Famine were described to members of the Irish Folklore Commission in the 1930s and 1940s. Pádraig Ó Diomasaigh of Cill Conaidhrean, who was born just after the Famine in 1854, explained that:

After the Famine Lord Dunsandle evicted, wasn't he called Lord Leveller? From the cross at Buacín there was terrible levelling of houses, about 40 houses.[125]

Some landlords did also use other strategies to rid their estates of unwelcome tenants. On the Lansdowne estate in county Kerry, for instance, the infamous land agent, William Steuart Trench—who was Adair's uncle—used assisted emigration to remove about 4,600 persons from the estate in the years after the Great Famine.[126] The threat of eviction was often used to ensure prompt payment of rent, and the large number of notices to quit that were issued may also explain the widespread perception of the Irish landlords as rampant serial evictors. Indeed, the number of notices to quit that were issued greatly exceeded the number of evictions in any one year. For instance, 5,531 notices to quit were issued in 1876 while only 553 tenants were evicted in that year. Landlords appear to have adopted the practice of issuing notices to quit as a matter of course to all of their tenants as a means of ensuring that they did not fall into arrears. It has been estimated that one million notices to quit were issued between 1850 and 1886, so that

---

123 Vaughan, *Sin, Sheep and Scotsmen*, 11–14.
124 Ibid. 62–3. Evicted tenants who were readmitted to their houses and holdings as caretakers did so without holding any lease.
125 Cathal Poirteir, *Famine Echoes* (Dublin, 1995), 234.
126 Lyne, *Lansdowne Estate in Kerry*, 195.

each tenant received—on average—two eviction notices over this period.[127] Although comparatively few of those who were issued with notices to quit actually were evicted, the receipt of such a document surely generated a certain amount of stress among tenant farmers, who remembered the mass evictions of the Famine period. As Alexander Richey, Professor of Law at Trinity College Dublin, explained in 1880: 'every notice to quit brought home to the tenant the power of the landlord to evict him; every use by a landlord of his legal power for the purpose of raising the rent . . . was a conclusive proof that this power might be harshly and inequitably used.'[128]

In Pomfret's account of landlord–tenant relations in Ireland, the dominant image is that of the rack-renting landlord who charged exorbitant rents of his hard-pressed tenants. However, the evidence of rent levels in Victorian Ireland does not substantiate this view of landlord behaviour. In general terms, rents increased significantly during the late eighteenth and early nineteenth centuries, but then fell back after 1850. Certainly, there were landlords who did screw up the rent on their properties (the Earl of Castlestuart was accused of increasing some of his rents by 500 per cent).[129] Similarly, Sir John Benn Walsh raised the rents on his Cork and Kerry estates by 55 per cent between 1829 and 1847, and then by a further 41 per cent between 1847 and 1866, but this was the exception rather than the rule.[130] Irish rents were generally lower than rents in England, and they do not appear to have kept pace with inflation.[131] Vaughan has carried out a study of rent increases on eleven estates (at least five of which were of more than 10,000 acres) and found that as a whole the average rental increase between the early 1850s and the late 1870s was just under 20 per cent.[132] This tallies with anecdotal evidence presented by Hoppen showing that the Duke of Abercorn's rents remained stable between 1837 and 1867; that rents collected on the Earl of Gosford's properties increased by only 8.8 per cent between 1850 and 1870; and that Lord Londonderry's rents had been 'reduced in the Famine years and never raised since'.[133] Moreover, rental increases appear to have fallen significantly behind increases in the prices for agricultural produce and cattle. Vaughan has calculated that the value of agricultural output increased by about 70 per cent between the end of the Famine and the beginning of the Land War, so that the increased profits from farming were generally falling into the hands of the large farmer class, rather than the supposedly predatory landlords.[134] The accumulation of wealth by the large farmer class in provincial Ireland in the

---

[127] Vaughan, *Landlords and Tenants in Mid-Victorian Ireland*, 24, n. 20.
[128] Hoppen, *Elections*, 129.
[129] Vaughan, *Landlords and Tenants in Mid-Victorian Ireland*, 45.
[130] Donnelly, 'The Journals of Sir John Benn Walsh', 89. Benn Walsh was the father of the 2nd Lord Ormathwaite who owned the estates in 1881.
[131] Vaughan, *Landlords and Tenants in Mid-Victorian Ireland*, 46, 51.
[132] Ibid. 48.   [133] Hoppen, *Elections*, 112.
[134] Vaughan, *Landlords and Tenants in Mid-Victorian Ireland*, 51.

post-Famine period had important implications for the distribution of political power in the Irish countryside, which will be discussed below. The myth of the rack-renting landlord appears to have originated in the small but well publicized number of steep rent increases, and in the random and sporadic manner in which rent increases were introduced on an estate, which almost seem to have been designed to generate maximum hostility.[135]

However, Pomfret was correct to assert that Irish landlords did not reinvest in their estates to the same extent as their fellow landowners in the rest of the United Kingdom. On British estates, it was the general practice for landowners to build houses and out-offices, to drain land, construct roads, and erect fences. John Steadyman of Wearywork Hall, for example, spent 14 per cent of his rents on repairs, drainage, local charities, and subscriptions to the Cidershire Foxhounds and the Boggymore Harriers.[136] In 1907, R. J. Thompson estimated that English and Welsh landowners spent as much as 27 per cent of receipts on improvements before 1881. A more recent study suggests that English landowners reinvested about 20 per cent of their rental receipts in their estates.[137] Irish landowners, on the other hand, appear to have invested between 4 and 11 per cent of their rental income in their estates, leaving them far behind their British colleagues in this respect.[138] In part, this can be explained by the high level of indebtedness that most Irish landlords experienced during the second half of the nineteenth century. It has been estimated that their average net income was as little as 40 per cent of their receipts, with just over 60 per cent taken up with taxes (12 per cent), estate management (6 per cent), improvements (11 per cent), interest on encumbrances (17 per cent), and the upkeep of the Big House (17 per cent).[139] Some landlords paid as much as 43 per cent of their gross receipts on the interest repayments for their mortgages, so that they were not in a position properly to manage their estates in a similar manner to British landlords.[140] Not all Irish landlords were as extravagant as Lord Dufferin, who spent £26,000 on yachts between 1852 and 1872, but many of them persisted in living beyond their means and accumulated large debts that greatly reduced their annual incomes.[141] Extravagance won out over improvements, and the Irish landlords failed properly to reinvest in their estates.[142] As Vaughan concludes: 'If a quarter of the rents had gone back to the tenants in the form of loans, gifts, new houses, and drained fields, the tenants would have been inextricably tied to their landlords.'[143]

---

[135] Hoppen, *Elections*, 113.
[136] Steadyman is the fictitious 'typical £5,000-a-year squire' invented by John Bateman. See Bateman, *Great Landowners of Great Britain and Ireland*, pp. xxiv–xxv.
[137] Vaughan, *Landlords and Tenants in Mid-Victorian Ireland*, 123.
[138] Ibid. 122–3.   [139] Ibid. 118.
[140] The Earl of Granard, for instance. See Dooley, *Decline of the Big House in Ireland*, 80.
[141] Vaughan, *Landlords and Tenants in Mid-Victorian Ireland*, 119.
[142] Ibid. 221.   [143] Ibid. 129.

It may be, then, that the underlying cause of the Land War was not the predatory behaviour of the Irish landlords but the failure of the Irish landlord class as a whole to naturalize its rule and position in Irish society in a manner comparable to landowners on the other side of St George's Channel. A cultural gulf separated most of the Irish landlords from their tenants because they were mainly Protestant while the tenant farmer class was overwhelmingly Catholic. In this context, it was more difficult for the Irish landlords to forge connections with the Catholic community, and thereby to win support for their rule. In England, on the other hand, where landlords usually shared the same religious beliefs as their tenants, it was easier for them to achieve hegemony.

Far from sharing a religious or ethnic identification with their tenants, however, the Irish landlord class were strongly identified with Protestantism. Of the landlords under review, twenty-nine of them (10 per cent) were patrons of livings who controlled access to vicarages.[144] Moreover, a number of the great landowners were senior members of the Church of Ireland: the Venerable Frederic Falkiner Goold owned 10,966 acres (valued at £3,090) in Limerick and was also Archdeacon of Raphoe (until his death in 1877), and the Revd Lord O'Neill (whose father had been rector of Kilmore, county Armagh) owned 65,919 acres in Antrim (valued at £44,000) and was prebendary of St Michael's, Dublin. Many others were closely related to leading figures in the Church of Ireland: the 4th Earl of Bandon was the Bishop of Tuam's nephew; Cornwallis Robert Ducarel Gun Cunninghame was the Bishop of Clogher's grandson; Ralph Smyth was the Bishop of Meath's grandson; and Lord George Hill's son married the Archbishop of Dublin's daughter. Many of the younger sons of landed families became Protestant clerics: according to one survey, 6 per cent of younger sons entered the church.[145] Other landowners in my study married into the church: seventeen (6 per cent) married the daughters of Protestant clerics, and thirty-seven of them (13 per cent) were related in some way to Episcopalian clergymen (as their sons, brothers, nephews, and fathers). As Chapter 6 of this book demonstrates, the Church of Ireland was essentially the church of the Irish landed elite.[146] Perhaps, then, the cultural divide between most landlords and most tenants did play a part in the landed elite's failure to achieve hegemony. If more of them had converted to Catholicism, they would have been in a position

---

[144] The patron of a living was an individual who owned the living or patronage of an Episcopalian church and had the power to appoint its vicar and officials.

[145] Dooley, *Decline of the Big House in Ireland*, 76.

[146] Of course, two of the landlords in this study were Papal Counts, and a significant number of the smaller landlords—probably those with estates of less than 2,000 acres—were Catholics. But the landlord class as a whole was strongly Protestant, and its self-appointed leaders (in landlord defence organizations after 1879) were overwhelmingly Episcopalian. Of 44 landlords in my sample who were the members of landlord's defence organizations, for instance, only one was Catholic. See L. P. Curtis, 'Landlord Responses to the Irish Land War, 1879–1987', *Eire/Ireland*, Fall–Winter (2003).

to associate more regularly with their tenants, and to empathize with their world view.[147] Indeed, it is striking that so few landlords did convert, especially when it is recalled how many converted to Protestantism in the eighteenth century to avoid the implications of the penal laws. In the rather different circumstances of the late nineteenth century, landlords could perhaps have saved themselves by becoming either Catholics or nationalists.

A survey of landlords' obituaries and notices about them in the *Irish Times*, however, suggests that some of them had naturalized their rule in Ireland. John Grey Vesey Porter, who supported Home Rule, and owned estates in counties Fermanagh, Longford, and Tyrone: 'was kindly and generous to his tenants, and voluntarily gave them several reductions in their rents. He spent a very large sum of money in carrying out extensive improvements in the village of Lisbellaw, where he established a good library and market house.'[148] At the coming of age of the Earl of Huntingdon's son in 1862, the tenants on the county Waterford estate presented a congratulatory address to him 'feeling it to be not only a duty, but also an expression of the unanimous feeling of your happy and contented tenantry . . . We trust your lordship may ever follow in the footsteps of your honoured father, of whom it may be truly said that he is "the farmer's patron and the poor man's friend".'[149] When Lord Castletown died in 1883, 'he commanded the respectful esteem of his tenantry . . . Among the poorest of the poor his name was revered and his good deeds were extolled'.[150] And when Viscount Gough's son, Hugh, returned from his travels in October 1876, he was met by a crowd of 'hundreds' at Gort railway station, and the Gort Temperance Band, who struck up 'Steer my bark to Erin's Isle' as he stepped from the train and was guided to his open carriage:

From this a number of his Lordship's tenantry, yielding to the impulse of their generous natures, had detached the horses, yoking themselves to it instead, and, with the Temperance band playing in front, dragged the carriage towards the town . . . Cheer succeeded cheer as they proceeded through the principal streets of the town, followed by the immense multitude of people which the occasion had brought together. Every window was ablaze with cheerful faces, whose voices, responding to the impulse of their hearts, cried 'welcome, welcome'.[151]

---

[147] Rosamund Ffrench, the daughter of one of the landlords under review (Robert Ffrench), whose family owned 10,121 acres in Galway (valued at £3,703) in 1876 converted to Catholicism in the 1890s and regularly cycled from her house at Monivea to mass at Skehana. Through her contact with the Catholic community there, it came to her attention that a small tenant farmer's wife (Margaret Jordan) had suffered several miscarriages and was once again pregnant. Ffrench paid for Mrs Jordan to travel to Dublin where, with medical assistance, she gave birth to a son at Holles Street Hospital in January 1907. Later, Ms Ffrench stood as godmother to the child, Michael Jordan, who could not have been born without the landlord's intervention. Such acts undoubtedly transformed the way in which landlords were viewed, and Rosamund Ffrench continues to be remembered in Skehana as a 'good' landlord. Interview conducted by the author with Margaret Campbell at Carlisle (8 Nov. 2008). Michael Jordan (1907–86) was the author's grandfather.

[148] *Irish Times*, 10 Oct. 1903. Porter's estates encompassed 21,660 acres.

[149] Ibid. 9 Dec. 1862.   [150] Ibid. 27 Jan. 1883.   [151] Ibid. 14 Oct. 1876.

Of course, if a study of landlordism in nineteenth-century Ireland was conducted only on the basis of reports in the *Irish Times*, a very rose-tinted and distorted impression of landlord–tenant relations would emerge, but even so these examples do suggest that at least some of the landlords—some of the time—were reasonably popular with their tenants.[152]

In general terms, however, even sympathetic commentators like Vaughan have argued that the Irish landlords did not behave as an aristocracy should.[153] They did not play a leadership role in their communities; they did not support their tenants during periods of scarcity; they did not invest in improving their estates; and they did not attempt to integrate their tenants into their social world. This failure to naturalize their rule and position in rural Ireland meant that they were unable to maintain law and order in Ireland in the manner of English landlords in England. English landlords were viewed as reliably maintaining law and order in their communities, while Irish landlords appeared to be foolishly and unnecessarily pouring fuel on the flames of agrarian conflict. Lord John Russell believed that twenty gentlemen 'like those we have in Hampshire and Sussex would set the Irish countryside aright', while Edward Horsman, who was the Irish Chief Secretary in 1855, even went as far as to suggest that 'outrageous' Irish landlords 'deserved to be murdered'.[154] Later in the nineteenth century, Arthur Balfour complained to Lord Salisbury: 'What fools the Irish landowners are . . . some stupid, some criminal, many injudicious.'[155]

It is a staple of popular nationalist opinion in Ireland that the British state and the Irish landlord class were closely allied and mutually supportive of one another. Gilbert Morrissey, a member of the Irish Republican Brotherhood at Craughwell, county Galway, epitomized this view in his statement to the Bureau of Military History: 'If the people were not fighting against the British forces proper, they were making a fair stand against its henchmen, the tyrant landlord class, their agents and bailiffs, who were backed up and protected by the Royal Irish Constabulary.'[156] While this view of the relationship between the British state and Irish landlordism might hold for pre-Famine Ireland, it does not hold for post-Famine Ireland. Indeed, the Famine marked a critical turning-point in British perspectives of Irish landlordism. British politicians expected Irish landlords to pay for Irish problems and when they so spectacularly failed to do so during the Famine years, British political opinion became extremely critical of the landlord's position.[157] And, yet, there is some truth in Morrissey's statement. Even after almost 300 years of living in Ireland, the landed elite continued to be regarded as British and as the representatives and allies of the British state in Ireland. Thomas Fennell, a Catholic Head

---

[152] We also need to be aware that daylight affection may have concealed moonlit disaffection.
[153] Vaughan, *Landlords and Tenants in Mid-Victorian Ireland*, 221.
[154] Hoppen, *Elections*, 167.   [155] Cannadine, *Decline and Fall*, 65.
[156] Gilbert Morrissey witness statement, MA BMH WS 1,138.
[157] Hoppen, *Elections*, 167.

Constable in the Royal Irish Constabulary, believed that the primary function of the Royal Irish Constabulary after the Land War (1879–81) was to protect the Irish landlord class, and he observed that: 'The enforcement of the various Coercion Acts, the protection of landlords and their agents, of "emergency men", land grabbers, and all the other duties in connection with evictions and boycotting became the chief work of the Force for years.'[158] The Irish landed elite had—for the most part—originated in the early modern period as a colonizing class, and they continued to be regarded as such well into the nineteenth century. Popular nationalist memory recalled that the Irish landlord class had gained their land by dispossession and regarded their continued tenure as illegitimate. It may be that the decline of Irish landlordism was caused primarily by the Irish landlords' failure to transcend its roots in colonization and dispossession.

IV

Irish landlordism was far from dead even after the Land War. The wave of evictions during the conflict revealed that landlords were quite prepared to meet the challenge of the Land League. As we have seen, almost 30,000 families were evicted between 1880 and 1887, revealing that the landlords had resources of toughness, resilience, and cruelty to draw upon, and that they were determined to get rid of insolvent and defiant tenants.[159] During the 1880s, a number of new organizations were established to uphold and—where necessary—defend landlord's rights. The Irish Land Committee (established in November 1879), the Orange Emergency Committee (formed in December 1880), the Property Defence Association (founded in December 1880), and the Irish Loyal and Patriotic Union (set up in May 1885) all represented the interests of the Irish landed class during the crisis of the 1880s. These organizations resisted boycotting conspiracies, petitioned the government on behalf of landlords, and dispatched emergency men to besieged estates so that landowners could sell livestock at auction and perform other necessary chores.[160] Of the landlords under review, forty-four (15 per cent) of them were leading figures in each of these organizations, and it is striking that a number of prominent peers served on the executive committees of at least three different associations.[161] The ethos of

---

[158] Rosemary Fennell (ed.), *The Royal Irish Constabulary: A History and Personal Memoir* (Dublin, 2003), 90. Fennell is discussed further in Ch. 3. 'Emergency men' were estate employees recruited by landowners from property defence organizations to work on their estates when local residents refused to do so because of the threat of boycotting and intimidation.

[159] Curtis, 'Landlord Responses to the Irish Land War', 151. Some 29,100 families were evicted between 1880 and 1887, and no more than 5% of these were readmitted as caretakers compared with 17% of the 6,850 families evicted during the previous decade.   [160] Ibid. 170–85.

[161] These were the Duke of Abercorn and Lords Ardilaun, Bandon, Castletown, Clonbrock, Cloncurry, Courtown, Donoughmore, Erne, Farnham, Longford, Rosse, and Rossmore. Ibid. 186.

these organizations was articulated by Captain Cosby who owned a great estate in the Queen's county: 'I do not intend to die without a struggle.'[162]

It has also been suggested that the impact of the Land Acts on the fortunes of Irish landlords was not as dire as has been suggested. Gladstone's second Land Act (in 1881) resulted in landlords losing only about £1.4 million during its first decade.[163] Given that the Irish landlords had received an income from rent of £354 million between 1851 and 1880, this was perhaps not a substantial loss.[164] It is even possible that the 1881 Land Act worked to the advantage of Irish landlords by stabilizing their income from rents.[165] The Wyndham and Birrell Land Acts did greatly accelerate land purchase, but in 1914 the Irish landlords still owned almost half (42 per cent) of their tenanted land.[166] Even where sales had taken place, landowners were paid a substantial capital sum that they could profitably reinvest. Under the Wyndham and Birrell Land Acts, the Irish landlords were probably paid more than £180 million between 1903 and 1921, and they had already received £25 million under the terms of land legislation passed between 1870 and 1896 leading Dooley to suggest—perhaps rather optimistically—that the Irish landlords were 'at least as well off' after purchase as they were before.[167] The rationale for the Wyndham Land Act had been to allow landlords to sell their tenanted land, but to retain their demesne farms so that they could remain on the land as substantial farmers, which many of them did into the 1920s and thereafter.[168] Notwithstanding these qualifications, however, it is clear that the Irish landlords' political and economic power was ebbing inexorably away after the Land War. The situation was, however, different in Ulster, where many landlords shared the same religion and politics as their tenants. For this reason, landlord power in Ulster remained significant at the local level long after it had declined in the rest of Ireland, and landlords continued to play an important role in Unionist politics in Ulster (and later in Northern Ireland) up to the beginning of the Great War and beyond.[169] Ulster landowners also had social and political links with the business community, and they constituted an integral part of the Unionist movement at the beginning of the twentieth century.[170]

Some landlords did become nationalists in an attempt to find a new role for the Irish landlord class as the leaders rather than the enemies of nationalist Ireland. Chief among these was Charles Stewart Parnell, the leader of the Irish Parliamentary Party in the 1880s. Similarly, John Shawe-Taylor, a Galway landlord, was a prominent advocate of the advisability of landlords becoming

[162] Ibid. Cosby owned an estate of 10,110 acres in Queen's county (valued at £7,077) in 1876.
[163] Vaughan, *Landlords and Tenants in Mid-Victorian Ireland*, 37.   [164] Ibid. 21.
[165] Ibid. 37.   [166] Campbell, *Land and Revolution*, 91.
[167] Ibid. 89, n. 21; Dooley, *Decline of the Big House in Ireland*, 144, 274.
[168] See Cannadine, *Decline and Fall*, 103–6.
[169] Ibid. 173, 176. Of 181 county council seats in the 9 Ulster counties in 1899, Unionists (many of whom were landlords) won 86 (48%) of the total number of seats.
[170] L. P. Curtis, 'Incumbered Wealth: Landed Indebtedness in Post-famine Ireland', *American Historical Review*, 85 (1980), 366.

nationalists. In his estimation, the trajectory of nineteenth-century land legislation suggested that the power of the landed elite would eventually be lost. If the landlords were to retain a role in Irish public life, they would have to sell their estates to the tenants, and once the 'wretched land business' was out of they way, they could 'take a hand in the social & national uplifting of the Country'.[171] The inspiration behind Shawe-Taylor's conversion to a pro-land-reform position may have been his encounter with five Galway Irish Republican Brotherhood men as they returned to their farms after they had assassinated a local landlord, Walter Bourke, at Castledaly, on 6 June 1882. Although Shawe-Taylor saw each of the men and recognized them, he did not give evidence against them, fearing that he would be assassinated next if he did so. He may also have felt that Bourke, a Catholic landlord who famously attended mass carrying a rifle, and who was in the process of evicting some of his tenants, was deservedly unpopular.[172] If other members of the landlord class had had similar experiences they may have also converted to Home Rule and land reform. On the other hand, an encounter with Fenian assassins might have reinforced their stalwart Unionism.

Horace Plunkett, who was the third son of the 16th Baron Dunsany who owned a substantial estate (which Horace's older brother inherited), also saw the end of landlordism as an opportunity for the Irish landlords to

fulfil the true functions of an aristocracy . . . My appeal . . . is that they should recognise this fact, and take their new position as men who, working among others in a rural community, have by their wealth and education special advantages which they desire to use for the common good.[173]

Too few of the Irish landlords became nationalists to ensure their political survival and instead the vast majority of them became stalwart Unionists.[174] This intransigence had also been spotted by Gustave de Beaumont in the 1830s when he observed that:

there is in this aristocracy something more surprising and extraordinary than its vices; I mean the delusions by which it imposes on itself, the faith that it has in the holiness of its rights and the legitimacy of its titles, the indignation which it displays when the least of its privileges is disputed.[175]

[171] Campbell, *Land and Revolution*, 77.

[172] Martin Newell witness statement, MA BMH WS 1,562; Jim Fahy, 'Looking West', RTÉ radio broadcast (18 Feb. 1988); Campbell, *Land and Revolution*, 77–8; Eugene Hynes, *Knock: The Virgin's Apparition in Nineteenth-century Ireland* (Cork, 2008), 205. The Bourke case does suggest, however, that conversion to Catholicism might not have been enough to improve the relationship between landlords and their tenants.

[173] Horace Plunkett, *Noblesse Oblige: An Irish Rendering* (Dublin, 1908), 26.

[174] Dooley, *Decline of the Big House in Ireland*, 218. Earlier in the nineteenth century, the Irish landlords had proven themselves to be more inclined to try to convert their tenants to Protestantism than to convert to Catholicism themselves. Irene Whelan, 'The Bible Gentry: Evangelical Religion, Aristocracy, and the New Moral Order in the Early Nineteenth Century', in Crawford Gribben and Andrew Holmes (eds.), *Protestant Millennialism: Evangelicalism and Irish Society, 1790–2005* (Basingstoke, 2006). [175] De Beaumont, *Ireland: Social, Political and Religious*, 203.

Time was perhaps against the great Irish landowners in 1881. Most of them (78 per cent) were aged over 40, and the vast majority of them were in their fifties, sixties, and seventies.[176] Almost all of them had been born before the Famine, many of them during the 1820s and the 1830s—arguably a golden age for Irish landlordism—when many Big Houses were being built, and before serious indebtedness had set in.[177] The optimism and opulence of their pre-Famine Ireland may have shaped their world view, and made it difficult for them to adjust to the new facts and realities of the new Ireland. Those landlords who were able to navigate a new path for landlordism tended to be substantially younger (Charles Stewart Parnell was aged just 35 in 1881), and to be more open to accepting the new circumstances in which Irish landlords now found themselves. For the majority of Irish landlords, clinging to the memory of an imagined golden age made more sense than actually imagining a new one. If history was offering them an opportunity to become the leaders of nationalist Ireland, they were perhaps too rooted in the past to envision a new future.

Although only about 275 Big Houses were destroyed by fire during the War of Independence (1919–21) and the Irish Civil War (1922–3), their fate suggests the almost complete destruction and silencing of the Irish landlord class and their Big Houses by 1923.[178] In her novel *The Last September* Bowen describes the fate of three imaginary Big Houses in county Cork that were burned down and finally silenced by the Irish Republican Army during 'the Troubles':

For in February . . . the death—execution, rather—of the three houses, Danielstown, Castle Trent, Mount Isabel, occurred in the same night. A fearful scarlet ate up the hard spring darkness; indeed, it seemed that an extra day, unreckoned, had come to abortive birth that these things might happen. It seemed looking from east to west at the sky tall with scarlet, that the country itself was burning . . . Then the first wave of silence that was to be ultimate flowed back, confident, to the steps.[179]

---

[176] Of 259 of the great Irish landowners in 1881 about whom information is available, 4% were aged between 0 and 20; 5% were aged between 21 and 30; 13% were aged between 31 and 40; 17% were aged between 41 and 50; 23% were aged between 51 and 60; 19% were aged between 61 and 70; 15% were aged between 71 and 80; and 4% were aged between 81 and 100.

[177] Of 731 major nineteenth-century Irish houses listed in Mark Bence-Jones's (admittedly incomplete) guide, 512 can be assigned to the first half of the century and 113 to the second (Hoppen, *Elections*, 115).

[178] The 275 Irish Big Houses that were burned during the War of Independence and the Irish Civil War constituted about 4% of the 6,500 (or so) Big Houses in Ireland at the end of the nineteenth century (Dooley, *Decline of the Big House in Ireland*, 286–7, 236). On some Irish estates, soviets were formed during the War of Independence. See, for instance, the case of the McNamara estate in county Clare discussed in the obituary of Henry Valentine McNamara, *Irish Times*, 30 Oct. 1925.

[179] Elizabeth Bowen, *The Last September* (London, 1929), in Seamus Deane (ed.), *The Field Day Anthology of Irish Writing*, ii (Derry, 1991), 1174–5.

2

Administration

In his influential book *The Greening of Dublin Castle* Lawrence McBride argues that the composition of the Irish administration—that is the Irish office and the senior members of the Irish Civil Service—was in a state of rapid transformation between 1892 and 1921:

In 1892 . . . [the Irish] administration was dominated by both a bureaucratic elite and rank and file civil servants who were Unionist in politics and Protestant in religion . . . Thirty years later, in 1921, the administration . . . [was] largely controlled by Nationalists and Catholics. This transformation was as comprehensive as it was complete because it extended across the whole spectrum of the Irish administration . . . from top to bottom.[1]

According to McBride, both Conservative and Liberal administrations appointed Irish-born Catholics and nationalists to senior positions in the Irish Civil Service. For the Liberal party, the aim of this policy was to prepare the Irish administration for the transfer of power that would inevitably follow the introduction of Home Rule. In their view, an established class of Catholic and pro-Home Rule civil servants would ensure a smooth transition from British to Irish rule. For the Conservatives, on the other hand, this policy was an attempt to legitimize the Act of Union (1801–1921), and to make the government of Ireland more representative and more acceptable to the Irish people. The appointment of Catholics to senior positions in the administration was, therefore, a key element of both Conservative and Liberal policies in Ireland in this period, and the result was—in McBride's view—the replacement of the old Protestant and Unionist establishment in Dublin Castle with a new Catholic and nationalist administrative elite.

McBride's hypothesis has been largely accepted by historians, and his book illuminates a great deal about British policy in Ireland between the first Home

---

[1] Lawrence McBride, *The Greening of Dublin Castle: The Transformation of Bureaucratic and Judicial Personnel in Ireland, 1892–1922* (Washington, DC, 1991), p. ix. An earlier version of this chapter was published as 'Who Ruled Ireland? The Irish Administration, 1879–1914', *Historical Journal*, 50 (2007), 623–44. However, since the publication of that article I have been able to conduct further research on the civil servants in the manuscript census returns for 1911—which became searchable online in Dec. 2007—and this has enabled me to gain more information on the religious affiliation of the civil servants, and so the data contained in this chapter are slightly different from those presented in the article.

Rule crisis (1886) and the signing of the Anglo-Irish Treaty (1921). However, McBride's arguments do not always tally with contemporary perceptions of the nature of Dublin Castle. For instance, when Sir Antony MacDonnell, a Catholic from a county Mayo landowning family, was appointed as under secretary for Ireland in 1902, he was surprised at the bigotry and suspicion that he encountered in Dublin Castle. In November 1902, he told his wife:

I went to the office at 11 am and made the acquaintance of the staff. The office is large: & some of the staff are able men: but I am not surprised at the popular idiom attacking the 'Dublin Castle'. . . In the Castle I see nothing but police[,] police [*sic*]. There is an atmosphere of suspicion and espionage. I could not stand it for any length of time and if I cannot improve it I must go.[2]

He felt that he was 'being watched' and that 'the landlord party view me with suspicion',[3] explaining 'Dublin is a big village and a dirty village in which gossip reigns supreme: and in which people are divided into sects & factions.'[4] After one meeting of the Local Government Board, he lamented that

No questions of importance were up for discussion: but those that were brought forward showed how the feud of Catholic & Protestant in the North of Ireland poisons the smallest relations of the people[.] The feud of Hindu & Mohamedan is not more bitter. Nor so enduring and persistent.[5]

Later he told a dinner party that he had been informed on his return to Ireland (from Bengal) that sectarian animosity was on the wane: if so, he said, 'it dies very hard'.[6] A less-sympathetic commentator on the British state in Ireland, D. P. Moran, the Catholic-Gaelic chauvinist and editor of the *Leader* newspaper also claimed that senior positions in the Irish Civil Service were dominated by Protestants and Unionists, and largely closed to Catholics and Nationalists.[7] Cumulatively, this evidence suggests that there may have been less of a 'greening' effect than McBride claims.

There are grounds, therefore, for revisiting McBride's hypothesis, and this chapter will re-examine his conclusions in the light of new evidence and a new approach. *The Greening of Dublin Castle* is a chronological account of the senior appointments made by each administration in Ireland between 1892 and 1921 based on a close reading of the correspondence of prime ministers, chief secretaries, lord lieutenants, under secretaries, Irish parliamentarians, and so on. My approach, on the other hand, is systematically to examine the social

[2] Antony MacDonnell to his wife, 18 Nov. 1902, Bodleian Library MS Eng. Hist. e. 216 (MacDonnell Papers), fo. 16^{r-v}.
[3] Antony MacDonnell to his wife, 16 Nov. 1902, ibid. fos 13^{v}–14^{r}.
[4] Antony MacDonnell to his wife, 21 Nov. 1902, ibid. fo. 22^{r}.
[5] Antony MacDonnell to his wife, 18 Nov. 1902, ibid. fo. 20^{r}.
[6] *Leader*, 16 May 1903, quot. McBride, *Greening of Dublin Castle*, 108.
[7] 'Light on the Local Government Board', *Leader* (Jan. 1907), quot. McBride, *Greening of Dublin Castle*, 18–19.

background of the top civil servants (the members of the Irish office, department heads, and their immediate subordinates) at two key points—1891 (before the 'greening' process had got under way) and 1911 (by which point the introduction of Home Rule was inevitable)—and to assess the extent to which a 'greening' process had taken place over this period.[8] Before going on to look at the senior members of the administration, however, it will first be necessary to provide a profile of the leading figures in the Irish administration (the lord lieutenant, chief secretary, and under secretary) and I will now turn to an examination of those individuals who held these positions in each of the four censal years of 1881, 1891, 1901, and 1911.

I

The most powerful individuals in the government of Ireland at the end of the nineteenth and the beginning of the twentieth centuries were the lord lieutenant, the chief secretary, and the under secretary. Although the lord lieutenant was technically the head of the Irish administration and the chief secretary was increasingly the most influential member of this triumvirate, the centre of power in the Irish administration remained unclear.[9] Indeed, during the period between 1895 and 1908, power appeared to flow between the three positions. Over the seven years between 1895 and 1902, the lord lieutenant, Cadogan, who had a seat in cabinet, was arguably the most powerful man in Ireland; during 1902–4, the chief secretary, Wyndham, dominated the Irish administration; and from 1904 to 1908, the under secretary, MacDonnell, decisively influenced Irish policy. John Dillon maintained that any one of a group of five administrators—the lord lieutenant, chief secretary, attorney general, lord chancellor, or under secretary—could dominate the Irish office depending on their personality or ability.[10] Certainly, there was a tension between the position and the person; and, as Antony MacDonnell demonstrated, an ambitious and single-minded personality could redefine the nature of the office he held.

Technically, however, the head of the Irish administration was the lord lieutenant or viceroy, who represented the Crown, was responsible for the peace and security of Ireland, and had the power to appoint individuals to most of the senior positions in the Irish Civil Service.[11] He was appointed by the prime

---

[8] See Appendix for the methodology and sources used for this chapter.

[9] Kieran Flanagan, 'The Rise and Fall of the Celtic Ineligible: Competitive Examinations for the Irish and Indian Civil Services in Relation to the Educational and Occupational Structure of Ireland, 1853–1921', DPhil (University of Sussex, 1978), 488.

[10] Eunan O'Halpin, *The Decline of the Union: British Government in Ireland, 1892–1920* (Dublin, 1988), 7.

[11] R. B. McDowell, *The Irish Administration, 1801–1914* (London, 1964), 52. For a list of the Lord Lieutenant's patronage rights over selected appointments in 1883, see Flanagan, 'The Rise and Fall of the Celtic Ineligible', 692.

minister and was always a peer, although he could not be a Roman Catholic.[12] At the beginning of the nineteenth century, he usually held a seat in cabinet, but by 1900 real administrative power had devolved to the chief secretary. In 1905, for instance, Arthur Balfour, the prime minister (and a former Chief Secretary), was forced to intervene in a dispute between Lord Dudley, the lord lieutenant, and Walter Long, the chief secretary, and explain to Dudley that: 'If. . . you ask me whether, in cases of differences, the views of the Chief Secretary should prevail, I can only answer yes. There can be but one head of the Irish administration.'[13] Even so, confusion did remain, and two twentieth-century Lord Lieutenants (Cadogan and French) held seats in cabinet, while one of them (Cadogan) laboured under the 'not uncommon viceregal illusion that his was the crucial post in Irish government'.[14] Increasingly, however, the position of Lord Lieutenant became symbolic. In most cases, he sat at the viceregal court surrounded by chamberlains, aides de camp, and gentlemen in waiting, spending his annual salary of £20,000 on the hosting of levées, balls, and dinners.[15]

In real terms, the chief secretary held the most powerful position in Irish society between 1879 and 1914. As the office of lord lieutenant declined in importance, the chief secretary became more and more influential. By the end of the nineteenth century, he was the political head of the Irish administration, the minister responsible for Irish affairs, and was also usually (although not always) a member of the cabinet.[16] When in Dublin, he lived at the chief secretary's lodge in the Phoenix Park (next to the viceregal lodge), and was paid £4,500 per annum. The chief secretary had two major tasks. First, to devise legislation for Ireland on matters as diverse as education, home rule, land reform, and social welfare. And second, to direct and oversee the administration of thirty or so Irish departments. As such, the chief secretary wielded enormous power in Ireland. In 1902, for instance, George Wyndham was able to call on £180 million of Government credit to finance the transfer of the ownership of the land of Ireland from the landlord to the tenant; and as a result more than 200,000 tenant farmers became the owners of their farms.

The chief secretary's office was at the centre of the Irish administration at Dublin Castle, and contained three main divisions: financial, judicial, and administrative. All the financial estimates of Irish departments passed through the finance division of the chief secretary's office, and were reviewed there before being forwarded to the Treasury in London. The judicial division controlled law and order in Ireland, and maintained contact with the Attorney General, the heads of the Dublin Metropolitan Police, the Royal Irish Constabulary

---

[12] McDowell, *Irish Administration*, 52; McBride, *Greening of Dublin Castle*, 5.
[13] O'Halpin, *Decline of the Union*, 5–6.   [14] Ibid. 14.
[15] McDowell, *Irish Administration*, 53–4. On the Lord Lieutenant's various entertainments, see 'A Native', *Recollections of Dublin Castle and of Dublin Society* (London, 1902).
[16] O'Halpin, *Decline of the Union*, 6.

and the prisons, as well as the local magistracy. Finally, the administration division managed all correspondence with English departments and oversaw personnel matters.[17] Such a wide range of responsibilities took their strain on chief secretaries, and George Otto Trevelyan (chief secretary, 1882–4) even found that his hair turned white while he was in office.[18] Despite the heavy administrative workload, the chief secretary was forced to spend most of his time in London attending parliamentary sessions and guiding Irish legislation through the House of Commons.[19] Indeed, it was often the case that the only time chief secretaries spent in Ireland was during the parliamentary recess, and so their experience of Ireland could be quite limited. Birrell (chief secretary, 1907–16) spent very little time in Ireland and his under secretary (Matthew Nathan) often had to adopt a persuasive tone in order to encourage him to visit Dublin. In March 1915, for instance, Nathan wrote to Birrell,

The weather is fine now. I should like to see you as it is long since I [*sic*] have had any talk together. Don't you think you might come over & stay with me for Easter. Charlie Hobhouse & his wife are coming I believe, but we shall be quite quiet & you shall see no one you don't want to see if I can help it.[20]

While the chief secretary was in London, the under secretary, who was the highest-ranking civil servant in Ireland, supervised the day-to-day running of the chief secretary's office.[21]

The under secretary was the permanent head of the Irish Civil Service and he occupied the pivotal post in the Irish government. Technically, his role was bureaucratic (while that of the chief secretary was political), but in practice the lines between bureaucratic and political roles were blurred. Sir West Ridgeway (under secretary 1887–93) was effectively replaced by John Morley (chief secretary 1892–5) because it was felt that he was too closely identified with the coercive policies of Arthur Balfour.[22] By the same token, David Harrel was appointed under secretary because he was regarded by the Liberal administration as sympathetic to Home Rule.[23] In 1904, Sir Antony MacDonnell even appeared to be dictating the Conservative administration's Irish policy when he drafted and published a devolution scheme that later forced Wyndham's resignation.[24] But the under secretary's role was chiefly administrative: he supervised the work of all government departments under Dublin Castle control, and was responsible for all administrative issues ranging from law and order to education. Because

[17] McBride, *Greening of Dublin Castle*, 5–8.
[18] McDowell, *Irish Administration*, 59.   [19] Ibid. 57.
[20] Matthew Nathan to Augustine Birrell, 24 Mar. 1915, Bodleian Library MS Eng. c. 7033 (Birrell Papers), fo. 67ᵛ. Charles Hobhouse was Postmaster General of the GPO in London.
[21] McBride, *Greening of Dublin Castle*, 8.   [22] O'Halpin, *Decline of the Union*, 10.
[23] McBride, *Greening of Dublin Castle*, 50–1.
[24] Antony MacDonnell is not included in my study because he was under secretary between 1902 and 1908.

he was permanently resident in Ireland, he was regarded by many observers as the real centre of power at Dublin Castle. The Dublin *Evening Post* explained in 1869:

Let no one attempt to persuade Mr. Gladstone, or Mr. Gladstone's advisers, that the Under Secretary to the Lord Lieutenant is only a chief clerk, or an amanuensis. During at least three-fourths of the year, the Under Secretary is *the* Executive of Ireland. Office business is not the department of the Lord Lieutenant; the Chief Secretary and the law officers will be absent in Parliament, the Lord Chancellor will be engaged in his court, and the whole routine of administration, as well as the whole correspondence between the Government and its Irish supporters upon matters of either local or general interest, must remain with the Under Secretary.[25]

Under secretaries also tended to remain in office for substantially longer periods than chief secretaries (because they were supposedly non-political appointments), thereby increasing their personal identification with the government. Between 1853 and 1907, for instance, there were only nine under secretaries while there were twenty-eight chief secretaries.[26] Because they were responsible for overseeing the entire administration of Ireland, they were also extremely overworked. Thomas Burke (under secretary 1869–82) told W. E. Forster (chief secretary, 1880–2) in June 1881: 'since December 1878 with the exception in two instances of a few occasional day's absence in the West of Ireland on urgent private business, I have not been absent from Dublin for a single day, and have, in addition, to attend my office on Sundays and holidays'. Forster later confirmed, in a letter to the Treasury, that Burke was 'more overworked than any official I have ever been brought in contact with'.[27] Indeed, when Burke and his chief secretary (Cavendish) were assassinated in the Phoenix Park in 1882, many believed that Burke was the real target of the assassins.[28] It was a high price to pay for £2,000 per annum.

During the period between 1881 and 1911, there were twelve individuals who occupied these positions. The vast majority were Protestants (eleven or 91.5 per cent). In most cases they were Episcopalian, but Lord Aberdeen (Lord Lieutenant in 1886 and 1905–15) was a Presbyterian, Augustine Birrell (chief secretary, 1907–16) was a Nonconformist, and James Dougherty (under secretary 1908–14) was a former Presbyterian minister. W. E. Forster (chief secretary 1880–2), who was allegedly 'the most hated man in Ireland' during the spring of 1882, was the son of a Quaker minister and anti-slavery campaigner, although he converted to Anglicanism when he was expelled from the Society of Friends for marrying Jane Martha Arnold (who was Matthew Arnold's sister).[29] They were also generally British born: three-quarters of them had been born in

---

[25] Flanagan, 'Celtic Ineligible', 518.   [26] Ibid. 520.   [27] Ibid. 523.
[28] Ibid., 529.
[29] T. W. Moody and Richard Hawkins (eds.), *Florence Arnold-Forster's Irish Journal* (Oxford, 1988), pp. xii–xv.

England (seven) or Scotland (two), while three of them were Irish born. David Harrel (under secretary 1893–1902) was the son of an Episcopalian land agent in county Down; James Dougherty was the son of an Ulster Presbyterian doctor; and Thomas Henry Burke was the son of a Trinity College Dublin educated Catholic landowner in county Galway as well as being Cardinal Wiseman's brother in law. However, all four lord lieutenants and all four chief secretaries were British born (six in England and two in Scotland) and Protestant (seven were Episcopalian and one was Nonconformist). This point was not lost on John Redmond, who observed in 1905 that no Irishman had held the office of chief secretary since 1871.[30] The senior members of the Irish administration were—during the period under review—actually British.

Only one of the most senior Irish administrators during this period, T. H. Burke, was Catholic. He was also the only senior administrator who had come up through the ranks. Lord lieutenants and chief secretaries were generally MPs or the members of influential British landed families who were promoted to a senior position in Ireland en route to high political office at Westminster. Arthur Balfour, for instance, served as chief secretary for Ireland between 1887 and 1891, and later became prime minister (1902–5). Under secretaries, while not ostensibly political appointments (as they stayed in office even when the administration changed), were generally recruited from outside the Civil Service. David Harrel, for example, who had served as a police officer and Resident Magistrate, was promoted from the chief commissionership of the Dublin Metropolitan Police to under secretary (1893–1902). Similarly, James Dougherty had been a Professor of Mathematics at Magee College in London-derry before being appointed assistant under secretary (1895–1908) and then under secretary (1908–14). West Ridgeway (under secretary 1887–93), the son of an Anglican clergyman, was an army officer who had served in the Afghan War and was a former senior member of the Indian Civil Service (like Antony MacDonnell) before being appointed to the top of the Irish administration. Only Burke, who had been born in 1829, and worked as a clerk in the Chief Secretary's Office after 1847, had come up through the ranks of the Civil Service to hold one of the most influential positions in Ireland.

Most of the senior administrators in Ireland were from powerful and wealthy British landed families. Seven of them were born into substantial landed families (five of whom inherited the family estate), and one (West Ridgeway) married into a landed family. In all cases, except that of T. H. Burke, these were landed estates that were located in England and Scotland. For example, the Earl of Aberdeen owned substantial estates in Aberdeenshire, and the Earl of Zetland (lord lieutenant 1889–92) owned huge estates in England and Scotland.[31] The

[30] Flanagan, 'Celtic Ineligible', 512, n. 56.
[31] The Earl of Aberdeen owned 62,422 acres (valued at £44,112), and the Earl of Zetland owned 68,170 acres (valued at £49,324).

two Conservative chief secretaries under review were also from considerable landed families: Arthur Balfour (chief secretary 1887–91) owned 87,196 acres in England and Scotland, while George Wyndham's family owned 109,935 acres in England. Altogether, two-thirds of the most powerful men in late nineteenth- and early twentieth-century Ireland were from substantial landed backgrounds. It is interesting that all of the lord lieutenants and chief secretaries during this period (who were landed) were drawn from the British (rather than the Irish) landed class. As suggested in Chapter 1, the British state does appear to have been suspicious of the great Irish landowners and to have regarded them as less capable than their British counterparts.

Most of the senior administrators were educated at the Clarendon schools: two chief secretaries attended Eton and two lord lieutenants attended Harrow. Three other administrators went to English Protestant schools: Birrell attended Amersham Hall School, Aberdeen went to Cheam School, and Harrel attended the Royal Naval College, Gosport. At least half of them received a university education. Five attended Oxbridge, with the most popular colleges being the same as those frequented by the great Irish landowners: Trinity College, Cambridge (Zetland and Balfour) and Christ Church, Oxford (Cowper). Aberdeen attended both Oxford (University College) and St Andrews, while only one (Dougherty) was educated at an Irish university, The Queen's University (Belfast). Two of them became army officers (West Ridgeway and Wyndham), and Wyndham attended Sandhurst before joining the Coldstream Guards. Almost all of them (eleven or 92 per cent) were the members of London and Dublin clubs. Most popular were the Carlton (four), Travellers (four), Whites (three), Athenæum (three), Reform (two), Brooks's (two), and National Liberal (one), while some of them were also members of the Devonshire (one), United Service (one), and Army and Navy (one). Although less popular than the London clubs, some were members of Dublin clubland: Wyndham was a member of the Kildare Street Club and West Ridgeway was a member of the Royal St George Yacht Club at Kingstown. In terms of their education and their social networks, then, the senior Irish administrators were closely integrated into the British political and landed elites.

Given that the majority of the population of Ireland was Catholic, it is clear that the Irish office, which was governed by British and Irish Protestants, was not representative of the population over which it ruled. Indeed, according to one under secretary, Sir Robert Hamilton, 'the majority of the country . . . [was] never represented in the Government at all, while the Anti-Irish party always was', leading to the inevitable result that Dublin Castle 'came to be identified largely in the public mind with that party which the people regarded as their political enemies'.[32] According to an article in the *Dublin University Magazine*,

[32] R. G. C. Hamilton, 'The Irish Question for the Administrative Standpoint', *Speaker*, 4 (13 May 1893), 536.

published in 1858, 'Ireland sends a body of representatives to England, and England sends back a staff of officials to Ireland'.[33] A generation later, Birrell famously characterized Dublin Castle as ' "switched off" from the current of National life and feeling' in his speech introducing the Irish Council Bill in 1907.[34] Certainly, McBride's 'greening' argument does not apply to the ruling administrators in the Irish office, where the proportion of Catholics was less in 1911 than it had been in 1881 when Burke (who had been appointed in 1869) was under secretary. Admittedly, Antony MacDonnell had served as under secretary between 1902 and 1908, but it is clear that Irish-born Catholics were largely excluded from the most sensitive and influential positions in the Irish administration.

The lord lieutenant, chief secretary, and under secretary presided over an extensive administration that consisted of forty government departments in 1914. Of these, eleven were United Kingdom departments which had Irish branches, and twenty-nine were Irish departments which dealt only with Irish affairs. Broadly speaking, the UK departments were responsible for imperial matters—defence and finance, for example—while the Irish departments were responsible for public health, education, agricultural development, and so on. Of the Irish departments, six were controlled by the Treasury, while ten departments (including those concerned with law and order, policing, prisons, and lunatics) were under the direct control of the Chief Secretary's Office. The chief secretary also formally controlled three other departments—the Congested Districts Board (CDB), the Department of Agriculture and Technical Instruction (DATI), and the Local Government Board—but in practice he played only a small part (if any) in the administration of these departments. Most of the departments were housed in Dublin Castle which facilitated the close interaction of senior civil servants, and led Wyndham to characterize the government of Ireland as 'conducted . . . by continuous conversation'.[35] The Irish Civil Service was staffed by more than 26,000 officials. Of these, about 2,500 to 4,000 were employed in the Irish-based departments with 23,000 to 24,000 working in the Irish branches of UK departments (this included about 20,000 employees of the post office).[36] Some of the Irish-based departments were bigger than others: eight departments had a staff of more than 100 and accounted for 83 per cent of the total workforce (the Land Commission alone had 550 employees),

---

[33] *Dublin University Magazine*, 51 (Apr. 1858), 466.

[34] Augustine Birrell, *Things Past Redress* (London, 1937), 206.

[35] McDowell, *Irish Administration*, 29–31. McBride states that there were 'some thirty' Irish-based departments (11 under the direct control of the chief secretary and 11 under his 'partial' control) and 13 others that were the branches of UK departments (McBride, *Greening of Dublin Castle*, 6). The discrepancies arise both because the number of departments changed over time, and because some small and unimportant departments were not counted.

[36] According to McBride, 'approximately' 4,000 civil servants served in the Irish departments, and 23,000 in the Irish branches of English departments (*Greening of Dublin Castle*, 20).

while seventeen Irish-based departments were staffed by only 9 per cent of the total.[37]

The Irish Civil Service had expanded a great deal during the nineteenth century. During the first half of the century, this was largely caused by the British state's attempt to maximize the human and material resources at its disposal in Ireland. Consequently, a number of important reforms were introduced to increase administrative efficiency, encourage economic growth, and to improve the welfare of the Irish population. In 1831, the Board of Works was reorganized; in 1836, the Royal Irish Constabulary, a centralized police force was formed; in 1847, a Poor Law System was established; and in the 1830s and 1840s, a national primary and tertiary education system was set up. This was followed by a second major series of reforms in the aftermath of the Land War (1879–81) that aimed further to integrate Ireland into the British state. Four major departments were established: the Land Commission (1881), the Congested Districts Board (1891), the Department of Agriculture and Technical Instruction (1899), and the National Insurance Commission (1911). These four departments alone employed more than half of the total staff of the twenty-nine Irish departments. As there was increased demand for trained civil servants, the civil and military apparatus of the British Empire was opened to competitive entry: the Indian Civil Service in 1855, the home Civil Service and sections of the Irish Civil Service in 1870, and the army establishment at Woolwich and Sandhurst (also in 1870). Owing to these administrative reforms, the number of Civil Service officers and clerks in Ireland increased tenfold (from 990 to 9,821) between 1861 and 1911.[38]

Broadly speaking, the 4,000-strong staff of the twenty-nine Irish departments can be divided into three main groups. First, the rank and file, which consisted of almost 3,500 clerks, each of whom probably earned about £100 per annum. Most of these entered the Civil Service through the open competitive examinations for second-division clerkships. In addition, a small number joined the Civil Service through the open competition for first-division clerkships, but such openings were comparatively rare in Ireland.[39] McDowell estimates that in 1914 there were over 500 clerks in the Irish departments that were recruited through the second-division examination, but fewer than twenty who had entered the Irish Civil Service via the first-division examination.[40] This appears to have been because the administration preferred to recruit top civil servants from outside

---

[37] McDowell, *Irish Administration*, 34–5.

[38] John Hutchinson, *The Dynamics of Cultural Nationalism: The Gaelic Revival and the Creation of the Irish Nation State* (London, 1987), 258–60.

[39] McBride, *Greening of Dublin Castle*, 20–4. On scarcity of first-division clerks, see Flanagan, 'Celtic Ineligible', 597. Candidates for first-division clerkships needed to have already had a university education, and individuals recruited in this manner by the Home Civil Service often went on to become department heads. In Ireland, however, most individuals were recruited via the less-demanding examination for second-division clerkships.

[40] McDowell, *Irish Administration*, 39.

the Irish Civil Service rather than from the ranks of the first-division clerks, as in the rest of the United Kingdom.[41] By the beginning of the twentieth century, the majority of clerks were Catholic, and a significant proportion of them were women.

Second, there were about 650 members of the professional staff—inspectors, legal advisers, auditors, and the like—who had a professional training and were usually recruited from outside the Civil Service through a limited competition examination.[42] For example, the vice-president of the newly formed Department of Agriculture and Technical Instruction (DATI) canvassed universities in the United States and the United Kingdom in search of recruits for professional staff positions in 1900–2, and only one of his fifteen nominees was recruited from the ranks.[43] John Campbell, a Scottish expert on agriculture, was typical of these new recruits as he was invited from the University of Leeds, where he was a Professor, to become assistant secretary in the DATI. The majority of the professional staff appears to have been Protestants. An article on the composition of the Local Government Board, for instance, claimed that only thirteen (28 per cent) of the forty-seven professional staff were Catholic.[44] The members of the professional staff probably earned between £400 and £1,000 per annum, were often the members of gentlemen's clubs, and tended to live in comfortable Dublin suburbs.[45]

Finally, at the top of the Irish Civil Service were the seventy-five or so highest-ranking civil servants. These were the heads of the departments and the officials who held positions that were immediately subordinate to the department head. They were responsible for putting legislative policy into effect, and for the day-to-day administration of public services. Usually, they were left to run their departments without interference. If an overzealous chief secretary attempted aggressively to intervene in the running of a department, several large boxes of correspondence would usually be sent to him by the head of department for his attention and comment; and in most cases the chief secretary adopted a less interventionist role and instead asked to be kept apprised of developments through the under secretary.[46] Unlike the rank and file of the Civil Service, which was opened to competitive examination in 1870, recruiting to the top jobs in the Irish Civil Service was generally done by nomination or nomination with limited competition.

The top civil servants were responsible for making decisions that would affect thousands of people's lives. The resident commissioner of the board of national

[41] Hutchinson, *Dynamics of Cultural Nationalism*, 270–1.

[42] McBride, *Greening of Dublin Castle*, 16–17. According to McBride, less than 10% of the professional staff were recruited from the ranks through limited competition examination.

[43] Ibid. 17.

[44] 'Light on the Local Government Board', *Leader* (Jan. 1907), quot. McBride, *Greening of Dublin Castle*, 18–19.

[45] Ibid. 19.   [46] Ibid. 11.

education, for instance, controlled £180 million in grants in aid to almost 8,200 national schools; he supervised the operation of the schools in terms of curriculum, evaluation, and teachers' salaries and therefore influenced the lives of the 500,000 or so national school students (most of whom were Catholic).[47] Similarly, the Estates Commissioners—appointed under the Wyndham Land Act—oversaw the way in which £180 million would be spent on land purchase, and made critical decisions as to the prices that tenants would pay and that landlords would receive. The top civil servants also influenced the way in which important public issues (especially health, land reform, and education) were handled. Edward Maziere Courtenay, one of the Inspectors of Lunatic Asylums, played a leading role in reforming the entire character of asylums in Ireland during his period of tenure.[48] And William Starkie, the resident commissioner of the board of national education (1899–1920), was described by *The Times* as a major influence on the educational reforms of the first two decades of the twentieth century.[49]

Who were the top ranking civil servants? I have compiled a study of the highest-ranking civil servants: the Lord Lieutenants, Chief Secretaries, Under Secretaries, the heads of departments and their immediate subordinates. My study examines the social composition of the leading civil servants in two censal years—1891 and 1911—and I have been able to compile information about seventy-seven of them in 1891, and ninety-one in 1911. Altogether—as there was a certain amount of overlap—I have compiled substantial biographical information about 165 of the highest ranking civil servants. Of the 165 civil servants under review, all were men except for one: Marie Louise Dickie was a Dublin-born member of the Church of Ireland who had been promoted to the position of commissioner of national health insurance in 1911 at the age of just 39.[50] Women were not excluded from the Civil Service and there were many women among the rank and file and the professional staff. By 1914, about sixty women were working in the Irish departments as inspectors in the Local Government Board, inspectors of Reformatory schools, and officials in the National Health Insurance Commission.[51] However, there was resistance to the recruitment of women to higher positions, as Dougherty explained to the Royal Commission on the Civil Service in 1913: 'public opinion in Ireland . . . [insisted] on the segregation of the sexes'.[52] The prevalence of this

[47] Ibid. 64.   [48] *Irish Times*, 23 Dec. 1912.   [49] *The Times*, 22 July 1920.
[50] Dickie had obtained both a degree and an LLB, and was an inspector of boarded out children before her appointment (without competitive examination) as a Temporary Inspector in the Local Government Board (at £200 per annum) in 1902. She was made permanent in 1906 and held the position of Inspector until 1911 when she was appointed a Commissioner of National Insurance (at an annual salary of £1,000), a position which she still held in 1922. At the time of the census in 1911, she was married to Alexandre Alfred Dickie, a Louth-born Presbyterian barrister who was 43 years of age. They had been married for 12 years and had one son.
[51] McDowell, *Irish Administration*, 35.
[52] *Royal Commission on the Civil Service, Fourth Report, Evidence* HC (1914) [Cd. 7340], xvi. 189, 206.

view among the top civil servants may explain why there was only one woman among the senior civil servants in Ireland between 1891 and 1911.

The vast majority of the top-ranking civil servants (79 per cent) were Irish born, with just under one-fifth (19 per cent) born in either England (15 per cent) or Scotland (4 per cent), and a couple born in Canada and Australia.[53] In terms of religious composition, almost two-thirds were Protestant (66 per cent) and slightly more than one-third were Catholic (34 per cent). This is in a population where the Catholic population (in 1891) was more than 75 per cent and where the Episcopalian population (in 1891) was almost 13 per cent (see Tables 2.1 and 2.2). This study demonstrates that Episcopalians were over-represented in the elite of the Civil Service: they composed about 13 per cent of the total population, but 58 per cent of the highest-ranking civil servants. Catholics, on the other hand, were under-represented: although they accounted for about 75 per cent of the total population, only 34 per cent of the highest-ranking civil servants were Catholics. Similarly, Presbyterians—who accounted for about 10 per cent of the population—were under-represented, with only 5 per cent of the highest-ranking civil servants being Presbyterians. Although Nonconformists constituted less than 3 per cent of the general population, they

Table 2.1. Religious Denominations in Ireland (by per cent)

Year	Catholic	Episcopalian	Presbyterian	Methodist	Other
1881	76.54%	12.36%	9.1%	0.94%	1.06%
1891	75.4%	12.75%	9.46%	1.18%	1.21%
1901	74.21%	13.03%	9.94%	1.39%	1.43%
1911	73.86%	13.13%	10.04%	1.42%	1.55%

Source: W. E. Vaughan, *Irish Historical Statistics Population, 1821–1971* (Dublin, 1978), 49.

Table 2.2. The Religious Composition of the Senior Civil Servants, 1891–1911

Religion	Number
Episcopalian	79 (58%)
Catholic	47 (34%)
Presbyterian	7 (5%)
Nonconformist	4 (3%)
Number (known)	137
(Not known	28)

[53] Data are available on the birthplace of 94 of the 165 civil servants under review: 74 were born in Ireland; 14 in England; 4 in Scotland; and 1 each in Australia and Canada.

were over-represented in the senior ranks of the Civil Service, with 3 per cent of the top administrators being Nonconformists.

In some departments, it was common practice to appoint one Catholic and one Protestant to senior positions. In the General Prisons Board in 1891, for instance, Patrick Joseph Joyce, a Catholic landowner from county Galway, was one of the Inspectors, while the other was Lord George Hill, who owned a substantial estate in Donegal.[54] They may, however, have had more in common than first appearances suggest. Hill was disliked as a landlord for his ruthlessness, and Joyce's brother, Walter, also a landowner, was disliked so much by local farmers that they shot him dead at Menlough, county Galway, in 1922.[55] Indeed, a significant proportion of the top civil servants either owned land or were members of landed families (either by birth or by marriage). Twelve (7 per cent) of the civil servants owned land themselves: half of them owned estates of fewer than 5,000 acres, while one owned an estate of between 5,000 and 10,000 acres; and five (42 per cent) owned estates of more than 20,000 acres. A much higher proportion were from landed families: almost one-third (31 per cent) were either born into or married into landed wealth. Table 2.3 shows the acreage of estates owned by senior civil servants' families, which demonstrates that these administrators were drawn from different sections of the landlord class. Almost one-third (31.5 per cent), were members of landed families with fewer than 1,000 acres; while one-quarter (23.5 per cent) were members of mid-range landed families; almost one-fifth (17.5 per cent) owned between 5,000 and 10,000 acres; and more than one-quarter (27.5 per cent) were in the elite of the landowning class with more than 10,000 acres. What is perhaps striking about these figures is the fact that most of the landed administrators (72.5 per cent)

Table 2.3. Acreage of Estates Owned by Senior Civil Servants' Families
(percentages are in brackets)

Acreage	Number
0–499	9 (17.5%)
500–999	7 (14%)
1,000–4,999	12 (23.5%)
5,000–9,999	9 (17.5%)
10,000+	14 (27.5%)
Number	51

[54] Hill owned 24,190 acres (valued at £1,308).

[55] On Hill, see W. E. Vaughan, *Landlords and Tenants in Mid-Victorian Ireland* (Oxford, 1994), 30; on Joyce, see Bernard McHale (ed.), *Menlough Looking Back: A Parish and Sporting History* (Menlough, 1991).

were from families with less than 10,000 acres. In general terms, administrators tended to come from the less-well-off landed families.

A significant proportion of the highest-ranking civil servants had been educated at both secondary and tertiary levels, and possessed the necessary technical and professional skills to run their departments. Data were available on the secondary education of fifty-six of them—although it is likely that most of them received some sort of secondary education—and the results are presented in Table 2.4. More than one-fifth (21 per cent) went to English Protestant public schools, and more than one in ten (11 per cent) attended English Catholic public schools.[56] Altogether, then, one-third of the top-ranking civil servants had received an English public school education. A further fifth (18 per cent) had attended other English Protestant schools (Windermere College, Gosport, and Manchester Grammar), and more than one-quarter were graduates of Irish Protestant schools (Royal Belfast Academical Institution, St Columba's, Dublin, and Kilkenny College). One-quarter (25 per cent) had been educated at Irish Catholic schools, and were graduates of Clongowes, Blackrock, and Belvedere, all of which groomed candidates for both the Indian and the Irish Civil Services.

Almost half (45 per cent) of the civil servants under review had received a university education. As Table 2.5 demonstrates, Oxbridge was a popular choice, as were some of the other English and Scottish universities (King's College, London, St Andrews, Edinburgh, and Manchester), but the vast majority (59 per cent) were graduates of Trinity College Dublin. The University of Dublin clearly fed many of its graduates into the elite of the Irish Civil Service. Less than one-fifth (19 per cent) attended the new universities established in Ireland during the nineteenth and early twentieth centuries (The Queen's Colleges, the Royal

Table 2.4. Secondary Education of Senior Civil Servants

(percentages are in brackets)

Type of school	Number
English Public School	12 (21%)
English Catholic Public School	6 (11%)
English Protestant School	10 (18%)
English Catholic School	1 (2%)
Irish Protestant School	15 (27%)
Irish Catholic School	14 (25%)
Number	56

Note: Two of them attended more than one secondary school.

[56] The Protestant public schools included Eton, Harrow, Haileybury, St Paul's, Repton, and Radley, while the Catholic public schools included Downside, Oscott, and Stoneyhurst.

Table 2.5. Tertiary Education of Senior
Civil Servants
(percentages are in brackets)

University	Number
Oxbridge	14 (19%)
Other English University	2 (3%)
Other Scottish University	2 (3%)
Trinity College Dublin	44 (59%)
Queen's Colleges	5 (7%)
National University of Ireland	2 (3%)
Royal University of Ireland	7 (9%)
Number	74

Note: Some individuals went to more than one university.

University, and the National University of Ireland). A significant proportion of them had also received a vocational or professional training (sometimes in addition to a degree but occasionally instead of a degree): sixty of the 165 civil servants under review (36 per cent) had some professional training—legal, medical, military, and as engineers, accountants, and so on—which provided them with the expertise to oversee the work of their departments.

The majority of top-ranking civil servants in the 1890s were in their forties or fifties, with a smaller number in their thirties and their sixties.[57] Most of them were the first-born sons in their families (53 per cent), while just under one-fifth were second- (18 per cent) or third-born (16 per cent) sons. Almost half of them (47 per cent) had been born into 'elite' families, and were the sons of landowners, clergymen, professionals, civil servants, Resident Magistrates, doctors, army officers, journalists, and engineers.[58] Almost all of them were married (86 per cent), and one in six (16 per cent) married into families that were listed in *Walford's County Families* (1879 and 1918 editions), thereby consolidating their establishment status.[59] Like the rest of the Irish population, most of them married when they were in their twenties or thirties, although a small proportion married late in life.[60] Sir Lawrence Dowdall, the principal clerk in the Chief Secretary's Office, for instance, married in

[57] In 1891 (out of a total of 46), 9% were aged between 30 and 39; 45% were aged between 40 and 49; 33% were aged between 50 and 59; 11% were aged between 60 and 69; and 2% were aged between 70 and 79.

[58] Data on the father's position or occupation were available for 78 of the 165 civil servants under review, and it is likely that many more of them had also been born into privilege.

[59] Seven of them married the daughters of peers, and five of them married the daughters of Church of Ireland clergymen (one of whom was the Archbishop of Dublin).

[60] Of 70 civil servants, 40% married when they were aged between 20 and 29; 41.5% when they were aged between 30 and 39; 14% when they were aged between 40 and 49; 1.5% when they were aged between 50 and 59; and 3% when they were aged between 60 and 69.

1914, when he was 63 years of age. On average, married civil servants had between one and four children, and comparatively few of them had childless marriages.[61] The average age at death was 74, with most of them living into their sixties, seventies, and eighties, and a small proportion going strong into their nineties.[62]

The comparatively high age at death was undoubtedly influenced by the fact that the top-ranking civil servants were extremely well off. Their average salary was in excess of £1,000 (£1,096. 13s. 6d.) at a time when other sections of Irish society earned substantially less. The lowest salary of the civil servants under review was £364, and the highest was £2,000. Most of them lived in prosperous and comfortable parts of Dublin. In fact, many of them lived within walking distance of one another at addresses on Fitzwilliam Square, Upper Mount Street, Leeson Street, Leeson Park, Morehampton Road, Raglan Road, Percy Place, Herbert Park, Ailesbury Road, and Earlsfort Terrace.

The top civil servants' houses became important meeting places where they met one another socially and often transacted business. When John Dillon needed to meet Nathan in 1914, and was not prepared to set foot in Dublin Castle, they arranged to meet at Land Commissioner William Bailey's house at Earlsfort Terrace, one of the social centres of Dublin at the time. Indeed, Bailey's obituary in the *Irish Times* said that his house was a 'delightful rendezvous of diverse talents. He assembled there men of all schools of thought and action, and, whether the subject of discussion was theology or Home Rule, Tariff Reform or Cubism, his own cheerful common-sense and large-minded tolerance always created an "atmosphere of settlement".'[63] Many of them also lived in the suburbs of Blackrock, Foxrock, Monkstown, Glenageary, Howth, Shankill, and Kingstown. Crosthwaite Park in Kingstown was a popular address, and it was here that Robert Edwin Matheson, the registrar of the census office, lived next door to the family of the playwright John Millington Synge.[64]

Indeed, the senior administrators often socialized with one another. Maurice Headlam, an Englishman who was Treasury Remembrancer, recalled an invitation from Lady Lyttelton, whose husband Neville was the commander

---

[61] Of 47, 2% had no children; 17% had 1 child; 17% had 2 children; 21% had 3 children; 17% had 4 children; 9% had 5 children; 6.5% had 6 children; 6.5% had 7 children; and 4% had 8 children.

[62] Of 105, 1% died when aged between 40 and 49; 6% between 50 and 59; 26.5% between 60 and 69; 34% between 70 and 79; 26% between 80 and 89; and 6.5% between 90 and 99.

[63] Nathan to Birrell, 26 Nov. 1914, Bodleian Library MS Nathan 462 (Nathan Papers), fo. 165ʳ; McBride, *Greening of Dublin Castle*, 184; *Irish Times*, 17 Apr. 1917. Bailey was reported by his obituary to have known, over a thirty-year period, 'nearly everybody of distinction in politics, art, and letters'.

[64] Matheson's daughter, Cherrie, was responsible for breaking John Millington Synge's heart in the 1890s.

Table 2.6. Club Membership of Senior Civil Servants
(percentages are in brackets)

Club	Number
London	
Athenæum	14 (18%)
Carlton	12 (16%)
Reform	9 (12%)
Brooks	5 (7%)
Royal Societies	5 (7%)
National Liberal	4 (5%)
Boodles	2 (3%)
Army and Navy	4 (5%)
Dublin	
Kildare St	19 (25%)
Sackville St	3 (4%)
Royal St George Yacht Kingstown	20 (26%)
St. Stephens' Green	17 (22%)
University	24 (32%)
Number	76

in chief of the forces in Ireland, to watch a Home Rule demonstration in 1912:

Lady Lyttelton had arranged that we should go to an hotel in Sackville Street to lunch and view the Home Rule 'demonstration' to which a quarter of a million people were to go: we were to be incog. of course, and the General went to play golf. We all drove down in cars, in beautiful sunshine, through crowded streets to the Imperial Hotel, where we found a large party—Sir Henry Robinson, Vice-President of the Local Government Board, Hanson, of the Board of Works . . . Sir F. Moore of the Glasnevin Botanical Gardens and his wife (most *sympatisch*) and son, and several others. We had an enormous lunch, beginning (as all our Irish meals, I find, begin) with oysters. And then we sat in the sun on the balcony and watched the procession and speech-making, though we were too far away to hear the speeches.[65]

The civil servants also networked and met one another at the various gentlemen's clubs in London and Dublin (Table 2.6). Nearly half (46 per cent) were members of London or Dublin clubs, and almost one-third (30 per cent) subscribed to more than one club. In London, the most popular clubs were the Athenæum, Carlton, and Reform. But, because the majority of civil servants were Irish born and lived permanently in Dublin, the Dublin clubs were the most popular. The Kildare Street Club, which we have already come across as a popular haunt for the Irish landlord class, was also frequented by many senior civil

[65] Maurice Headlam, *Irish Reminiscences* (London, 1947), 30–1.

servants. Headlam recalled playing games of squash with his friend, Philip Hanson, a Yorkshireman, at the Kildare Street Club.[66] The Dublin University Club was also popular, and underlines the fact that a substantial proportion of senior Irish civil servants were graduates of Trinity. Yachting was a popular leisure activity among civil servants, and more than a quarter of them were members of the Royal St George Yacht Club at Kingstown.[67] Finally, the St Stephen's Green Club was popular mainly among Catholic civil servants who were sympathetic to Home Rule, but also included Protestant members (William Moore Johnson, the Solicitor General in 1881, for example) and Catholic Unionists (including Thomas O'Hagan who was Lord Chancellor in 1881).[68]

It should also be noted that the Statistical and Social Inquiry Society of Ireland was an important meeting place for Irish civil servants.[69] At least six of the civil servants under review were officers of the Society, and it provided a forum where they could formulate possible solutions to some of the public issues (mental illness, poverty, education, and so on) which they oversaw.[70] It also provided a useful meeting place for establishing networks and perhaps securing future promotions. Daniel Simpson Doyle, a Catholic solicitor who had been educated at Clongowes and the National University of Ireland, for instance, probably came to the attention of senior civil servants through his membership of the Society. Certainly, this placed him within influential Dublin Castle networks, and may have even played a part in his appointment as Assistant Registrar-General in the General Register Office.

The various leisure pursuits of the civil servants were quite different from those of the Irish landlord class. To be sure, some of them did enjoy hunting and shooting. Peter O'Brien, the Attorney-General, was a well-known figure at the Kildare hunt;[71] and Frederick Wrench, the former land agent, brother-in-law of Sir Henry Bellingham, and Estates Commissioner, listed shooting and stalking as some of his recreations. But he was also a keen photographer

[66] Ibid., 55.
[67] On the day of W. E. Forster's final departure from Ireland at the end of his chief secretaryship, a group of Invincibles were waiting to assassinate him on the platform of Westland Row station where he was due to take the 6.45 boat train for Kingstown. However, his private secretary, Henry Jephson, suggested that they go to Kingstown by an earlier train so that they could have lunch in the Royal St George Yacht Club before going on board the mail boat, and so he eluded his attackers. Moody and Hawkins, *Florence Arnold-Forster's Irish Journal*, p. xviii.
[68] McBride, *Greening of Dublin Castle*, 16.
[69] On the Statistical and Social Inquiry Society, see Mary Daly, *The Spirit of Earnest Inquiry: The Statistical and Social Inquiry Society of Ireland, 1847–1997* (Dublin, 1997). Landlords and businessmen were also members of the society.
[70] Stanislaus John Lynch, a Catholic Land Commissioner, was a former president of the society and read a number of papers on land purchase to its members. See *Irish Times*, 18 Mar. 1915.
[71] Ibid. 8 Sept. 1914.

and bred prize-winning pedigree stock.[72] Indeed, most of the civil servants in my sample list the more thoughtful and intellectual pursuits of photography, antiquarianism, collecting old prints and drawings, book hunting, and reading among their hobbies. Sir Bernard Burke of the Office of Arms and keeper of the State Paper Office was the son of the founder of Burke's *Peerage*. William Richard Dawson, one of the Inspectors of Lunatic Asylums, had an interest in archaeology and was also a keen photographer, fisherman, and mountaineer. A relatively recent invention—the motor car—had been taken up by some of them, and Sir Henry Robinson (vice chairman of the Local Government Board), William Bailey (the Estates Commissioner), and Henry Doran (of the CDB) were all keen motorists, who often drove around the west of Ireland together, partly as recreation and partly as observers of the way life was lived there (Birrell often travelled with them).[73] As we have seen, yachting was popular, and many of the civil servants—both Protestant and Catholic—were keen golfers. Joseph Glynn, who was chairman of the National Health Insurance Commission as well as a Catholic solicitor, chairman of Galway county council, Gaelic Leaguer, and author of a *Life of Matt Talbot*, played golf, as did the Unionist, Sir Henry Robinson.

II

To what extent did the social composition of the Civil Service change between 1891 and 1911? The first point that strikes one is a slight decline in the proportion of Irish-born civil servants between 1891 and 1911. In 1911, only 79 per cent of the top-ranking civil servants had been born in Ireland as compared with 86 per cent in 1891. The shortfall was taken up by English- and Scottish-born civil servants, the proportion of which increased from 11 per cent to 19 per cent over the same period. This was probably partly because Horace Plunkett, the vice president of the DATI had deliberately sought out experts on agricultural and technical matters from British and North American universities. As we have seen, he appointed a young Scottish Presbyterian Professor of Agricultural Science, John Campbell, as the assistant secretary of the Department. However, the proportion of Catholic and dissenting civil servants did increase (see Table 2.7). The proportion of Catholic civil servants increased slightly from 33 per cent to 37 per cent, even if Catholics were still under-represented in terms of the general population. Similarly, the proportion of Presbyterian civil servants increased substantially by 8 per cent, as did that of Nonconformists (by 2.5 per cent). These increases were at the expense of

[72] For instance, Wrench's three-year-old chestnut hackney stallion, Fitzrose, won a prize at the Royal Agricultural Show at Carlisle in July 1902. Ibid. 8 July 1902.
[73] McBride, *Greening of Dublin Castle*, 157.

Table 2.7. The Religious Composition of the Senior Civil Servants in 1891 and 1911

Religion	1891	1911
Episcopalian	35 (65%)	44 (50.5%)
Catholic	18 (33%)	32 (37%)
Presbyterian	0	7 (8%)
Nonconformist	1 (2%)	4 (4.5%)
Number	54	87
(Not known	23	4)

Episcopalians whose numbers declined markedly by 14.5 per cent (although they were still very much over-represented in terms of the general population). Certainly, McBride's 'greening' hypothesis seems to be at least partially supported by these data.

The new recruits to the top Civil Service jobs were educated at different schools and universities than their predecessors. Table 2.8 suggests two trends. Protestant civil servants in 1911 were more likely to have been educated at English Public School or at English Protestant schools than at Irish Protestant schools. And Catholic civil servants were more likely to have been educated at Irish Catholic schools (notably Clongowes, Belvedere, and Blackrock) than at English Catholic public schools. These data suggest a certain amount of social mobility as young Irish Catholics, groomed for the Civil Service at elite Irish Catholic schools, began to take their place among the administrative elite. There are also some significant changes in the tertiary education of top civil servants in 1891 and 1911 (see Table 2.9). Oxbridge retains its importance with broadly the same proportion of graduates in the Irish Civil Service in 1911 as in 1891. Graduates from other British universities increased significantly, however, probably due to Plunkett's decision to recruit technical and agricultural experts

Table 2.8. The Secondary Education of the Senior Civil Servants in 1891 and 1911

Type of school	1891	1911
English Public School	4 (16.5%)	7 (18%)
English Catholic Public School	5 (21%)	3 (8%)
English Protestant School	4 (16.5%)	8 (20.5%)
English Catholic School	0	1 (2.5%)
Irish Protestant School	6 (25%)	9 (23%)
Irish Catholic School	5 (21%)	11 (28%)
Total Protestant	14 (58%)	24 (61.5%)
Total Catholic	10 (42%)	15 (38.5%)
Number	24	39

Table 2.9. Tertiary Education of the Senior Civil Servants
in 1891 and 1911

Type of university	1891	1911
Oxbridge	5 (16%)	9 (18%)
Other British University	0	4 (8%)
Trinity College Dublin	24 (75%)	24 (49%)
Queens Colleges/		
University College Dublin/		
National University of Ireland	1 (3%)	6 (12.5%)
Royal University	1 (3%)	6 (12.5%)
European University	1 (3%)	0
Number	32	49

from British universities (King's College London, St Andrews, Edinburgh, and Manchester, all of which were more highly regarded than Oxbridge for science). However, the most significant change between 1891 and 1911 is the decline in importance of Trinity College Dublin. Whereas three-quarters of university-educated Irish civil servants were graduates of Trinity in 1891, by 1911 fewer than half had been educated at Trinity. Recruits were coming instead from the new universities—The Queen's Colleges (which was popular with Presbyterians and Nonconformists) and the Royal University and National University of Ireland, which were popular with Catholics. This is real evidence of social mobility and a significant change in the composition of the administrative elite. Whereas 6 per cent of civil servants in 1891 had been to these universities, this had increased to 25 per cent by 1911.

As well as evidence of change, there is evidence of continuity. At the most fundamental level, twelve of the 91 civil servants in 1911 (13 per cent) had been civil servants in 1891 so that there was a thick strand of continuity in the

Table 2.10. The Age of the Senior Civil
Servants in 1891 and 1911

Age	1891	1911
0–19	0	0
20–9	0	0
30–9	4 (9%)	6 (9%)
40–9	21 (45%)	15 (21.5%)
50–9	15 (33%)	22 (31.5%)
60–9	5 (11%)	24 (34%)
70–9	1 (2%)	2 (3%)
80–9	0	1 (1%)
Number	46	70

administrative elite. Because the Civil Service was a job for life, once an individual was in position, they could not easily be removed unless they moved sideways or upwards. The high level of continuity is reflected in Table 2.10, which shows the ages of the top civil servants in 1891 and 1911. This clearly shows a steady increase in the age-profile of the Irish civil servants: whereas most of them were in their forties and fifties in 1891, the majority were in their fifties and sixties twenty years later. Indeed, this table underlines the fact that a significant number of the top civil servants in 1911 were already in post in 1891. Given that about one in eight of the top civil servants in 1911 were the same individuals who had held the top jobs in 1891, there was much less scope for a general 'greening' than McBride suggests.

For McBride, Birrell's chief secretaryship (1907–16) was the critical turning-point in the 'greening' of the Irish Civil Service: 'The period of Birrell's administration largely marked the greening of Dublin Castle. Irish civil servants were becoming more broadly representative of the people they served.'[74] The evidence presented here suggests, however, that the 'greening' process had a long way to go in 1911, after the most radical and innovative phase of Birrell's chief secretaryship.[75] In 1911, the majority of top civil servants were still Protestant, and more than half were Episcopalian, while Catholics were still under-represented in terms of their numbers in the general population. In other sectors of the administration, there was much greater Catholic advancement. Among the rank and file of the Irish Civil Service, for instance, which was opened to competitive examination in 1870, the proportion of Catholic officers and clerks increased from 39 per cent in 1861 to 61 per cent in 1911.[76] Why was there not a comparable change in the composition of the elite of the Irish administration?

III

Contemporaries frequently asserted that deficiencies in the provision of education for Catholics in nineteenth-century Ireland explained why so few of them were appointed to senior positions in the Irish Civil Service. Arthur Balfour, for instance, commented that 'there were no Catholic Irishmen sufficiently educated

---

[74] McBride, *Greening of Dublin Castle*, 190.

[75] Admittedly, Birrell's chief secretaryship had five years still to run in 1911, but the 1907–11 period was his most active, and once the Great War had begun opportunities for transforming the Irish administration were more limited.

[76] Hutchinson, *Dynamics of Cultural Nationalism*, 263. It is important to note that this increase in the proportion of Catholic civil servants occurred during a period when the total Catholic population of Ireland was in decline (from 77.7% of the total population in 1861 to 73.9% in 1911). James Lowry Whittle even contends that 13,022 (60%) of 21,542 civil servants were Catholic in 1866. See James Lowry Whittle, *Freedom of Education: What it Means* (Dublin, 1866), 12.

and qualified for government posts', and that this explained the lack of 'greening' at the highest levels of the Irish Civil Service.[77] It is necessary therefore to examine the extent of secondary and tertiary education provision for Catholics in late nineteenth-century Ireland in order to assess the validity of this hypothesis. It is true that during the nineteenth century, Protestants (and particularly Episcopalians) were much more likely than Catholics to receive a secondary education. In fact, notwithstanding the decline in the number of Protestant schools from the 1830s onwards, by 1861, 1.1 per cent of Episcopalians were receiving a secondary education compared with only 0.4 per cent of Presbyterians, and 0.2 per cent of Catholics. In other words, one in every 93 Episcopalians was at secondary school as opposed to one in every 443 Catholics.[78] Episcopalians were, therefore, at a considerable advantage in competing for jobs in the Civil Service and the professions.

However, the provision of Catholic secondary education greatly improved in the second half of the nineteenth century. The number of Catholic secondary schools more than doubled between 1850 (when there were twenty-one schools) and 1870 (when there were forty-eight schools).[79] Moreover, at the top of the (Catholic) secondary sector were a number of elite institutions that prepared students for university entrance and for the entrance examinations for the major professions: the Indian and home Civil Services, the army, police cadetships, and so on.[80] Of these schools, the most important was Clongowes Wood (founded in 1814) but, by the end of the nineteenth century, Belvedere, Blackrock, and Castleknock had become almost as prestigious and influential. The critical turning-point in the provision of Catholic secondary education was the introduction of the Intermediate Education Act of 1878. This Act provided £27,500 and £32,000 each year to the students and managers of secondary schools on the basis of payment by results achieved in examinations run by the Intermediate Education Board. Members of all religious denominations and both sexes could apply, thereby opening the possibility of a secondary education to both women and Catholics. The Act resulted in nothing less than a revolution in Catholic participation in secondary education.[81] Up to this point, Catholic secondary schools were run from their own financial resources, and the Act provided badly needed funding.[82] As a result, the number of Catholic pupils attending secondary school almost trebled between 1871 and 1911 (increasing from 12,274 pupils in 1871 to 31,742 in 1911) and the proportion of Catholics receiving a secondary education increased from 50 per cent of the total number of secondary school students to 73 per cent over the same period.[83]

[77] McBride, *Greening of Dublin Castle*, 84.   [78] Flanagan, 'Celtic Ineligible', 62–3.
[79] Senia Paseta, *Before the Revolution: Nationalism, Social Change and Ireland's Catholic Elite* (Cork, 1999), 29.   [80] Hutchinson, *Dynamics of Cultural Nationalism*, 260.
[81] Flanagan, 'Celtic Ineligible', 45.   [82] Ibid. 62.
[83] Hutchinson, *Dynamics of Cultural Nationalism*, 260.

By the middle of the nineteenth century, there were three different universities operating in Ireland. The most prestigious of these was Trinity College Dublin, founded by Queen Elizabeth in 1591 as an essentially Anglican institution (although Catholics and Dissenters were allowed to graduate after 1793). During the nineteenth century, the student body was largely drawn from the Protestant professional classes mainly because the Irish landlords tended to attend Oxbridge (as we have seen in Chapter 1).[84] The Catholic hierarchy was opposed to Catholics attending Trinity until 1970, and this ensured that very few Catholics graduated from the university. In fact, about twenty Catholics attended Trinity each year between 1860 and 1900 (this was between 7 per cent and 9 per cent of the annual intake).[85] In general, these were from professional backgrounds and had attended one of the 'elite' secondary schools (Clongowes, Blackrock, and so on). Episcopalians, on the other hand, accounted for more than 80 per cent of students attending Trinity (approximately 200–50 students each year), and between 10 and 20 students were from a Presbyterian background (3 per cent to 6 per cent of annual intake).[86]

The Queen's Colleges were established at Belfast, Cork, and Galway in 1849 'to supply the want, which had long been felt in Ireland, of an improved Academical education equally accessible to all classes of the community without religious distinction'.[87] As a state university, professors were nominated by the Irish administration and more than £25,000 was allocated to the colleges each year after 1855.[88] However, the Catholic hierarchy objected to The Queen's Colleges because they were unable to control appointments and curriculum, and in 1850 the Synod of Thurles—under the leadership of Cardinal Paul Cullen—condemned the colleges as a danger to the faith and morals of Catholics.[89] Consequently, Protestants were much more likely to attend The Queen's Colleges than Catholics: in 1866, for instance, 25 per cent of the student body were Catholic, and 75 per cent Protestant.[90] Indeed, Presbyterians appear to have benefited most from The Queen's Colleges as they composed more than one-third of the undergraduate population of the colleges between 1859 and 1872.[91]

Some Catholics did attend The Queen's Colleges, however, as William O'Malley, Home Rule MP for Connemara between 1895 and 1918, later recalled:

Before leaving home in 1869 for London my father was anxious that I should go to the Queen's College, Galway, but as the Bishops and priests had condemned these

---

[84] Flanagan, 'Celtic Ineligible', 133.
[85] *First Report of the Royal Commission on Trinity College Dublin, and the University of Dublin*, Appendix, section B, HC (1906) [Cd. 3176], lvi. 20.   [86] Flanagan, 'Celtic Ineligible', 150.
[87] *Report of the Commissioners Appointed to Inquire into the Progress and Condition of the Queen's Colleges at Belfast, Cork and Galway*, HC (1857–8) [2413], xxi. 1.
[88] Flanagan, 'Celtic Ineligible', 137–8.   [89] Ibid. 142.
[90] Ibid. 146, 154. In fact, of 288 entrants to the three Queen's colleges in 1864–5, only 73 (25%) were Catholic.   [91] Flanagan, 'Celtic Ineligible', 151.

'godless' colleges, my mother, who would never go contrary to the wishes of the Church, was strongly opposed to the idea. However . . . Several young fellows from Connemara, whose parents were not influenced by the priest, went to the Queen's College. Two of these became distinguished. The late Sir Peter Freyer, who won the Gold Medal from All Ireland, and who after several years in India, set up for himself in London as a specialist in stone diseases . . . And Joseph Pye . . . was also a student of the Galway Queen's College . . . [He] carried all before him in the examinations and became an M.D. and one of the College Professors.[92]

The third university system in mid-nineteenth-century Ireland was the Catholic University (which later became University College Dublin), established in 1854. It was funded entirely by public subscription and had no state endowment. Despite this, it had an annual expenditure of £6,000, which was about the same as each of The Queen's Colleges individually. But it was unable to attract significant numbers of middle-class Catholic students: between 1868 and 1873, there were about 125 students each year. In part, the university's failure to attract students was because it lacked facilities. Dr O'Dwyer, the bishop of Limerick, explained in 1902:

All I have to say about it my lord, is this—as a University institution it is simply a burlesque. It is a house on the side of the street. It is number something in St. Stephen's-green but there are neither libraries, laboratories, museums, nor any of the apparatus of a University college connected with it.[93]

In 1879, the state of third-level education for Catholics in Ireland was transformed by the University Education (Ireland) Act which created the Royal University of Ireland. The Royal University was an examining body rather than a teaching institution. In other words, the university had the power to grant degrees to whoever passed its exams, irrespective of where they had been educated. This provided a cheap and accessible degree for Catholics (a whole degree could cost between £3 and £10 in examination fees), which had the blessing of the Catholic hierarchy. For the first time, the university provided the opportunity of university education to a large section of the Catholic population, and the numbers presenting for examination each year increased from 728 in 1881 to 4,136 in 1908.[94]

Finally, the university system in Ireland was rationalized and reformed by the Irish Universities Act of 1908. This created two new universities: the National University of Ireland, encompassing The Queen's Colleges at Cork and Galway, and University College Dublin (formerly the Catholic university); and The Queen's University, Belfast which was composed of the former

---

[92] William O'Malley, *Glancing Back* (London, 1933), 287–8. T. P. O'Connor, another Home Rule MP, ignored the Catholic church's 'fatwa' on Queen's College Galway and attended the university.
[93] *First Report of the Commissioners on University Education (Ireland)*, evidence, HC (1902) [Cd. 826], xxxi. 19–20.   [94] Paseta, *Before the Revolution*, 12.

Table 2.11. Numbers of Catholics in Selected Professions, 1861–1911

Profession	1861	1911
Legal	873 (34%)	999 (44%)
Medical	971 (35%)	1,092 (48%)
Civil service officers and clerks	420 (39%)	5,998 (61%)
Schoolteachers	11,034 (57%)	12,721 (69%)
Architects, accountants, and engineers	498 (31%)	1,618 (46%)

Source: Census of Ireland, 1861 and 1911; John Hutchinson, *The Dynamics of Cultural Nationalism: The Gaelic Revival and the Creation of the Irish Nation State* (London, 1987), 262.

Queen's College, Belfast. From 1908 onwards, the National University of Ireland provided Catholics with the first state-funded teaching university of which the Roman Catholic hierarchy approved. As a result of all of these reforms, about 1,000 Catholic students were graduating each year from the Irish universities from the 1880s onward. By 1900, then, there was probably a pool of 20,000 or so university-educated Catholics capable of taking up a position in the Irish Civil Service if recruitment via first-division clerkships had been adopted in Ireland as it was in the rest of the United Kingdom. Arthur Clery, a young University College Dublin-educated barrister, confirmed that this was the case in his 1910 essay 'The Plague of B.A.'s': 'No greater nonsense was, indeed, ever uttered than to say there are no educated Catholics to fill public positions. The fact is, that the positions are there, the educated Catholics are there . . . [but they] are never introduced to one another.'[95] Indeed, some educated Catholics had already joined the various professions in Ireland (see Table 2.11). It would be incorrect, therefore, to assume that the low representation of Catholics in the top-ranks of the Civil Service was due to a lack of educated Catholics in Irish society. By 1900, this argument could not be substantiated and it is necessary to look elsewhere to find an explanation of the slow pace of 'greening' at the highest levels of the Irish Civil Service.

IV

Contemporaries viewed the Irish administration as dominated by the Irish Protestant middle class. The *Leader* newspaper undertook a series of investigations into the composition of the elite of the Irish Civil Service, and found that the senior administrators were overwhelmingly Irish Protestants (and usually Episcopalians). In an article on the Prison Service, for example, the *Leader*

[95] Arthur Clery, *Dublin Essays* (Dublin and London, 1919), 59.

claimed that the four largest prisons were governed by Protestant officials and that only one of these had a Catholic serving as deputy-governor. Of ten smaller prisons, seven had Protestant governors. According to D. P. Moran, the newspaper's editor, the chief problem in the Irish administration was that department heads acted as 'croupiers for their religion':

In the past . . . the Irish were treated as nothing . . . At present . . . the spirit of serf-dom and indifference which distinguished the older generation does still exercise a depressing influence over the younger men [who are heads of departments]. There is a tendency with them to slip into the old groove. The great majority of the superior positions being in the hands of the anti-Irish, there is little encouragement to Irishmen, especially Catholics, to work for anything. The sceptre of authority is wielded by those people as if they appeared to be convinced that the Irish are really an inferior breed, and, therefore, not supposed to look above their present level.[96]

The Revd J. W. Whigham of Ballinasloe, county Galway, the Presbyterian Moderator in 1885–6, found a similar state of affairs in his examination of the Irish Civil Service.[97] Presbyterians had been discriminated against during the eighteenth century by sacramental tests, and they also appear to have been viewed by the largely Episcopalian establishment as second-class citizens during the second half of the nineteenth century. In the Local Government Board in 1881, for instance, Whigham discovered that 16 (73 per cent) officers were Episcopalian, while 5 (22.5 per cent) were Catholic, and only

Table 2.12. The Religious Denomination of the Irish Administration *c*.1881

Department	Catholic	Episcopalian	Presbyterian
Judges	5	11	1
County Court Judges	6	14	2
Resident Magistrates	25	53	2
Royal Irish Constabulary County Inspectors	9	30	0
Royal Irish Constabulary District Inspectors	37	188	5
Royal University senators	17	9	8
Intermediate education	4	3	2
National education	10	6	3
Board of Works	3	18	0
Local Government Board	5	16	1
Lunatic Asylums	5	19	0
Land Commission (chief)	3	2	0
Land Commission (assistant)	7	3	0

Source: Revd Thomas Hamilton, *History of the Irish Presbyterian Church* (Edinburgh, 1887), 191.

[96] *Leader*, 11 Mar. 1905. Quot. McBride, *Greening of Dublin Castle*, 19.
[97] Whigham's figures were reproduced in Thomas Hamilton, *History of the Irish Presbyterian Church* (Edinburgh, n.d. [1887?]), 191.

one (4.5 per cent) was Presbyterian (see Table 2.12).[98] Irish MPs held a similar view. According to John Redmond, 'Large masses of the [Episcopalian] Protestants are, no doubt, frightened by the [Home Rule] Bill. I do not wonder at it. They have had in their hands for generations a monopoly of all power and place and patronage.'[99] T. W. Russell, the Liberal MP for south Tyrone, explained Unionist opposition to the Irish council bill in a similar manner:

From the magistrates up through the whole gamut of officials these gentlemen [Unionists] have occupied posts for the whole period of the Union. They oppose the Bill because they see that their privileges—they have no rights in the matter—are in danger. It is because the old system is going—the system of administration by patronage and jobs; that is the sole ground upon which they can logically oppose the Bill.[100]

The British state in Ireland since the Act of Union (1801) had been largely based on its alliance with the landlords and the Irish Protestant middle class. Indeed, the Protestant middle class regarded themselves as the members of a privileged, governing minority who were intent on maintaining their position in Irish society. Edward Stephens, a Protestant solicitor in Dublin during the early years of the twentieth century, recalled that his grandparents:

By living very quietly . . . did not in any way detach themselves from the privileged minority, the Protestant governing class, which was held together by inter-marriage, by tradition, and by fear of the Roman Catholic majority in the country. This minority controlled the opportunities for rising professional men in Ireland. Its members were quick to recognize among their number, and to advance by their support, the conventional clever young men who were likely to prove useful in upholding their privileges.[101]

The Protestant middle class appears to have regarded Catholics as second-class citizens. According to Stephens, when his family moved to Crosthwaite Park in Kingstown, the home of a number of prominent civil servants including Robert Edwin Matheson and Stanislaus Murphy:

The members of the family group felt themselves to be socially superior to many of their neighbours, and were very careful to avoid making friends quickly with anyone . . . [Our] new home . . . was well suited to the maintenance of their aloofness, except that our mother found an unforeseen difficulty in preventing my brother, my sister, and me from picking up young acquaintances. To her it seemed much more important that we should understand and be guided by class and religious differences, than that we should

---

[98] The proportion of Presbyterians and Nonconformists in the Irish establishment did increase significantly between 1881 and 1911. See the discussion of this point in Conclusion.

[99] McBride, *Greening of Dublin Castle*, 57.

[100] Ibid. 137. The Irish Council Bill aimed to give Ireland a limited measure of political independence when it was introduced—unsuccessfully—in 1907.

[101] Andrew Carpenter (ed.), *My Uncle John: Edward Stephens's Life of J. M. Synge* (Oxford, 1974), 18.

enjoy naturally the company of other children . . . It was inevitable that we should be taken frequently into the park, across which the houses of the two terraces confronted each other. Here we found nurses and other children with whom we should have been delighted to have played . . . but our mother thought that some of . . . [the] children might be vulgar, and a few might even be Roman Catholics.[102]

It might be suggested that Stephens's mother, a member of the Plymouth Brethren and John Millington Synge's sister, was particularly vociferous in her views, but Elizabeth Bowen, who spent her childhood winters in Dublin, also recalled the sense of ethnic segregation that she felt there:

The world my parents inhabited, and the subworld of its children, was still late-Victorian. Their friends were drawn from the Bar, from Trinity College, from among the prelates of the Church of Ireland or landed people quietly living in town . . . Roman Catholics were spoken of by my father and mother with a courteous detachment that gave them, even, no myth. I took the existence of Roman Catholics for granted but met few and was not interested in them. They were, simply 'the others,' whose world lay alongside ours but never touched.[103]

Indeed, it is likely that one of the only occasions when members of the Protestant middle class actually met Catholics was when they addressed their servants, since many well-to-do Protestants tended to employ servants who were Irish-born Catholics. A survey of thirty-one Protestant civil servants who occupied senior positions in the Irish administration in 1911 (and who could be identified in the 1911 census), for instance, revealed that twenty-three (or 74 per cent) of them had servants who were exclusively Catholic.[104]

Catholic observers also noted that the Catholic and Protestant middle class rarely had anything to do with one another. George Noble Plunkett's children who grew up as Catholics on Fitzwilliam Street had a similar experience, as his daughter Geraldine recalled:

In Fitzwilliam Street we were always on the outside, surrounded by people who didn't like us. Unionists and bootlickers to the administration, and, mainly because of Pa's political activities, we were regarded with deep suspicion. Most of the children there were not allowed to play with us. Some of them spat at us or called us names when we passed by.[105]

---

[102] Ibid. 63–4.

[103] Elizabeth Bowen, *Bowen's Court and Seven Winters* (London, 1984), 48.

[104] Altogether 49 of the senior civil servants in 1911 included in this study had servants and could be identified in the 1911 census. Of 31 Protestant civil servants, 23 employed exclusively Catholic servants, 5 employed exclusively Protestant servants, and 3 employed both Catholic and Protestant servants. Of 18 Catholic civil servants, 17 employed exclusively Catholic servants, and 1 employed a Protestant servant.

[105] Honor O Brolchain (ed.), *All in the Blood: A Memoir of the Plunkett Family, the 1916 Rising and the War of Independence by Geraldine Plunkett Dillon* (Dublin, 2006), 45. George Noble Plunkett was an art historian and director of the National Museum of Ireland between 1907 and 1916 and under his directorship annual visits to the museum increased from 100 to 3,000 annually. His political activities in the 1870s and 1880s were of the Home Rule variety.

Similarly, Arthur Clery believed that Irish society was deeply segregated between Protestant and Catholic at the beginning of the twentieth-century:

Perhaps the most surprising aspect of the religious question in Ireland . . . is the way in which the Catholic and the Protestant live socially apart . . . Socially I happen to belong . . . to something like the middle of the Irish upper middle-class . . . I have only once in my life dined in a Protestant house . . . With trifling and accidental variations, this is, I believe, the general experience of Catholics of my own class and any classes below it . . . Catholic society is conducted on a like basis of separateness. In Dublin, at any rate, neither religion feels the want of the other socially; each is self-sufficing.[106]

C. P. Curran, one of Clery's friends and fellow students at University College Dublin, confirms Clery's characterization to be correct, and adds that: 'the coincidence of religion and politics had established two self-sufficing circles rotating on independent axes.'[107] Middle-class Irish society, then, was often deeply divided along sectarian lines, and it would seem that the predominantly Episcopalian establishment was keen to maintain this segregation within the top ranks of the Irish Civil Service.

D. P. Moran believed that the only way to make Dublin Castle representative of the people of Ireland was to release the senior positions of the Civil Service to open competition.[108] Although the rank and file of the Civil Service had been opened to competitive examination in 1870, the top jobs in the Civil Service were still filled according to a complex procedure of nomination and appointment. Of 1,611 principal positions in the Irish administration, 622 (39 per cent) were made by direct nomination, and 766 (48 per cent) were made after limited competition examination. Only 219 (13 per cent) were made after open competition examination that admitted all candidates.[109] This system of recruiting to senior positions was very different from that in the rest of the United Kingdom (after 1870).[110] In 1911, for instance, only about a dozen of 435 senior staff in eleven departments in the Home Civil Service had been recruited from outside the Civil Service.[111] The vast majority of senior civil servants in the United Kingdom (excluding Ireland) were recruited by open competition to first-division clerkships.[112] How did recruiting to the senior positions in the Irish Civil Service work?

---

[106] Clery, *Dublin Essays*, 45–6. Clery suggests that the demarcation of Protestant and Catholic is less marked among the upper middle class and the aristocracy.

[107] C. P. Curran, *Under the Receding Wave* (Dublin, 1970), 128. These divisions may have been less marked in rural and small-town Ireland. Kevin O'Shiel, who became a leading Sinn Feiner in 1917, grew up in Omagh where his father, Francis, was the captain of the local golf club and prided himself on his family's 'cosmopolitan Catholicism' and their social interaction with Protestant neighbours (interview conducted by the author with Prof. Eda Sagarra—O'Shiel's daughter—at Trinity College Dublin (23 Jan. 2003)).

[108] McBride, *Greening of Dublin Castle*, 104.   [109] Ibid. 14–15.

[110] See R. K. Kelsall, *Higher Civil Servants in Britain: from 1870 to the Present Day* (London, 1955; repr. 1998).

[111] Ibid. 107.   [112] Ibid. 13; 20.

Technically, the lord lieutenant had wide-ranging powers to appoint most of the senior members of the Civil Service (including the members of the Irish Office, and those in charge of policing, prisons, hospitals, and so on), although these appointments were usually made by the chief secretary.[113] However, some appointments were beyond the control of the chief secretary. The Treasury, for instance, was responsible for appointing the Treasury Remembrancer in Ireland, and the GPO in London controlled senior appointments to the Post Office in Dublin. Heads of departments were also extremely influential in making appointments and usually maintained that they were in the best position to decide who should be appointed or promoted to key positions.[114]

However, the senior members of departments had different views as to what kinds of people should be recruited. Henry Robinson, the vice president of the Local Government Board (1898–1920) believed that Irish Catholic civil servants were brilliant but impulsive and therefore required the steadying hand of 'stolid' Englishmen and wise Scotsmen to run a department properly. In 1913, he commented retrospectively on the appointments he had made since 1898:

Politics and religion find their way into many matters of local government in some parts of Ireland, and as things stood then our staff was nearly all Irishmen and knew almost too much of the political and religious aspects of affairs. I was therefore very anxious to leaven them if I could with a few Englishmen and Scotchmen . . . I have seen the characteristics of the three, English, Irish, and Scotch, and, working together, they make a really perfect combination. The Englishmen we have had from the upper division examination have been stolid, sensible, highly competent persons. The Scotchman is a rock of common-sense, accurate, and cautious. The Irishman is brilliant, resourceful, and quick, but he is rather impulsive and wants the steadiness of the English and Scotch.[115]

These public (and dubiously essentialist) remarks concealed Robinson's real view that more Unionists should be appointed to the top jobs.[116] Given his views, it is not surprising that Robinson favoured the traditional method of recruitment by nomination without examination. He claimed that men of 'imperturbable good temper . . . and great tact' were required in the Local Government Board, and that the best recruiting strategy was to appoint an official on a temporary basis, see how he or she got on, and, if the results were favourable, appoint them to a permanent position.[117]

Thomas Patrick Gill, on the other hand, the Catholic and pro-Home Rule permanent head of the Department of Agriculture, held a different view. He favoured recruiting from the ranks, and explained that:

I attach myself more importance to rearing and breeding than to subsequent education. I mean if they come from a good home, from a decent stock of people with right

---

[113] For a list of the positions in the Civil Service over which the lord lieutenant had powers of appointment, see Flanagan, 'Celtic Ineligible', 692.

[114] McBride, *Greening of Dublin Castle*, 14.   [115] Quot. ibid. 79.

[116] O'Halpin, *Decline of the Union*, 18.   [117] McDowell, *Irish Administration*, 37–8.

traditions, you will have a chance of getting better original material; and when I speak of decent traditions, I am not speaking of aristocratic traditions, though I include them in my idea. I think the home of a farmer or a working-class home, in which independence, religion, honesty, truthfulness, loyalty, and these old principles were not merely names, but were revered and practised, would be just as likely to give you the original qualities... I don't think that merely putting in a few years in a university and letting a man pass a brilliant examination at the end will make him a much better man for exercising control over a staff and for getting the best qualities out of a staff.[118]

Gill's views were, however, unusual, and most department heads favoured recruiting from outside the Civil Service by direct nomination or through first division examination. Starkie, the resident commissioner of the national education board and a Catholic Unionist, for instance, explained that his preferred candidates were those first-division men 'able to write satisfactory letters on important subjects'.[119] Broadly speaking, recruiting to the top of the Civil Service was in the hands of a variety of different individuals (the lord lieutenant, the chief secretary, the Treasury, the various department heads) and, for this reason, there was no single recruiting policy. Indeed, the motivations for appointments to the top of the Irish Civil Service were contradictory and diverse, rather than coherent and dictated by a single purpose. The different arms of the state had different interests, and this generated a complex pattern of recruitment.[120]

There was considerable interest in senior Civil Service appointments as they were extremely well paid and influential positions. As John Morley (chief secretary 1892–5) explained in 1892 when there was a vacancy in the Land Commission, 'the flies cluster pretty thick about such a pot of honey as this'.[121] Similarly, when there was a vacant Judicial Commissionership in 1906, James Bryce (chief secretary, 1906–7) told his under secretary (MacDonnell) that one of the candidates (Bodkin) 'keeps writing to beg for the post'.[122] Indeed, a variety of different interest groups and networks immediately made themselves known whenever a senior position became vacant. However, the first qualification for appointment was that the candidate was a part of the Dublin Castle network and known to the senior staff. William Le Fanu recalled that when he became commissioner of Public Works in 1863 he had 'been much pressed to do so by my friends in the Irish Government'.[123] Because appointments were based on hearsay, it was impossible to get a foot on the ladder if the applicant was not known to

---

[118] *Royal Commission on the Civil Service, Fourth Report, Evidence,* 227.

[119] McDowell, *Irish Administration,* 40.

[120] According to Maguire, Dublin Castle in 1912 was 'a labyrinth of dispersed authority' (Martin Maguire, *The Civil Service and the Revolution in Ireland, 1912–1938* (Manchester, 2008), 19).

[121] McBride, *Greening of Dublin Castle,* 42.

[122] James Bryce to Antony MacDonnell, 13 Aug. 1906, Bodleian Library MS Eng. Hist. c. 350 (MacDonnell Papers), fo. 28ᵛ.

[123] William Richard Le Fanu, *Seventy Years of Irish Life* (London, 1893), 210.

the prime movers. For this reason, there were a number of cases where private secretaries to either the Chief Secretary or the Lord Lieutenant went on to be appointed to prestigious positions. Wyndham's private secretary, Philip Hanson, an English-born Episcopalian, was appointed a commissioner in the Board of Works. Similarly, Birrell's private secretary, Charles Beard, was promoted to the secretaryship of the Land Commission. And Lord Aberdeen's personal physician, William John Thompson, a Methodist, later became Registrar General of Ireland.

The members of families with a connection to the Civil Service were in a particularly strong position. Of the 165 civil servants under review, eighteen (11 per cent) were related to other senior members of the Civil Service. In other words, more than one in ten of the senior staff were related to one another. William Lawson Micks, the secretary and later permanent member of the CDB, first joined the Civil Service as a clerk in the Church Temporalities Commission (at the age of 21 in 1872), where his uncle, James Anthony Lawson, was a commissioner.[124] Similarly, William Evelyn Wylie, who had won the large Gold medal—a prestigious academic award—while at Trinity College Dublin, was appointed as a Judicial Commissioner in the Land Commission in 1920, where his uncle, James Owen Wylie, had also been a Judicial Commissioner. Edmund Thomas Bewley, Judicial Commissioner in the Land Commission, was Lord Ashbourne's brother in law; and Malachy Kelly, the Chief Crown Solicitor for Ireland, married his predecessor's daughter. William Starkie of the national education board had a brother, Robert, who was a police officer, private secretary to the Inspector General (1893–5), and finally Resident Magistrate for Cork (1905–20).[125] Some Church of Ireland households provided a number of senior civil servants. In 1911, William Henry Drennan, for instance, presided over a household at 61 Lansdowne Road where he and three of his sons were senior members of the Irish administration.[126]

Such was the extent of family connection within the elite of the Civil Service that some positions were even regarded as hereditary. Maurice Headlam, the Treasury Remembrancer, described the vice president of the Local Government Board as a 'hereditary' office because Henry Robinson's father had been vice president before him.[127] This may have been overstating the case, but it is

---

[124] Micks's association with the CDB was such that his obituary stated that: 'The name of Mr. W. L. Micks spelled "Congested Districts Board" for many years in Ireland.' *Irish Times*, 5 Apr. 1928.

[125] Occasionally family connections were disadvantageous. On 7 Dec. 1914, Robert Starkie met Nathan and asked to be considered for higher appointment, claiming that 'had it not been for his brother being in a big spending Department he would probably have been made Treasury Remembrancer'. MS Nathan Papers 467, fo. 60ʳ.

[126] William Henry was assistant registrar of deeds; his eldest son, William Trimble, was senior clerk in the Land Registry; his next son, John Thomas, was assistant secretary at the Land Commission; and his youngest son, Victor Vivian, was a clerk in the Land Registry.

[127] Headlam, *Irish Reminiscences*, 31.

clear that some families did provide several generations of senior officials. Richard Bourke of Thornfield, county Limerick, an Inspector in the Local Government Board, was the son of the Governor-General of New South Wales, and the father and grandfather of senior staff in the Local Government Board.[128] One of his sons (John Ulick) was a Resident Magistrate, and the other (Edmund) a commissioner in the Local Government Board, while his grandson (Richard) was a temporary inspector in the Board. The Bourkes were probably not unusual in being a small Protestant landed family that provided four generations of senior administrators for the British state.[129] Indeed, there appears to have been a strong sense of inherited position among the Irish Protestant middle class. John Millington Synge's family, for instance, who did not regard the writing of plays as a respectable pursuit, was keen for him to take up an occupation 'appropriate to his inherited position in society'.[130] Similarly, the sponsors of applicants for senior Government positions often invoked heredity in support of their candidates. In 1915, for instance, G. H. Shannon, a Resident Magistrate, asked Nathan if his son might be appointed to the Resident Magistracy: 'Mr. Shannon urged his own services as Resident Magistrate and the theory of heredity in favour of . . . [his son's] application.'[131]

As McBride has correctly pointed out, both Liberal and Conservative administrations after 1892 were concerned to appoint candidates who were acceptable to the nationalist movement (the Irish Parliamentary Party, as well as newspapers like the *Leader*). Members of the Irish Parliamentary Party took a pledge each year that they would not accept a position in the Irish administration or use their influence to secure a candidate's appointment to a paid government position. This pledge was designed to protect MPs from the allegation that they were place-hunters, and to insulate them from the petitioning letters of nationalist supporters who wanted jobs in the public service.[132] Even so, the senior members of the Irish Parliamentary Party (IPP) strongly influenced appointments to the Civil Service.[133] Geraldine Plunkett Dillon, whose father, Count George Noble Plunkett was appointed by Lord Aberdeen as the Director of the National Museum in 1907, recalled that after the Liberal victory in 1906, Redmond 'had been telling Irishmen that they should apply for such positions'.[134]

---

[128] Sir Richard Bourke was Governor-General of New South Wales between 1831 and 1838.
[129] The Bourkes owned 948 acres (valued at £763).   [130] Carpenter, *My Uncle John*, 55.
[131] Memorandum of meeting with G. H. Shannon, RM, 13 Jan. 1915, Bodleian Library MS Nathan 467, fo. 96ʳ.   [132] McBride, *Greening of Dublin Castle*, 46–7.
[133] James McConnel confirms that the members of the IPP played a part in influencing Government appointments. See McConnel, ' "Jobbing with Tory and Liberal": Irish Nationalists and the Politics of Patronage, 1880–1914', *Past and Present*, 188 (Aug. 2005).
[134] O Brolchain, *All in the Blood*, 89, 90. Intriguingly, Geraldine suggests that it was Lady Aberdeen who 'took care of most of the business, so it was from her that Pa got a letter saying that he had been appointed.'

Indeed, most Home Rule MPs did use their influence to get jobs for their friends, families, associates, and constituents in the Irish Civil Service.[135] In fact, Dublin Castle appears to have operated on the assumption that members of the Irish Party were integral to the recruiting process. For instance, T. F. Rahilly, a junior clerk in the Accountant General's office in Dublin told Tom O'Donnell, the Home Rule MP, that the Accountant General: 'Volunteered the information himself to me that the way of making sure of my getting the transfer is to get some Nationalist MP to say a word in my favour to the Chancellor, the ex-Attorney General.'[136] John Dillon's postbag was regularly full of begging letters from his fellow MPs asking him to use his influence to gain appointments for constituents, friends, and family members. Such was the extent of Home Rule MPs attempting to influence the recruiting process at Dublin Castle that Denis Kilbride was forced to write to Dillon to tell him that the Estates Commissioners were becoming annoyed at the volume of correspondence they were receiving from Home Rule MPs recommending individuals for vacancies at the Land Commission.[137] Michael McCartan's papers demonstrate that he spent much of his time during the 1890s trying to secure patronage for his constituents.[138] Moreover, Redmond, Dillon, and Devlin were also prominently involved in advising the government—and particularly the under secretary Matthew Nathan—as to how Ireland should be governed during the third Home Rule crisis and the early years of the Great War.[139] It is also possible that the IPP leaders used their influence in support of their own families: in 1912, for instance, Redmond's son in law, Max Sullivan Green was appointed to the prestigious position of vice chairman of the General Prisons Board, with an annual salary of £1,200.

The various administrations also had to ensure that they did not alienate the support of Unionists. To be sure, some landlords and Unionists were concerned that appointments were tending to favour nationalists and Catholics rather than Protestants and Unionists. The Duke of Abercorn, the owner of enormous estates in Donegal and Tyrone, was outraged by the Conservative administration's appointments to the Land Commission in the late 1890s. In a letter to the lord lieutenant, Cadogan, Abercorn fumed: 'It is beyond comprehension . . . how Gerald Balfour could have selected [as land valuer] such a man as Mr. Teeling, who is an acknowledged Home Ruler with very advanced principles.'[140] He must have been even more outraged in 1903 when Wyndham appointed pro-tenant

[135] James McConnel, 'The View from the Backbench: Irish Nationalist MPs and their Work, 1910–14', PhD thesis (Durham University, 2002), 156.

[136] Ibid. 160–1.

[137] Ibid. 160, 159. Apparently P. A. Meehan, William Delany, and Tom O'Donnell were prominently involved in attempting to influence the recruiting process at both the Estates Commissioners and the Congested Districts Board.   [138] Ibid. 156.

[139] John Redmond, John Dillon, and Joe Devlin were the leading figures in the IPP between 1900 and 1918, and will be discussed in Ch. 4.

[140] McBride, *Greening of Dublin Castle*, 73. Abercorn owned estates of 76,500 acres.

officials to two of the three top jobs in the Estates Commissioners, which had enormous powers to decide the value of estates for sale under the Wyndham Land Act. Having said that, tenants believed that the value of land had gone up considerably under the terms of the Wyndham Land Act (in comparison to earlier land purchase legislation), and landlords were also getting a 12 per cent bonus on the total purchase price of their estates.[141] Indeed, Unionist concerns about Catholic appointments were probably exaggerated. There was a sense that even a small number of Catholic appointments would turn the administration against them: J. P. Mahaffy, the Provost of Trinity College Dublin, made this argument in 'The Romanization of Ireland' published in July 1901.[142]

But, on balance, appointments often still favoured Protestants and Unionists, rather than Catholics and nationalists. It should also be noted that, in addition to the Unionist party, there were many strong Unionist and pro-landlord forces in the administration not least of which were pro-Unionist heads of department like Robinson. A small number of the civil servants under review were well-known Freemasons, and it is likely that many more were also members. Masonic influence over appointments was noted by contemporaries and believed to be a key reason why Catholics were prevented from taking their share of senior appointments.[143] Indeed, it is probable that well-positioned Masons like Sir Laurence Charles Dowdall, the principal clerk in the chief secretary's office and a former private secretary to three successive chief secretaries (Balfour, Morley, and Wyndham), were able to influence appointments and promotions in the Chief Secretary's Office. Similarly, many senior civil servants were members of the Kildare Street Club (as we have seen), a strongly Protestant and Unionist establishment, and whenever positions became vacant, club members were keen to influence appointments. Birrell told Nathan in 1914: 'There is a pertinacity about the Kildare Street Club type of man which is very noticeable . . . They crop up with their suggestions [for appointments] at critical moments and always with the same object—to cripple the Home Rule movement.'[144]

Both Conservative and Liberal administrations did appoint Catholics to senior positions. Wyndham appointed John Ross of Bladensburg, a convert to Catholicism, as chief commissioner of the Dublin Metropolitan Police, and he made Michael Finucane, an Irish-born Catholic who had worked in the Indian Civil Service, as one of the three Estates Commissioners in 1903. He also appointed Sir Antony MacDonnell, a Catholic whose brother was a member

[141] Campbell, *Land and Revolution*, Chs. 2 and 3.

[142] J. P. Mahaffy, 'The Romanization of Ireland' in *Nineteenth Century*, 50 (July 1901).

[143] See R. J. Smith, *Ireland's Renaissance* (Dublin, 1903), pp. ii–iii, 313, 343. On Freemasonry in Ireland, see Ramsay Colles, *In Castle and Court House: Being Reminiscences of 30 Years in Ireland* (London, 1911), 179–187. Colles founded the journal *Irish Masonry, Illustrated* in 1901.

[144] McBride, *Greening of Dublin Castle*, 183–4.

of the Irish Parliamentary Party, as his under secretary.[145] But he appointed many Protestants and Unionists to senior positions in the Civil Service, too. All twenty-one assistant land commissioners, appointed in 1903 to administer the new Land Act, for instance, were Protestants. Indeed, McBride calculates that of seventy key appointments to the Civil Service over the decade of Conservative government between 1895 and 1905, only fifteen (21 per cent) were Catholic. Similarly, Liberal administrations appointed both Catholics and Protestants. John Morley substantially altered the composition of the magistracy during his chief secretaryship by appointing 554 Catholics as magistrates (out of a total of 637 appointments), and thereby changed the ratio of Protestants to Catholics on the bench from 4:1, to 2:1.[146] But Birrell appointed N. R. Wilkinson, an English Protestant with no knowledge of heraldry, to the Office of Arms after the theft of the so-called Irish crown jewels in 1908; he made Charles L. Matheson (brother of R. E.) a Serjeant at Law;[147] and Richard Maunders, a Unionist, was appointed Registrar of Deeds and Titles in the same year.[148] If the British state had wanted substantially to 'green' Dublin Castle, they could have opened up the senior positions to competitive examination as in the rest of the United Kingdom. Why did they not do this? To answer this question, it is necessary to examine the social background of those Irish Catholics who were appointed to influential positions in Dublin Castle.

V

The first point that is striking about the Catholic civil servants under review is the large proportion of them who were from landowning families.[149] Fourteen of the Catholic civil servants in this survey (36 per cent of the total) were born into a landed family. Two more married into landed families, making a total of sixteen (41 per cent) with landed connections.[150] The sizes of the estates of the fourteen born into landed families are enumerated in Table 2.13. In general, they were from the lower end of the landlord class: almost half (46.5 per cent) were born into estates of fewer than 1,000 acres; and 85 per cent were from

---

[145] Mark Antony MacDonnell, a surgeon at Liverpool, was Home Rule MP for the Leix division of Queen's county, 1892–1906.

[146] John Morley, *Recollections*, i (London, 1917), 339; McBride, *Greening of Dublin Castle*, 48–9, 69.

[147] According to McBride, Matheson was appointed by Birrell after a number of appointments of Catholics to the judiciary in order to reassure Unionists (*Greening of Dublin Castle*, 171).

[148] Ibid. 11, 155, 190.

[149] Of the 165 civil servants under review, we know the religion of 138, and 47 of these (34%) were Catholic.

[150] It is significant that the proportion of landed Catholic civil servants is higher (41%) than the proportion of civil servants generally who were landed (31%). When Catholics were recruited, they were more likely than Protestant civil servants to be from a landed background.

Table 2.13. The Size of
Estates of Catholic Senior
Civil Servants Born into
Landed Families

Acreage	Frequency
0–499	1 (8%)
500–999	5 (38.5%)
1,000–4,999	5 (38.5%)
5,000–9,999	2 (15%)
10,000+	0
Number	13

landed families who owned fewer than 5,000 acres. Admittedly, there was a minority (15 per cent) with estates of between 5,000 and 10,000 acres, but there were no Catholic civil servants born into the higher end of the landlord class (those who owned estates of more than 10,000 acres). Thomas Henry Burke, the Catholic under secretary who was murdered by the Invincibles in the Phoenix Park in 1882 was from a landed family in the west of Ireland, as was one of his successors as under secretary, Sir Antony MacDonnell. Many of these Catholic landlord families must have used ingenious strategies to retain their land during the enforcement of the penal laws, and it is interesting that one of the Catholic civil servants from a landowning background, William Butler, a commissioner of intermediate education, published a book on this subject, *Confiscation in Irish History* (1917).[151]

Typical of the Catholic landlord class from which so many Irish civil servants were recruited were the Considines of Pallasgreen, county Limerick. Sir Heffernan Considine (1816–85) owned 950 acres (valued at £1,211) in Limerick, and was a magistrate, deputy lieutenant, and (sometime) high sheriff in the county. His eldest son, Heffernan, who was educated at Stoneyhurst and Lincoln College, Oxford, became a Royal Irish Constabulary officer, a Resident Magistrate, and assistant Inspector General of the Royal Irish Constabulary.[152] His younger brother, Thomas Ivor, trained as a doctor and worked as assistant medical officer at Dundrum Asylum for the so-called 'criminally insane' before being appointed (without examination) to the top of the Civil Service as one of the Inspectors of Lunatic Asylums in 1910 (at the age of 42) on a salary of £1,000. A sister, Mary, married Lieutenant Colonel William MacCarthy-O'Leary of Millstreet, county Cork, and an officer in the South Lancashire Regiment, who was killed during the Boer War. And two of Heffernan's sons fought in the Great War,

---

[151] Butler was the son of Thomas Butler of Ballycarron, Golden, county Tipperary, who owned 2,335 acres (valued at £1,897) and was a Trinity College Dublin-educated Resident Magistrate.
[152] For a full discussion of Heffernan Considine's career, see Ch. 3.

one of them, Heffernan James Considine of the Royal Irish Regiment, losing his life in 1916. The Considine family provided at least two generations of loyal servants to the Crown in Ireland, and were intermarried with Catholic MPs, barristers, and landowners.[153] Thomas Ivor was in many respects untypical of the Catholic population of Ireland. He was from a prosperous landowning family (although not prosperous enough for him not to have to work), and he, therefore, shared the class interests of Irish Protestant landlords. Furthermore, his family had proved their loyalty to the British state, and to a certain extent were rewarded for this, and successful because of this. When he died in 1912, Heffernann Considine's obituary noted that he had: 'served his country with conspicuous ability, courage, and firmness during the worst days of the Irish Land War. He was a most efficient, high-minded public official in whom everyone connected with the Executive Government of Ireland had the fullest confidence.'[154]

Loyalty was an important criterion when appointments were made to the top of the Irish Civil Service. When the Duke of Abercorn was recommending the appointment of the Presbyterian John Ross to the vacant judicial position on the Land court in 1896, he told Cadogan, 'a man should be chosen who has fought and sacrificed for his [*here the word 'country' is crossed out*] party, who has shown his own personal worth by his political actions'.[155] This was especially the case when Catholics were appointed. In 1902, Wyndham was determined to appoint Sir Antony MacDonnell, perhaps the most talented administrator of his generation, as under secretary for Ireland. Despite the fact that MacDonnell had been recommended by the former Viceroy of India (Lord Lansdowne) and the president of the India council (George Hamilton), the Prime Minister (Arthur Balfour) was concerned that MacDonnell being Catholic might be disloyal. Wyndham then interviewed MacDonnell and told Balfour: 'He [MacDonnell] is a landlord. He repudiates a Parlt for Ireland . . . He is sound on law and order and contemptuous of the methods as well as of the aims of Redmond's party. He is fearless and as straight as a dart.'[156] MacDonnell was duly appointed. Similar problems arose when Horace Plunkett wanted to appoint T. P. Gill as the secretary to the DATI. Gill, a journalist and former Home Rule MP, had alarmed the chief secretary by writing a series of articles criticizing the government's Transvaal policy. Plunkett strongly defended Gill in a letter to an intermediary—Lady Betty Balfour, the chief secretary's wife—and explained that Gill did not have 'an "anti-English" craze or even conscious bias . . . I suppose . . . a man of his origin and history must have a virulent nationalist bacillus in his blood which become active whenever he breathes an atmosphere in

[153] Thomas Ivor's uncle (on the mother's side) was Thomas MacMahon a Trinity College Dublin-educated barrister from county Clare; and Heffernan's father in law was John Hyacinth Talbot of Castle Talbot, county Wexford, a former MP for New Ross.

[154] *Irish Times*, 13 Feb. 1912.   [155] McBride, *Greening of Dublin Castle*, 74–5.

[156] Wyndham to Balfour, 13 Sept. 1902 British Library, Arthur Balfour Papers MS 49,804.

which such bacilli thrive'. This pseudo-scientific explanation of Gill's fluctuating disloyalty appears to have satisfied the chief secretary's wife, and he was appointed to the post.[157]

Most of the Catholics who were appointed to senior positions in the Civil Service appear to have come from backgrounds that were demonstrably loyal to the British state in Ireland. More than half of them (54 per cent) had been born into elite families, where their fathers were landowners, senior civil servants, Resident Magistrates, magistrates, lawyers, medics, military officers, engineers, and so on. Seven of them (18 per cent) had brothers who also held elite positions as landowners, police officers, judges, MPs, and barristers. Some of the Catholic civil servants in this study were part of the largely Protestant social networks that emerged like spokes from the centre of the wheel of Dublin Castle. Thomas Burke, for instance, was, according to his 'dear friend', William Richard Le Fanu, 'one of a little club of twelve members who for some years dined once a month at each other's houses, and among whom were my brother [Joseph Sheridan Le Fanu] and myself'.[158] Some of them had married into the Irish Protestant middle class: Joseph Edmund Devlin, for instance, was an assistant secretary in the Local Government Board, and a Monaghan-born Catholic, whose wife Edith was a Dublin-born Anglican. A very large proportion of the Catholic civil servants, then, were not members of a newly mobile Catholic middle class, but members of an established Catholic landowning and professional elite for whom promotion to the top of the Civil Service (or similar position) was probably a foregone conclusion. Indeed, during the last quarter of the nineteenth century, educated Catholics were under a great deal of pressure to become Unionists as Geraldine Plunkett Dillon remembers:

Pa told me that it was not easy for a young Catholic man to be a Nationalist at that time, particularly if he had intellectual interests or any education. Most cultural institutions were in the hands of the Unionists, and it was represented to young Catholics that it was merely ignorance that prevented them from taking a larger part in the affairs of the country, a silly patriotic ignorance, and that as soon as they gave it up and recognised England's greatness and their own menial position, they would have their reward.[159]

Some of them had perhaps manifested the zeal of the convert in their loyalty to the British state. Peter O'Brien, the Catholic Attorney General in 1888–9, was from a substantial landed family. His father, John, had been Liberal MP for Limerick city (1841–52) and made his fortune in business before buying into land (5,575 acres valued at £1,953 in county Clare). One of his brothers, James, was a magistrate who inherited the family estate, and another brother, Jerome,

---

[157] McBride, *Greening of Dublin Castle*, 82–4.
[158] Le Fanu, *Seventy Years of Irish life*, 255, 143. Le Fanu also occasionally attended fancy-dress parties disguised 'as an Irish peasant', which suggests the distance between the Protestant middle class and the native Catholic population.   [159] O Brolchain, *All in the Blood*, 19–20.

was an officer in the 28th Foot. Peter was educated at Trinity College Dublin before becoming a barrister at Middle Temple, and working as registrar to his uncle, who was a Queen's Counsel. This appears to have led to an appointment as junior Crown counsel, then 3rd serjeant, and then into the Irish office as solicitor general (in 1887–8). O'Brien's ongoing success, however, was enhanced by the fact that he had become a staunch Unionist following the introduction of the first Home Rule Bill. According to *The Times*: 'Mr. O'Brien was unable, like a great number of educated Roman Catholics, to follow Mr. Gladstone in his conversion to Home Rule.'[160] Instead, O'Brien became a Judge with the reputation for extensively using the Crown's right to ask jurors (who were suspected of sympathizing with the defendants) to stand down, earning him the sobriquet 'Peter the Packer'.[161] In one case, that of the trial of those accused of the Maamtrasna murders in county Galway in 1884, O'Brien had annotated a list of the prospective jurors with the letter 'C' next to those whom he believed to be Catholic.[162] Such blatant sectarianism, together with his assumption that all Catholic jurors were probably disloyal and sympathizers with the Maamtrasna murderers, suggests that O'Brien may have internalized the British state's view of Irish Catholics. It would seem that Irish Catholics with the exception of those from landed and professional backgrounds were to be regarded as disloyal and potentially suspect.

VI

This survey of the composition and recruiting practices of the elite of the Irish Civil Service suggests a more complex pattern than that presented by McBride in *The Greening of Dublin Castle*. Whereas McBride sees a relatively straight-forward transition from Protestant and Unionist administrators to Catholic and nationalist ones, this chapter suggests that there were a variety of sometimes contradictory impulses dictating recruiting practices. In part, this was because there were a number of different individuals who decided who should be appointed to senior positions ranging from the lord lieutenant and chief secretary, to the various department heads, and to senior officials in the GPO and the Treasury in London. It would have been unlikely that all of these interests and individuals would agree on the types of individuals who should be recruited to the top of the Irish Civil Service. Even so, some clear recruitment patterns are evident.

---

[160] *The Times*, 8 Sept. 1914.
[161] The Crown could ask an unlimited number of jurors to stand down if they were suspected of sympathizing with those they were empowered to try, while the defence lawyers could ask only 20 jurors to stand down, if they were suspected of being biased against the defendants.
[162] Jarlath Waldron, *Maamtrasna: The Murders and the Mystery* (Dublin, 1992), 179.

McBride was clearly right to state that successive British administrations appointed Catholics to senior positions during this period. The proportion of Catholics at the top level of the Irish Civil Service did increase slightly (from 33 per cent to 37 per cent) between 1891 and 1911 due to the influence of both Liberal and Conservative chief secretaries who wanted to make the Irish administration more representative of the Irish population as a whole. However, the vast majority of Catholic recruits were not as representative of the Irish Catholic population as McBride suggests. There were approximately 6,500 landlords in Ireland, in a population of almost 5 million, and so landowners constituted a tiny proportion of the Irish population. Yet almost half (41 per cent) of Irish Catholic civil servants had landed connections. This was because landowners were an extremely powerful class in nineteenth-century Ireland; because the younger sons of the smaller landlords did not have sufficient private income to sustain an appropriate lifestyle and required well-paid salaried work; and because the British state regarded Catholic landowners as loyal servants of the Crown. In the aftermath of the Land War (1879–81) and the rapid development of the Home Rule movement in the 1880s, the British state appears to have regarded Irish Catholics as suspect and potentially disloyal. Irish Catholic landowners, however, because they generally shared the interests of their class rather than their ethnic group were regarded as supporters of the British State and were therefore much more likely to be recruited to the top of the Irish Civil Service than any other section of Catholic Irish society.

The elite of the Irish Civil Service had been dominated by Englishmen and members of the Irish landlord and Protestant professional classes since the beginning of the nineteenth century. In an open letter to the lord lieutenant in 1905, Barry O'Brien, the Home Ruler and first historian of Dublin Castle wrote: 'It is notorious that the highest positions in the government of Ireland have been and are filled by Protestants, almost wholly to the exclusion of those who professed the religion of the nation.'[163] Given the nature of the Civil Service, where positions were held for life and where vacancies occurred only when existing members either died or retired, change in the composition of the elite of the Civil Service was always going to be slow. However, government objections that there were insufficient educated Catholics capable of taking up senior positions must be regarded as a smokescreen. By 1900, there were perhaps 1,000 Catholic graduates emerging from the Irish universities each year, and some of these were already serving in the top jobs. Moreover, by 1911, the majority of clerks and officials in the lower-ranks of the Civil Service were Catholic, and if the recruiting practices of a head of department like T. P. Gill

---

[163] R. Barry O'Brien, *England's Title in Ireland: A Letter Addressed to his Excellency the Lord Lieutenant of Ireland* (London, 1905), 36–7.

had been followed many of these could have been recruited from within the Civil Service to the senior positions.

The vast majority of senior civil servants in the rest of the United Kingdom were recruited by open competition to class I clerkships.[164] This system enabled the Home Civil Service to discriminate against candidates on a class, rather than ethnic, bias. The examination for first-division clerkships could only be passed by candidates who had received a third-level education, meaning that most first-division clerks were drawn from significantly higher social groups than second-division clerks.[165] In due course, it was the first-division clerks who tended to become the heads of departments, and their immediate subordinates, and promotion from second- to first-class clerkships was rare. According to one senior civil servant, Sir Albert Flynn, writing in 1928:

I say emphatically and with a full sense of responsibility that, in my experience, these conditions [of lower division clerks being given an opportunity to be promoted to the higher class], though admitted in theory, are most insufficiently observed in practice. The different classes of the Civil Service are treated as 'castes', determined by a man's entrance examination, and special promotion into the upper caste is very rare.[166]

That the British state did not apply this recruiting system to Ireland suggests that the motivating impulse behind discriminatory recruiting practices in Ireland was ethnic, rather than class, discrimination. Had the government wanted to keep lower-class Irish men and women, both Catholic and Protestant, out of the top levels of the administration, the system of recruiting first-division clerks, as practised in the rest of the United Kingdom, could have been adopted. However, the government's determination to appoint senior civil servants in Ireland without competitive examination of any kind suggests that recruits were being vetted according to their ethnicity and perceived disloyalty, rather than class.

The Irish administration and the professions more generally had been dominated by the Irish Protestant middle class for generations. Table 2.11 demonstrates that Catholics remained under-represented in the professions up to 1911. As yet, however, very little systematic work has been done on the professions in nineteenth- and twentieth-century Ireland, with the exception of some work on the legal profession and a recent flowering of pioneering work on the origins of the accountancy profession in Ireland conducted by M. Annisette, Margaret Ó

---

[164] Kelsall, *Higher Civil Servants in Britain*, 13, 20.

[165] See Kelsall's analysis of the social background of the fathers of first- and second-division clerks in 1911 (ibid. 25).

[166] Sir Albert Flynn, quot. ibid. 45. According to Kelsall's figures, 'the annual promotion prospect proportion [from second- to first-class clerkships] in the ten-year period 1902–11 was about 0.12%' (ibid. 40).

hÓgartaigh and Philip O'Regan.[167] Broadly speaking, this work suggests that the Institute of Chartered Accountants in Ireland, which was established in 1888 by members of the Irish Protestant middle class, used social closure strategies to ensure that new recruits to the professional association were of 'good social standing and repute'. Almost all (twenty-seven of thirty-one or 87 per cent) of the founding members of the Institute of Chartered Accountants were Protestants, and the proportion of Catholics does not appear to have increased over the first thirty years of the Institute, suggesting that Irish Catholics were regarded as not possessing sufficient social standing or repute to become accountants.[168] Indeed, because prospective members of the Institute needed to be sponsored by an existing member, and because the required training as an articled clerk demanded an initial payment of £50 and up to five years of unpaid training, it was unlikely that there would be too many Catholic recruits.[169] By 1901, the profession appeared to be favouring mainly the sons of existing members: in that year, for instance, 30 per cent of the Belfast members of the Institute were fathers and sons, and many of the articled clerks were also sons of existing members.[170]

This suggests a parallel with those Church of Ireland families that provided large numbers of senior civil servants, and suggests that the Irish professions at the beginning of the twentieth century remained dominated by a small number of Protestant families. Moreover, the members of the professions were also joining together with the senior civil servants and businessmen in places like the Kildare Street Club and at elaborate dinners at places like the Shelbourne Hotel. Indeed, on the evening on which the Institute was established a 'a large and influential' group of friends including barristers, solicitors, bankers, and merchants gathered for a dinner at the hotel 'in a very recherché style'.[171] Such social events consolidated the sense of identity of the Irish Protestant middle class that dominated the top of the Irish administration and of many of the professions.

Richard Jarrell has also shown that nineteenth-century Irish scientists were overwhelmingly members of the Irish Protestant middle-class.[172] Jarrell defines

---

[167] Daire Hogan, *The Legal Profession in Ireland, 1789–1922* (Dublin, 1986); M. Annisette and Philip O'Regan, 'Joined for the Common Purpose: The Establishment of the Institute of Chartered Accountants in Ireland as an all-Ireland Institution', *Qualitative Research in Accounting and Management*, 4 (2007), 4–25; and Margaret Ó hÓgartaigh, 'Irish Accounting, Business and Financial History', *Accounting, Business and Financial History*, 18 (Mar. 2008), 7–19.

[168] Philip O'Regan, ' "Elevating the Profession": The Institute of Chartered Accountants in Ireland and the Implementation of Social Closure Strategies, 1888–1909', *Accounting, Business and Financial History*, 18 (Mar. 2008), 40; Margaret Ó hÓgartaigh, 'Irish Accounting, Business and Financial History', 7–19.

[169] O'Regan, 'Elevating the Profession', 44.   [170] Ibid. 46.   [171] Ibid. 41.

[172] Richard Jarrell, 'Differential National Development and Science in the Nineteenth Century: The Problems of Quebec and Ireland', in Nathan Reingold and Marc Rothenberg (eds.), *Scientific Colonialism: A Cross-cultural Comparison* (Washington, DC, 1987).

Irish scientists as those who taught science or worked for the government in a scientific capacity or who published scientific articles. During the nineteenth century, he found that of 118 scientists either from Ireland or who worked in Ireland, eighty were alumni or teachers at Trinity College Dublin and thirty-eight others were from elsewhere or educated at other colleges. Of these 118 scientists, Jarrell estimated that almost all of them were 'Anglo-Irish or Protestants', and that only about one in eight (13 per cent) was Catholic.[173] This again suggests that Catholics may have been denied access to some professions.

Discrimination is always almost impossible to prove since it operates in an informal manner, and tends to be based on the shared assumptions of employers, rather than on any policy document that is written down and left in wait for future historians. But absence of evidence is not evidence of absence, and it is likely that many of the young educated Catholics in Ireland at the beginning of the twentieth century had a similar experience to that of Patrick Shea when he was principal officer in the Ministry of Education in Northern Ireland in the 1950s:

One day at lunch a group of us got to talking about how a forthcoming vacancy would be filled. The conversation was no more serious than gossip about anticipated events of that sort ever is, until one of the company said, in the most matter-of-fact way: 'Of course, Paddy, you being an RC, I suppose we can leave your name out of the reckoning.' I felt a pang of disappointment, not so much because of what had been said. The speaker was an old friend, a kind, liberal-minded man; his comment, simply and perhaps rather innocently, gave expression to what he regarded as an accepted fact of life. But I was disappointed and I was angry that his remark aroused no response from the others; the conversation went on as though it had not been made . . . At that moment, for the only time in my long career, I felt isolated from those with whom so much of my life had been spent.[174]

One of the purposes of this book is to explore what young Catholic men and women did with their similar feelings of anger, frustration, and injustice when they felt the glass ceiling of discrimination push down upon their hopes and ambitions. The next chapter will examine what opportunities were available to Catholics among the officer class of the Royal Irish Constabulary.

---

[173] Ibid. 346, 347. However, there were some eminent Irish Catholic scientists—Sir Robert Kane, W. K. Sullivan, and Nicholas Callan, among others—and Jarrell also suggests that the Catholic church and Irish nationalists might have identified science with colonialism and therefore directed their communities away from it. Greta Jones also suggests that the Catholic church's suspicion of some scientific developments might have led it to use some of its control over third-level education in Ireland to discourage developments in the teaching and practice of science ('Catholicism, Nationalism and Science', *Irish Review*, 20 (Winter/Spring 1997), 47).

[174] Patrick Shea, *Voices and the Sound of Drums: An Irish Autobiography* (Belfast, 1981), 179.

3

Policing

The previous chapter explored the extent to which there was a 'greening' of the Irish Civil Service between 1891 and 1911, and found that the proportion of Catholic administrators did increase slightly during this period. This chapter looks instead at another arm of the British state in Ireland—that of the Royal Irish Constabulary—and asks if there was a parallel 'greening' process taking place among the leaders and the officer class of the Irish police force. In 1870, there were two arms of the police force in Ireland: the Royal Irish Constabulary which numbered about 13,000 men, and the Dublin Metropolitan Police Force which numbered about 1,000 men; although this chapter is concerned only with the former.[1]

The Land War (1879–81) inaugurated a prolonged period of agrarian conflict and political disaffection in Ireland, and the officers of the Royal Irish Constabulary were responsible for policing this crisis. Police officers were extremely powerful, then, as they were responsible for upholding 'law and order' at the front line in a country where there was considerable opposition to both the distribution of land and the legitimacy of the state. In addition, they were responsible for writing monthly reports on the political and agrarian conflicts in their counties, as well as on more general social and economic matters, which were sent to the senior members of the Irish Office in Dublin Castle. In this respect, the officers of the Royal Irish Constabulary were doubly responsible for both 'policing the crisis' and for compiling information about political and agrarian disaffection in their localities, since their reports were the main method by which the government was informed about developments in the Irish countryside; and they formed the basis on which subsequent Irish policy was devised by Dublin Castle.

I

In an influential article, William Lowe and Elizabeth Malcolm argue that the Royal Irish Constabulary became 'domesticated' between its formation in 1836 and its disbandment in 1922:

[1] W. E. Vaughan, 'Ireland *c*. 1870' in W. E. Vaughan (ed.), *A New History of Ireland,* v *Ireland under the Union*, i *1801–1870* (Oxford, 1989), 765.

[I]t was naturalized by becoming in its composition more truly representative of the Irish population; it was attached to home as its duties became more routine, more akin to house-keeping than to peace-keeping; and it was tamed because its ability to use force was greatly diminished . . . [T]he Royal Irish Constabulary was by the early years of the twentieth century very much a civil police force, reflecting very accurately in its composition the socio-economic structure of Irish society and in its operations the needs of small, relatively law-abiding, rural communities.[2]

Lowe's and Malcolm's 'domestication' argument is based on three main points. First, that the responsibilities of the Royal Irish Constabulary became gradually more civil (and less 'military') as the nineteenth century progressed. Increasingly, police constables were as concerned with the collecting of agricultural statistics and with dog licence enforcement as they were with the prevention of agrarian and political 'crime'. As H. A. Blake observed in 1881, the Royal Irish Constabulary did 'everything in Ireland, from the muzzling of a dog to the suppression of a rebellion'.[3] Second, that the Royal Irish Constabulary (which was an armed police force) tended to use arms less and less, so that 'there was a feeling within the force that the seldom-seen carbines were a pointless trapping and that policemen were no longer properly trained in their use'.[4] Lowe's and Malcolm's third—and most important—point is that the 'religious composition of the [rank and file of the] Constabulary [was] . . . consistently more than 70 per cent catholic, and thus very close to the recorded catholic proportion of the population during 1861–1911'.[5] Indeed, over each decade between 1841 and 1911, they demonstrate that the proportion of Catholic recruits was between 66 per cent and 79 per cent, so that by 1914 81 per cent of the rank and file of the Royal Irish Constabulary were Catholics.[6]

In a later article, Lowe has applied a modified version of this argument to the officers of the Royal Irish Constabulary.[7] Unlike the police forces in the rest of the United Kingdom, most of the officers of the Royal Irish Constabulary were not recruited from the ranks of the force but through a cadet system introduced in 1842.[8] In order to become an officer in the Royal Irish Constabulary, it was necessary to be nominated by the Lord Lieutenant, Chief Secretary, or the Inspector General to compete in an examination for a cadetship.[9] If the

---

[2] William J. Lowe and Elizabeth L. Malcolm, 'The Domestication of the Royal Irish Constabulary, 1836–1922', *Irish Economic and Social History*, 19 (1992), 27.

[3] Quot. ibid. 29.   [4] Ibid. 31.   [5] Ibid. 35.

[6] Lowe's and Malcolm's study is based on an analysis of a 10% stratified sample of all policemen (excluding officers) enrolled between Jan. 1837 and Aug. 1920, and includes 'slightly more' than 7,000 individual cases. The period 1837–51 is considered as one decade (ibid. 33). See also Brian Griffin, 'Religion and Opportunity in the Irish Police Forces, 1836–1914' in R. V. Comerford, et al. (eds.), *Religion, Conflict and Coexistence in Ireland* (Dublin, 1990), 221.

[7] William J. Lowe, 'Irish Constabulary Officers, 1837–1922: Profile of a Professional Elite', *Irish Economic and Social History*, 32 (2005), 19–46.

[8] Stephen Ball (ed.), *A Policeman's Ireland: Recollections of Samuel Waters, RIC* (Cork, 1999), 4.

[9] Between 1866 and 1898, the Inspector General had the privilege of nominating one-third of all cadetships (and he usually used this power to put forward the sons of needy police officers). After

candidate succeeded in obtaining a sufficiently high score in the examination, he would become a cadet for a period of about six months' training at the Royal Irish Constabulary depot in Phoenix Park, before being appointed as a Sub- (later a District) Inspector.[10] Some police officers were recruited from the ranks, but the vast majority were recruited from outside the force through the cadet system.

Between 1836 and 1866, for instance, only eighty-four (18 per cent) of the 474 Sub-Inspector vacancies were filled from the ranks by promot- ed head constables.[11] For this reason, as Lowe acknowledges: 'Throughout 1842–1921 cadet appointments predominated, accounting for nearly two-thirds (65.4 per cent) of [officer] appointments', and the vast majority of these cadets (70 per cent to 80 per cent) were Protestants.[12] As a result, the Royal Irish Constabulary officer corps 'was not as "green" as the rest of the Castle adminis- tration that was taking shape [between 1892 and 1922]'.[13] However, the gradual reform of the recruiting mechanism for Royal Irish Constabulary officers in 1867 (when one-quarter of entry-level officers were to be recruited from the ranks) and 1895 (when the quota of District Inspectors to be recruited from the ranks was increased to one-half) meant that 'rankers began to make steady progress in the 1870s . . . [and they] achieved near parity [in officer appoint- ments] during 1901–10'.[14] Because the majority of promoted head constables were Catholic, this resulted in a certain amount of 'greening' of the officer corps.[15]

Lowe also argues that the equitable award of favourable and unfavourable records to both Protestant and Catholic Royal Irish Constabulary officers 'showed progress toward fairness characteristic of a "neutral and impartial state"', and that Catholic officers advanced more quickly than their Protes- tant colleagues to the position of first-class District Inspector.[16] This evidence suggests that, once Catholics had been admitted to the officer corps of the force, they were not treated differently from Protestant officers, and that 'reli- gion did not bestow a permanent advantage'.[17] Lowe therefore concludes his discussion of Irish police officers by suggesting that a process of professionalization

---

1898, the power of nomination for cadetships was solely in the hands of the Chief Secretary and the Lord Lieutenant. See Brian Griffin, 'The Irish Police, 1836–1914: A Social History', PhD thesis (Loyola University of Chicago, 1991), 247–8.

[10] In the 1850s, cadets spent between 4 and 5 months in training at the depot but by the early 1900s the training period had been extended to 8 months (ibid. 269). [11] Ibid. 246.

[12] Lowe, 'Irish Constabulary Officers', 31, 33. Lowe, together with his two graduate research assistants (Jessica McLaughlin and Michelle Sheldon), has carried out a study of the records of the 1,220 police officers contained in the RIC officers' register, and these data form the basis of his article. Table 3 (ibid. 34) depicts the proportion of Catholic and non-Catholic cadets between 1837 and 1921, which indicates that between 70% and 80% of cadets were non-Catholic and between 10% and 20% were Catholic. [13] Ibid. 46.

[14] Ibid. 31. [15] Ibid. 22, 32, 33, 34, 42, 46.

[16] Police officers were first appointed as third-class Sub- (or district) inspectors, and proceeded to second- and first-class before becoming county inspectors (ibid. 40–2). [17] Ibid. 42.

(if not domestication) was taking place among Royal Irish Constabulary officers:

the Constabulary's professional elite was . . . part of the modernisation of Irish public service careers. The dominance of Protestants in cadet appointments shows that, even in the twentieth century, religion and its attendant political and social associations with the ruling establishment remained a powerful though diminishing barrier to officer status. The personnel register data reveal that, by the late nineteenth century, Catholics were making progress as a proportion of officer appointments, especially among rankers [that is, officers who had been recruited from the ranks]. In the three decades preceding the War of Independence, rewards and punishments were administered fairly and Catholics and rankers were very successful in advancement to the rank of 1st class district inspector. These are encouraging indicators of movement towards a modern professional environment that, despite differences of religion and social background, tempered establishment influence and treated men equitably within the officer ranks in the high-profile R.I.C. Catholics and rankers could and did enjoy successful Constabulary officer careers working alongside Protestant former cadets.[18]

In this way, the Royal Irish Constabulary introduced 'merit-based practices that, over time, liberalised entry to Constabulary officer positions' and thereby 'contributed to the long-term weakening of the political power of the Protestant establishment'.[19]

In a recent monograph, however, Elizabeth Malcolm presents a rather different view of the officers of the Royal Irish Constabulary.[20] Although she agrees with Lowe that between 1837 and 1921 one-third of the officers of the Royal Irish Constabulary were Catholic, and that there was increased recruitment from the ranks from the 1890s onwards, she suggests that Catholic officers were less likely to be promoted to the senior positions in the force than their Protestant counterparts:

[P]romoted Catholic officers were clearly at a disadvantage as regards their Protestant colleagues. Protestants . . . were more likely to reach the higher ranks of the force. Between 1837 and 1921[,] of the Royal Irish Constabulary's first-class county inspectors[,] 71 per cent were Protestant and only 29 per cent Catholic. As overall about one-third of officers were Catholic, this might seem a fairly representative figure. But of these Catholic county inspectors fully 80 per cent were appointed in 1920–21. In other words, there was a rush to appoint Catholics to senior positions only in the final days of the Royal Irish Constabulary's existence. Prior to then Protestants had been dominant.[21]

According to Malcolm, the 'religious and political prejudices' (that Lowe suggested were declining in importance) continued to influence the process of promotion to senior positions in the Royal Irish Constabulary up to 1920–1. Indeed, Malcolm's view of the Royal Irish Constabulary appears to have been

18 Ibid. 46.   19 Ibid. 20.
20 Elizabeth Malcolm, *The Irish Policeman, 1822–1922: A Life* (Dublin, 2006).
21 Ibid. 63, 149–150.

revised considerably since the publication of her co-authored article (with Lowe) in 1992. Far from regarding the Irish police as becoming increasingly 'domesticated', she now suggests that the Royal Irish Constabulary retained the centralized and military character of a European gendarmerie: 'The centrally controlled, paramilitary Royal Irish Constabulary, with its wide-ranging responsibilities was far more like a European-style *gendarmerie* than it was a locally regulated, unarmed English borough or county constabulary, primarily concerned with the prevention and detection of non-political crime.'[22]

Broadly speaking, Lowe and Malcolm present two very different views of the officers of the Royal Irish Constabulary. For Lowe, the Royal Irish Constabulary officers were becoming gradually professionalized. By the end of the nineteenth century, they were increasingly recruited from the ranks; many of them were promoted Catholic head constables; they were behaving more like a respected profession than establishment elite; and the processes of recruiting and promotion were becoming increasingly impartial and meritocratic.[23] Malcolm, on the other hand, presents a more negative portrait of the officers of the Royal Irish Constabulary. Although there was increased recruitment from the ranks, and 'a rough balance in [Catholic and Protestant] appointments' from the 1890s onwards, the senior positions in the force continued to be the preserve of Protestants until the crisis of 1920–1.[24] According to Malcolm, the professionalization of the Royal Irish Constabulary was tempered by the enduring influence of political, religious, and class-based discrimination at the top level of the force. This chapter will explore the social composition of the senior officers of the Royal Irish Constabulary between 1881 and 1911 and consider which model (either that of Lowe or Malcolm) best characterizes the nature of the officer class of the Royal Irish Constabulary during this period.[25]

[22] Ibid. 40–1.

[23] In his paper at the American Conference of Irish Studies in June 2001, Lowe concluded: 'The extension of advancement opportunities based on experience, performance, and merit (democratization) [in the RIC officer corps] *versus* class and connections does not result in what we usually think of as an elite' and he characterized the RIC officers as 'respectable professionals' rather than an 'establishment elite'. See William J. Lowe, 'RIC Officers, 1879–1922: Respectable Professionals or Establishment Elite?' (unpub. paper delivered at ACIS (American Conference for Irish Studies) conference, New York City, June 2001), 19–20.

[24] Malcolm, *Irish Policeman, 1822–1922*, 62.

[25] This chapter adopts a different approach and methodology to that of both Lowe and Malcolm. Whereas Lowe examines the composition of the RIC officer corps as a whole between 1837 and 1921 (1,220 individuals), and Malcolm analyses a 10% random stratified sample of RIC officers over the same period (122 individuals), this chapter explores the social background of the senior officers of the RIC in 1881, 1891, 1901, and 1911. I have defined the senior RIC officers as the six individuals who held the top jobs (the Inspector General, the Deputy Inspector General, the Assistant Inspector Generals (of which there were three at any one time), and the private secretary to the Inspector General) and all of the County Inspectors of the Irish counties and ridings. Altogether, 129 individuals held these positions in 1881, 1891, 1901, and 1911. The number of senior police officers changed over time as some counties were divided into two Ridings therefore requiring an additional County Inspector. In 1881 and 1891, there were 40 senior officers; in 1901, there were

II

Before going on to look at the social background of the senior officers of the Royal Irish Constabulary between 1881 and 1911, I will first consider the background of those individuals who held the position of Inspector General between 1836 and 1922 as these men were effectively the leaders of the force during this period. The Inspector General played a key role in influencing Irish policy and in recruiting officers to the force. Before 1898, for instance, the Inspector General controlled one-third of the nominations to take the cadet examination, providing him with enormous power over recruiting to the officer class of the Royal Irish Constabulary.[26] He was also in a strong position to influence the Irish policy of the government. In January 1902, for instance, Neville Chamberlain, who was Inspector General between 1900 and 1916, and the inventor of snooker, concluded his monthly report on the state of the country with a call for the introduction of coercive legislation to 'establish confidence in the power of the law'.[27] This was duly introduced—albeit after some debate and disagreement—two months later in March 1902.

Between 1836 and 1922, there were eleven permanent Inspector Generals who served in Ireland.[28] Of these, nine (82 per cent) had previously been senior army officers who were recruited from outside the force.[29] Many of them had experience of serving in the colonies before their appointment to the Royal Irish Constabulary. General Sir Duncan McGregor (Inspector General, 1838) had served in Egypt; Colonel Sir John Stewart Wood (Inspector General, 1865–76) had been in India and Afghanistan; Colonel Robert Bruce (Inspector General, 1882–5) had played his part in suppressing the Indian mutiny; Colonel Neville Chamberlain had experience of India and Afghanistan; and Major-General Sir Henry Tudor (Inspector General, 1920–2) had participated in the South African War (1899–1902). The strong military credentials of the leading officers of the Royal Irish Constabulary were not lost on the rank and file members of the force. Thomas Fennell, for instance, observed that: 'The Inspector General had always . . . been a military officer of the rank of Colonel and, in the early years of

42; and in 1911, there were 43. My study does not examine the background of the lesser police officers who were Sub- (later District) Inspectors. For the methodology and sources used to compile the data for this chapter, see Appendix.   [26] Lowe, 'RIC Officers, 1879–1922', 3–4.

[27] Inspector General monthly report (Jan. 1902), National Archives, London (NAL), Colonial Office (CO), 904/74.

[28] Major George Warburton served temporarily as Inspector General in 1838 and he is not included in this sample.

[29] Five Inspector Generals were the members of prominent military families (whose fathers were also army officers): Lieutenant-General James Shaw-Kennedy (Inspector General, 1836–8); Sir Henry John Brownrigg (Inspector General, 1838–65); Colonel Sir John Stewart Wood (Inspector General, 1865–76); Lieutenant Colonel George Hillier (Inspector General, 1876–1882); and Colonel Sir Neville Chamberlain (Inspector General, 1900–16).

the Force, his deputy and assistants had also been military officers. From the very beginning, then, the R.I.C. was organised and ruled from a military standpoint, rather than as a civil force.'[30]

There were, however, two exceptions to the military rule. Sir Andrew Reed (Inspector General, 1885–1900) and Sir Thomas James Smith (Inspector General, 1920) had both been County Inspectors (who joined the force as cadets) before being promoted to the top rank in the Constabulary. Smith was Inspector General for little more than two months (between 11 March and 15 May 1920) while Reed served as Inspector General for fifteen years and was arguably the most influential Inspector General during the history of the Irish Constabulary. Reed was regarded favourably by the rank and file, partly because he played a part in reforming the day-to-day life of the rank and file of the force. Fennell recalls that:

He was the most competent of any of the Officers who filled the position, before or after him . . . He was an officer of broad outlook and effected many appreciative reforms in the service. The military officers had not his administrative experience as a police officer. A mind fashioned in military service could not be as fit to rule a police force . . . as that of an officer who had graduated in that Force.[31]

Reed was recruited to the Royal Irish Constabulary in an unusual manner. In 1859, the Lord Lieutenant, the Earl of Carlisle, visited Queen's College, Galway and told the president of the college that he wanted to give an appointment (to the public service) to a particularly promising student. The president suggested Reed who was the son of a Church of Ireland land agent and a part-time tutor at the Erasmus Smith school in Galway. Reed accepted the offer and became a Sub-Inspector in the Royal Irish Constabulary in 1859 and a County Inspector in 1868, when he was also asked by the Inspector General, Sir John Stewart Wood, to become his private secretary. Between 1868 and 1879, Reed served under both Wood and his successor, Hillier, as private secretary to the Inspector General. In 1882, Reed was appointed Assistant Inspector General and in 1885 he became the first Inspector General to be promoted from within the force. During his term of office, he reformed the daily experience of rank-and-file policemen, and improved the possibilities for promotion for Catholic policemen:

Restrictions on men entering public houses for refreshment, whether on or off duty, were removed to the extent that, when not on duty, they were free to do so. Knowing the sameness of their daily lives, he ordered that men should have perfect freedom

---

[30] Rosemary Fennell (ed.), *The Royal Irish Constabulary: A History and Personal Memoir* (Dublin, 2003), pp. 24, xiii, 176–7. Fennell was a Catholic sergeant and head constable in the force who served in Mayo, Donegal, King's county, Armagh, and Sligo between 1875 and his retirement in 1905. This account of his experiences was written in the 1930s when was in his late 70s, possibly embittered by his failure to become an officer, and perhaps trying to make his role in the force acceptable to nationalist Ireland.   [31] Ibid. 24–5.

to enjoy themselves, to sing and dance and engage in any pastime not forbidden by regulations and, as far as possible, make their barracks their home. This was a departure from the unwritten law that men's noses should be always on the grindstone . . . Most convincing, perhaps, of his capability as head of the Irish police was an order by him that the police should be courteous towards the public making enquiries or desiring their assistance, and [he] directed County Inspectors not to recommend any man for promotion who failed to carry out these instructions . . . Above all other improvements that marked his rule, was the competitive system for a portion of the promotions to the various grades. In these competitions, Catholics gained 90 per cent of the places assigned to each . . . [and this] enable[d] Catholics to win promotion by their own ability.[32]

Reed was also responsible for opening half the District Inspectorships to promotion from the ranks in 1895, which was described by one officer as the 'greatest reform he carried out' because this system 'gave the young men of the force an opportunity of advancement . . . It also . . . immensely increased the educational qualifications and professional knowledge of the men in the ranks'.[33] However, Reed was very much the exception to the rule. Wyndham regarded him as 'useless' and appointed Colonel Neville Chamberlain to be his successor who, as an army officer (who was the son of an army officer), fitted much more closely the typical profile of an Inspector General in Ireland. According to Wyndham, Chamberlain would oversee 'a gradual screwing up of efficiency'.[34]

Reed was also untypical of Inspector Generals in that he was Irish born. Of the ten Inspector Generals about whom information is available: four were born in England, two in Scotland, and four in Ireland. Almost two-thirds of Inspector Generals were, therefore, British; while just two-fifths were Irish. Two of the Irish Inspector Generals were born in Derry (Bruce and Byrne) while one was born in King's county (Smith), and one in Galway (Reed). The vast majority (ten or 91 per cent) of Inspector Generals—whether British or Irish—were Episcopalian: only one of the eleven was Catholic (Sir Joseph Aloysius Byrne, who succeeded Chamberlain in August 1916 and served until March 1920). It is striking that the first Catholic head of the Irish police force was appointed eighty years after the establishment of the Constabulary and in the aftermath of a major rebellion against British rule in Ireland. In every other respect, however, Byrne was typical of the profile of Inspector Generals. Before his appointment to the Royal Irish Constabulary he had served in the South African War (where he had been wounded at the siege of Ladysmith) and he had ascended to the rank of Brigadier-General. He was promoted from outside the force, although he did have an uncle (John Peter Byrne) who was a former

[32] Ibid. 25–6.
[33] Starkie to Miss D. M. Reed, 18 July 1915, quot. Lowe, 'RIC Officers, 1879–1922', 5–6.
[34] George Wyndham to Arthur Balfour, 26 Nov. 1900, in J. W. Mackail and Guy Wyndham, *Life and letters of George Wyndham*, ii (London, 1925), 410.

District Inspector and a Resident Magistrate. Whereas many Inspector Generals were the sons of army officers, Byrne was the son of a Catholic doctor in Derry (Dr Joseph Byrne). Most of the Inspector Generals, then, were British-born, Episcopalian former army officers. The next section of the chapter will explore the background of their immediate subordinates: the senior officers and County Inspectors.

III

All of the senior Royal Irish Constabulary officers were men: women were not permitted to join the Royal Irish Constabulary at either officer or rank-and-file levels. As Table 3.1 demonstrates, the majority (81 per cent) of senior officers over the period between 1881 and 1911 were Protestant (77 per cent were Episcopalians and 4 per cent were Dissenters), while only one-fifth (19 per cent) were Catholic. Protestants were, therefore, enormously over-represented in terms of their numbers in the Irish population as a whole, while Catholics were seriously under-represented among the senior officers. Most of them (109 or 84 per cent) were Irish born, although about one-sixth (twenty or 16 per cent) had been born in England (nineteen) or Scotland (one). It is necessary, therefore, to separate the figures on religious affiliation of those who were born in Ireland, and those who were born in Britain (see Table 3.2).

Table 3.1. Religion of Senior Police Officers, 1881–1911

Denomination	Number
Episcopalian	99 (77%)
Catholic	24 (19%)
Presbyterian	5 (3.5%)
Methodist	1 (0.5%)
Number	129

Table 3.2. Religion of Irish- and British-born Senior Police Officers, 1881–1911

Denomination	Irish-born	British-born
Episcopalian	81 (74%)	18 (90%)
Catholic	22 (20%)	2 (10%)
Presbyterian	5 (5%)	—
Methodist	1 (1%)	—
Number	109	20

Table 3.3. Age of Senior Police Officers
in 1881 and 1911

Age	1881	1911
0–19	—	—
20–9	—	—
30–9	—	—
40–9	14 (35%)	10 (24%)
50–9	17 (42.5%)	28 (66.5%)
60–9	6 (15%)	4 (9.5%)
70–9	3 (7.5%)	—
Number	40	42

This does not radically transform the picture, but it does reveal the tendency of the British government to appoint English Catholics to the Royal Irish Constabulary, a point to which I will return later in the chapter.[35] Of the Irish-born senior officers, the majority were recruited from the eastern province of Leinster, largely because they were reared in close proximity to the Dublin Castle networks that enabled candidates to win nominations to take the examination for a cadetship.[36] Those who were raised further away from Dublin (in Ulster or Connacht) were least successful in their quest for cadetships. The vast majority of officers under review were recruited via the cadet system. Of the 129 senior officers, 120 (93 per cent) had been cadets or were appointed directly as Sub-Inspectors; five (4 per cent) were recruited from outside the force (these were senior officers); and only four (3 per cent) were head constables who had been promoted from the ranks.

Police officers tended to be middle-aged by the time they were promoted to the position of County Inspector (see Table 3.3). The 'officer list' operated according to seniority, and—assuming officers did not receive any 'unfavourable records' or criticisms from Dublin Castle—they could expect to become a County Inspector after twenty or so years on the force.[37] This meant that in both 1881 and 1911 the majority of senior officers were in their forties and fifties. The age profile of the senior officers in 1911 was slightly higher (with more in their fifties than forties), but a retirement rule had been put in place so that there were no longer

[35] Although it is clear that there were even more Protestants among the Irish-born County Inspectors than there were among the cohort as a whole (80% as opposed to 77%).

[36] Of 109 officers about whom information is available, 41 (38%) were born in Leinster, 31 (28%) in Munster, 19 (17%) in Ulster, and 18 (17%) in Connacht.

[37] According to Griffin, Sub-Inspectors had to wait an average of 25 years before being promoted to County Inspector ('The Irish Police, 1836–1914', 289). Clifford Lloyd, the Special Resident Magistrate, believed that promotion was overly slow and that 'by the time an officer reached the rank of County Inspector, much individuality had been knocked out of him. He was frequently past his work, and still more often quite unsuited to it from a police point of view' (ibid. 290).

any officers in their seventies. In 1911, the eldest serving officer was Heffernan Considine, who was 65 years of age and due to retire that year, whereas in 1881 the oldest serving officer had been Alexander Wilson Hutchinson Heard (of Kinsale, county Cork) who was aged 74 when he retired in October 1882. Despite the dangers of the job (which became more pronounced as the nineteenth century progressed), the age at death of the senior officers was very high. Of eighty-six individuals about whom information is available, most died in their fifties (21 per cent), sixties (30 per cent), and seventies (31 per cent), with a small number surviving into their eighties (12 per cent) and even their nineties (5 per cent).[38] The eldest surviving senior officer in my sample was Rowland Francis Nichol Fanning, a Dublin-born Catholic, who served as both Assistant Inspector General (1876–82) and Deputy Inspector General (1882–6) before his death in February 1919 at the age of 92 (having received a Knighthood in 1886 for his 'long and meritorious service').

There was a high price to be paid by some County Inspectors—particularly during the Land War (1879–81) and the Irish Revolution (1916–23)—and one member of my sample (Alexander Gray) was killed during the Easter Rising at Ashbourne in 1916.[39] Another—Albert Augustine Roberts—was seriously wounded at Amiens Street, Dublin, on 22 June 1920 during the War of Independence. There were also a number of suicides among the senior officers of the Royal Irish Constabulary—perhaps due to the difficulties of being a member of a force that was often regarded in a negative light by large sections of the Catholic Irish population—and one County Inspector in my sample committed suicide. William Lennon, a member of the Church of Ireland from county Wicklow, took his own life on 15 January 1897, at the age of 52. His father, who had also been a police officer, had committed suicide in March 1867 (when he was 65 and William was 22), and this appears to have influenced the decision of the son to take the same course. However, as with all cases of suicide, it is impossible to unravel the complex sequence of events that leads to a person taking their own life.[40]

In part, the comparatively high age at death was a function of the relatively prosperous lives of high-ranking police officers. County Inspectors earned between £350 and £450 each year after the reforms of 1882: the starting salary for a County Inspector after 1882 was £350, which increased each year by £20

[38] One of the County Inspectors in my sample (1% of the total) died in his 40s. He was Frederick Augustus White, a Carlow-born Catholic, who died in Nov. 1893 at the age of 48.

[39] Gray was wounded on 28 Apr. 1916 and died of his wounds on 10 May 1916. For a full list of police officers killed in action, see Jim Herlihy's *Royal Irish Constabulary Officers: A Biographical Dictionary and Genealogical Guide, 1816–1922* (Dublin, 2005), 337–44. On Gray, see Terence Dooley, 'Alexander "Baby" Gray and his Death at the Battle of Ashbourne, April 1916', *Riocht na Midhe* (2003).

[40] On suicide in Victorian and Edwardian Ireland more generally, see Georgina Laragy, 'Suicide in Ireland, 1831–1921: A Social and Cultural History', PhD thesis (National University of Ireland, Maynooth, 2005).

until it reached the maximum annual salary of £450.[41] After retirement, they were entitled to a pension which ranged from (in my sample) £254 (paid to George Hill Wray when he retired in 1886) and £1,800 (paid to Andrew Reed when he retired in 1900). On average, the ninety-one County Inspectors about whom information is available received £493 each year after their retirement. Most of them also left a reasonable sum in their wills. On average, the fifty-six County Inspectors about whom information is available left £6,299 each in their wills, ranging from the £21 left by Wellington Colomb to the £90,593 left by Heffernan Considine. It is true that some police officers believed that they were not well paid—Thomas Hartley Montgomery even murdered the cashier of his local bank and stole £1,500 to pay off his debts—but in comparison to other sections of Irish society they made a comfortable living.[42] These salaries enabled County Inspectors to live in relatively prosperous houses. Many of them rented former landlords' houses in the counties in which they were stationed. For example, Samuel Waters recalled that 'Ballyard House [in county Kerry], which I eventually settled in, was a very comfortable mansion, at a moderate rent, which included the shooting over a large tract of mountain'.[43] And, after retirement, many of them appear to have lived in the same comfortable suburbs of Dublin as the senior civil servants. Interestingly, a number of retired County Inspectors lived at different addresses on Morehampton Road in Donnybrook in the 1890s and early 1900s where they would have rubbed shoulders with the senior civil servants.[44]

A substantial proportion of the senior officers were born into what might be described as 'elite' families. At least fifty (39 per cent) of the 129 senior officers were the sons of police officers, landlords, army officers, clergymen, magistrates, doctors, land agents, or Resident Magistrates.[45] A very large proportion of them were the sons of police officers, and there was a strong tendency in the Royal Irish Constabulary to nominate police officers' sons for cadetships. During the period when the Inspector General had the power to nominate candidates for one-third of the available cadetships (1866–98), he tended to nominate the sons of police officers. This enabled the Inspector General to nominate the sons of officers who he knew were experiencing financial or other difficulties but it also

---

[41] See the discussion of officers' salaries in Griffin, 'The Irish Police, 1836–1914', 288–9.

[42] On Montgomery, see ibid. 288; Ball, *A Policeman's Ireland*, 7. Although police officers were well paid in comparison with other sections of Irish society, some of them did experience financial difficulties because they attempted to emulate the lifestyle of the landlords with whom they socialized.   [43] Ball, *A Policeman's Ireland*, 75.

[44] For example, Thomas Ross died at 11 Morehampton Road in Aug. 1912; Thomas Robert Barry died at 45 Morehampton Road in Aug. 1895; and Daniel Corley Jennings died at 18 Morehampton Road in Nov. 1896.

[45] Of the 50 'elite' fathers, 23 (46%) were police officers; 12 (24%) were landlords; 7 (14%) were army officers; 6 (12%) were Episcopalian clergymen; 1 (2%) was a land agent; 2 (4%) were doctors; 6 (12%) were magistrates; and 2 (4%) were Resident Magistrates. There is some overlap between these categories (some fathers held more than one of these positions).

ensured that these candidates were loyal and familiar with the lifestyle and duties of a police officer. This explains why the age restrictions on candidates for the cadet examination were different for the sons of police officers than they were for other candidates. Of the 129 senior police officers (in 1881, 1891, 1901, and 1911), forty (31 per cent) were related to other members of the Royal Irish Constabulary. Almost one-fifth (18 per cent) were the sons of police officers, and three (2 per cent) had grandfathers who were police officers. Almost one in ten (ten or 8 per cent) had brothers who were in the force, and seventeen (13 per cent) had sons who became police officers. There was almost a sense that membership of the officer class of the Royal Irish Constabulary became a hereditary position for some families. This was literally the case with William Henry, whose father (also William) resigned from his Sub-Inspectorship on 31 March 1841, in favour of the appointment of his son, who was appointed Sub-Inspector the following day. But it was less formally the case with many more families who provided two and even three generations of personnel for the Royal Irish Constabulary. James Robert Gibbons (County Inspector, 1869–86), for instance, was the son of Inspector James Gibbons, who had been shot dead during an incident in the Tithe War at Carrickshock, county Kilkenny, on 14 December 1831. In 1869, James Robert's own son, James Samuel Gibbons, became a police officer (after completing a degree at Trinity College Dublin), and was later appointed vice chairman of the General Prisons Board. There were many similar cases of families providing several generations of police officers.

It should perhaps be stated, however, that not all police officers came from wealthy and influential backgrounds. According to the *Daily Express*, cadet officers tended to be 'gentlemen of good families, birth, and education, but who, being for the most part without private means, could not support themselves if appointed to the army'.[46] An officership in the army was expensive and, in many cases, members of the British and Irish Protestant middle class could not afford to send their sons into the officer class of the army, and instead sent them into the Royal Irish Constabulary. For instance, the Manchester clergymen, Revd Crane, had two sons who he sent to Oxford but could not afford to then place them in the army. Charles Paston Crane, who became a police officer and later a Resident Magistrate, recalled: 'My elder brother and I had taken our degrees together [at Exeter College, Oxford] and we both had similar tastes—he ought to have been a soldier and so ought I, but the necessity of a further two years at Sandhurst put the idea out of the question.'[47] Instead, his father applied for a nomination for his two sons—Charles Paston and Hubert William—from the Chief Secretary, James Lowther, and they both became police officers. George Edward Hillier (Deputy Inspector General, 1867–76, and Inspector General, 1876–82) observed in 1872 that: 'the young gentlemen we are getting into

46 *Daily Express*, 27 Oct. 1858, quot. Griffin, 'The Irish Police, 1836–1914', 253.
47 C. P. Crane, *Memories of a Resident Magistrate, 1880–1920* (Edinburgh, 1938), 12.

the service now—clergymen's sons, professional men's sons, and magistrate's sons—are about the same class of men as are entering the army. Of course, there is not the same éclat attached to our service, but our men are in the same social position.'[48]

A survey of the previous occupations of forty-three of the senior police officers under review suggests that many of them were drawn from lower middle-class backgrounds. Twelve (28 per cent) of them had been clerks in commercial and financial offices before joining the force. Alexander Heard had been a clerk in the Provincial Bank in Ennis and Frederick St Clair Ruthven had worked for the Bank of Ireland, while Thomas Whelan was a clerk with the Great Northern Railway at Doncaster and John Harcourt worked in a merchant's office in Waterford. Some of them (eight or 19 per cent) had also held clerkships in the Irish Civil Service. William Henry St Leger was a clerk in the Constabulary Office and Frederick James Ball had been a junior clerk in the Dublin Metropolitan Police court for almost seven years before becoming a cadet. Some of them (eight or 19 per cent) had been school teachers or private tutors. Ernest Mulliner worked as an assistant master at Leamington College for two years, while J. T. Brooke had been a private tutor at Guildford for six years before joining the force. Andrew Reed had been a School master at the Erasmus Smith School in Galway for five years (at the same time as he was completing his degree at The Queen's College), and William Charles Hetreed, an English-born Catholic, had worked at both St Brendan's, Killarney, and at Clongowes before becoming a police officer. As we might expect, some of them (nine or 21 per cent) had held rank-and-file positions in the forces—R. A. Smith had been a midshipman in the Navy for four and a half years, and Mason Alcock had been an ensign in the south Cork militia—before becoming police officers. None of these were the kinds of occupations that the son of a landowner or a wealthy professional would take up, and they suggest that a substantial proportion of the recruits to the senior officer class of the Royal Irish Constabulary was drawn from the British and Irish (usually Protestant) middle class.[49]

Senior police officers also consolidated their elite status by marrying into powerful (and often landed) families. The vast majority of senior officers did marry: of the 129 under review, 86 per cent were married while 14 per cent were unmarried.[50] Once policemen of any rank had married, they were no longer allowed to be stationed in the same counties as their wives' family or friends

---

[48] Griffin, 'The Irish Police, 1836–1914', 254. It is likely, however, that Hillier was incorrect and that most police officers were drawn from less well-to-do social backgrounds than army officers.

[49] Griffin has surveyed the previous occupation of 174 (34%) of the 519 cadets who became police officers between 1852 and 1914 , and found that 'practically all of these had been involved in clerical or teaching work' (ibid. 260).

[50] Unlike the Irish landlords, most of the married County Inspectors appear to have had children. Information is available for ten individuals who had one (1), two (1), three (4), seven (2), eight (1), and ten (1) children. The average number of children was 4.7.

(neither were they allowed to be stationed in counties where their own family or friends resided). George Birmingham explains why this was so in his novel *Irishmen All*:

It is not possible to respect the law properly in the person of Tommy Jackson . . . if you happen to be Tommy's father and to have smacked him when he was young and small. Even for Tommy's cousins and school-fellows, who ran races with him long ago and watched him struggling with the multiplication table, it is very hard to realise that the law when Tommy represents it is really a majestic thing. The governing powers, understanding this, have decreed that no policeman shall serve in his own locality. The recruit from County Donegal is sent to a barrack in Wexford. If, when he is there, he marries a County Wexford young lady, he is immediately sent away to County Kerry, lest his wife's relations, getting to be familiar with him, should come to regard the law as a common thing.

In England no such regulations exist, and a man may be a policeman in the village in which he is born. That is because the law is regarded in England in an entirely different way. The English people love it as a creation of their own, a thing devised by themselves for their own convenience. The more familiar they are with it the better, and no harm can possibly come of intimacy with policemen. The Englishman loves law rather more than less after he has spent the evening smoking with a constable and seen that officer with his coat unbuttoned and his feet in carpet slippers. The majesty of the law is a force kept in reserve and only used to overawe malefactors. But in Ireland everyone is a potential malefactor. We are not supposed to love the law which was made for us and not by us. It is desirable only that we should fear it. Therefore everything that can be done is done to prevent our coming to regard it as an intimate and familiar thing. The police, though it is not possible to surround them with a halo of mysterious sanctity, are kept remote as may be from the ordinary life of the people among whom they live.[51]

However, police officers were encouraged to develop friendly relations with some members of their local communities and, in particular, the landlords who resided in their counties. In 1872, this was made a *sine qua non* of further promotion for Sub-Inspectors who were informed in the *Royal Irish Constabulary Rules* published in that year that a prerequisite of promotion would be that they had 'cultivated a friendly intercourse with the gentry in [their] . . . neighbourhood'.[52] Police Inspectors often socialized with landlords. William Nott-Bower recalled that when he was stationed at Rathkeale, county Limerick in the 1870s, he spent his time with members of the 'old Irish families' engaged in 'Hunting, shooting, entertaining, dancing, [and] hating work of any kind . . . they were the most delightful of companions'.[53] In 1899, the Duke of Ormonde invited 160 guests to a 'house party' at Kilkenny Castle in honour of the Duke and Duchess of York (later King George V and Queen Mary) who were visiting Kilkenny. The guest list included peers, landlords, army officers, clergymen, and also ten Royal Irish

[51] George Birmingham, *Irishmen All* (London and Edinburgh, 1913), 51–2.
[52] Griffin, 'The Irish Police, 1836–1914', 279.
[53] Sir William Nott-Bower, *Fifty-two Years a Policeman* (London, 1926), 28.

Constabulary District Inspectors.[54] John Regan, a Catholic District Inspector, recalled that police officers were invited as a matter of course to join the County Club at Ennis:

The fact that I was a cricketer seemed to be known, as on the day after my arrival I was invited to meet the secretary of the County Club of which the cricket club was an offshoot. Membership of the County Club was confined to landlords throughout the county, their agents and lawyers, military and police officers and a few other officials. I expected to see amongst the members many frightened individuals whose main pre-occupation in life had always been trying to escape the assassin's bullet, but instead saw only men who appeared to think of little else but hunting, shooting, fishing and to a lesser degree, cricket and other games. Many of them, I thought, had an unlimited capacity for consuming Irish whiskey.[55]

In counties where the local landlords did not organize a lively social scene around the Big House, however, the police Inspector's lot could be a miserable one. A Claremorris Head Constable told the 1914 Royal Irish Constabulary Inquiry that the west of Ireland 'is not a desirable place for a District Inspector, as there is very little society for him in it, and the country is poor and backward, and there are no hunting grounds in it'.[56] Similarly, Garrow Green found Crossmolina (in county Mayo) an uncongenial post and wrote the following warning to prospective cadets:

Take heed all ye English aspirants for cadetships, especially those who have healthy gregarious instincts, and [who] fresh from your luxurious homes and social delights hanker after the sword of the R.I.C. Use all your diplomacy and interest to avoid being consigned to one of these ultima Thules, for they are the very abomination of desolation. The stagnation of them, the horrible environment, the misery and lethargy of the people, the absence of all inducement to even live save in the performance of uneventful duties and the mere animal instinct, must be experienced to be even imagined. I believe there are still worse states of exile in India, but trust me that the unhappy wretch who is relegated to one of these awful places can only exist in the hope of getting out of them.

I once met one of ours, in a northern train; a thorough-bred English gentleman, and ex-scholar of Oxford, who had been lately emancipated from some ghastly station in Donegal. His account was pitiable. He had been forty miles from the nearest railway, had only a hard-worked country doctor to speak to, the parson being an acidulated book-worm, and the only magistrates small shopkeepers. I asked him about field sports. 'Oh,' said he, 'there's lots of wild shooting, but after a time one gets to loathe the very look of the interminable black bog, and I had no one to give the birds to.' The same applied to fishing also, and his only resources were his piano and scribbling magazine sonnets of a weird and mournful character.[57]

---

[54] Terence Dooley, *The Decline of the Big House in Ireland: A Study of Irish Landed Families* (Dublin, 2001), 52–3.

[55] Joost Augusteijn, *The Memoirs of John M. Regan: A Catholic Officer in the RIC and RUC, 1909–1948* (Dublin, 2007), 49.   [56] Quot. Griffin, 'The Irish Police, 1836–1914', 299.

[57] G. Garrow Green, *In the Royal Irish Constabulary* (Dublin, 1905), 86–7.

However, Garrow Green had a much happier experience at Shinrone, county Tipperary—largely because the local gentry created a lively social scene—as he explains:

I had scarcely shaken down, when from all sides the local gentry—even some from a distance—flocked to call. Carriages and traps were constantly at the door, and there was a never-ending hail of cards for At Homes, Tennis Parties, Afternoon Dances, Balls and Receptions, besides invitations to hunt, shoot and fish, and so many kind attentions from everyone that I consigned the miseries of the past three years to oblivion and prepared to enter on a fresh lease of life . . . Besides the upper ten, there existed, as usual in Ireland, a lower strata, who kept up a sort of minor court among themselves. Though their pretensions to family may have been more dubious, they were eminently respectable and had such hospitable houses that they contributed very considerably to an undercurrent of merry-making, filling up all the gaps between larger functions.[58]

A key factor in the recruiting of police officers was a concern that they would be of the appropriate social background to enable them to socialize with the local landlords. As John Regan recalled 'The necessity for a nomination for the exam had the effect of keeping out what may be termed "undesirables" ' while the examination itself which he took in 1908, 'seemed to differentiate between nominated candidates by loading the dice in favour of those in hunting and fishing circles. The three essay subjects were (1) Horse breeding in Ireland, (2) Salmon fishing in Ireland, and (3) Describe an Irish Jaunting Car and a typical Irish Jarvey [a hackney-coach]'.[59] Unsurprisingly, then, the members of landed families were often successful in their applications to become police officers. Almost one-fifth of the senior police officers under review (twenty-two or 17 per cent) were landlords, the sons of landlords, or the members of landed families.[60] In general, they tended to come from the smaller landed families (as Table 3.4 demonstrates). In fact, those senior police officers who came from 'estates' of fewer than 500 acres could more accurately be described as large farmers (rather than landlords)—although they are distinct from the tenant-farmer class in that they owned their land in the 1870s—and these large farms were often deemed to be extremely valuable. Sinclair Dickson Smith Chatterton of Mount Olive in Raheny might have owned just 25 acres in county Dublin but it was valued at £105; William Crawford Gore Moriarty was born on a farm of 74 acres in Roscommon, but it was valued at £295; and Robert Allman Smith's father, the Rector of Omagh, owned 215 acres valued at £162 in Tyrone. These farms would have been regarded as extremely valuable by the local farming community, most of whom rented farms valued

[58] Ibid. 119; 124.

[59] Augusteijn, *Memoirs of John M. Regan*, 37–8. Regan gained second place in the exam.

[60] It is likely that more of the officers under review came from landed backgrounds but it is impossible to confirm the backgrounds of some County Inspectors.

Table 3.4. The Size of the
Family Estate of Senior
Police Officers who were
Born into Landed Families

Acreage	Frequency
0–99	4 (18%)
100–499	3 (14%)
500–999	4 (18%)
1,000–1,999	5 (23%)
2,000–2,999	4 (18%)
3,000–4,999	—
5,000–9,999	—
10,000+	2 (9%)
Number	22

at between £5 and £20, and who regarded farms valued at £50 and over as 'large'.[61]

It is noteworthy that the landlords who owned the big estates of more than 10,000 acres very rarely sent their sons into the police force. Only two of the senior officers under review came from the big estates. William Townsend Gun was the second son of Townsend Gun who owned 11,819 acres at Causeway, county Kerry, and William's older brother, Wilson, inherited the family estate. Similarly, Robert Bruce's elder brother, Sir Henry Hervey Bruce, inherited the family estate of 21,514 acres at Downhill, county Derry, and Robert joined the army and was later appointed Deputy Inspector General (1877–82) and Inspector General (1882–5). This was a familiar pattern—that the younger sons should go into the professions—but the big landowners normally sent their non-inheriting sons into the army or the church, rather than into the police force. It seems that the great landowners regarded a cadetship in the Royal Irish Constabulary as perhaps not quite prestigious enough for their sons, and the army was their preferred option.

The less-well-off landlords who owned middle-sized estates probably could not afford to send their sons into the army, and the Royal Irish Constabulary provided them with respectability, a measure of power, and a steady income. More than half (59 per cent) of the senior police officers who came from landed backgrounds were born into what might be described as middle-sized estates of between 500 and 3,000 acres. Robert Grove Annesley is typical of those police officers who came from this background. His father was a former army officer who owned

[61] See the discussion of farm size and valuation in Fergus Campbell, *Land and Revolution: Nationalist Politics in the West of Ireland, 1891–1921* (Oxford, 2005), 310–11.

1,757 acres in county Cork, and was well-to-do but not sufficiently wealthy to provide a private income for his sons and daughters. One of his daughters was married off to Lieutenant Henry Albert Platt; his eldest son, Richard, who had been educated at Eton and Trinity College Dublin, inherited the estate in 1863; and his youngest son, Robert, became a cadet in 1854. Indeed, it was the general pattern that the younger and non-inheriting sons of these middle-sized landlord families joined the force. For instance, Arnold Philip Carden was the fourth son of Andrew Carden who owned 2,709 acres at Barnane, county Tipperary.[62] Similarly, Francis Blake Lopdell was the youngest son of John Lopdell of Raheen Park, Athenry, who owned 1,365 acres in Galway; and Francis became a cadet while his eldest brother, John Joseph, inherited the family estate. A considerable proportion of senior police officers were, therefore, drawn from the families of the middle-sized landlords in Ireland.

A significant proportion of senior police officers also married into landed families: more than one in ten (fifteen or 12 per cent) of the officers under review married into landed families. In many cases, they married the daughters of prominent individuals in the counties where they were stationed. Garrow Green devotes a chapter of his memoir to his unsuccessful quest to marry the daughter of an army colonel destined to inherit £40,000 in the county in which he served.[63] There are many cases of officers in my sample marrying a local landowner's daughter in a county where he was stationed. Plunkett De Courcy Ireland (County Inspector, 1869–87), for instance, married Ada Hall of Merton Hall, Borrisokane, county Tipperary (whose father owned 369 acres valued at £279) in 1871, after spending most of his career serving in Tipperary. Some of these landed families owned farms of fewer than 500 acres.[64] For instance, Francis Nesbitt Cullen married Emily Margaret Finucane, whose father, Andrew, owned forty-three acres at Ennistymon, county Clare; and Alex Gambell married Sarah Faris of Corr, Crossdoney, whose family owned 379 acres in county Cavan. Even so, some of the senior police officers married into much bigger landed families. Charles Ewen Cameron (Assistant Inspector General, 1889–1901), who was prominently involved in monitoring the United Irish League's expansion in 1898–1900, was married to Sarah, Marchioness Conyngham, whose family

[62] However, Henry James Bourchier was the first son of John Bourchier and he did inherit the family estate of 845 acres (valued at £981) at Bruff, county Limerick as well as becoming a police officer: this may have been because Bourchier's father was comparatively young and did not die until 1885 when Henry had been a police officer for almost twenty years (he became a cadet in 1866).

[63] Garrow Green, *In the Royal Irish Constabulary*, 36–40.

[64] Of the 15 officers under review who married into landed families: 7 (46.8%) married into estates of less than 499 acres; 4 (26.8%) married into estates of between 500 and 1,999 acres; 3 (19.9%) married into estates of between 2,000 and 4,999 acres; and 1 (6.5%) married into an estate of more than 10,000 acres.

owned 166,710 acres in counties Kent, Donegal, Clare, and Meath. It is also significant that the brothers and sisters of senior police officers often married into landed families. For instance, William Crawford Moriarty's sister married into the family of Helenus White, the owner of 1,542 acres at Mount Sion, county Limerick, so that Moriarty's brothers-in-law were Limerick landowners. Undoubtedly, the influence of these landed connections on senior police officers informed the Constabulary's view of the unfolding land agitation in late nineteenth-century Ireland. Indeed, Thomas Fennell believed that the primary function of the Royal Irish Constabulary after the Land War (1879–81) was to protect the Irish landlord class,[65] and landowners certainly believed that this was the case. Garrow Green even recalled that one Kerry landowner 'considered the police less as conservators of the public peace than as supporters of a class'.[66]

In the view of the Inspector General in 1882, the officers of the Royal Irish Constabulary were men 'of very superior education'.[67] The data available on the senior officers' secondary education, however, are patchy and it is difficult to draw out any pattern from the evidence. Data are available for only six individuals. Three attended schools in England: E. M. Wynne attended Eton; Heffernan Considine went to Stoneyhurst; and Neville Chamberlain went to Brentwood School. The other three attended Irish schools: Andrew Reed was educated at the Erasmus Smith school in Galway; Bourchier went to St Columba's in Rathfarnam; and Henry Thynne was educated by the Christian Brothers. It is likely that many more of them received a secondary education but that information is not available. According to *The Times*, forty-three (16 per cent) of the 276 police officers in September 1890 were university graduates.[68] However, only thirteen (or 10 per cent) of the senior police officers appear to have received a third-level education. This perhaps suggests that the senior officers were less likely to have received a university education than the less-senior District Inspectors. The dissonance between the two sets of evidence might, on the other hand, be attributed to the slightly later date of *The Times* survey (1890) than my start date (1881) because it is clear that the proportion of senior police officers who received a university education did increase over time. Of my sample, almost one-half (five or 42 per cent) attended Oxbridge; one-quarter (three or 25 per cent) attended Trinity College Dublin, and one-quarter attended The Queen's Colleges; and, finally, one (8 per cent) attended the Royal University. Most of the senior officers under review appear to have become clerks or teachers—rather than going to university—before joining the force.

[65] Fennell, *Royal Irish Constabulary*, 90.
[66] Garrow Green, *In the Royal Irish Constabulary*, 30.
[67] Griffin, 'The Irish Police, 1836–1914', 268.
[68] Quot. ibid. According to *The Times*: 25 attended Trinity College Dublin; 9 attended Oxford; 2 attended Cambridge; and 5 were qualified barristers.

IV

How did the profile of the senior police officers change over time? As we have seen, there was a certain amount of 'greening' of the senior officers in the Irish Civil Service between 1891 and 1911, but was there a comparable 'greening' of the senior officers of the Royal Irish Constabulary between 1881 and 1911? Tables 3.5–3.7 suggest that far from a 'greening' process taking place, the proportion of Irish-born Catholic police officers was in decline and, in fact, an 'orangeing' or reverse 'greening' appears to have been taking place. In 1881, more than one-quarter (27.5 per cent) of the senior police officers were Irish-born Catholics, but by 1911 Irish Catholics accounted for less than one in ten of senior officers (9 per cent). In terms of the total population, Irish-born Catholics had been under-represented in 1881, and were obviously even more under-represented by the eve of the Great War.

Table 3.5. The Religion of Senior Police Officers, 1881–1911

Religion	1881	1891	1901	1911
Episcopalian	29 (72.5%)	32 (80%)	38 (90%)	32 (74.5%)
Catholic	11 (27.5%)	8 (20%)	4 (10%)	6 (14%)
Presbyterian	—	—	—	4 (9.5%)
Methodist	—	—	—	1 (2%)
Number	40	40	42	43

Table 3.6. The Ethnicity of Senior Police Officers, 1881–1911

Ethnicity	1881	1891	1901	1911
English	3 (7.5%)	2 (5%)	6 (14%)	12 (28%)
Scottish	1 (2.5%)	—	—	—
Irish	36 (90%)	38 (95%)	36 (86%)	31 (72%)
Number	40	40	42	43

Table 3.7. The Religion of Irish-Born Senior Police Officers, 1881–1911

Religion	1881	1891	1901	1911
Episcopalian	24 (69%)	29 (78%)	32 (89%)	22 (71%)
Catholic	11 (31%)	8 (22%)	4 (11%)	4 (13%)
Presbyterian	—	—	—	4 (13%)
Methodist	—	—	—	1 (3%)
Number	35	37	36	31

Over the same period, the proportion of Dissenters (Presbyterians and Methodists) increased significantly from zero to almost one in eight (11.5 per cent), which was broadly similar to the proportion of Dissenters in the total population. The proportion of Episcopalian senior police officers remained more or less the same (increasingly slightly from 72.5 per cent in 1881 to 74.5 per cent in 1911), and the proportion of Irish-born Episcopalians was more or less the same as their numbers in the Irish population. However, the increase in the proportion of English-born officers between 1881 and 1911 is particularly striking. In 1881, only one in twelve (7.5 per cent) of the senior police officers was English born but this had increased to more than one-quarter (28 per cent) by 1911 (ten of them were Episcopalians and two of them were Catholics). Three broad patterns can, therefore, be identified: first, a substantial decline in the proportion of Irish-born Catholic senior police officers; second, a substantial increase in the proportion of senior police officers from an Irish dissenting background; and third, a significant increase in the proportion of English-born senior police officers.

There were also significant changes in the educational experience of the senior police officers between 1881 and 1911. In 1881, only two (5 per cent) of the senior officers had received either a third-level or a vocational education, whereas in 1911 this had increased to eleven (26 per cent).[69] Of the 1911 cohort, three had attended Oxford, one gained his degree from Cambridge, three were graduates of Trinity College Dublin, and the Royal University and The Queen's College (at Belfast) provided one each (one is not known). This indicates that the traditional English universities were an important source of English-born recruits for the senior officer class of the Irish police force. Both Charles Paston Crane and his brother Hubert William had studied history at Exeter College, Oxford, before becoming cadets in the Royal Irish Constabulary; and Ernest Mulliner gained his degree from Clare College, Cambridge, before joining the force. Some prosperous Irish Catholics were also Oxford graduates, although these were more unusual: Heffernan Considine, for instance, was a graduate of Lincoln College, Oxford. Trinity College Dublin, on the other hand, was a source of Irish-born Protestant recruits to the force. Henry Browne Morell (a Presbyterian), and Ross Carthy Rainsford and Courtney Chamberlain Oulton (both Episcopalians) were Trinity graduates who became cadets. The new universities also provided Presbyterian recruits for the Royal Irish Constabulary: Alexander Gray was a graduate of The Queen's College, Belfast, and William Millar had gained his degree from the

[69] In 1881, 1 officer had received a degree and 1 a vocational qualification; in 1891, 2 had gained degrees; in 1901, 3 had obtained degrees; and in 1911, 10 had degrees, and 1 had a vocational qualification.

Royal University. Educational reforms were, therefore, enabling the members of previously marginal groups to gain prestigious professional positions in Ireland. At a broader level, these data suggest that the officer class of the Royal Irish Constabulary was becoming more professionalized during this period, even if the senior police officers were not as well educated as has been generally assumed by historians. The next section of the chapter will examine the ways in which police officers were recruited.

V

The vast majority of officers of the Royal Irish Constabulary were recruited through a cadet system that was introduced in 1842, and very few officers were recruited from the ranks. In order to become a cadet, candidates had to be nominated to take an examination by the Lord Lieutenant, the Chief Secretary, or the Inspector General of the Royal Irish Constabulary. If the candidate then scored sufficient marks in the examination, he would go on to six months' training at the Royal Irish Constabulary depot in Phoenix Park and then be posted to a district where he would become a Sub- (later District) Inspector. The critical recruiting mechanism was, therefore, the process by which an individual was able to receive a nomination from the Lord Lieutenant, Chief Secretary, or Inspector General to take the cadet examination. As we have seen, between 1866 and 1897, the Inspector General had the power to nominate one-third of all cadetships, and usually used this power to nominate the sons of police officers. The other two-thirds of nominations during this period were in the gift of the Lord Lieutenant and the Chief Secretary. From 1 January 1898, however, the Lord Lieutenant and the Chief Secretary had the power to nominate all of the cadet recruits to the Royal Irish Constabulary.[70]

As with the senior positions in the Irish Civil Service, no official records were kept of these nominations (although letters from potential candidates to the Chief Secretary are contained in the Chief Secretary's Office Registered Papers, and in the various collections of Chief Secretary's private papers that survive). It is necessary, therefore, to examine closely the evidence that does survive on the process of nomination from the 1860s onwards, as well as the identity of those who were recruited in order to ascertain the general patterns of recruitment to the officer class of the Royal Irish Constabulary. Given that nominations for cadetships had to be personally made by the senior members of the Irish government, the first step was to be a part of the Dublin Castle networks that

[70] Griffin, 'The Irish Police, 1836–1914', 248.

would enable the potential candidate to be personally known to those who had the power to nominate. Sir William Nott-Bower, who became a police officer in 1872, for instance, records that he received a nomination because his father was an 'old friend' of W. E. Forster, then an influential Liberal politician who would become Chief Secretary for Ireland in 1880.[71]

Family loyalty to the state and particularly to the military also played a part in securing nominations. Alfred Thomas Gilley used this as the entire basis of his letter of application for a cadetship to the Chief Secretary:

That your Lordship may fairly judge of my claims I may add that my grandfather served in the 7th Fusiliers through the Peninsular War. My father served for 20 years in the same corps and I have lost two brothers in the army—one served through the late war in India and was unfortunately killed in that country, the other a lieut in the Royal Engineers died on foreign service.[72]

Similarly, the Revd Thomas Burrowes, rector of Hutton in Somerset, successfully applied for a nomination for his son by outlining his family's services to the forces of the Crown. One of his great uncles, the chaplain of HMS Director, was drowned in 1797; another great uncle was 'blown from a battery' at Burtphare in 1825; a cousin was killed during the Crimean War; an uncle served for thirty years in India; and another cousin, a colonel in the Royal Horse Artillery, survived the Sikh War.[73] Such catalogues of family loyalty and sacrifice in the cause of the British state, and particularly the army, were often successful at securing nominations. Edward Mansergh, for instance, won a nomination for his brother by explaining to the Chief Secretary that his father, two uncles, and twelve granduncles had served in the army and navy, and that another uncle had died while serving as paymaster in the Irish Constabulary.[74] Cadetships were clearly regarded both as rewards for political service, and for family loyalty to the British state.

Freemasonry was reputed to be common in the Royal Irish Constabulary, and to be a strong factor in influencing promotion in the ranks as well as the recruiting of cadets. The extent of Freemasonry in the force is suggested by the fact that the oath which each member of the Royal Irish Constabulary had to swear concluded with the pledge 'that I will not, while I shall hold the said office, join, subscribe, or belong to any political society, whatsoever, unless the society of Freemasons'.[75] Samuel Waters was a Freemason and a good friend of Dowdall, the chief clerk in the Chief Secretary's Office, who was also a Freemason, and this suggests that there may have been strong interlinking networks of Freemasons throughout the various arms of Dublin Castle.[76] Certainly, this was the perception among the rank and file of the Royal Irish Constabulary. Constable O'Hara, serving in

[71] Nott-Bower, *Fifty-two Years a Policeman*, 26.
[72] Griffin, 'The Irish Police, 1836–1914', 252.   [73] Ibid.   [74] Ibid. 252–3.
[75] Oath quot. Fennell, *Royal Irish Constabulary*, 5.   [76] Ball, *A Policeman's Ireland*, 79, 94.

Armagh, told the 1882 committee of enquiry into the Royal Irish Constabulary that:

Freemasonry in the service is causing universal dissatisfaction. The Catholic portion of the service is prohibited by the head of their church from joining the craft, and they believe that the officers, who are nearly all Freemasons, do everything in their power to get a sub-constable who is a mason either promoted or transferred to a favourite station.[77]

Similarly, a letter to the *Freeman's Journal* from 'Justice' complained that 'the officers of the force, who are almost all Protestants and Freemasons . . . recognise only the claims and consider the interests of those who are of their own creed or who are brother masons'.[78] Although it is impossible to quantify the influence of Freemason networks on promotions and appointments, it is likely that such networks did play a significant role in the day-to-day life of the Royal Irish Constabulary and in the recruiting of the officers of the force.

It is striking that—unlike the police forces in the rest of the United Kingdom—Royal Irish Constabulary officers were vary rarely recruited from the ranks.[79] The main justification for this recruiting strategy was that the Royal Irish Constabulary was armed, and the recruiting mechanism in the Royal Irish Constabulary was therefore closer to that of an Infantry regiment than that for a police force in another part of the United Kingdom.[80] The commissioners responsible for considering the grievances of the Royal Irish Constabulary in 1882 explained that:

A semi-military force imposes duties on its officers which obviously require qualities different in some respects from those suited to purely civil forces. The officers of an armed force, in dealing with their own men and with the people, require habits of command and perfect tact, qualities with which education and social standing have a good deal to say.[81]

Quin John Brownrigg, the Sub-Inspector for Bray in 1872, further explained that:

None but well educated gentlemen could properly discharge a sub-inspector's duties. The moral influence of persons of good education and birth is felt more in this country than in perhaps any other. The tendency of police—especially detective—training is such, that it requires the guiding and restraining influence of officers of enlarged and liberal views.[82]

---

[77] Quot. Griffin, 'Religion and Opportunity', 224.   [78] Quot. ibid. 225.

[79] The position of Superintendent—which was analogous to that of Sub-Inspector—in the various English Constabularies, was always held by policemen who had progressed through the ranks rather than by gentlemen commissioned from outside the force. Griffin, 'The Irish Police, 1836–1914', 281.   [80] Ibid. 275–6.

[81] *Royal Irish Constabulary, Report of the Committee of Inquiry, 1883*, HC (1883) [C. 3577], xxxii. 17, 273.

[82] *Report of the Commissioners Appointed . . . to Enquire into the Condition of the Civil Service in Ireland on the Royal Irish Constabulary*, HC (1873) [C 831], xxii. 99, 229.

Other senior police officers appear to have agreed with this perception. Deputy Inspector General George Hillier told the 1872 Commission that he would 'look upon promotion altogether from the-ranks as so fatal that it is not to be contemplated—that it ought not to be contemplated'.[83] Neville Chamberlain (Inspector General, 1900–16) told the Royal Irish Constabulary Commissioners in 1914 that his twenty-seven years' experience in the army led him to believe that 'the direct commissioned officer is found to be a necessity'.[84]

The central argument put forward to justify the cadet system was, therefore, that a semi-military force needed to be officered by men of superior education and social status, men 'of enlarged and liberal views' who had 'moral influence', and who were capable of restraining the obtuse instincts of their more dim-witted inferiors in the rank and file of the force. However, as we have seen, the senior officers of the Royal Irish Constabulary were not particularly well educated. Very few of them had received a third-level education or gained a professional vocational qualification. To what extent had their training at the depot provided them with the requisite intellectual and moral qualities to lead the Royal Irish Constabulary?

In the 1850s, the cadets' training consisted of between four and five months at the depot in Phoenix Park which had been increased to eight months' training by the early 1900s.[85] Cadets received the same training as the rank and file of the force in drill, musketry, and police duties. In addition, they were given extensive horse-riding training by an ex-cavalryman and instructed in making statistical returns of crime, police accounts, and so on.[86] Charles Paston Crane recalled that:

An officer in the Royal Irish Constabulary was supposed to be a sort of 'Jack of all trades.' He had to know infantry drill, a certain amount of cavalry drill, sword exercise and musketry; to understand how to choose forage and how to shoe a horse; and he had to go through a short veterinary class and be a good rider. He had to be well up in criminal law and the law of evidence, and capable of instructing his men in all their duties. Moreover, he had to keep accounts and learn the Code of Regulations of the Force, a formidable work, which nearly drove him distracted by its multiplied instructions. It was a good training for young men.[87]

However, not all cadets took their training as seriously as Crane (who was later promoted to the Resident Magistracy). George Garrow Green characterized his depot training in the following terms:

I had gained distinction as a ring-leader in the pastime of 'haymaking,' [the prank of piling fellow cadets' furniture in a heap], had mastered the intricacies of the goose-step, had fired

[83] Ibid. 120, 250.

[84] *Royal Irish Constabulary and Dublin Metropolitan Police, Appendix to the Report of the Committee of Inquiry, 1914*, HC (1914) [Cd. 7637], xliv. 183, 547.

[85] Griffin, 'The Irish Police, 1836–1914', 269.   [86] Ibid.

[87] Crane, *Memories of a Resident Magistrate*, 17.

twenty rounds of balled cartridge at Sandymount—chiefly to the disturbance of the local mud—and was unrivalled in my sublime ignorance of both statute and common law, and the detection of criminals . . . I could form a hollow square, but of the necessary steps to be taken in a murder case my head was about equally empty.[88]

Indeed, one officer—Sir William Nott Bower—was given the following advice 'by an old and disgruntled Sub-Inspector' while at the depot: 'Never neglect any routine duty. Never take any responsibility which you can avoid. Never attempt any job which is not strictly your own. Then you will have a happy time in the police. But if ever you try to *do* anything, you will surely be *done*.'[89]

When they were posted to the various counties to take up the position of Sub- (later District) Inspector, many officers were not able effectively to discharge their duties. Inspector General Brownrigg complained in 1862 that 'many sub-inspectors are very irregular in their attendance at Petty Sessions, and further, that some are in the habit of giving only a limited attendance thereat'.[90] Six years later, Inspector General Wood observed that:

It is with regret that I am compelled to remark that, not only on my own inspections of counties, but also on those of the officers at head quarters, there has appeared a general want of knowledge, on the part of county and sub-inspectors, of the regulations bearing on their practical (I may say their daily official) duties. For example, when asked what orders have been recently issued regarding correspondence; the placing of men on the promotion list; the notice that should be taken of cases of intoxication in the force; the pay of the different grades and-ranks, and similar questions; the officers are generally at a loss for a correct answer, which clearly indicates that orders, when read, instead of being fixed in the memory, are laid aside and left to others, less responsible, to carry out; and hence the trouble is so often experienced at head quarters, in having to refer officers to existing orders which they have forgotten or neglected.[91]

In many cases, therefore, the cadets' training was insufficient to enable them to carry out the duties of a police officer and many officers were forced to rely on the skills of their inferiors (and particularly the Head Constables) to carry out their duties.

Many police officers were, therefore, not particularly competent. This was, in part, because of their poor education and brief training, but also because many of them did not take their duties seriously and instead indulged their leisure interests. Vere Gregory (a relation of Lady Gregory), who became a police officer after completing his degree at Trinity College Dublin in the 1890s, explained that: 'During the first twenty years of my service, and before the political situation became acute, there was probably no other profession in the world which afforded such scope and leisure for enjoying a maximum amount of sport at a minimum expense.'[92]

---

[88] Garrow Green, *In the Royal Irish Constabulary*, 24.
[89] Nott-Bower, *Fifty-two Years a Policeman*, 27.
[90] Quot. Griffin, 'The Irish Police, 1836–1914', 272.   [91] Quot. ibid. 272–3.
[92] Vere R. T. Gregory, *The House of Gregory* (Dublin, 1943), 151–2.

Nott-Bower also recalled that his duties were not exacting, and that he 'continued to indulge my taste [for theatricals] in Dublin, where I acted several times, under an assumed name, at the old Theatre Royal'.[93] John Regan even attended Petty Sessions with his hunting outfit under his police greatcoat so that 'Twenty or thirty cases of a petty nature could be concluded in fifteen or twenty minutes, [and then]...I would throw off my coat, get on the horse and make for the meet'.[94] Such was C. P. Crane's love of sport that when he encountered a man poaching salmon from the River Laune in the 1880s he did not arrest him but instead shouted encouragement and was 'as pleased as possible in watching the struggle'.[95]

In many cases, the serious work of policing was actually carried out by the Head Constables. The editor of the *Constabulary Gazette* regarded the cadet officers as the 'ornamental section of the force', while the day-to-day work of the force was actually carried out by the rank and file.[96] Neither was this only the view of a pro-reform voice within the Royal Irish Constabulary. Andrew Reed recalled the efficient work of his Head Constable when he first became an officer and acknowledged that 'I never liked to interfere [with his good work]'.[97] Garrow Green referred to his Head Constable as 'that grand vizier to an Irish police officer'.[98] Similarly, Samuel Waters remembered that his first Head Constable 'knew very little drill, had only a hazy perception of the technical regulations of the force, but he knew how to keep order in his subdistrict'. He also 'took all official care off my hands, did all my office work, kept all the accounts, and quite resented it if I proposed to do any office work'.[99] And John Regan recalled that his Head Constable at Ennis 'looked on me with a fatherly eye'.[100]

This division of labour aroused much resentment from the poorly paid members of the rank and file who often carried out the work of their superior officers. 'Goose Quill', for instance, wrote to the *Freeman's Journal* in 1866 to complain that 'juveniles fresh from school' gained officer status over the heads of senior rank and file, and that 'head constables have to instruct these recipients in police duties for years after [their] joining their stations'.[101] The editor of the Constabulary Gazette made a similar argument in his *Plea for Reform*:

A head constable becomes a DI, if he is lucky, with twenty-five years' service. But a youth from school enters into command and responsibility without any knowledge or training worth mentioning. He is enabled to do this by providing him with a head constable as a clerk and a guide...A head constableship is won only after many years of hard

[93] Nott-Bower, *Fifty-two Years a Policeman*, 35.
[94] Griffin, 'The Irish Police, 1836–1914', 296.
[95] Crane, *Memories of a Resident Magistrate*, 86.
[96] Quot. Griffin, 'The Irish Police, 1836–1914', 273–4.
[97] Reed recollections, quot. Lowe, 'RIC Officers, 1879–1922', 11.
[98] Garrow Green, *In the Royal Irish Constabulary*, 26.
[99] Ball, *A Policeman's Ireland*, 16; 29–30.   [100] Augusteijn, *Memoirs of John M. Regan*, 50.
[101] Quot. Griffin, 'The Irish Police, 1836–1914', 274.

and zealous labour, and when it is attained, what is its value?—clerk to an untrained officer... and a salary of two pounds a week.[102]

Thomas Fennell, a Head Constable himself, confirms: 'As a rule, he [the Head Constable] and the District Inspector got on well together and in most instances the District Inspector left the control of the station chiefly in the hands of the Head Constable.'[103]

The argument that promotion from the ranks was not encouraged in the Royal Irish Constabulary because promoted head constables did not have the requisite skills and education to carry out the duties of a police officer can, therefore, be ruled out. Police officers were not particularly well educated; the cadet training was not particularly useful; many of them spent their time engaged in leisure pursuits; and—in many cases—the real policing work was actually done by Head Constables. So, what was the real reason why promotion from the ranks was not allowed? The vast majority of the rank and file were Catholic (as were most Head Constables), and promotion from the ranks would effectively result in the proportion of Catholic police officers increasing rapidly. This was a cause for concern for the government—particularly after the Land War (1879–81) when an essentially Catholic nationalist movement attacked the authority of the British state in Ireland. Stephen Ball suggests that the reason why there were so few Catholic police officers was because the state believed that they might not be loyal servants of the Crown: 'the government perceived that the predominantly Catholic rank and file might be torn between attachment to their class or nation and their allegiance to the Crown.'[104] The testimony of several witnesses to the Commissions on policing in Ireland in 1872 and 1883 also suggests that promoted Catholic Head Constables (most of whom were Catholic) were regarded as potentially disloyal. Wellington Colomb, a Protestant Sub-Inspector and adjutant to the depot, for instance, told the 1872 Commission that he believed Head Constables should not be promoted because they would be unable to obtain as much local information about political 'crime' as the local gentry:

If an officer's duty was merely the detection of ordinary crime, supposing Ireland perfectly quiet at all times, then the [promoted] head constable might do the duty [of an officer]—that is, supposing he had only to look after robbers, burglars, and so forth; but there is a great deal of excitement in the country at times, such as in the Fenian excitement; then I think it is an advantage that the Sub-Inspector should be a gentleman, and in the habit of mixing with the gentry, for he thereby learns a great deal he would not otherwise know.[105]

Colomb's dubious assertion that the local gentry might have valuable information about political dissent and that this justified recruiting 'gentlemen' to

---

[102] Quot. ibid. 275.   [103] Fennell, *Royal Irish Constabulary*, 116.
[104] Ball, *A Policeman's Ireland*, 4.
[105] *Report of the Commissioners Appointed . . . to Enquire into the Condition of the Civil Service in Ireland on the Royal Irish Constabulary*, HC (1873) [C 831], xxii. 57, 187.

the senior officer class of the Royal Irish Constabulary probably concealed his real reason for opposing promotion from the ranks. Indeed, reading between the lines, it seems likely that Colomb's real concern about the behaviour of promoted Head Constables during a political crisis was not that they might be unable to gain information about the Irish Republican Brotherhood (IRB) from local landlords but because they might be tempted into becoming disloyal themselves, given the fact that the vast majority of Head Constables were Catholic and possibly sympathetic to Irish nationalism.

There was clearly a concern among senior members of the British government that Catholic policemen (officers and men) may not be loyal servants of the Crown, and might be swayed by views of their co-religionists, particularly during a period of disaffection. In September 1843, the Chief Secretary, Eliot, complained to the Home Secretary (Sir James Graham) that none of the last cohort of twelve or fourteen appointed police officers had been Catholic. Graham replied that this was necessary to combat the 'pernicious influence' of Catholic officers 'especially at the present moment, when the arts and power of the Roman Catholic priesthood are exerted to shake the fidelity of the armed force in Ireland, and in particular of the constabulary'.[106] Lord de Grey disagreed with Graham as to the reliability of Catholic officers, but observed that: 'As regards the men there is a difference. We know that some of them have been tampered with; and though I as lord lieutenant have nothing to do with the enrolment of recruits, I know that Colonel Macgregor did not feel it safe to increase the number of Catholics.'[107] A year later, the Home Secretary told the Duke of Wellington that the rank and file of the Royal Irish Constabulary were 'not held to be entirely trustworthy, on account of the large proportion of Roman Catholics, and the influence which daily intercourse with a disaffected population cannot fail to exercise, in a religious struggle, on members of the same communion'.[108]

Senior army officers—who may have held similar views to some of the senior police officers who were drawn from military backgrounds—often held frankly racist views of the native Catholic Irish. When a fellow officer was killed during the Nile expedition in 1884–5, Garnet Wolseley observed that: 'If only Stewart had died in battle in place of being murdered like an Irish landlord by a cowardly skulking reptile such as this country [the Sudan] and Ireland produce in large numbers!'[109] Later—while Wolseley was serving as commander in chief of the forces in Ireland—he described the Catholic Irish to his wife (in 1895) as:

a howling, begging lot of savages, who will not work except in their own lazy fashion, and to whom dastardly murder is no crime. Their murders are always of a cowardly nature. There is no question of a fair stand-up fight, but a sneaking rascal pots you in safety from behind a wall, and the whole cowardly population seek to screen him from the crime

---

[106] Griffin, 'Religion and Opportunity', 222–3.   [107] Ibid. 223.   [108] Ibid.
[109] Elizabeth A. Muenger, *The British Military Dilemma in Ireland: Occupation Politics, 1886–1914* (Dublin, 1991), 36.

he has committed, which he is quite willing to repeat any number of times until some hangman puts an end to his infamous career.[110]

While such views were not held by all of the officers in the British army, or by all of the senior members of the Royal Irish Constabulary, they were certainly held by some individuals and this must have resulted in some discrimination against Catholic applicants for senior positions in the police and the army.[111]

Such views seem to have influenced the recruiting of Catholic police officers. In 1850, for instance, only three (8 per cent) of the thirty-seven County Inspectors were Catholic; and between 1852 and 1858, there was never more than one Catholic County Inspector.[112] There is also evidence to suggest that the government may have been right to be suspicious of Catholic police inspectors' loyalty. Certainly, some Catholic police officers sympathized with the tenants' cause during the late nineteenth- and early twentieth-centuries. Patrick Shea's father was a Catholic sergeant at Delvin, county Westmeath, during the Ranch War and '[b]eing the son of a small farmer, like most members of the force, he had no enthusiasm for the role of protector of the property of landlords'.[113] Jeremiah Mee, a Catholic constable from County Galway, along with thirteen other constables, refused to allow Listowel barracks to be transferred to military control in June 1920 as a protest against the actions of the Black and Tans in the locality.[114] John Regan recalled being part of a large party of police summoned to enforce the eviction of an old woman in county Clare, on the eve of the Great War, who could not afford to pay her rent and had fallen behind in her payments: 'We hated the job and even offered to pay up the arrears.' However, he did not let sentiment prevent him from carrying out his duty:

The eviction did not take very long as there was little or nothing in the house to remove. The few sticks of furniture were placed on the roadside, where the evicted woman sat on a chair. The house was then locked up . . . It was a winter's day and it had started to snow . . . [T]he scene was heartrending. There . . . sat on the roadside the little old lady in her tattered shawl, on her only chair, amidst her few worldly possessions. Her little white dog was on her lap, and the snow kept falling, falling, falling. I knew then why landlords had been shot in Ireland.[115]

While being trained at Phoenix Park, Regan had also attended 'for instructional purposes' the eviction of a—presumably Catholic—tenant in county Kerry who

---

[110] Ibid.

[111] George Wyndham, who was chief secretary for Ireland, also described the people of the west of Ireland as 'reptiles'. See Campbell, *Land and Revolution*, 57. Nora Robertson reports that her father—an Irish Protestant army officer—'was quite without religious prejudice' (Nora Robertson, *Crowned Harp: Memories of the Last Years of the Crown in Ireland* (Dublin, 1960), 124).

[112] Griffin, 'Religion and Opportunity', 223–4.

[113] Patrick Shea, *Voices and the Sound of Drums: An Irish Autobiography* (Belfast, 1981), 4. Shea's father was also a Home Ruler.

[114] On the Listowel mutiny of June 1920, see Malcolm, *Irish Policeman, 1822–1922*, 160–9.

[115] Joost Augusteijn, *The Memoirs of John M. Regan* (Dublin), 71.

had barricaded himself inside his house, and it is possible that Regan was asked to assist with this violent eviction so that his loyalty could be assessed by his superiors.[116] Indeed, the government was particularly concerned with Catholic police officers' loyalty during the Land War (1879–81) and its aftermath, and this explains the declining proportion of Catholic police officers between 1881 and 1911.

As we have seen, despite the influence of Reed's reform in 1895 (which reserved half of the District Inspectorships for (the mainly Catholic) Head Constables), only six of the senior police officers were Catholic in 1911 although almost half (45 per cent) of the District Inspectors in 1914 were Catholic.[117] A glass ceiling appears to have remained in place, however, even for newly promoted Catholic District Inspectors as the proportion of Catholic County Inspectors in 1918 and 1922 remained low.[118] As with the senior civil servants, the only Irish-born Catholics to be promoted to the senior positions in the Royal Irish Constabulary were those individuals who were perceived to be loyal. Of all of the 129 senior police officers under review, twenty-four (19 per cent) were Catholic.[119] Two of these were English-born. Joshua Edward Leo Holmes was, in fact, second-generation Irish. His father, Jesse, had been born in Ireland in 1828, while Joshua was born at Marleybone, London, in 1858.[120] William Charles Patrick Hetreed was a native of Kent who became a cadet after working as a tutor at St Brendan's College, Killarney, and at Clongowes Wood College for almost three years. William later wrote an article for the *Clongownian* encouraging students at Clongowes to consider becoming cadets in the Royal Irish Constabulary.[121] His younger brother Vincent James also became a police officer after working as a clerk at the Land Commission for eighteen months.[122]

At least six (25 per cent) of the Catholic senior police officers had been born into 'elite' families. Four were the sons of police officers; two were the sons of landowners; two were the sons of magistrates; one was the son of

---

[116] Ibid. 46–7.   [117] Griffin, 'Religion and Opportunity', 224.

[118] John McCrory's study of the RIC demonstrates that only 11% of the senior police officers was Catholic in 1918 but that this had increased to almost one-quarter (27%) by 1922. 'Religion, Opportunity, and Change in the Royal Irish Constabulary: Analysis of the County Inspectorate, 1871–1922', BA thesis (Newcastle University, 2006).

[119] Of the 24, 21 were recruited as cadet officers; 1 (Heffernan Considine) was recruited from outside the force to become Deputy Inspector General; and 2 were promoted from the ranks (John Donovan and Michael Hurley). Donovan was a native of Kerry who became a Sub-Constable in 1833 and a Sub-Inspector in 1847 (when he was 35 years of age). Hurley was from Cork and became a Sub-Constable in 1854, a Sub-Inspector in 1881 (when he was 46 years of age), and private secretary to the Inspector General (Andrew Reed), between 1885 and 1893.

[120] Before becoming a cadet, Joshua had spent seven months working as a clerk in the GPO at Birmingham.

[121] William Hetreed, 'The RIC as a Profession', *Clongownian* (June 1898). Andrew Reed was Inspector General when Hetreed wrote this article.

[122] Vincent James Hetreed is not included in my sample because he did not become a County Inspector until July 1920.

an army officer; and another was the son of a Resident Magistrate.[123] The Catholic senior police officers were, therefore, not representative of the Irish Catholic population as a whole, being drawn either from the English Catholic community or the well-to-do Irish Catholic community. Indeed, at least four (18 per cent) of the (twenty-two) Irish Catholic senior officers were from wider landowning families.[124] With the exception of the two promoted Head Constables (Donovan and Hurley) and the two English-born Catholic Inspectors (Holmes and Hetreed), then, a significant proportion of the remaining twenty Catholic police officers were from the Irish Catholic landowning and professional classes, which were—broadly speaking—loyal to the Crown. Henry Roderick McDermott, for instance, was the son of Henry, a police officer, as well as being a relation of the landowning The MacDermott of Sligo. One of his brothers, Edward Joseph, also became a police officer and was later promoted to the Resident Magistracy (1892–1911), while his sister married Daniel Lyne, a medical doctor and magistrate from Castletownberehaven, county Cork. Catholic senior police officers tended to emerge from these Irish Catholic sub-communities that had connections to land and the professions, and had a history of loyalty to the British state in Ireland. Samuel Waters noted, for instance, that Heffernan Considine:

never, for a moment, allowed the question of religious feeling to affect, in the slightest degree, his official acts. He was a most scrupulous Catholic in his attention to all the claims of his Church; but he resented as a gross insult, any attempt, by priests or others, to influence him in the discharge of his public duties by an appeal to religion. A more perfect gentleman never lived, nor one who was animated by higher principles of justice and right.[125]

And John Regan, whose father was a District Inspector, explained in his memoir: 'I had been pro-British from my earliest years'.[126]

VI

Broadly speaking, the evidence presented in this chapter suggests that Malcolm rather than Lowe is correct in her interpretation of the nature of the officers of the Royal Irish Constabulary. According to Lowe, there was a 'greening' process taking place among the officers of the Royal Irish Constabulary—admittedly

---

[123] There is some overlap between these categories.
[124] Heffernan Considine owned 950 acres (valued at £1,211) in county Limerick; Myles Blake Burke was a relation of Sir Valentine Blake of Menlo Castle who owned 2,030 acres (valued at £350) in county Galway; Henry Roderick McDermott was a relation of Hugh Hyacinth MacDermott (The MacDermott) who owned 909 acres (valued at £236) in county Sligo; and William Arthur O'Connell (a descendant of Daniel O'Connell) owned 2,019 acres (valued at £946) in county Clare.
[125] Ball, *A Policeman's Ireland*, 82.
[126] Augusteijn, *Memoirs of John M. Regan*, 25–6. Regan's brother was a Catholic priest.

at a slower rate than among the rank and file—demonstrating that the force was becoming more representative of the Irish population as a whole. However, it is clear that at the top level of the Royal Irish Constabulary—the County Inspectorate and above—there was a glass ceiling beyond which most Irish-born Catholics were unable to ascend.

Although Lowe does not include the real number of Catholic and Protestant police officers in his article, he does describe the Royal Irish Constabulary officer corps as 'composed almost exactly of one-third Catholics and two-thirds Protestants'.[127] However, it is clear from the data presented in this chapter, that the proportion of Catholic senior officers between 1881 and 1911 was far lower (19 per cent) than that of Catholic police officers as a whole; and that the proportion of Catholic senior officers was actually in decline (from 28 per cent in 1881 to 14 per cent in 1911). This is significant because we know that the proportion of Catholic District Inspectors was increasing rapidly during this period owing to the opening of half of the entry-level officer positions to men promoted from the ranks in 1895 (who were, by and large, Catholic). Similarly, it is clear that whereas more than one-third of the Royal Irish Constabulary officers as a whole were 'rankers' (or men promoted from the ranks), only 3 per cent of the senior officers between 1881 and 1911 were men promoted from the ranks.[128] It may be that the reason why there were so few Catholics and rankers among the senior officers of the police force was because many of them had been promoted from the ranks when they were already relatively well advanced in years, and that there was insufficient time for them to reach the top of the seniority list and become County Inspectors.[129] That some Catholic rankers did make it to the top suggests that others also could have done so, but that there was some obstacle to their further promotion. Indeed, it is likely that the Royal Irish Constabulary—like the Irish Civil Service—were happy for Catholics to work at the junior and middle levels of the administration, but that they were to be prevented from taking up the senior positions where real power lay; and which might have required them to police and suppress a nationalist rebellion.

The detailed and systematic data presented here support Malcolm's assertion (based on her more impressionistic evidence) that Catholics were less able to reach the senior positions in the Royal Irish Constabulary than their Protestant colleagues. However, Malcolm does not explain why this was the case, although she does suggest that there were 'religious and political prejudices' that militated against Catholic advancement. This chapter suggests, on the other hand, that it was the government's belief that Catholic officers were potentially disloyal that—largely—prevented Catholics from advancing to the senior positions in the Constabulary. In addition, Malcolm suggests that Royal Irish Constabulary

---

[127] Lowe, 'Irish Constabulary Officers', 40.   [128] Ibid. 31.   [129] Ibid. 41–2.

officers' opposition to greater promotion from the ranks was based more on class prejudice than on political or religious discrimination:

RIC officers regarded themselves as 'gentlemen' and saw themselves as coming from a different class to their men. Promoting the sons of small farmers into the officer corps in large numbers was perceived by officers as a direct threat to their social standing. They were not prepared to treat such men as either professional or social equals.[130]

However, the presence of a significant number of members of the Protestant middle class (clerks and teachers and so on) among the senior officers of the Royal Irish Constabulary (and the relative absence of members of the Catholic middle class) suggests that opposition to promotion from the ranks was probably motivated more by ethnic discrimination than by class prejudice.

The evidence presented in this chapter also has implications for Lowe and Malcolm's account of the 'domestication' of the Royal Irish Constabulary as a whole. Much of the liberalization of the Royal Irish Constabulary during the late nineteenth century was as a result of Andrew Reed's period of tenure as Inspector General. It was Reed who improved the working conditions of the rank and file policemen, and encouraged them to develop better relationships with their local communities (rather than just with the local landowners); and it was Reed who opened half of the District Inspectorships to promoted Head Constables in 1895. According to Fennell: 'Sir Andrew Reed's enlightened rule of the Force, brought a much more liberal treatment of Catholics'.[131] However, Reed was not typical of the Inspector Generals who held office in Ireland between 1836 and 1922. He was one of only two Inspector Generals to be recruited from the ranks; and many of his colleagues regarded him as an oddity who should be replaced by a more hardline Inspector General with a more military state of mind. Indeed, if Reed had not become Inspector General it would be much harder to make the argument that the force as a whole was becoming more 'domesticated' during this period. Reed was exceptional, and if the British state had wanted to 'domesticate' or 'green' the Royal Irish Constabulary, it would have appointed more Inspector Generals like Reed and less like Chamberlain, who were from a military rather than a policing background.[132]

Indeed, notwithstanding Lowe and Malcolm's 'domestication' argument, almost all accounts of the Royal Irish Constabulary by members of the force emphasize its military nature. Sir William Nott-Bower recalls that 'Life at the

---

[130] Malcolm, *Irish Policeman, 1822–1922*, 148.   [131] Fennell, *Royal Irish Constabulary*, 57.

[132] In fact, Reed had objected to his own promotion to the position of Inspector General in 1885 as he was concerned that his appointment would appear discriminatory towards the Catholic deputy Inspector General, who was his senior. Reed accepted the position only when he was informed that if he did not do so the next Inspector General would be recruited from outside the force. Malcolm, 'Sir Andrew Reed' <http://www.oxforddnb.com/view/article/37886?docPos=2> (accessed 15 Nov. 2008).

Depot was very similar, in most respects, to life in the army'.[133] Garrow Green introduces his readers to the nature of the force in the following manner:

To readers unacquainted with the corps, I may say that it is a military police peculiar to Ireland, and officered in much the same way as the army. The uniform resembles that of the Rifle Brigade. A County Inspector, *i.e.* the officer commanding a county, wears the badges, and holds the relative rank of Colonel. The District Inspectors, his officers, command the various districts in such county, and wear the badges and hold the relative ranks of Major, Captain and Lieutenant. Their arms are swords and revolvers; those of the men, the rifle (Martini Carbine), bayonet and baton. The Royal Irish Constabulary may be termed, *de facto*, the Irish Garrison.[134]

And Clifford Lloyd, a Special Resident Magistrate, who worked closely with the force during the Land War (1879–81) observed that 'The Royal Irish Constabulary can best be described as an army of occupation, upon which is imposed the performance of certain civil duties'.[135]

It is also worth bearing in mind that Andrew Reed's reforms did not transform the ethos of the force as a whole. Although the majority of the rank and file were Catholics, the ethos of the force was determined by the senior officers (who were overwhelmingly Protestant), and rank and filers were forced to bow to the prevailing ideology. According to Fennell, most rank and file members of the Royal Irish Constabulary did not understand the real nature of the force when they first joined it:

It was only after ten or twelve years that they began to see that this Force was specially organised and equipped to sustain landlordism and keep the people in subjection. No matter how distasteful it was, they had then in most cases reached a time when they were obliged to continue. By that time, most men had married and had rising families.[136]

Indeed, Fennell goes on to explain that Catholic rankers often had to conceal their real feelings if they wanted to secure promotion:

Bigotry in the service was constantly in evidence not alone in the matter of promotion but in the behaviour and speech of Protestant members in the ranks. They were not afraid to give expression to their feelings on political matters and the stronger the opposition they evinced towards every National movement the better they thought was their chance of advancement, while Catholics had always to be carefully on their guard to say little or nothing, unless they were of the flunkey type—and there were a few of them around everywhere—who always joined with the Protestants in their views of everything having a political or anti-national tinge. Flunkeyism was one of the means adopted to gain favour in official circles by men having little else as a recommendation, who availed of every opportunity to show how worthy they were as loyal and reliable members. The better

---

[133] Nott-Bower, *Fifty-two Years a Policeman*, 26.
[134] Garrow Green, *In the Royal Irish Constabulary*, 5.
[135] Clifford Lloyd, *Ireland under the Land League: A Narrative of Personal Experiences* (Edinburgh and London, 1892), 51.   [136] Fennell, *Royal Irish Constabulary*, 10.

educated and more independent Catholics avoided discussion of subjects on which they were supposed not to have any views.[137]

Because promotion in the ranks of the force was usually at the discretion of the—mainly Protestant—County Inspectors, Fennell claimed that Catholic rankers who wanted to secure promotion had to be particularly careful to conceal any dissenting views:

Catholic members of the Force required to be careful to avoid anything in speech or action which would indicate that they held views different to the spirit that ruled in the service. Constant care in this respect, had, however, enabled men without embarrassment to cloak their private feelings, giving no inkling of what was at the back of their minds. For anyone who hoped to advance in the service, it was incumbent upon him to guard against even suspicion of holding any views not in conformity with those of the people in whose hands rested his advance.[138]

The fact that the majority of the rank and file of the Royal Irish Constabulary were Catholic does not necessarily mean that the ethos of the force was representative of the Irish population and becoming more 'domesticated'. It was the senior officers who determined the nature of the force—not the rank and filers or even the sub- or district inspectors—and this meant that the force continued to be run as a pro-landlord and essentially Protestant force.

The following account of the Royal Irish Constabulary in *Irishmen All* is suggestive:

I know a lady who speaks very bitterly about the Irish police. She is an enthusiastic gardener, and lives almost under the shadow of a constabulary barrack in which there is a large force of sergeants and men with a very smart District Inspector at the head of them. Every day for some weeks in the early summer of last year those men practised rifle-shooting quite after the manner of real soldiers on a piece of waste land just below the lady's lawn. The sound of the crackling shots ought to have been most consoling to her. She ought to have realised that the men were becoming more and more perfect in the art of hitting things with bullets. She ought to have remembered that there might at any moment be an outbreak of rebels in Tipperary, furious men bent on the destruction of civilisation, or a rising of loyalists in Ulster, equally determined to maintain Law and Order. In either event the security of her family silver, the glass in her windows, even perhaps her life, would depend on the ability with which the police could use their rifles. She ought not to have grumbled about their daily practice. But every night, when the rifle fire was over, a thief came quietly across the wall at the bottom of the lawn and dug up a plant or two. Sometimes he took a few choice rose-bushes, sometime half a dozen begonias, sometimes a carnation plant of rare and precious quality. The lady complained of the inefficiency of the police. This was unreasonable. The expert rifleman cannot be

---

[137] Ibid. 71.

[138] Ibid. 113. This strategy fits in with Scott's notion of the 'hidden transcript'. See James C. Scott, *Domination and the Arts of Resistance: Hidden Transcripts* (New Haven, Conn., 1990). County Inspectors decided on rankers' promotions. See Fennell, *Royal Irish Constabulary*, 22.

expected to catch thieves. Armed men, engaged in holding down a turbulent populace, have more important things to think of than begonias.[139]

Notwithstanding Lowe and Malcolm's 'domestication' argument, the Royal Irish Constabulary in early twentieth-century Ireland were insufficiently concerned with the stealing of begonias.

[139] Birmingham, *Irishmen All*, 43–4.

4

Politics

The previous two chapters have examined the social characteristics of the individuals who were responsible for devising, implementing, and upholding the policies of the British state in Ireland. As we have seen, the state and its representatives were extremely powerful in Ireland, and were responsible for transforming Irish society—in a variety of respects—between 1879 and 1914. However, the British state was not autonomous, and it was accountable for its actions to the elected representatives of the various political parties both in Ireland and in the rest of the United Kingdom. The Irish MPs—democratically elected by the Irish population—were therefore in a position both to pressurize the state to adopt or reject reformist policies in Ireland, and to oppose policies which they thought might be detrimental to what they perceived to be Irish interests.

The Irish political elite—defined here as the elected representatives of the Irish political parties—exercised a great deal of power and influence over the actions of the British state during this period. This chapter will examine who the Irish MPs were, and consider the extent to which the political elite was 'open' to the various political viewpoints and social groups in Irish society. Because political power is generally exercised by an organized group of political representatives in a political party, the chapter will focus on the composition of the main Irish political parties at the two key points of 1881 and 1911. In 1881, the three political parties in Ireland were the Conservative Party, the Liberal Party, and the Irish Parliamentary Party. And in 1911—following the first Home Rule crisis of 1885–6—the Irish representation was divided into the (anti-Home Rule) Irish Unionist Party and the (pro-Home Rule) Irish Parliamentary Party.

In late nineteenth- and early twentieth-century Ireland, then, the political elite was essentially divided into two competing sections: one Nationalist, and the other Unionist. Although Irish Unionism did not formally come into existence until after the Home Rule crisis of 1885–6, it is clear that the Irish Conservative Party and sections of the Irish Liberal Party were the precursors of the later Irish Unionist Party. The Irish Parliamentary Party, on the other hand, was the chief representative of nationalism in Ireland between 1874 and 1918. The power and influence of the Unionist and the Nationalist parties in Ireland were transformed during the period under review. Before 1886, the Liberal and the Conservative

Parties were the most influential political parties and—depending on whether there was a Liberal or a Conservative government in power—were in a position decisively to influence British policy in Ireland. After 1886, however, when the Irish Parliamentary Party entered into an alliance with the Liberal Party, the Nationalist and Unionist political representatives in the House of Commons were probably equally influential and both achieved a great deal for their respective communities. The Nationalists, for instance, played a key role in pressuring the government to introduce three Home Rule Bills (in 1886, 1893, and 1912), the Wyndham Land Act in 1903, and the 1908 University Act which transformed the provisions for third-level education for Catholics. The Unionists, on the other hand, were able to pressure the government to accept partition and the ultimate exclusion of six Ulster counties from Home Rule. Both the Nationalist and Unionist parties were also able to influence appointments to senior positions in the Irish administration. The Irish MPs—both Nationalist and Unionist—were, therefore, enormously powerful during the period under review, and capable of decisively influencing the behaviour of the British state in Ireland between 1879 and 1914.

We might expect the political elite in Ireland between the Land War (1879–81) and the Great War (1914–18) to have been one of the more 'open' elite groups in Irish society during this period. Technically, anyone could put themselves forward as a candidate (as long as he was a man), and the recruiting of MPs was not—ostensibly at least—as subject to discriminatory practices as were appointments to the higher echelons of the Civil Service or the police. Indeed, after the introduction of the secret ballot in 1872 and the reform of the franchise in 1868 and 1884–5, elections were relatively open and democratic at least by the standards of the time. However, the degree of 'openness' of the Irish political elite was restricted by three factors: first, the extent of the franchise; second, the fact that members of the British parliament did not receive a salary until 1911 and therefore required independent means; and third, by the often complex and restrictive procedures by which political parties recruited parliamentary candidates.

The electorate constituted only a minority of the Irish population before the introduction of universal adult male suffrage (and limited female suffrage) in 1918. In 1881, there were 103 MPs who were elected in borough constituencies under the terms of the 1868 Act, and in the county constituencies under the terms of the 1850 Act. The 1868 Act enfranchised occupiers in the borough constituencies with a valuation of 'over £4' while the 1850 Act enfranchised occupiers in the counties who owned property valued at £12 and over. Overall, in 1881, the Irish electorate constituted just 4.4 per cent of the total population (the comparable figure for England and Wales was 9.7 per cent).[1] The size

---

[1] B. M. Walker, 'The Irish Electorate, 1868–1915', *Irish Historical Studies*, 18 (Mar. 1973), 359, 402. I have included the parties and constistuencies which each MP named in the text represented (before 1922) in the footnotes.

of the electorate in Ireland trebled as a result of the introduction of the Representation of the People Act in 1884. Indeed, the electoral reforms of 1884–5 created a uniform householder and lodger franchise for the whole of the United Kingdom, and the level for both county and borough occupiers was set at £10 rateable value.[2] In social terms, the Irish electorate was expanded to include small farmers and agricultural labourers (cottagers only), and the denominational breakdown of the electorate became broadly similar to that in the population as a whole.[3] However, the legislation of 1884–5 did not introduce universal adult male suffrage. In particular, servants who resided with their employers and sons living with parents were not entitled to vote, and neither were women. Even so, the proportion of the Irish population now entitled to vote increased to 15.7 per cent in 1891, 16.4 per cent in 1901, and 15.7 per cent in 1911. This was broadly similar to that in the rest of the United Kingdom: in England and Wales, for instance, 16.6 per cent of the total population could vote in 1891, 16.4 per cent in 1901, and 17.7 per cent in 1911.[4]

Members of Parliament did not receive a salary until 1911 and this also restricted the kinds of people who were capable of putting themselves forward as candidates. Potential MPs needed to have substantial financial resources to fund their parliamentary and constituency duties, and this factor informed the process of selecting candidates. However, the Irish Parliamentary Party did pay a parliamentary salary to those of its members who could not afford to attend Westminster. In 1895, thirty-five Home Rule MPs received a stipend of between £200 and £500 per annum; in 1897—during more straitened times for the Home Rule movement—twenty-one MPs received £120 per year; and, following revived fortunes, half of the Home Rule members (between 1906 and 1910) received an average of £120 per year each.[5] Even so, attendance at Westminster could have a devastating effect on Home Rule MPs' professional and business lives, and, as Laurence Ginnell suggested in 1906, even the allowance was 'terribly meagre'.[6] However, when the British government introduced the policy of paying MPs an annual salary of £400 in 1911, the Irish Parliamentary Party initially decided not to accept it since to do so would have undermined the Party's commitment to not accepting position or patronage from the British state. But, by August 1911, the IPP reversed its decision in the face of Lloyd George's insistence that all MPs should accept this payment. Notwithstanding the Party's volte face, however, individual MPs could still find themselves in dire straits and J. J. Clancy, for instance, complained in 1918 that 'the money

[2] Ibid. 365.
[3] B. M. Walker, 'The Land Question and Elections in Ulster, 1868–1886', in James Donnelly and Samuel Clark, *Irish Peasants: Violence and Political Unrest, 1780–1914* (Manchester, 1983), 231–2.   [4] B. M. Walker, 'The Irish Electorate', 366, 403–5.
[5] James McConnel, 'The View from the Backbench: Irish Nationalist MPs and their Work, 1910–14', PhD thesis (Durham University, 2002), 269.   [6] Ibid. 270.

only paid their bare expenses'.[7] Financial considerations were also to the fore during the selection of Irish Unionist Party candidates as Alvin Jackson has explained: 'Running an Irish Unionist constituency was costly—and there was therefore an independent financial compulsion on selectors to opt for older, and wealthier, candidates.'[8] Broadly speaking, only those individuals with independent financial resources were in a position to put themselves forward as political candidates, and this greatly restricted the openness of the Irish political elite.

Finally, it is necessary to consider the process by which candidates for election were selected by the various parties between 1881 and 1911.[9] Before 1900, Irish Parliamentary Party candidates were selected by the central leadership of the party in Dublin. This occasionally required the leadership of the party to overrule a locally selected candidate. In 1885, for instance, a local man was nominated by a convention in county Tipperary but Parnell rejected their decision and imposed his own candidate—John O'Connor—on the constituency.[10] Indeed, T. P. O'Connor recalled how parliamentary candidates were selected by the IPP under the leadership of Parnell:

Probably never in the history of Parliamentary institutions was there a stranger method of electing the representatives of a nation. A meeting was held in a room of Morrison's Hotel, where Parnell habitually stayed when in Dublin. Parnell sat at the head of the table; around him were prominent members who lived in Dublin, of whom Mr. Healy was one; Parnell rarely took any part in the discussions. Names were submitted; such local information as could be got about them was mentioned; then, after a comparatively short discussion, the name was chosen, and the choice of that name by this small committee meant practically his election as member.

Arrangements were made for a convention to nominate the member. These conventions were presided over by a member of the Party; he came there with his written instructions, the first of which was to get the man through who had been chosen by the committee in Dublin. He had also in many cases a second or third name up his sleeve, so to speak. In some cases where a candidate was known as somewhat undesirable, the chairman was expected to take any and every measure to prevent his being chosen.

These conventions were preceded in many cases, of course, by very active wire-pulling, especially for the local candidate, and it required all the dexterity and the firmness of the chairman to get the choice of the committee adopted . . . It will be evident from these facts that this little committee in Dublin had the representation of Ireland entirely in its hands.[11]

[7] Ibid. 271. J. J. Clancy was Home Rule MP for north county Dublin, 1885–1918.

[8] Alvin Jackson, *The Ulster Party: Irish Unionists in the House of Commons, 1884–1911* (Oxford, 1989), 67.

[9] I have confined this discussion to how Home Rule and Unionist candidates were selected as there are less data available on how Conservative or Liberal candidates were selected.

[10] Alan O'Day, *The English Face of Irish Nationalism* (Dublin, 1977), 28. John O'Connor was Home Rule MP for South Tipperary, 1885–92, and for north Kildare, 1905–18.

[11] T. P. O'Connor, *Memoirs of an Old Parliamentarian*, 2 vols. (London 1929), ii. 14–16. O'Connor was Home Rule MP for Galway, 1880–5, and Liverpool, 1885–1929.

The IPP leadership more or less decided who Home Rule MPs would be before 1900 and this meant that the representatives of the Home Rule movement in London and Dublin, the personal friends and relations of IPP MPs, and members of the Irish community in London were at an advantage when it came to the selection of candidates.[12] Matthew Keating became a parliamentary candidate as a result of his 'judicious cultivation of parliamentary influences' as well as his 'activity at national meetings in London'; Stephen Gwynn tried to secure a position as a Home Rule MP by attending dinners at Sir James Matthew's house in London with the intention of meeting John Dillon (who was Matthew's son-in-law); and Dillon and Redmond's postbags were often filled with letters from first- and second-generation Irishmen in London who were keen to become Home Rule MPs.[13]

After 1900, however, the leadership of the IPP were no longer able to dictate who would become a parliamentary candidate. The constitution of the reunited Irish Parliamentary Party and the United Irish League—adopted in June 1900—stipulated that the United Irish League organization in the constituency had the power to select parliamentary candidates. The National Directory (which was composed of the leaders of the Party) did have the power to send one representative to each local convention but he was entitled to make a recommendation only if he was invited to do so by the convention.[14] This did not stop Redmond, Dillon, and the other leaders of the IPP from attempting to influence the selection of parliamentary candidates but it did greatly reduce their influence over who was selected. Stephen Gwynn, for instance, met with Redmond in his office in the House of Commons to ask if he might be put forward as a parliamentary candidate. According to Gwynn: 'He [Redmond] was very guarded, and said it was entirely a matter for the local conventions . . . All that he could do was let my disposition be known in places where a vacancy was probable.' Redmond does appear to have recommended Gwynn to two local conventions—in north Kildare in 1904 and west Clare in 1906—but in neither constituency was Gwynn successful although he was invited by a local priest to put himself forward at the convention in the latter constituency. Instead, at the Kilrush convention held on 10 January 1906, the delegates (who included 248 lay delegates and twenty priests) selected James Halpin with Gwynn coming a close second.[15] This case suggests two important points about the selection of Home Rule parliamentary candidates after 1900: first, that the

---

[12] O'Day, *English Face of Irish Nationalism*, 28.

[13] McConnel, 'The View from the Backbench', 116. John Redmond was Home Rule MP for New Ross, 1881–5, north Wexford, 1885–91, and Waterford city, 1891–1918. John Dillon was Home Rule MP for Tipperary, 1880–3, and east Mayo, 1885–1918.

[14] Fergus Campbell, *Land and Revolution: Nationalist Politics in the West of Ireland, 1891–1921* (Oxford, 2005), 42; McConnel, 'The View from the Backbench', 119.

[15] McConnel, 'The View from the Backbench', 117–18. James Halpin was Home Rule MP for west Clare, 1906–9.

Party leadership were unable to dictate who would be selected as they had done before 1900; but, second, that the leaders of the IPP were prepared to break the rules of the United Irish League (UIL) constitution and lobby for their preferred candidates.

Redmond justified his actions on the grounds that local conventions often selected men who were well known and well respected locally but who were not well suited to their work in the House of Commons.[16] After the death of William McKillop, Redmond explained his position to Canon Quin, one of the members of the south Armagh convention that would select McKillop's successor:

I am anxious, at the earliest possible moment, to consult you. Poor McKillop's death makes a vacancy in south Armagh, and I need not tell you of what enormous importance it is to Ireland that the vacancy should be filled up by some one competent to give us assistance in the House of Commons in our work. Some man should be chosen for his qualifications for this particular line of work, and not merely because he is a good fellow or a good Nationalist.[17]

Indeed, John Valentine, the leader of the UIL at Bristol, felt that Redmond's inability to dictate the selection of parliamentary candidates greatly reduced the quality of Ireland's representatives in the House of Commons:

I have referred to the selection of candidates for Parliament. In this work John Redmond showed his weakness. He spoke more than once of the necessity for suitable men, but seemed afraid of alienating supporters, and left matters to local people, who put forward, say, a farmer or a dealer who had been prominent in cattle driving, etc., independent altogether of fitness for Parliament; and thus the once great Irish Party ultimately had very few men who could assist Ireland's cause on the platform; some, indeed, were a hindrance to success.[18]

Gwynn echoed these comments and observed that the candidate who defeated him at the west Clare convention in 1906, James Halpin, was 'a decent, stout, strong farmer . . . whom I came to know and like' but he was 'no use in the world for the work at Westminster'.[19] Of course, the selection of well-known local candidates might have meant that not all Home Rule MPs after 1900 were powerful speakers and adept organizers in the House of Commons but it did mean that they were perceived to be effective representatives of the powerful farming and shopkeeping classes in the Irish countryside. Indeed, Halpin may have been deficient in the House of Commons but he was a very effective local constituency MP who as sometime Fenian, prisoner, Land Leaguer, National

---

[16] Redmond was also concerned that new recruits to the Home Rule party should be 'trustworthy', and this was a concern—in various ways—for all of the elite groups under review in this book. McConnel, 'The View from the Backbench', 122.

[17] Redmond to Quin, 31 Aug. 1909, quot. McConnel, 'The View from the Backbench', 122. William McKillop was Home Rule MP for south Armagh, 1906–9.

[18] John Valentine, *Irish Memories* (Bristol, 1927), 60.

[19] McConnel, 'The View from the Backbench', 122.

Leaguer, United Irish Leaguer, county councillor, Poor Law Guardian, and builder of the sea wall at Lahinch worked tirelessly for his constituents at both local and national levels. Men like Halpin played a critically important role in binding together the leadership and the rank and file of the Home Rule movement, and at representing the interests of large farmers and shopkeepers among the Irish establishment.

The selection of parliamentary candidates after 1900 was, therefore, the product of both the wishes of the local conventions and the IPP leadership who continually tried to influence the selection processes of local conventions. Even these local conventions, however, were not necessarily representative of the entire nationalist community in their various constituencies. Local conventions were composed of the officers of United Irish League branches and other nationalist organizations, as well as many members of the local clergy. William O'Malley recalled that when he was selected by a convention that met in 'the old city of the Tribes [Galway]': 'The selection was made by a small body of men—perhaps about thirty—the most important and respectable men in the constituency. There were several priests present.'[20] Given that UIL officers were often shopkeepers and large farmers, and that the local clergy played an important role in the decision-making process, this meant that local selecting conventions often tended to select the more conservative local candidates. After the death of John Roche in 1914, for instance, the East Galway UIL Executive selected James Cosgrave, a comparative unknown, rather than Martin Finnerty, who was one of the architects of the Ranch War in Ireland, as the Home Rule candidate for the constituency. Finnerty was undoubtedly the better-qualified candidate but he was also a member of the IRB and strongly in favour of using violent methods to implement rapid land redistribution in the west of Ireland, and it would seem that the local bourgeoisie and clergy preferred to select a socially conservative candidate over whom they might have more control.[21] The process of becoming a Home Rule MP was, therefore, a complicated business. Before 1900, it was necessary to be reasonably well known to the party leaders; and after 1900, it was necessary to be popular with local power brokers in the United Irish League, Ancient Order of Hibernians, and the Catholic Church as well as on good terms with the leaders of the Irish Parliamentary Party.

The situation was not dissimilar in the Irish Unionist Party. From 1886 onwards—when the Ulster Party came into existence—party candidates were selected by local constituency associations.[22] However—as with the Home Rule movement—local associations were not necessarily representative of local Unionist opinion. In 1900, for instance, the East Antrim constituency association

[20] William O'Malley, *Glancing Back* (London, 1933), 173–4.
[21] Campbell, *Land and Revolution*, Chs. 3, 4, and 5.
[22] Jackson, *Ulster Party*, 212, 213. Although, during the 1890s, Arthur Balfour often intervened in the selection of local Unionist candidates.

selected Colonel McCalmont as the Unionist candidate for the general election. A rival candidate—Dr King-Kerr—later pointed out that the constituency association had invited only a carefully vetted section of its membership to the nomination meeting at Ballyclare: 'There were 8900 electors in East Antrim' King-Kerr explained, 'would they allow 50 or 60 men who met in Bally-clare to select their representative? Was that fair?'[23] Whether it was fair or not, it was often the case that small groups of local Unionist activists select-ed parliamentary candidates. Moreover, because the provincial organization of the Unionist movement was not as extensive as that of the Home Rule movement, there were many constituencies where a local propertied clique basically decided who the Unionist candidate would be. It is certainly the case that after 1893 (and especially after 1905) the Ulster Party had to pay more attention to the concerns of rank and file Unionists but—even so—the man-agement and selection of local Unionist candidates was often in the hands of a small number of local landowners, businessmen, and professionals.[24] Broad-ly speaking, then, prospective parliamentary candidates were required to have independent means, and to be influential members of both local and national political networks if they wanted to become members of the Irish politi-cal elite. These factors do force us to consider the extent to which Ireland was a democracy on the eve of the Irish Revolution (1916–23). The next section of the chapter will examine who the members of the political elite were in 1881.

I

The Conservative Party in Ireland represented the interests of most of the Irish landlords and a large part of the Irish Protestant population, and particularly members of the Church of Ireland.[25] In fact, the party had three main objectives: to defend the Act of Union; to defend the established church; and to defend the interests of the Irish landlord class.[26] In the 1850s and 1860s, it had been the biggest political party in Ireland: in 1859, for instance, the Conservatives held more seats than any other Irish party. After the introduction of the secret ballot in 1872, however, the party had fallen into decline, although it still held twenty-four seats in 1881. The vast majority of Conservative MPs in 1881 were either Church of Ireland or Church of England (twenty-two or 92 per cent), with a minority of Presbyterian MPs (two or 8 per cent). None of the Conservative

    23 Ibid. 226. Colonel James Martin McCalmont was Unionist MP for east Antrim, 1885–1913.
    24 Ibid. 229, 322.
    25 K. Theodore Hoppen, *Elections, Politics and Society, 1832–1885* (Oxford, 1984), 266, 304–5.
    26 Andrew Shields, *The Irish Conservative Party, 1852–1868: Land, Politics and Religion* (Dublin, 2007), 211.

MPs in 1881 was Catholic. Broadly speaking, the Irish Conservative Party was opposed to the reforms demanded by the Catholic majority during the second half of the nineteenth century.[27] The Irish Conservative party was a part of the British Conservative party but its leadership did have a certain amount of freedom to develop their own policies.

Most of the Irish Conservative MPs were either landowners themselves or the members of landed families. Almost two-thirds of them were landowners (fifteen or 63 per cent) with a further quarter (six or 25 per cent) closely related to landowners. Overall, then, the Conservative MPs were generally drawn from landed families, most of whom (eleven or 52 per cent) owned estates of more than 10,000 acres. Maxwell Charles Close, for instance, owned a great estate in Armagh and Queen's county.[28] And John Mulholland owned almost 15,000 acres in counties Down and Tyrone.[29] However, some of the landed members of the Conservative Party owned even larger estates: Viscount Castlereagh owned 50,323 acres, and Sir Richard Wallace owned 72,307 acres.[30] The Protestant landowning class saw themselves as the natural leaders of Irish society. Indeed, when Viscount Crichton, the owner of a 30,294 acre estate, died—the *Belfast Newsletter* explained, 'It was natural that one of his lineage and associations should find a place in the House of Commons'.[31] William Humphrys Archdale was born into an estate of 5,627 acres, and when his relation Edward Mervyn Archdale resigned his north Fermanagh seat in 1903 the *Irish Times* noted that 'An Archdale . . . [had] represented County Fermanagh in the Irish and English Parliaments for a continuous period of 150 years'.[32]

A significant minority of Conservative MPs (four or 17 per cent) was also drawn from the world of big business. Sir William Ewart was a linen manufacturer at Belfast. In the mid 1840s, he had entered into partnership with his father and established 'one of the leading establishments in the great linen industry of Belfast' which boasted three mills, a bleach works, and a weaving factory. Ewart paid annual wages of £150,000 to his 6,000 employees, and when he died in August 1889 left £313,126 in his will.[33] Sir James Porter Corry was a Belfast shipbuilder whose ships sailed throughout the

[27] D. George Boyce, 'Trembling Solicitude: Irish Conservatism, Nationality and Public Opinion, 1833–86', in Boyce, Robert Eccleshall, and Vincent Geoghegan, *Political Thought and Ireland since the Seventeenth Century* (London, 1993), 124.

[28] Close was Conservative MP for Armagh, 1857–64 and 1874–85, and owned 12,765 acres (valued at £13,441).

[29] Mulholland was Conservative MP for Downpatrick, 1874–85, and owned 14,688 acres (valued at £19,424).

[30] Castlereagh was Conservative MP for Down, 1878–84 and Wallace was Conservative MP for Lisburn, 1873–84.

[31] *Belfast Newsletter*, 4 Dec. 1914. Crichton was Conservative MP for Enniskillen, 1868–80, and Fermanagh, 1880–5.

[32] *Irish Times*, 14 Mar. 1903. William Archdale was Conservative MP for Fermanagh, 1874–85. Edward Mervyn Archdale was Unionist MP for north Fermanagh, 1898–1903 and 1916–22.

[33] *Belfast Newsletter*, 3 Aug. 1889. Ewart was Conservative MP for Belfast, 1878–89.

world, and who left £55,499 in his will when he died in November 1891.[34] And James Chaine was a director of the Larne and Stranraer Boat Co. who was responsible for building Larne port and harbour, and who left £62,681 when he died in May 1885.[35] The Conservative Party—as well as being the party of traditional landed wealth—was also, to a certain extent, the party of new big businesses in the early 1880s. By 1881, the old landed elite were already beginning to join with the new business elite to form a new upper class although the landlords still had the upper hand in this alliance at that point.

Members of the professions—and especially lawyers and army officers—constituted half of the Conservative MPs in 1881. Many of these came from landed families. Sir Henry Hervey Bruce was an officer in the 1st Life Guards before succeeding to the family estate in Derry.[36] Similarly, a number of the Conservative lawyers came from landed families. Edward MacNaghten for example, was a barrister, and the second (and non-inheriting) son of Sir Edmund C. Workman-MacNaghten who owned substantial estates in Antrim, Armagh, and Derry.[37] However, it is possible that most of the solicitors and barristers who became MPs did so in the hope of benefiting from government patronage, since the senior Irish law officers were usually recruited from their ranks. David Robert Plunket became Solicitor General for Ireland (1875–7), and Paymaster General in 1880, before ascending to the top of the Irish Civil Service where he served as commissioner of public works, 1885–92.[38] Similarly, Edward Gibson became Attorney General for Ireland, 1877–80, and Lord Chancellor of Ireland with a seat in cabinet (1885–6, 1886–92, and 1895–1906).[39] In part, the high proportion of lawyers was probably also necessitated by the highly technical nature of land legislation in the last quarter of the nineteenth century that required legal men both to understand and to amend it. In addition, lawyers were effective public speakers and tended to frequent the same social circles as the Irish political elite in London and Dublin, making them accessible to the recruiting mechanisms of all the Irish political parties. There are also some similarities between the legal profession and politics in that both involve public speaking, performance, and the ability to represent the views of either a client or a constituency, and this might explain why 'almost everywhere lawyers are politically prominent'.[40]

The vast majority of the Irish Conservative MPs received both their secondary and university educations in England. Half of them (twelve or 50 per cent)

[34] Corry was Conservative MP for Belfast, 1874–85.
[35] Chaine was Conservative MP for Antrim, 1874–85.
[36] *Belfast Newsletter*, 9 Dec. 1907. Bruce was Conservative MP for Coleraine, 1862–74, and 1880–5, and owned 20,801 acres (valued at £11,397).
[37] MacNaghten was Conservative MP for Antrim, 1880–7 and his family owned 8,281 acres (valued at £8,937).   [38] Plunket was Conservative MP for Dublin University, 1870–95.
[39] Gibson was Conservative MP for Dublin University, 1875–85.
[40] Robert D. Putnam, *The Comparative Study of Political Elites* (New Jersey, 1976), 59.

had received a secondary education, with most (eight or 67 per cent) attending Eton. A further quarter attended English Protestant schools. Only one of the Irish Conservatives attended an Irish Protestant School: Sir William Ewart was a former pupil of Belfast Academy. Slightly more than one-half (thirteen or 54 per cent) of the Irish Conservatives had received a university education, with the vast majority of these (nine or 69 per cent) attending Oxford or Cambridge. As with the Irish landlord class, the most popular colleges were Christ Church, Oxford and Trinity College, Cambridge. One of the Irish Conservatives had studied at the universities of Bonn and Munich in Germany.[41] Only one-quarter of the Irish Conservatives in 1881 received their university education in Ireland, with just three (or 23 per cent) of those who had received a third-level education attending Trinity College Dublin.

The Irish Conservative MPs were also fully integrated into London clubland. All of the Tory MPs in 1881 were the members of at least one club in London, Dublin, or Belfast, while many of them held simultaneous membership of a number of clubs. Three of the Irish Conservatives in 1881, for instance, were the members of seven clubs at the same time.[42] Most popular was the Carlton Club in London: twenty-one (or 88 per cent) of them held memberships of this club which provided a forum for Irish Conservatives to meet with their English colleagues. The Athenæum, the Travellers, and St Stephens were also popular haunts of the Irish Conservatives in London. In Dublin, almost half of the Tories were members of the Kildare Street Club, where they could meet other members of the Irish landlord class, as well as the senior administrators of Dublin Castle. The ultra-Protestant Sackville Street Club was also popular with almost one-third (seven or 29 per cent) of the Conservative MPs. A significant minority (three or 13 per cent) were members of the Ulster Club in Belfast, reflecting the Northern origins of some of the Conservative MPs. However, the Irish Conservative Party—unlike its successor, the Irish Unionist Party—was very much an all-Ireland party, rather than a party rooted in Ulster society.

Despite their great wealth, some of the Conservative MPs appear to have maintained links with the Protestant working class and small tenant farmer class, particularly in Ulster. Even after the democratization of local government in 1898, a number of Conservative landowner-MPs served on the newly created county councils. Sir Henry Hervey Bruce was the chairman of Derry county council, 1899–1902; and Viscount Crichton (who became the 4th Earl of Erne in 1885) was the chairman of Fermanagh county council over the same period. In part, membership of the Orange order may have cemented links between the

---

[41] This was John William Ellison Macartney, MP for Tyrone, 1874–85.
[42] These were Viscount Castlereagh (Conservative MP for Down, 1878–84); David Plunket (Conservative MP for Dublin University, 1870–95); and Thomas Taylor (Conservative MP for county Dublin, 1841–83).

elite of the Conservative party, and the less well-to-do Protestant community. In fact, the Earl of Erne succeeded his father-in-law, the Earl of Enniskillen, as the Imperial Grand Master of the Orange Order in 1885; Bruce was the Grand Master of the Orangemen of Derry; and when John William Ellison Macartney died in 1904, the local Orange Lodge sent a wreath to his funeral.[43] But the Conservative MPs—and particularly those representing big business—were also prominently involved in local 'good works' that may have consolidated their links with the Protestant working class. Corry—an elder of the Presbyterian church—was instrumental in the building of Elmwood Church in Belfast, and contributed funds to the Belfast Town Mission; the Belfast Sailor's Home; Malone Protestant Reformatory; Belfast Royal Hospital; and the Association for the employment of the industrious blind.[44] Similarly, William Ewart built 500 houses next to his mills for his employees, and he also assisted in the building of schools (notably the National School on the Crumlin Road where two of his mills were located). Apparently, Ewart believed that education would improve the relations between capital and labour, and his longevity on Belfast Corporation (to which he was connected for twenty-eight years) suggests that this may have been more than empty rhetoric.

The Irish Liberal party was a much more amorphous political organization than the Conservative party. A number of diverse sections of Irish society support-ed the Liberal Party and became its representatives including a small proportion of the landlord class (and especially Catholic landowners); businessmen who were attracted by the party's 'free trade' policy; Presbyterians and Dissenters who were alienated by the Episcopalianism and pro-landlord policies of the Conservative party; and some sections of the Catholic middle class and particularly barristers who hoped to gain position from the patronage of the wider British Liberal party. Indeed, the Liberal Party was effectively the party for Catholics in Ireland before the formation of the Home Rule party in 1874.[45] Unlike the Conservative Party, the Liberals did not have an extensive organization throughout Ireland and instead relied on patronage from Liberal governments for survival.[46] This meant that the number of MPs elected in Ireland was erratic, and that the high water mark of Liberalism in Ireland coincided with the election of Liberal governments in the mid-nineteenth century. In 1859, the Liberals won fifty seats, and in 1868, sixty-six seats.[47] However, by the early 1880s, they were in a steep decline owing to the emergence of the Home Rule movement which won the support of Catholic landowners and farmers who had formerly voted Liberal. The sixteen Liberal MPs in 1881 were mostly based in Ulster because the Home

---

[43] *Belfast Newsletter*, 17 Feb. 1904.   [44] *Belfast Newsletter*, 30 Nov. 1891.

[45] Although a recent book is concerned with identifying a strand of 'popular liberalism' in Irish politics between 1876 and 1906, the Irish Liberal Party and its provincial support bases are surprisingly not discussed. See Eugenio Biagini, *British Democracy and Irish Nationalism, 1876–1906* (Cambridge, 2007).   [46] Hoppen, *Elections*, 277, 258.

[47] Ibid. 273.

Table 4.1. The Occupational Breakdown of the Members of Irish Political Parties, 1881–1911

Occupation	Conservative	Liberal	Home Rule 1881	Home Rule 1911	Unionist
Business	4 (17%)	7 (44%)	13 (21%)	18 (22%)	6 (30%)
Landowner	15 (63%)	3 (19%)	17 (28%)	5 (6%)	2 (10%)
Landed family	6 (25%)	5 (31%)	13 (21%)	4 (5%)	3 (15%)
Farmer	—	—	2 (3%)	7 (9%)	—
Shop-grazier	—	—	—	8 (10%)	—
Labourer	—	—	—	—	—
Artisan	—	—	—	5 (6%)	—
Clerk	—	—	—	—	—
Professional	12 (50%)	9 (56%)	42 (69%)	44 (54%)	14 (70%)
Number	24	16	61	82	20
Of professionals					
Journalist	—	—	10 (16%)	14 (17%)	1 (5%)
Lawyer	6 (25%)	5 (31%)	22 (36%)	19 (23%)	10 (50%)
Army officer	6 (25%)	—	5 (8%)	2 (2.5%)	3 (15%)
Reverend		2 (13%)	1 (2%)	—	—
Engineer	—	—	1 (2%)	2 (2.5%)	—
Surveyor	—	—	1 (2%)	—	—
Doctor	—	1 (6%)	1 (2%)	4 (5%)	—
Civil servant	—	1 (6%)	1 (2%)	—	—
Academic	—	—	—	1 (1.3%)	—
Land agent	—	—	—	1 (1.3%)	—
Auctioneer	—	—	—	1 (1.3%)	—

Note: Some individuals have more than one occupation.

Table 4.2. The Religion of the Members of Irish Political Parties, 1881–1911

Religion	Conservative	Liberal	Home Rule 1881	Home Rule 1911	Unionist
Episcopalian	22 (92%)	6 (37.5%)	10 (16.5%)	6 (7%)	12 (60%)
Catholic	—	4 (25%)	50 (82%)	75 (90%)	—
Presbyterian	2 (8%)	5 (31.25%)	1 (1.5%)	1 (1.5%)	7 (35%)
Nonconformist	—	1 (6.25%)	—	1 (1.5%)	1 (5%)
'Don't know'	—	—	2*	—	—
No. (known)	24	16	61	83	20

Note: The two Home Rule MPs in 1881 whose religious affiliation I could not identify were Benjamin Whitworth (Liberal/Home Rule MP for Drogheda, 1865–9, Kilkenny City, 1875–80, and Drogheda, 1880–5) and Eugene Collins (Liberal/Home Rule MP for Kinsale, 1874–85).

Table 4.3. Acreage of Landed Members of Irish Political Parties, 1881–1911

Acreage	Conservative	Liberal	Home Rule 1881	Home Rule 1911	Unionist
0–499	1 (5%)	2 (25%)	4 (13.3%)	2 (22%)	1 (25%)
500–999	1 (5%)	—	7 (23.3%)	—	—
1,000–4,999	2 (9.5%)	2 (25%)	12 (40%)	5 (56%)	—
5,000–9,999	6 (28.5%)	2 (25%)	6 (20%)	2 (22%)	1 (25%)
10,000+	11 (52%)	2 (25%)	1 (3.3%)	—	2 (50%)
Number	21	8	30	9	4

Table 4.4. Club Membership of Irish MPs, 1881–1911

	Conservative	Liberal	Home Rule 1881	Home Rule 1911	Unionist
London					
Athæneum	3 (13%)	2 (15%)	—	—	—
Bachelors	—	—	1 (3%)	—	1 (5%)
Brooks	—	1 (8%)	2 (6%)	—	—
Carlton	21 (88%)	—	—	—	18 (95%)
Conservative	2 (8%)	—	—	—	—
Constitutional	1 (4%)	—	—	—	10 (53%)
Devonshire	—	3 (23%)	6 (17%)	2 (7%)	—
National	2 (8%)	—	—	—	—
National Lib	—	2 (15%)	8 (22%)	16 (59%)	—
Reform	—	12 (92%)	16 (44%)	3 (11%)	—
Royal Auto	—	—	—	5 (19%)	—
Royal Yacht	—	—	1 (3%)	—	—
St Stephens	4 (17%)	—	—	—	3 (16%)
Turf	2 (8%)	1 (8%)	—	1 (4%)	—
Travellers	3 (13%)	—	—	—	—
Dublin					
Catholic	—	—	1 (3%)	—	—
Friendly Bros	1 (4%)	—	—	—	2 (11%)
Kildare St	10 (42%)	3 (23%)	2 (6%)	1 (4%)	1 (5%)
Royal Yacht	1 (4%)	2 (15%)	—	2 (7%)	1 (5%)
Sackville St	7 (29%)	—	—	—	1 (5%)
Stephen's Grn	1 (4%)	4 (31%)	5 (14%)	5 (19%)	1 (5%)
University	2 (8%)	1 (8%)	1 (3%)	—	3 (16%)
Belfast					
Ulster	3 (13%)	1 (8%)	—	—	9 (47%)
Ulster Reform	—	3 (23%)	—	—	—
Union	—	1 (8%)	1 (3%)	—	4 (21%)
Royal Ulster Yacht	—	—	—	—	1 (5%)
Number	24	13	36	27	19
Percentage of party who were members					
of clubs	100%	81%	58%	33%	95%

Table 4.5. The Secondary Education of the Members of Irish Political Parties, 1881–1911

School	Conservative	Liberal	Home Rule 1881	Home Rule 1911	Unionist
British					
Public school	8 (67%)	—	2 (6%)	1 (2%)	7 (47%)
Catholic public school	—	1 (11%)	10 (28%)	6 (10%)	—
Protestant school	3 (25%)	—	—	—	1 (7%)
Catholic school	—	—	3 (8%)	1 (2%)	—
Irish					
Protestant school	1 (8%)	7 (78%)	2 (6%)	2 (3%)	7 (47%)
Catholic school	—	1 (11%)	23 (64%)	51 (86%)	—
Number	12	9	36	59	15

Note: Some MPs attended more than one secondary school.

Table 4.6. The Tertiary Education of the Members of Irish Political Parties, 1881–1911

University	Conservative	Liberal	Home Rule 1881	Home Rule 1911	Unionist
British					
Oxbridge	9 (69%)	2 (29%)	3 (12%)	4 (15%)	2 (20%)
Other	—	1 (14%)	5 (19%)	4 (15%)	1 (10%)
European	1 (8%)	1 (14%)	1 (4%)	3 (11%)	—
Australian	—	—	—	1 (4%)	—
Irish					
Trinity College Dublin	3 (23%)	3 (42%)	14 (54%)	6 (22%)	4 (40%)
Queen's Colleges of Ireland	—	1 (14%)	3 (12%)	5 (19%)	4 (40%)
University College Dublin	—	—	—	3 (11%)	—
Catholic University of Ireland	—	—	3 (12%)	2 (7%)	—
Royal University of Ireland	—	—	—	4 (15%)	—
Number	13	7	26	27	10

Note: Some individuals attended more than one university.

Rule movement had not yet established itself in the north-east of the country.[48] As the so-called Home Rule invasion of Ulster gathered pace—culminating with

[48] Although 7 of the 16 Liberal MPs represented constituencies outside Ulster: Stuart was MP for Waterford; Allman was MP for Bandon; Lyons was MP for Dublin city; J. J. Ennis was MP for Athlone; W. M. Johnson was MP for Mallow; Charles Russell was MP for Dundalk; and Sir Rowland Blennerhassett represented Galway city between 1865 and 1874 and one of the county

Table 4.7. The Age of the Members of Irish Political Parties in Ireland, 1881–1911

Age	Conservatives	Liberals	Home Rule 1881	Home Rule 1911	Unionists
0–19	—	—	—	—	—
20–9	1 (4%)	1 (6%)	2 (3%)	3 (4%)	—
30–9	3 (13%)	2 (13%)	21 (36%)	12 (15%)	3 (16%)
40–9	8 (33%)	6 (38%)	11 (19%)	20 (25%)	6 (31.5%)
50–9	5 (21%)	5 (31%)	21 (36%)	19 (23%)	4 (21%)
60–9	7 (29%)	1 (6%)	3 (5%)	23 (28%)	6 (31.5%)
70+	—	1 (6%)	1 (1%)	4 (5%)	—
Number	24	16	59	81	19

Tim Healy's victory in Monaghan in 1883—the last remaining support base for Irish liberalism was eroded; and at the 1885 general election the party ceased to exist.[49]

In 1881, the Liberal Party won support from a broad constituency. About one-third (six or 37.5 per cent) of the Liberal MPs were Episcopalian; slightly less than a third (five or 31.25 per cent) were Presbyterian; exactly one-quarter were Catholic; and one of the sixteen Liberal MPs was a Nonconformist. It is clear, therefore, that the Liberal Party was the party that was most popular with Presbyterians and Nonconformists in 1881 but that it also appealed to both Episcopalians and Catholics. Indeed, the Irish Liberal Party was the only party in this study that drew significant support from both the Catholic and the Protestant communities. In Ulster, the Liberals' support for land reform won support from both Catholic tenant farmers and Presbyterian tenant farmers. Some Presbyterian ministers were enthusiastic supporters of land reform and it was a Presbyterian minister, the Revd N. M. Brown of Limavady, who coined the term 'the three Fs' (meaning 'free sale, fair rent, and fixity of tenure') that encapsulated the aims of agrarian agitators in the 1870s and 1880s.[50] At its peak, then, the Liberal Party in Ireland was able to win the support of Protestant businessmen and professionals (some of whom were Presbyterians and Dissenters), Presbyterian tenant farmers, and Catholic professionals, some of whom stood to gain from the Liberal Party's patronage.[51]

The Liberal party included fewer MPs from landed backgrounds (three or 19 per cent were landowners themselves) than any of the other Irish parties in 1881. Those Liberal MPs that did come from landed backgrounds, tended

Kerry constituencies in the Liberal interest between 1880 and 1885. Most of the Liberal MPs outside Ulster represented urban constituencies.

[49] Hoppen, *Elections*, 271. Tim Healy was Home Rule MP for Wexford borough, 1880–3; Monaghan, 1883–5; south Derry, 1885–6; north Longford, 1887–92; north Louth, 1892–1910; and north east Cork, 1911–18.

[50] Graham Greenlee, 'Land, Religion and Community: The Liberal Party in Ulster, 1868–1885', in Eugenio Biagini (ed), *Citizenship and Community: Liberals, Radicals and Collective Identities in the British Isles, 1865–1931* (Cambridge, 1996), 254.   [51] Ibid. 274.

to be drawn from the lesser landed families: half of the landed Liberal MPs were from families that owned estates of less than 5,000 acres. In fact, the landowners who became Liberal MPs tended to be Catholics like Sir Rowland Blennerhassett who owned a substantial estate in county Kerry.[52] What is perhaps most striking about the Irish Liberal Party, however, is the high proportion of representatives from big business. Whereas there were only three representatives of big business among the Conservative MPs (Ewart, Corry, and Chaine, amounting to one in eight of the total), almost one-third (five or 31 per cent) of the Irish Liberal MPs were from substantial business backgrounds (some Liberal MPs owned smaller businesses too). James Dickson was a Presbyterian linen manufacturer at Dungannon; James Nicholson Richardson was a Quaker linen manufacturer who owned the Bessbrook Spinning Co.; Richard Lane Allman was the joint-owner of Allman and Co., distillery, and Allman, Dowden and Co., brewery; William Findlater was a member of Findlater and Co., brewers; and John Givan was a solicitor whose father was a prominent linen manufacturer at Castlecaulfield, county Tyrone.[53] The Liberal Party was, therefore, the party that was most representative of the members of the new business elite in Ulster in 1881, some of whom were Presbyterians and Nonconformists.

As with the other parties, over half (nine or 56 per cent) of the Liberal MPs were professionals with lawyers constituting almost one-third (31 per cent) of the total. The presence of lawyers need not surprise us, since these were simply those legal men who hoped to benefit from the patronage of Liberal (rather than Conservative) administrations. It was, however, the Catholic lawyers who joined the Liberal party in the hope that it might be beneficial to their future legal careers. Charles Russell, for example, was a Catholic barrister who was appointed as Attorney General for Ireland by Gladstone in 1886, and also by Morley in 1892–4.[54] The Liberal Party also appealed to more religious leaders than any of the other Irish parties between 1881 and 1911. The Revd John Kinnear, for instance, had been the Presbyterian minister at Letterkenny for thirty years before he became the member of parliament for Donegal.[55] And Henry Windsor Villiers Stuart had been the vicar of Napton-on-the-Hill, Warwickshire for almost twenty years before he was elected to the House of Commons.[56] There were also some medical doctors who became Liberal MPs. Robert Spencer Dyer Lyons, for instance, was a prominent physician who worked in the Richmond,

[52] Sir Rowland was Liberal MP for the borough of Galway, 1865–74, and Kerry, 1880–5, and owned 8,390 acres (valued at £2,145).

[53] James Dickson was Liberal MP for Dungannon, 1880–5; Richardson was Liberal MP for Armagh, 1880–5; Allman was Liberal MP for Bandon, 1880–5; Findlater was Liberal MP for Monaghan, 1880–5; and Givan was also Liberal MP for Monaghan, 1880–3.

[54] Russell was Liberal MP for Dundalk, 1880–5, and south Hackney, 1885–94.

[55] Kinnear was Liberal MP for Donegal, 1880–5.

[56] Stuart gave up Holy Orders in 1871 before his election to the House of Commons. He was Liberal MP for Cappoquin, county Waterford, 1873–85.

Whitworth, and Hardwick hospitals in Dublin, was a Fellow of the Royal College of Surgeons, and wrote influential medical reports.[57]

The vast majority of the Irish Liberal MPs who had received a secondary education, did so in Ireland. Slightly more than half (nine or 56 per cent) of them had attended a secondary school, while only one was educated in England (at Stoneyhurst).[58] Indeed, most of the Liberal MPs attended secondary school in Ulster, reflecting the Northern roots of Irish liberalism in the early 1880s. Three MPs were graduates of the Royal Belfast Academical Institution, and two others were former students at the Royal School, Dungannon. Charles Russell, the Catholic Liberal barrister, however, had gained his secondary education at Castleknock. Less than half of the Liberal MPs in 1881 (seven or 44 per cent) had gained a university education. Unlike the Irish Conservatives, more than half of the Liberal MPs (four or 57 per cent), who had received a third-level education, attended Irish universities. Trinity College Dublin was most popular, while one of the Liberal MPs gained his degree from The Queen's College, Belfast.[59] Two of the Liberal MPs—both of whom were from substantial landed backgrounds—attended Oxford. Sir John James Ennis attended Christ Church, as did Sir Rowland Blennerhassett. Blennerhassett also studied at the universities of Louvain, Munich, and Berlin.[60]

Like their Tory counterparts, most of the Irish Liberal MPs (thirteen or 81 per cent) were the members of at least one club in London, Dublin, or Belfast. Most of the Irish Liberals were the members of Liberal clubs in London: twelve (92 per cent) were members of the Reform Club; two (15 per cent) were members of the National Liberal; two (23 per cent) were members of the Devonshire; and one (8 per cent) was a member of Brooks's. These clubs provided a forum for Irish Liberals to associate with their British colleagues. But the Irish Liberals also socialized in some of the same clubs as the Irish Conservatives: two (15 per cent) were members of the Athenæum, and one (8 per cent) was a member of the Turf. In Dublin, almost one-quarter of the Irish Liberals (three or 23 per cent) were members of the Kildare Street Club, where they could mix with Irish Tories, landlords, and senior civil servants. Almost one-third (four or 31 per cent) of the Irish Liberals were also members of the Stephen's Green Club in Dublin, which was popular with Irish Home Rulers. A significant proportion of the Irish Liberals frequented Belfast clubland: three (or 23 per cent) were members of the Ulster Reform Club, while one (8 per cent) was a member of the Union, and another was a member of the Ulster Club. Broadly speaking, the range of clubs to which the Irish Liberals belonged suggests the diverse range of support that the party attracted. The Irish Liberal Party included orthodox Liberals, Irish

---

[57] Lyons was Liberal MP for Dublin city, 1880–5.

[58] This was Sir Rowland Blennerhassett.

[59] This was Andrew Marshall Porter, Liberal MP for Derry, 1881–3.

[60] Ennis was Liberal MP for Athlone, 1868–74 and 1880–4, and owned 10,935 acres (valued at £7,403).

Home Rulers, and Irish Liberal Unionists, and so the Party members socialized in a range of different social milieu. It should also be emphasized that by the early 1880s, the Irish Liberal party was largely an Ulster phenomenon.

The third main party in Ireland in 1881 was the Irish Parliamentary Party (or Home Rule party). Broadly speaking, the party stood for a limited form of political independence within the British Empire, and represented moderate, constitutional nationalism in Ireland between 1874 and 1918. The Home Government Association was first established at Bilton's Hotel in Dublin on 19 May 1870 by the Donegal-born Protestant barrister, Isaac Butt.[61] This was then superseded by the Home Rule League, founded at the Rotunda in Dublin in November 1873. A number of Home Rulers won by-elections from 1871 onwards and, following the general election of February 1874, there were fifty-nine Home Rule supporters (some of whom were nominal) in the House of Commons. During the first nine years of its existence—from its foundation to the death of Butt in 1879—the Home Rule movement stood for the establishment of an Irish parliament which would have domestic autonomy within a federated United Kingdom.

Following Butt's death, Charles Stewart Parnell, the Wicklow Church of Ireland landowner, was elected chairman of the Irish Parliamentary Party in May 1880, and he presided over the development of the National League (that replaced the proclaimed Land League in 1882) as the IPP's constituency organization in the Irish countryside. By the mid-1880s, the National League had established itself in every Irish parish, had a mass membership, and played its part in returning the eighty-six MPs that were committed to Home Rule for Ireland at the December 1885 general election.[62] Parnell's conception of Home Rule was similar to that of Butt and envisaged an Irish parliament that controlled domestic matters but which remained subordinate to the British House of Commons. Parnell was also concerned that Protestants and landowners would play a part in the projected new Home Rule Ireland and—to this end—he was also elected president of the Irish National Land League founded in Dublin on 21 October 1879. The paradox of a landowner supporting an organization that was committed to the destruction of landlordism can be explained by the fact that Parnell envisaged an Ireland where Protestant landowners sold their land to their tenants—thereby removing the main cause of conflict between landlord and tenant (and indeed Protestant and Catholic)—so that they could then take a leading role among the leadership of nationalist Ireland. Parnell's support for land reform had the added bonus of fusing together the land and national struggles so that the mass support for land reform evident at the early

[61] Butt was MP for Youghal, 1852–65, and Home Rule MP for Limerick, 1871–9.
[62] For the best study of the National League, see Stephen Ball, 'Policing the Land War: Official Responses to Political Protest and Agrarian Crime in Ireland, 1879–91', PhD thesis (University of London, 2000).

Land League meetings in county Mayo in 1879 could be mobilized behind the Home Rule movement. Consequently, between 1879 and 1885, the campaign for Home Rule was converted from an essentially Dublin-based political party into a nationwide mass movement.[63]

The pro-Home Rule MPs who held seats in 1881 were overwhelmingly Catholic (fifty or 82 per cent), although there was a minority of Episcopalians (ten or 16.5 per cent) and one Presbyterian (1.5 per cent). As we have seen, the leader of the Irish Parliamentary Party in 1881 was Charles Stewart Parnell. Indeed, almost half of the Home Rule MPs were either landowners (seventeen or 28 per cent) or closely related to landowners (thirteen or 21 per cent). Most of these (76.6 per cent) came from comparatively small landed families who owned less than 5,000 acres, with only about one-quarter (seven or 23.3 per cent) of the landed Home Rule MPs owning more than 5,000 acres (and just one or 3.3 per cent owning an estate of more than 10,000 acres). The vast majority of these were members of the Catholic landowning class that, as we have seen, were extremely influential among the administrative elite. Some of these had been Conservatives who defected to Butt's Home Rule party in the 1870s. Sir Joseph Neale McKenna, for instance, was a Catholic landlord who had actually defeated Butt at Youghal in 1865 before joining his party.[64] Others were former Liberal MPs who converted to Home Rule, some of whom had even been members of O'Connell's Catholic Association.[65] James Patrick O'Gorman Mahon, for example, had played a part in O'Connell's election campaign in Clare in 1828; and was a grandson of The O'Gorman, who owned an estate in county Clare.[66]

Indeed, the members of the Catholic landowning class appear to have regarded themselves as the natural leaders of the Catholic community in Ireland. The O'Donoghue was the head of one of the few old Celtic houses that had survived the penal laws and owned a substantial estate in county Kerry.[67] Similarly, Denis Maurice O'Conor was the son of The O'Conor Don, and owned land himself.[68] Other Home Rule MPs were from landowning families, rather than being landowners themselves. John Redmond was the grandson of Patrick Walter Redmond, who owned an estate in county Wexford.[69] Redmond's father, William Archer, was Patrick's second son and did not inherit the family estate,

[63] On the gestation of Home Rule, see Jackson, *Home Rule: An Irish History, 1800–2000* (London, 2003), Chs. 2, 3, and 4.

[64] McKenna was Home Rule MP for Youghal, 1865–8, 1874–85, and south Monaghan, 1885–92 and his nephew was Sir Reginald McKenna. See Martin Farr, *Reginald McKenna: Financier among Statesmen* (London, 2007). McKenna owned 1,581 acres (valued at £504).

[65] The Catholic Association was established in May 1824 to campaign for Catholic emancipation.

[66] Mahon was Liberal MP for Clare, 1830–1 and Ennis, 1847–52, and Home Rule MP for Clare, 1879–85 and Carlow, 1887–91. The O'Gormans owned 863 acres (valued at £275).

[67] O'Donoghue was Liberal/Home Rule MP for Tipperary, 1857–65 and Tralee, 1865–85, and owned 9,463 acres (valued at £868).

[68] O'Conor was Liberal/Home Rule MP for Sligo, 1868–83, and owned 2,010 acres (valued at £1,583). The O'Conor Don was Liberal MP for Roscommon, 1831–47, and owned a 12,650 acre estate in 1876.   [69] Patrick Walter Redmond owned 2,026 acres (valued at £1,313).

instead becoming a civil servant and later an MP (Liberal for the borough of Wexford, 1872–80).[70]

Many of the professionals who were Home Rule MPs were also the members of Catholic landlord families. Patrick Leopold Martin, for instance, was a barrister whose father-in-law, Michael Cahill, owned land in Kilkenny.[71] John Aloysius Blake was a senior civil servant (he was the Inspector of Fisheries for ten years) and the son of Andrew Blake of Waterford, who owned a small amount of land in county Kilkenny.[72] Charles Henry Meldon was a barrister, and the 3rd (and non inheriting) son of James Dillon Meldon, who owned a substantial estate.[73] A number of Catholic landowners were also officers in the army. Colonel Francis O'Beirne was a Captain in the 2nd Dragoon Guards who served in the Oude campaign of 1858–9, before inheriting the family estate in county Leitrim.[74]

The Home Rule MPs of 1881 were—by and large—loyal to the British state in Ireland, and this was expressed in their tendency to serve in the British army. At least five (or 8 per cent) of them had served as officers in the British army, and many of them were drawn from families that had a tradition of service in the British army. The Redmond family, for instance, exemplify this tendency. Patrick Walter Redmond owned an estate—as we have seen—in Wexford. His eldest son, Lieutenant General John Patrick Sutton Redmond (who was born in 1824) became an officer in the 61st Foot before he inherited the family estate. The second son, William Archer Redmond, completed a degree at Trinity College Dublin (in 1847) and then joined the Irish Civil Service, before becoming Liberal MP. William's eldest son, John, attended Clongowes and Trinity College Dublin, became Home Rule MP for New Ross (in 1881), and was called to the English and Irish bars (in 1886 and 1887). And John's younger brother, Major William Hoey Kearney Redmond, who was also educated at Clongowes and Trinity College Dublin, became Home Rule MP for north Wexford in 1883, and an officer in the Royal Irish Regiment—killed in action in the Great War in 1917. Then John's son, Captain William Archer Redmond, also became an MP (after being educated at Clongowes and Trinity College Dublin) and served as an officer in the Irish Guards during the Great War. In this respect, the social

---

[70] John Redmond eventually inherited the family estate from his uncle, Lieutenant General John Patrick Sutton Redmond; and it was alleged that he charged too high a price when he sold the estate to the tenants (Patrick Maume, *The Long Gestation: Irish Nationalist Life, 1891–1918* (Dublin, 1999), 69; Paul Bew, *John Redmond* (Dundalk, 1996)).

[71] Martin rose to a high position in his profession (he was a QC) and left £56,532 in his will. He was Home Rule MP for Kilkenny, 1874–85. Cahill owned 2,249 acres (valued at £1,480).

[72] Blake was Liberal/Home Rule MP for Waterford City, 1857–69, county Waterford, 1880–84, and county Carlow, 1886–7. Andrew Blake owned 389 acres (valued at £331).

[73] Meldon was Liberal/Home Rule MP for Kildare, 1847–85. James Dillon Meldon owned 7,677 acres (valued at £7,743).

[74] O'Beirne was Home Rule MP for Leitrim, 1876–85, and owned 7,910 acres (valued at £3,421).

background of the Catholics in the Home Rule party in 1881 was similar to that of the Irish-born Catholics in the Irish Civil Service and the officer class of the Royal Irish Constabulary in the 1880s and the 1890s.

As with the other parties, the majority of the Home Rule MPs in 1881 (forty-two or 69 per cent) was drawn from the professions, and particularly the legal profession (twenty-two or 36 per cent of the total). Lawyers were essential to the Home Rule party since they could understand the intricate technical details of the land legislation passed by the British government after 1870. But these legal men—like their colleagues in the Conservative and Liberal parties—may have viewed their involvement in politics as a route to upward social mobility. Although there was less patronage available for Home Rule lawyers than there was for the lawyers in other parties, some of them did benefit from their political involvement. Patrick Leopold Martin was a barrister whose political career may have influenced his appointment as QC in 1877, and helped him to establish a lucrative private practice. Similarly, Arthur O'Connor was a barrister who became QC in 1899, and a county court Judge for Durham in 1900–11, and for Dorset, 1911–20.[75] He was regarded as one of the 'ablest' Irish members in the House, and chaired a commission of inquiry into industrial unrest in 1917. Charles Henry Meldon was called to the Irish bar in 1863, and appointed QC in 1877.[76] Tim Healy was called to the Irish bar in 1884, appointed QC in 1899, and a bencher of King's Inns in 1905.[77] Rowland Ponsonby Blennerhassett became QC in 1894, and a bencher in 1903.[78] Some of the lawyer-Home Rulers in 1881 were also appointed to senior positions in the Irish Civil Service. Richard O'Shaughnessy was called to the Irish bar in 1866, and later appointed as the Registrar of Petty Sessions clerks in 1883, and as a commissioner of public works, 1891–1903.[79] A stint in Home Rule politics might not be as advantageous to a legal career as a spell in Conservative (and later Unionist) politics, but there were clear advantages to be gained by the lawyer-Home Rule MPs in 1881.

However, it is clear that some of the Home Rule barrister-MPs were elected to parliament before they became barristers. Indeed, altogether nine Home Rule MPs became students at the King's Inns following their election to Westminster: A. M. Sullivan, Tim Healy, Edmund Leamy, Timothy Harrington, J. J. Clancy, John Deasy, M. J. Kenny, John Redmond, and William Redmond.[80] Perhaps

---

[75] O'Connor was Home Rule MP for Queen's county, 1880–5 and east Donegal, 1885–1900.

[76] Meldon was Liberal/Home Rule MP for Kildare, 1847–85.

[77] Healy was one of the few Irish MPs, 1881–1911, to hold an influential position after the Irish Revolution (1916–23): he was Governor General of the Irish Free State, 1922–8.

[78] Ponsonby Blennerhassett was Home Rule MP for Kerry, 1872–85.

[79] O'Shaughnessy was Liberal/Home Rule MP for Limerick city, 1874–83.

[80] Kenneth Ferguson, *King's Inns Barristers, 1868–2004* (Dublin, 2005), 71. A. M. Sullivan was Home Rule MP for Louth, 1874–80, and Meath, 1880–2; Edmund Leamy was Home Rule MP for Waterford city, 1880–5, north east Cork, 1885–7, south Sligo, 1888–92, and north Kildare, 1900–4; Timothy Harrington was Home Rule MP for Westmeath, 1883–5, and the harbour division of Dublin, 1885–1910; John Deasy was Home Rule MP for Cork city, 1884–5,

these individuals felt that their successful political careers might enhance their chance of becoming successful barristers in either London or Dublin. There were also some medical doctors in the Irish Parliamentary Party. John Dillon, for instance, had a medical degree although he did not practise medicine. Indeed it is striking, given the extensive involvement of doctors in later twentieth-century Irish politics, that so few MPs between 1881 and 1911 were drawn from the medical profession. Perhaps the fact that a political career would not enhance the career prospects of an ambitious young doctor explains the lack of medic-politicians during this period. It was also possible to practise law on a part-time basis whereas medical practice required a more permanent commitment of time.

A number of Home Rule MPs in 1881 were journalists and newspaper proprietors. As with lawyers, journalists were often articulate public speakers who moved in the same circles as the leaders of the political parties in London, Dublin, and Belfast, making them likely recruits to the world of politics. There may also be some examples of newspaper proprietors using politics as a route to upward social mobility. Earl Spencer, for instance, regarded Edmund Dwyer Gray—who owned the *Freeman's Journal* and the Belfast *Morning News*—as over-egging his commitment to nationalist politics in order to make greater profits from his newspapers:

Gray is a man who plays a grave & most false game for he does not at heart believe in the policy of the Extreme men in Irish politics, & yet he is always pandering & Flattering their policy & themselves. His sole object is to make his paper pay. I confess that I have the lowest possible opinion of him.[81]

However, it is more likely that journalists and newspaper proprietors were recruited by the various political parties in order to secure the control of influential and opinion-forming newspapers. Some of the Home Rule MPs in 1881 were journalists of international stature: James Joseph O'Kelly worked for both the *New York Herald* and the *London Daily News*. And O'Kelly's brother, Aloysius, was an artist and illustrator who was responsible for many of the drawings of events during the Irish Land War that were published in the *Illustrated London News*.[82]

Alvin Jackson has suggested that the Irish Parliamentary Party—with one or two exceptions—was unable to attract the support of big business.[83] Similarly, Paul Bew claims that individuals with substantial business interests did not

and west Mayo, 1885–93; Matthew Joseph Kenny was Home Rule MP for Ennis, 1882–5, and mid-Tyrone, 1885–95; William Archer Redmond was Home Rule MP for east Tyrone, 1910–18, and Waterford city, 1918–22.

[81] Spencer to Gladstone, 25 Aug. 1882, quot. O'Day, *English Face of Irish Nationalism*, 46. Gray was Home Rule MP for Tipperary, 1877–80, Carlow, 1880–5, and the St Stephen's Green division of Dublin, 1885–8.

[82] J. J. O'Kelly was Home Rule MP for Roscommon, 1880–5, north Roscommon, 1885–92 and 1895–1916. See Niamh O'Sullivan, *Aloysius O'Kelly: Reorientations: Painting, Politics and Popular Culture* (Dublin, 1999). [83] Jackson, *Ulster Party*, 68.

become Home Rule MPs because they were 'anti-home rule or at any rate lukewarm about it'.[84] However, the Irish Parliamentary Party in 1881 did include a significant number of businessmen. To be sure, many of the businessmen in the Irish Parliamentary Party in the 1880s were small provincial shopkeepers like the Kilmallock merchant, William Henry O'Sullivan, and the Cork merchant, John Daly.[85] In 1881, however, a number of prominent businessmen *were* members of the Irish Parliamentary Party. John Francis Smithwick was a member of the prominent brewing family.[86] Joseph Gillis Biggar was a Belfast Presbyterian provisions merchant with an annual income of £4,000 who amassed a small fortune, leaving £37,341 in his will in 1890.[87] According to T. P. O'Connor, Biggar 'had the reputation of a millionaire; as a matter of fact he left something like £30,000—and that was enough to make a man among the members of the Irish Party a millionaire'.[88] Similarly, Henry Joseph Gill was 'a wealthy publisher' and bookseller in Dublin.[89] Donald Horne MacFarlane was a Scottish-born East India merchant and William Shaw was the Chairman of the Munster Bank who—admittedly—declared himself bankrupt in January 1886.[90] Mitchell Henry was a partner in the cotton trading firm of A. and S. Henry and Co. of Manchester (with branches in Bradford, Belfast, Leeds, Huddersfield, Glasgow and family connections to cotton manufacturers in Philadelphia) before he bought Kylemore Castle and a large estate in Connemara, apparently because he was attracted by the good angling in the locality.[91] His father was 'a great Manchester merchant and manufacturer' and Henry was reputed to be 'an immensely wealthy man' who had invented Henry's Fluid Magnesia.[92] John Orrell Lever—described by T. P. O'Connor as 'a grotesque and almost incredible candidate for an Irish seat'—owned the Atlantic Royal Mail Steam Navigation Co., known as the 'Lever Line'.[93] And John Barry owned the

[84] Paul Bew, *Ideology and the Irish Question: Ulster Unionism and Irish Nationalism, 1912–1916* (Oxford, 1994), 10. Jackson's and Bew's comments on the lack of businessmen in the IPP are made about the Party during the third Home Rule crisis of 1912–14, but I will consider their applicability to the Home Rule MPs in both 1881 and 1911.

[85] O'Sullivan was Home Rule MP for Limerick, 1874–85 and Daly was Home Rule MP for Cork city, 1880–4. O'Sullivan left £3,830 in his will.

[86] Smithwick was Home Rule MP for Kilkenny city, 1880–6.

[87] *Freeman's Journal*, 20 Feb. 1890. Biggar was Home Rule MP for Cavan, 1874–90.

[88] O'Connor, *Memoirs of an Old Parliamentarian*, ii. 60.

[89] O'Day, *English Face of Irish Nationalism*, 20. Gill was Home Rule MP for Westmeath, 1880–3, and Limerick, 1885–8.

[90] Shaw's obituary declared that he was 'a conspicuous failure in public and commercial life' (*Freeman's Journal*, 21 Sept. 1895). MacFarlane was Home Rule MP for Carlow, 1880–5 and Shaw was Liberal/Home Rule MP for Bandon, 1868–74 and Cork, 1874–85.

[91] Henry became a Liberal Unionist in 1886, served as Liberal/Home Rule MP for Galway, 1871–85, and owned an estate of 9,252 acres (Tim Robinson, *Connemara: The Last Pool of Darkness* (Dublin, 2008), 77).

[92] O'Malley, *Glancing Back*, 285. For Henry's obituary, see *Irish Times*, 23 Nov. 1910.

[93] Lever was Liberal/Home Rule MP for the town of Galway, 1859–65 and 1880–5 (O'Connor, *Memoirs of an Old Parliamentarian*, i. 38).

linoleum company of Barry, Ostleve, and Co., reported to be the largest company of its kind.[94]

Some of the Home Rule MPs who were newspaper proprietors were also extremely wealthy. Edmund Dwyer Gray owned the *Freeman's Journal* and the Belfast *Morning News*, and left £89, 611 in his will when he died in March 1888. And Thomas Sexton was also a former chairman of the *Freeman's Journal* who became the chairman of Boland's Mills after he retired from the press, and left £23,371 when he died in November 1932.[95] Jackson, therefore, is surely wrong to suggest that: 'the Nationalist Party failed singularly to attract big business into its ranks... The feebleness of the party's business lobby deprived it of prestige and wealth, and weakened its claim to embrace all sections of Irish society.'[96] There may have been no linen barons in the Irish Parliamentary Party, but some of the Home Rule MPs in 1881 had amassed considerable wealth from their manufacturing and entrepreneurial endeavours.

More than half (thirty-six or 58 per cent) of the Irish Home Rulers had received some form of secondary education. In most cases, this education was in Ireland rather than in other parts of the United Kingdom. However, a significant minority of Home Rule MPs had been educated in England. In particular, some of those Home Rulers from Catholic landowning families attended English Catholic Public Schools, including Stoneyhurst, Downside, and Oscott: ten (or 28 per cent) of the Home Rulers in 1881 had attended one of these schools. Two of the Irish Home Rulers (who were from landed backgrounds) had even attended the Clarendon schools: Sir Alan Henry Bellingham was an old Harrovian and Colonel David La Touche Colthurst was an old Etonian.[97] The vast majority (twenty-three or 64 per cent) of the Irish Home Rulers had attended Irish Catholic schools. More than one-fifth (eight or 22 per cent) had attended Clongowes, while two others attended St Vincent's College, Castleknock. The remainder were graduates of the provincial diocesan colleges, and two had gained their education from the Christian Brothers' schools.[98] In addition, two of the Home Rulers attended Irish Protestant schools: Joseph Gillis Biggar attended Belfast Academy, and James Carlisle McCoan had attended Dungannon School.[99] The diverse educational experience of the Irish Home Rulers in 1881 suggests the diverse membership of the party that included prosperous Catholic landowners, provincial shopkeepers and farmers, and a handful of Protestants merchants and intellectuals.

[94] See 'John Barry' by Daniel Crilly in the *Weekly National Press*, 19 Sept. 1891. Barry was Home Rule MP for Wexford, 1880–93.

[95] Sexton was Home Rule MP for Sligo, 1880–6, west Belfast and north Kerry, 1892–6.

[96] Jackson, *Ulster Party*, 68.

[97] Bellingham was Home Rule MP for Louth, 1880–5 and Colthurst was Home Rule MP for Cork, 1879–85.

[98] The diocesan colleges included St Jarlath's of Tuam; St John's, Waterford; and St Patrick's, Carlow.   [99] McCoan was Home Rule MP for Wicklow, 1880–5.

Less than half of the Irish Home Rulers in 1881 (twenty-six or 42 per cent) had attended university. In most cases, they gained their degrees from Irish universities. More than half of these (fourteen or 54 per cent) had attended Trinity College Dublin—despite the fact that a significant number of them were Catholic—and this reflects the presence of loyal landed and professional Catholics in the early Home Rule movement. However, the 'new' universities were also significant providers of Home Rule MPs: three (or 12 per cent), including John Dillon, had attended the Catholic University; and a further three (or 12 per cent) had attended The Queen's Colleges, one each at Belfast, Cork, and Galway. A significant minority of the Home Rulers (almost one-third) received their university education in England. Three of them, including Charles Stewart Parnell (and all drawn from landed backgrounds), had attended Oxbridge; and five others (19 per cent) were graduates of the University of London. Denis Maurice O'Conor, for instance, completed a law degree there before practising as a barrister in London, as did Edward Purcell Mulhallen Marum and Andrew Commins.[100] The University of London was clearly regarded by these Home Rulers as a stepping stone to a successful legal career in the metropolis.

The Irish Home Rulers in 1881 were much less likely to be the members of London or Dublin clubland than their contemporaries in the Irish Conservative and Liberal parties. Whereas all of the Irish Tories were members of at least one club, as were the vast majority (thirteen or 81 per cent) of the Irish Liberals, only slightly more than half (thirty-six or 58 per cent) of the Home Rulers were the members of clubs. Certainly, the Irish Home Rulers were not as clubbable as their more 'establishment' colleagues in the Conservative and Liberal parties but they were hardly socially isolated either. Through his wife, Bessie, T. P. O'Connor 'became a figure in the social life of the time' and John Dillon also enjoyed dining out in London in the 1890s.[101] Some of the Home Rule MPs also made their mark on the gentlemen's club scene in London. Robert Steven, a former political secretary of the National Liberal, recalled that 'John O'Connor could always tell a good story and delight the social circle with a happy and graceful speech'.[102] Some of the Irish MPs were also the members of more exclusive clubs and sub-groups: John O'Connor, for instance, was a member of the 'Exiles', a small private bohemian club that met at Simpson's restaurant on the Strand.[103]

Nevertheless, the fact that the Home Rulers were less clubbable than their Liberal and Conservative counterparts also reflected the comparative poverty of some of the provincial Home Rulers, many of whom were provincial farmers and shopkeepers rather than prosperous barristers, businessmen, and landlords.

---

[100] O'Conor was Home Rule MP for Sligo, 1868–83; Marum was Home Rule MP for Kilkenny, 1880–90; and Commins was Home Rule MP for Roscommon, 1880–1900.
[101] McConnel, 'The View from the Backbench', 259.   [102] Ibid. 260.
[103] Ibid. n. 112.

Indeed, this distinction is evident in the locations where the Home Rule and Conservative or Unionist MPs lived while in London. The Unionists tended to own impressive residences on Eaton Square, while many of the Home Rulers lived in less-prestigious suburbs of London. Joseph Gillis Biggar, for instance, lived at Clapham Common while Edward Carson owned an impressive residence at Eaton Place.[104] Although some of the leading figures in the Home Rule party, including the Redmond brothers and Edward Blake, lived in Kensington, most of the other Home Rulers lived in Clapham, Pimlico, Lambeth, or Southwark (where many other Irish immigrants also lived). Usually, the less well-to-do Home Rulers lived together in cheap boarding houses and guesthouses, and some of them appear to have had difficulty affording to pay their rent. In 1908, for instance, John Redmond received a letter from D. D. Sheehan's landlady saying that he had left without paying 'for apartment and board'.[105]

Given the importance of the alliance with the British Liberal Party (as well as the Liberal origins of many of the Irish Home Rulers), it is not surprising to find those Irish Home Rulers who did hold club membership in the various Liberal clubs in London. Most popular were the Reform, National Liberal, Devonshire, and Brooks's Club, although there were a handful of Home Rulers in the Bachelors' Club and the Thames Royal Yacht Club. In Dublin, there were a very small number (two or 6 per cent) of Home Rulers in the Kildare Street Club, but the St Stephen's Green Club was by far the most popular Dublin club among the Irish Home Rule MPs (five or 14 per cent of them held memberships). Only one of the Irish Home Rulers was a member of a Belfast club. Paradoxically, Colonel Francis O'Beirne was a member of the Union club in Belfast. In the early years of the Home Rule movement, the party still attracted—as we have seen—a significant number of MPs from landed backgrounds, some of whose commitment to Home Rule was at best tenuous. Moreover, the distinction between Irish Liberals and Irish Home Rulers was quite blurred and some of the Home Rulers in 1881 were nominal rather than committed.

II

To what extent did the composition of the Irish political parties change between 1881 and 1911? As we have seen, the structure of Irish politics was transformed by the Home Rule crisis of 1885–6. The Irish Liberal Party ceased to exist after the 1885 general election, and its members either became Home Rulers or Unionists. In fact, most of the Protestant businessmen who were Liberals

---

[104] Carson was Unionist MP for Dublin University, 1892–1918, and the Duncairn division of Belfast, 1918–21.

[105] McConnel, 'The View from the Backbench', 263. D. D. Sheehan was Home Rule MP for Mid-Cork, 1901–18.

before the Home Rule crisis switched to Unionism thereafter because they felt that their business interests would be jeopardized by Home Rule. Thomas Sinclair, for instance, who was the Presbyterian managing director of one of the biggest companies in Ireland—Kingan's Pork Packers of Belfast—and a founder of the Ulster Reform Club, felt betrayed by Gladstone's conversion to Home Rule and subsequently became the first president of the Liberal Unionist association between 1886 and 1890.[106] Similarly, Catholic Liberals who had supported the party because of its position on land reform and the possibility of patronage now switched to the Home Rule party because it offered land reform, patronage, and the possibility of political independence. The first Home Rule Bill also precipitated the establishment of a formal Unionist movement in Ireland, and the Irish Conservative Party became the Irish Unionist Party after 1885–6. In 1911, the Irish MPs were divided into two political parties: the Irish Unionist Party, that had twenty members, all of whom—with one exception—sat for Ulster constituencies; and the Home Rule party, that had increased from sixty-two MPs in 1881 to eighty-three MPs in 1911.

The Home Rule party was significantly more Catholic in 1911 than it had been in 1881. Whereas fifty (or 82 per cent) members of the party had been Catholic in 1881, seventy-five of the Home Rule MPs in 1911 (90 per cent) were Catholics. There was undoubtedly a slight 'greening' of the Home Rule party between 1881 and 1911; and the proportion of Catholics in the Home Rule party in 1911 was broadly similar to that in the general population. There was also a slight decline in the proportion of Episcopalians. In 1881, ten (or 16.5 per cent) of the Home Rulers had been either Church of Ireland or Church of England, by 1911 the number of Episcopalians had declined to six (or 7 per cent). The proportion of Presbyterians and Nonconformists in the party remained broadly the same (at between 1.5 and 3 per cent). The decline of Protestant Home Rulers (from 18 per cent to 10 per cent) reflects the general development of Irish nationalism into an essentially Catholic movement, representing the aspirations of the Irish Catholic population rather than those of the Irish population as a whole.

Even so, it is significant that a minority of the Home Rulers (eight or 10 per cent) in 1911 were Protestant, and that the parliamentary representation was not exclusively Catholic. Given the familiar Unionist complaint that Home Rule would be 'Rome Rule'—and that the Roman Catholic church would exercise undue influence in a Home Rule Ireland—it was important to the leaders of the IPP to demonstrate that they were not likely to discriminate against Protestants. John Redmond's mother, Mary Hoey, came from a Protestant background, and his second wife, Ada Beesley of Leamington, was also a Protestant, and he made

---

[106] Philip Ollerenshaw, 'Businessmen and the Development of Ulster Unionism, 1886–1921', *Journal of Imperial and Commonwealth History*, 28 (Jan. 2000), 35–64. Sinclair was reputed to be the author of the Ulster Solemn League and Covenant in 1912.

strong efforts to ensure that Protestant MPs were put forward in the Home Rule interest.[107] In 1910, he personally intervened to make sure that William Abraham, who was a Congregationalist, was elected for a Dublin constituency, and he also endeavoured to ensure that Anthony Donelan was returned again after he lost his seat in 1911.[108] It is possible that if the party leadership had retained control of the recruitment of MPs after 1900, more Protestants might have been Home Rule MPs in 1911: local conventions, which were under clerical control, were unlikely to select Protestant candidates. Interestingly, however, a number of the Protestant Home Rulers eventually converted to Catholicism. Joseph Gillis Biggar became a Catholic, and T. P. O'Connor explained his conversion as political rather than spiritual in intent:

[he] had been carried away, perhaps by political rather than religious feeling, so far as to take the plunge into the Catholic Church. I have always thought that his change was due not so much to religious conviction as to a desire to be in thorough sympathy with the people he loved so much.[109]

Similarly, Anthony Donelan converted to Catholicism just before his death in 1924, and although Stephen Gwynn did not convert, his wife did, and they reared their children as Catholics.[110]

In terms of the occupational breakdown, the most obvious change between 1881 and 1911 was the decline in the influence of landowners on Irish nationalist politics. Whereas almost half (49 per cent) of the Home Rule MPs in 1881 had been either landowners or their close relations, only one in ten (11 per cent) of the Irish MPs in 1911 were the members of landed families. It is also significant that it was the middle-sized landowners (who owned between 1 and 5,000 acres) who retained political influence in 1911, with the smallest landowners (with under 1,000 acres) and the biggest landowners (with more than 5,000 acres) in decline. Some of the landowners who remained influential in the Home Rule party in 1911 were Protestant. Captain Anthony John Charles Donelan was an army officer who owned a small amount of land in county Cork. But the majority of landowners who were Home Rulers in 1911 were Catholic. Emblematic of these landlord-MPs was Patrick Joseph Power who owned estates in Waterford and Tipperary.[111] Like other members of the Catholic landowning class, Patrick

---

[107] Bew, *John Redmond*, 6, 14.

[108] McConnel, 'The View from the Backbench', 65. *The Times* explained Donelan's conversion to Home Rule in Freudian terms: 'Almost unconsciously, despite his Conservative leanings and his ardent Protestantism, he became a convert to Home Rule.' *The Times*, 17 Sept., 1924. Donelan was Home Rule MP for east Cork, 1892–1911, and east Wicklow, 1911–18, and owned 143 acres (valued at £80). Abraham was Home Rule MP for west Limerick, 1885–92, north east Cork, 1893–1910, and the harbour division of Dublin, 1910–15.

[109] O'Connor, *Memoirs of an Old Parliamentarian*, ii. 60.

[110] McConnel, 'The View from the Backbench', 64, 63. Stephen Gwynn was Home Rule MP for Galway, 1906–18.

[111] Power was Home Rule MP for Waterford, 1884–1913, and owned 3,418 acres in Waterford and Tipperary (valued at £1,000).

had been educated at Stoneyhurst, while his father, Pierce, was a graduate of Trinity College Dublin (in 1833). However, some representatives of the great Catholic landowners did survive in the Irish Parliamentary Party in 1911. Sir Thomas Henry Grattan Esmonde, for instance, owned substantial estates in King's county, Kilkenny, Tipperary, Waterford, Wexford, and Wicklow, and was a senior whip of the Irish Parliamentary Party.[112]

The shortfall was taken up by farmers, who increased from about one in thirty of the Home Rule MPs (3 per cent) in 1881 to almost one-tenth (9 per cent) in 1911. If we include the shopkeeper-graziers in the farming category, the increase in the number of MPs from farming backgrounds was even more significant (increasing from 3 per cent in 1881 to 19 per cent in 1911). The increased number of farmer-MPs was initially caused by the Land War of 1879–81 which propelled the farmers and shopkeepers of rural Ireland to the forefront of local political life and conjoined the struggles for Home Rule and land reform. Following the proclamation of the Land League in 1881, the National League was established in 1882 and its branches—dominated by farmers and shopkeepers—became the constituency organization of Parnell's Irish Parliamentary Party during the 1880s. The formation of the United Irish League in 1898 and its expansion into a mass movement—which forced the factions of the Irish Parliamentary Party to reunite in 1900—also changed the composition of the Home Rule party. After 1900, it was local conventions—dominated by local farmers, shopkeepers, and priests—who selected parliamentary candidates, and they were generally inclined to select farmers and shopkeepers who were influential in local political forums (county councils, boards of poor law guardians, United Irish Leaguers, members of the Gaelic Athletic Association, and the Gaelic League) as their political representatives.

In general, the farmer-MPs in 1911 were large farmers or graziers rather than poorer small farmers. Peter Ffrench was 'an extensive farmer' who employed workmen on his farm;[113] John Hackett was a 'gentleman farmer' at Longford pass, county Tipperary;[114] and William P. Delany was a grazier at Roskeen who left £4,239 when he died in March 1916.[115] However, there were some nationalist MPs who were drawn from the small farmer class, most notably Laurence Ginnell.[116] A significant number of the Irish MPs were shopkeepers,

---

[112] Esmonde, who was a grandson of Henry Grattan, had been an officer in the Royal Artillery, and briefly defected to Sinn Fein in 1907–8 before becoming a senator in the Irish Free State in 1922. He was Home Rule MP for south Dublin, 1885–91, west Kerry, 1891–1900, and north Wexford, 1900–18, and he owned 8,057 acres (valued at £4,563) as well as being the chairman of the National Bank. For a discussion of his business involvements, see Ch. 5.

[113] *Wexford Free Press*, 9 Nov. 1929; *The People*, 9 Nov. 1929. Ffrench was Home Rule MP for north Wexford, 1893–1918.

[114] *Thom's Irish Who's Who* (Dublin, 1923), 100–1. Hackett was Home Rule MP for mid-Tipperary, 1910–18.

[115] Delany was Home Rule MP for the Ossory division of Queen's county, 1900–16.

[116] Ginnell was MP for north Westmeath, 1906–18.

publicans, and merchants who also occupied farms. John O'Dowd was a merchant and farmer; and Patrick Guiney was a farmer and businessman at Newmarket, county Cork, whose brother owned the Commercial Hotel at Kanturk.[117] Those shopkeepers who also farmed land—known to contemporaries as 'shopkeeper-graziers'—tended to occupy farms of a substantial size. Francis Edward Meehan was a merchant and farmer at Manorhamilton who occupied an extensive farm of land.[118] Similarly, Patrick Aloysius Meehan owned five shops, a post office, a dairy, and a large farm.[119] Apparently, he also 'gave a large amount of employment' to the people of Maryborough.[120] During the second half of the nineteenth century, the large farmers and shopkeepers were gradually becoming one of the most economically powerful sections of provincial Irish society, and many of them became Home Rule MP, thereby also becoming members of the Irish establishment.

However, often the large farmers and shopkeeper-graziers who became MPs had identified themselves with the struggle of the farming class as a whole for rent reductions and land purchase. Patrick Guiney, for instance, was described by his obituary as 'possessing a sound grasp of local affairs, and [he] took more than a passing interest in the welfare of the poor'.[121] And Denis Kilbride, who occupied a 900 acre farm (that was valued at £450), was evicted in 1887 for his role in organizing the Plan of Campaign on the Lansdowne estate in the Queen's county.[122] The Marquis of Lansdowne had offered the tenants on his county Kerry estates a rent reduction of one-third, but refused to do the same on his Queen's county estates. Kilbride led the tenants' campaign for a rent reduction on the Luggacurran estate:

The majority of the tenants were small men, but the estate became of the highest importance in the campaign by reason of the fact that two such strong and substantial farmers as Mr. Kilbride and Mr. [James] Dunne [who occupied 1,400 acres on the estate], casting all personal considerations to the wind, threw in their fortunes with those of their humble neighbours, with a nature utterly devoid of selfishness.[123]

Both Kilbride and Dunne were subsequently evicted—along with the rest of the tenants—and Kilbride went on to become a Home Rule MP and a lifelong campaigner for land reform as his obituary explained:

Mr. Kilbride's name will always be associated with the Irish Land War. He was one of the few now surviving captains of the struggle, which finally won the land of Ireland for

---

117 O'Dowd was Home Rule MP for south Sligo, 1900–18 and Guiney was Home Rule MP for north Cork, 1910–13.
118 F. E. Meehan was Home Rule MP for north Leitrim, 1908–18.
119 P. A. Meehan was Home Rule MP for Queen's county, 1906–13.
120 McConnel, 'The View from the Backbench', 29. Maryborough is now Portlaois.
121 *Cork Evening Echo*, 13 Oct. 1913.
122 Kilbride was MP for south Kerry, 1887–95, north Galway, 1895–1900, and south Kildare, 1903–18.   123 *Nationalist and Leinster Times*, 1 Nov. 1924.

the people, and created a great peasant proprietary, which is the bone and sinew of the nation's future.[124]

Similarly, Michael Meagher, a farmer from Tullaroan, county Kilkenny, devoted himself to campaigning on behalf of evicted tenants and successfully agitated for the redistribution of grazing land among small farmers in the midlands counties.[125] Of course, it is also necessary to point out that many of the Irish MPs who were members of the professions had been born into farming households (probably reasonably prosperous ones that could afford to send their children to secondary school and university), and so they were committed to advancing the cause of the Irish farming class in the House of Commons. John Cullinan was a journalist whose father Charles was a merchant and farmer at Bansha, county Tipperary.[126] And Thomas O'Donnell was a barrister whose father Michael was a farmer at Liscarney, county Kerry.[127]

Many of the Home Rule MPs had family connections with the Catholic church in Ireland. Michael Reddy, for instance, was a farmer whose brother was an Archdeacon.[128] John Redmond, John Philips, and Tom Lundon all had sisters who were nuns; one of Stephen Gwynn's sons was a Jesuit and his daughter was a nun; James O'Mara's brother was a Jesuit; James Halpin's brother in law was a priest; and John Dillon, John Fitzgibbon, and E. P. O'Kelly all had sons who were priests.[129] Some of the MPs were related to senior members of the Catholic church: Tim O'Sullivan was a nephew of Dr Charles O'Sullivan, the bishop of Kerry; John Hackett was the cousin of Dr Sheehan, the Bishop of Waterford; and J. P. Boland was a nephew of the assistant bishop of Dublin.[130] Indeed, as Chapter 6 demonstrates, most of the Catholic priests in Ireland were recruited from the farming community, and there were strong connections between the Catholic church, the farming community, and the Home Rule movement. Many of the senior members of the Irish Parliamentary Party were extremely devout Catholics. John Redmond attended mass every Sunday at the Catholic church on Kensington High Street; J. P. Boland jogged to mass 'every day of his life'; and William Martin Murphy 'was an ardent Catholic who . . . went to Mass every morning all his life'.[131] When P. A. Meehan, who was a daily communicant, died in 1913, his parish priest described him as a 'saintly man' and observed

---

[124] Ibid. Interestingly, Kilbride's brother, Joseph, was a Resident Magistrate.
[125] *Kilkenny People*, 31 Dec. 1927. Meagher was Home Rule MP for north Kilkenny, 1906–18.
[126] Cullinan was Home Rule MP for south Tipperary, 1900–18.
[127] O'Donnell was Home Rule MP for west Kerry, 1900–18.
[128] Reddy was Home Rule MP for the Birr division of King's county, 1900–18.
[129] John Philips was Home Rule MP for south Longford, 1907–17; Tom Lundon was Home Rule MP for east Limerick, 1909–18; James O'Mara was Home Rule MP for south Kilkenny, 1900–7, and later defected to Sinn Fein; E. P. O'Kelly was Home Rule MP for east Wicklow, 1895, and west Wicklow, 1910–14; and Tim O'Sullivan was Home Rule MP for east Kerry, 1910–18.
[130] McConnel, 'The View from the Backbench', 54.
[131] Ibid. 52; O'Connor, *Memoirs of an Old Parliamentarian*, ii. 58. J. P. Boland was Home Rule MP for south Kerry, 1900–18.

that he had never met anyone who had 'got so many masses said for the souls in purgatory'.[132] William O'Malley also observed that the priests of Connemara had supported him throughout his tenure as MP for west Galway: 'from the day I became M.P. for Connemara until the end of 1918, when the young priests helped to unseat me, I found the priests of Connemara, without exception, to be good friends of mine.'[133]

There was a significant increase in the proportion of artisans who were nationalist MPs between 1881 and 1911 (increasing from none to five (6 per cent of the total)). This perhaps reflects the development of the labour movement in Ireland following the formation of the Irish Transport and General Workers' Union (ITGWU) in 1909 which led to the establishment of the Irish Labour Party in 1912. Among the labourer-MPs, the most prominent was Eugene Crean, a carpenter from Cork city.[134] Crean distinguished himself in the House of Commons by attacking the leader of the Unionist party, Colonel Edward Saunderson. According to Crean's obituary:

Though he never figured very largely in the British parliament, he was ever ready to defend the Irish and Ireland when the occasion arose. At such times he showed that he possessed forceful eloquence and an advocating style, which earned him the reputation of being a 'born fighter' . . . His eagerness to uphold the honour of his country is best illustrated by the fact that he caused an uproar in the said parliament by assaulting Colonel Saunderson, a Tory M.P., who had referred to the Irish representatives as 'Irish dogs'.[135]

However, it is clear that the poorer sections of Irish society—the small farmers, artisans, and labourers—were not strongly represented among the nationalist political elite between 1881 and 1911 and this appears to have influenced the position which the Home Rule party took on industrial conflict. Some of the Home Rule MPs were connected with the labour movement and made public statements supporting the cause of labour particularly in its struggle with the directors of the big Irish railway companies. William Field, J. P. Nannetti, Joseph Devlin, Eugene Crean, and William Abraham were all connected with the cause of labour in early twentieth-century Ireland.[136] During the all-Ireland rail strike of August 1911, for instance, Devlin stated that 'he was heartily in sympathy with those railway employees who were making an effort . . . to better

[132] McConnel, 'The View from the Backbench', 53.   [133] O'Malley, *Glancing Back*, 174.
[134] Crean was Home Rule MP for the Ossory division of Queen's county, 1892–1900, and south east Cork, 1900–18.
[135] *Cork Weekly Examiner*, 21 Jan. 1939. Crean would not be the last Irish MP to assault a Conservative MP in the House of Commons. In 1972, Bernadette Devlin punched the Conservative Home Secretary Reggie Maudling in protest against the events of 'Bloody Sunday'.
[136] McConnel, 'The View from the Backbench', 40. William Field was Home Rule MP for the St Patrick's division of Dublin, 1892–1918; J. P. Nannetti was the Home Rule MP for College Green, Dublin, 1900–15; 'wee' Joe Devlin was Home Rule MP for north Kilkenny, 1902–6, west Belfast, 1906–18, and the Falls division of Belfast, 1918–22.

their conditions', and that he hoped there 'would be a satisfactory conclusion of the great industrial war'. Later he told the House of Commons that 'the cause of the strike was the conduct of the railway directors and the scandalous wages they paid' and that he was 'sorry the strike did not go on, for the railway directors would have been beaten'.[137] However, the Irish Party did not have a clear pro-labour policy and tended to shy away from supporting militant strike activity.

The acid-test of the IPP's position on the struggle of labour versus capital came in the summer of 1913 when William Martin Murphy and a group of Dublin employers dismissed (or 'locked out') any of their employees who were members of the ITGWU. By September, 20,000 mainly unskilled Dublin workers were either on strike or locked out. During this conflict, which lasted from August 1913 to its conclusion in January 1914, when most of the demoralized workers were forced to withdraw from the ITGWU and return to work, the IPP tended to condemn the leader of the ITGWU, James Larkin, rather than the leader of the employers, William Martin Murphy. In part this was because Larkin was perceived to be a socialist and a serious threat to the power and ideology of the Catholic church. 'Saintly' P. A. Meehan, for instance, denounced Larkin for allegedly attempting 'to subvert the faith and religion of our Catholic people'.[138] The Catholic hierarchy took a similar view of Larkin and the striking workers and offered no support to the demoralized Dublin working class. Some of the Home Rule MPs were also members of the Dublin business community and connected with William Martin Murphy, and this might explain their failure to support the striking workers. P. J. Brady, J. P. Boland, and Sir Walter Nugent were all connected to the Dublin business community, and, of course, William Martin Murphy himself was a former member of the IPP.[139] A number of other Home Rule MPs were connected with the wider world of business in both Ireland and Britain: according to the *Directory of Directors* in 1910, nine Home Rule MPs held eighteen directorships between them on the boards of firms like the Irish Industrial Printing and Publishing Co. and the Anglo-Serbian Trading Co.[140]

There were clearly strong networks binding together Home Rule politics, Catholic business interests, and the Catholic church. William O'Malley observed that William Martin Murphy and Tim Healy were 'related to each other by ties of blood or marriage, but they were also related by business ties. They were of mutual advantage to each other'.[141] And T. P. O'Connor also explained that William Martin Murphy's involvement in politics had been 'useful to him from a commercial point of view, as the fortunes of tramways

---

[137] McConnel, 'The View from the Backbench', 43.   [138] Ibid. 46.

[139] William Martin Murphy was Home Rule MP for Dublin between 1885 and 1892.

[140] MPs were recruited onto boards of directors because of the status and contacts that they could provide for the entrepreneur. McConnel, 'The View from the Backbench', 266–7.

[141] O'Malley, *Glancing Back*, 60.

depended largely on the sanction of Parliament'.[142] In fact, William Martin Murphy was a member of the 'Bantry band' or 'Bantry gang', a group of Home Rule MPs, nationalist journalists, and businessmen who hailed from Bantry in county Cork. Murphy was 'a loyal disciple' of A. M. Sullivan, the former editor of the *Nation*, and he grew up alongside the Healy brothers (Tim and Maurice, both of whom were MPs), and with the Sullivans and their children.[143] Indeed, it may be that Murphy's close connection with the 'Bantry band' as a young man, and the deep influence of A. M. Sullivan upon him, played a part in making him a Home Ruler rather than a Unionist when most of his friends in big business were vigorously defending the union. Both Murphy and Tim Healy were also devout Catholics with strong connections to the Catholic hierarchy which were economically beneficial to Murphy. In particular, the enormous amount of church building in nineteenth-century Ireland during the 'devotional revolution' provided a great deal of work for Murphy—who started out as a building contractor—and allowed him to accumulate sufficient capital to begin building his business empire.[144] The Irish establishment may have been dominated by Protestant business, landed, and professional networks emerging from the Big House, the Kildare Street Club, and Dublin Castle but there were also strong Catholic Home Rule patronage networks that clustered around influential Catholic politicians, businessmen, and bishops.

A minority of Home Rulers, however, did support Larkin. T. P. O'Connor stated that 'all my sympathies are with the workers'; Charles Diamond told Dillon that if he owned a Dublin newspaper that it would support Larkin; and Richard McGhee explained that: 'When a conflict between the working classes of Dublin even with Larkin at their head and such scoundrels as William Murphy takes place I am with the working classes every time.'[145] Notwithstanding these statements, the IPP did nothing to support the striking workers in 1913 and this probably reflects the fact that the party was composed of businessmen, professionals, provincial farmers, and shopkeepers but contained very few small farmers, artisans, and labourers (either urban or rural). Indeed Diamond alluded to this in his correspondence with Dillon in October 1913: 'there is a sort of feeling that many of the Irish Party are more in sympathy with the farmers and

---

[142] O'Connor, *Memoirs of an Old Parliamentarian*, ii. 55.

[143] Frank Callanan, *T. M. Healy* (Cork, 1996), 7–8. Maurice Healy was Home Rule MP for Cork city, 1885–1900, 1909–10, north east Cork, 1910, and Cork city, 1910–18.

[144] On the devotional revolution, see Ch. 6.

[145] McConnel, 'The View from the Backbench', 50–1. Charles Diamond was a newspaper magnate and Home Rule MP for north Monaghan between 1892 and 1895; Richard McGhee was the son of a poor tenant farmer and Home Rule MP for south Louth between 1896 and 1900 and for mid-Tyrone between 1910 and 1918. On Charles Diamond, see Joan Allen, 'Keeping the Faith: the Catholic Press in Victorian Britain and the Preservation of Celtic Identity', in Richard Allen and Stephen Regan (eds.), *Irelands of the Mind* (Cambridge, 2008). Diamond was a wealthy and influential figure who owned more than 40 newspapers throughout the United Kingdom.

the shopkeepers than with the great body of the workers, whose condition is in many cases deplorable.'[146]

The proportion of professionals in the Home Rule party declined over this period (from 69 per cent to 54 per cent), but the professions remained the single largest occupational grouping in the Irish Parliamentary Party. Lawyers could still benefit from a political career, and of the nineteen Home Rule lawyers in 1911, one became QC, five became KCs, and one became a circuit court judge. John Joseph Mooney was a barrister who was appointed a member of the Advisory committee under the Defence of the Realm Act, 1911–14; Hugh Alexander Law was a Protestant barrister who served in the Ministry of Munitions, 1915–16; James Carrige Rushe Lardner was a barrister who became a KC in 1921, and was a member of the British Treasury committee investigating the application of the Insurance Act to Ireland; and John Muldoon was a barrister who became a KC in 1913.[147] Some Home Rule lawyers, on the other hand, found that their legal careers were damaged by the long absences required in order to attend the House of Commons. Michael McCartan, a Belfast solicitor, told Dillon in 1897 that he had decided to resign his seat because 'ruin [is] staring me in the face' and explained that 'since I entered Parliament it took every penny of my fees remaining and my parliamentary allowance to make ends barely meet and it blighted a bright professional prospect'. Apparently, McCartan's Belfast rivals had used his parliamentary career against him by telling potential clients that he would be likely to be at Westminster when they needed him.[148] Perhaps a political career was advantageous to a legal career in London—and to the quest for political patronage—but might be disadvantageous to a legal practice in the Irish provinces.

There was also a slight increase in the proportion of journalists and newspaper proprietors between 1881 and 1911 from ten (or 16 per cent) to fourteen (or 17 per cent). It is significant, however, that the journalists who were Home Rule MPs in 1881 tended to work in the national or international press (Gray and Sexton were chairmen of the *Freeman's Journal*, and Justin McCarthy was the editor of the *Morning Star*), whereas the journalist-MPs in 1911 tended to own provincial newspapers. Indeed, it is likely that the journalist-MPs in 1911 were recruited by the Irish Parliamentary Party to ensure that the provincial Irish press remained solidly behind the Home Rule movement. J. P. Farrell founded, owned, and edited the *Longford Leader*; John Patrick Hayden owned and edited the *Westmeath Examiner*; and William Doris founded and edited

---

146 McConnel, 'The View from the Backbench', 50.
147 Mooney was Home Rule MP for south Dublin, 1900–6, and Newry, 1906–18; Law was Home Rule MP for west Donegal, 1902–18; Lardner was Home Rule MP for north Monaghan, 1907–18; and Muldoon was Home Rule MP for north Donegal, 1906, east Wicklow, 1907–11, and east Cork, 1911–18.   148 McConnel, 'The View from the Backbench', 269.

the *Mayo News*.[149] Other journalist-MPs had made their name on the national and the international stage: Edmund Haviland Burke, for instance, was a war correspondent for the *Manchester Guardian*.[150] A number of other MPs were on the boards of directors of provincial newspapers: William Duffy and William O'Malley were both members of the board of directors of the Galway newspaper, the *Connacht Tribune*, that was established in 1909; Thomas Condon was a director of the *Clonmel Nationalist*; Esmonde was a director of the *Enniscorthy Echo*; and Walter Nugent and John Muldoon were directors of the *Freeman's Journal*.[151] Control of a newspaper also provided Home Rule MPs with a great deal of patronage and some of them received begging letters from young university-educated nationalists asking for jobs on their newspapers.[152] There was also a slight increase in the proportion of MPs who were medical doctors: from one (2 per cent) in 1881 to four (5 per cent) in 1911, suggesting the increasing influence of doctors in Irish politics at the beginning of the twentieth century.

The proportion of businessmen in the IPP remained broadly the same (increasing from 21 to 22 per cent), but if the shopkeeper-graziers are included in the business section, the proportion of businessmen-MPs increased significantly from about one-fifth (21 per cent) in 1881 to about one-third (32 per cent) in 1911. However, there were significantly less representatives of big business among the Home Rule MPs in 1911 than there had been in 1881. Of the eighteen businessmen-MPs in 1911, only three can be characterized as representing big business. Samuel Young was the owner of Young, King, and Co., distillers, Belfast and Limvady and the chairman of the firm of Bernard Hughes Ltd., bakers and millers. He was the wealthiest member of the IPP in 1911, and—arguably—the one very substantial businessman who was a Home Rule MP at that time.[153] According to T. P. O'Connor, 'one of his favourite jokes was that he had avenged the wrongs of Ireland largely by the amount of bad Irish whisky [*sic*] he had induced Englishmen to drink'.[154] However, Matthew Keating, who began his working life as a miner before entering commercial life in London in the 1890s, ended his career as the Director of Irish Shell Ltd in the Irish Free State.[155] And

[149] Farrell was Home Rule MP for west Cavan, 1895–1900, and north Longford, 1900–18; Hayden was Home Rule MP for south Roscommon, 1897–1918; and Doris was Home Rule MP for west Mayo, 1910–18. [150] Burke was Home Rule MP for King's county, 1900–14.
[151] O'Malley, *Glancing Back*, 268; McConnel, 'The View from the Backbench', 266–7.
[152] See, for instance, the letter from Tom Kettle to William O'Brien dated 2 Sept. 1899 asking for a job working on the *Irish People*, University College Cork Archives, William O'Brien papers, UC/WOB/PP/AJC/59. Kettle eventually followed his father into politics and became Home Rule MP for east Tyrone, 1906–10.
[153] Bew, *Ideology and the Irish Question*, 9; Maume, *Long Gestation*, 245. Young was Home Rule MP for east Cavan, 1892–1918.
[154] O'Connor, *Memoirs of an Old Parliamentarian*, ii. 58–9.
[155] Keating was Home Rule MP for south Kilkenny, 1909–18.

Sir Walter Richard Nugent was a Catholic landowner who became a director of the Midland Great Western Railway and the Bank of Ireland, as well as the president of the Dublin Chamber of Commerce.[156] It is also worth pointing out that some of the professionals in the IPP in 1911 were born into substantial business families. John Pius Boland was a barrister whose father, Patrick, owned Boland's mills in Dublin.[157] Even so, Bew and Jackson are broadly speaking correct to characterize the Home Rule party in 1911 as lacking significant business interests among its ranks. The vast majority of businessmen in the party were small provincial shopkeepers like Timothy O'Sullivan, a Killarney merchant; William J. Duffy, a publican, shopkeeper, and grazier at Loughrea; and James Peter Gilhooly, a Bantry draper.[158] Broadly speaking, it is clear that the provincial Catholic middle class were more and more represented among the Irish political elite in 1911. Large farmers, shopkeepers, publicans, drapers, merchants, shopkeeper-graziers, and newspaper proprietors dominated provincial Irish society in the decades after the Land War (1879–81) and, by 1911, they constituted an extremely influential group in the Irish Parliamentary Party.

In terms of education, more of the Home Rule MPs in 1911 (fifty-nine or 73 per cent) had received a secondary education than their colleagues in 1881 (thirty-six or 58 per cent). But they tended to have attended less prestigious schools. Whereas ten (or 28 per cent) of the Home Rulers in 1881 had attended English Catholic public schools, only six (or 10 per cent) had done so in 1911. Undoubtedly, this reflects the declining importance of Catholic landowners in the Home Rule party in 1911. Similarly, less Home Rule MPs in 1911 had attended the elite Catholic schools in Ireland. The number of Home Rule MPs who had attended Clongowes, for instance, declined from eight (or 22 per cent) in 1881 to seven (or 12 per cent) in 1911. Catholic Home Rule MPs in 1911 tended to have gained their secondary education from the more accessible Diocesan and Christian Brothers' schools, rather than the expensive elite Catholic schools (like Clongowes, Castleknock, Blackrock, and so on). The proportion of MPs who had attended the Christian Brothers' Schools—which were more accessible to less well-to-do Catholic families—increased from two (or 3 per cent) to seven (or 9 per cent). Once again, this reflects the declining importance of Catholic landowners, and the increasing influence of the provincial bourgeoisie in the Home Rule party by 1911.

Whereas the proportion of Home Rule MPs who received a secondary education increased between 1881 and 1911, the proportion of Home Rulers

[156] Nugent was Home Rule MP for south Westmeath, 1907–18 and he inherited an estate of 7,218 acres that had been valued at £4,637 in 1876 as well as being a director of numerous businesses and banks (including the Bank of Ireland in 1920). He later became the president of Dublin Chamber of Commerce (in 1929) and was a senator in the Irish Free State.

[157] Boland was Home Rule MP for south Kerry, 1900–18.

[158] O'Sullivan was Home Rule MP for east Kerry, 1910–18; Duffy was MP for south Galway, 1900–18; and Gilhooly was Home Rule MP for west Cork, 1885–1916.

attending a third-level institution declined from twenty-six (or 42 per cent) to twenty-seven (or 33 per cent). The types of universities attended by Home Rule MPs also changed between 1881 and 1911. More than half (fourteen or 54 per cent) of the Home Rule MPs in 1881 who had received a university education had done so at Trinity College Dublin while less than one-quarter (six or 22 per cent) of the university-educated Home Rule MPs in 1911 were Trinity graduates. Once again, this probably reflects the declining importance of the Catholic landowning class in the leadership of the Home Rule movement by 1911. Instead, many of the Home Rule MPs attended the Royal University (up from none to four or 15 per cent) with The Queen's Colleges (up from three to five) and the Catholic University (down from three to two) more or less holding their own. However, it is striking that the proportion of Home Rulers who had attended Oxbridge remained broadly similar (three or 12 per cent in 1881, and four or 15 per cent in 1911). Two of the Protestant writers and intellectuals who were members of the party in 1911 had attended Oxford: Stephen Gwynn was a graduate of Brasenose College; and John Gordon Swift MacNeill gained his degree from Christ Church.[159] Yet, it is clear that a third-level education was becoming less and less important to Home Rule MPs between 1881 and 1911. It may be that the local conventions who selected Home Rule candidates after 1900 felt that a stint as an officer of the local United Irish League or as the member of a county council was a better qualification for becoming a political representative than having attended university.

Indeed, the Irish Parliamentary Party in 1911 was composed of two sections. On the one hand, there was a leading group, including Redmond, Dillon, Devlin, T. P. O'Connor, and a handful of their confidantes and advisers, who were well-known in 'high' political circles in London and Dublin, and who decided what policies the IPP would adopt. On the other hand, there were the vast majority of Home Rule MPs, many of whom had been selected by local conventions, and who tended to be strong farmers or shopkeepers who were immersed in local nationalist politics. The former lived lives more like their counterparts in the House of Commons while the latter lived lives more like their constituents, and the two sections of the party bound together the political leadership at Westminster with the social groups in the provinces that provided the votes for the party. In this respect, the IPP was a relatively democratic organization that was—to a certain extent—representative of the social groups in provincial Ireland that elected it to power. Arthur Lynch observed these two sections of the IPP in his autobiography:

John Redmond had a much greater reputation in this country than in Ireland. That is quite natural, for he had been so immersed in the politics of the House of Commons that he had become infiltrated with all its traditions, and he always seemed to me to have a

[159] Gwynn was Home Rule MP for Galway city, 1906–18 and MacNeill was Home Rule MP for south Donegal, 1887–1918.

greater respect for British institutions than for those which he was endeavouring to set up in his own country . . . As to the rank and file [of the IPP] . . . they were an excellent body of men, most of whom had done good work in the strenuous Land League days, and in personal intercourse they were genial in their manner and of helpful disposition. They were all good sportsmen, and here is a point which we have always taken for granted, though it perhaps deserves to be emphasised, though they were none of them rich, they were all of them incorruptible. No motive save that of the honour of Ireland, as they saw it, ever swayed their votes.[160]

T. P. O'Connor also admired the self-sacrifice of the local Home Rule MPs:

as to the rank and file of the Party, they were practically paupers. I look back on several of their figures, and there is an ache in my heart when I think of how pathetic and how essentially noble most of them were. They were nearly all married men with small businesses of their own. These businesses had to be managed by their wives, for they were rarely able to go to Ireland while the House of Commons was sitting.[161]

William Duffy, the Loughrea shopkeeper, typifies the hard-working and dedicated service which many of the Home Rule MPs provided for their constituents. According to the *Connacht Tribune*:

Living among them he is familiar with every grievance, and it is a noteworthy fact that when he is in Loughrea, he is kept just as busy—if not busier—than if he were in Parliament. From early morning till eve evicted tenants with grievances, and others, are calling on him to lay the facts of their particular case or grievance before him.[162]

In response to locally expressed grievances and concerns, Home Rule MPs asked questions about local matters in the House of Commons, and so the ordinary people of Ireland were able to express their views—through the Home Rule MPs—in the British House of Commons. A large number of questions were asked—according to one survey, 464 oral and written questions were advanced by Home Rule MPs during twelve weeks in 1910—and the questions and answers were often published in the local nationalist newspapers so that the people of provincial Ireland could see democracy in action.[163]

In many cases, the route to becoming an Irish Home Rule MP in 1911 was via local activism rather than attending university: almost half (thirty-two or 39 per cent) of the Home Rule MPs in 1911 had been (or continued to be) members of the Land League, the National League, or the United Irish League. In other words, a significant proportion of the Home Rule Party—although

---

160 Arthur Lynch, *My Life Story* (London, 1915), 262–3, 264.
161 O'Connor, *Memoirs of an Old Parliamentarian*, ii. 61–2.
162 *Connacht Tribune*, 14 Aug. 1909, quot. McConnel, 'The View from the Backbench', 179. Duffy's mother, from whom he inherited the family business in Loughrea, was reputed to have helped out poor farmers and labourers in south Galway during the years of the Great Famine. Interview conducted by the author with the late J. B. Donohoe, a local historian, at Loughrea (16 May 1996).   163 McConnel, 'The View from the Backbench', 187.

generally not farmers themselves—participated in agrarian agitation, and this involvement played a significant part in their election as Home Rule MPs. Moreover, a significant proportion had been imprisoned as a result of their involvement in agrarian conflict (fifteen or 18 per cent); and a spell in jail appears to have become the *sine qua non* for success in Irish Home Rule politics after the Land War (1879–81). Involvement in local government was the next step for local political activists who had been involved in the land wars and wanted to ascend into national political life. More than one-third (twenty-eight or 34 per cent) of the Home Rule MPs in 1911 were or had been members of local boards of poor law guardians, town councils, county councils, or urban and rural district councils. Those local activists who made their name in these local forums were then given the opportunity to put themselves forward for election to Westminster. Patrick Guiney, for instance, made his name 'as a member of several public boards [where] he gave evidence of possessing a sound grasp of local affairs' and thereby 'came into prominence as a member of local boards'.[164]

Given the critical role that the IRB played in the land agitation of the 1870s, 1880s, and 1890s, it is not surprising that many members of the Home Rule party in 1911 were also former Fenians. As many as thirteen or 16 per cent of Home Rulers in 1911 had been sworn into the Brotherhood, and many of them were not reluctant to trade on their past involvements when seeking election. McConnel's figures on the number of Home Rule MPs who had been involved in the IRB are slightly higher: by his reckoning, twenty-one of the eighty-three Home Rule MPs in 1909 were former Fenians and four others were suspected of being so. The revival of agrarian conflict by the United Irish League in 1898, and the changes in the way in which Home Rule MPs were recruited strongly influenced the proportion of former Fenians who became MPs: of the twenty-one former Fenian MPs in 1909, ten had been elected after 1900. This former Fenian element that was making its way into the Irish establishment at the beginning of the twentieth century was there because the IRB had been closely involved in agrarian conflict in rural Ireland from the late 1870s onwards. Indeed, the strong former-IRB element in the party reflects the increasingly local profile of many Home Rule MPs after 1900 rather than anything else. The Fenianism of these Home Rule MPs had been tamed and become a badge of honour rather than a means of communicating with the real thing or influencing policy in a Fenian direction.[165] By 1911, it may have become little more than a sub-group or a social network—rather like William Le Fanu's dining club—described in Chapter 2—except consuming pints of porter rather than flutes of champagne—that bound the rank and file of the party together.

[164] *Cork Evening Echo*, 13 Oct. 1913.
[165] McConnel, 'The View from the Backbench', 14, 24–5, 32, 37.

Because many of the Home Rule MPs in 1911 were less well-off and more-constituency based than their predecessors in 1881, fewer of them were the members of London or Dublin clubland: thirty-six (or 58 per cent) held club memberships in 1881 whereas this had declined to twenty-seven (or 33 per cent) by 1911.[166] Indeed, fewer members of the Home Rule party in 1911 were the members of clubs than any of the other parties under review. Those Home Rulers who were the members of London clubland tended to frequent the Liberal clubs: sixteen were members of the National Liberal, three were members of the Reform, and two were members of the Devonshire. Some of the Irish Home Rulers (five or 19 per cent) were also members of the Royal Automobile Club, and one of the Home Rulers was a member of the Turf Club. In general, it was the leading members of the Irish Parliamentary Party who were the members of London clubland. In Dublin, the most popular club among the Home Rulers was the St Stephen's Green Club—five (or 19 per cent) of them were members of this club—and two others were members of the Royal St George Yacht club in Kingstown that was also frequented by many senior members of the Irish Civil Service. Interestingly, Sir Walter Richard Nugent who was a Catholic landowner and businessman, was a member of the Kildare Street Club. However, he was an anomalous member of the Home Rule party who tended to associate with the Protestant members of the party, Stephen Gwynn and Hugh Law, and who was drawn from the loyal Catholic landlord Home Rule tradition.[167] None of the Irish Home Rulers in 1911 was the member of any of the Belfast Unionist clubs.

Although most of the Home Rulers in 1911 lived permanently in Ireland (fifty-nine or 71 per cent), a significant minority (eleven or 13 per cent) resided in England or Scotland. Some of these were the leading figures in the Party who worked in London (T. P. O'Connor, for instance), but a substantial proportion of the Home Rule MPs in 1911 were the representatives of the Irish diaspora in Britain. Joseph Patrick Nannetti had founded the Home Rule organization in Liverpool when he worked there in his youth as a printer. He later returned to live in Dublin, but continued to act as a trustee of the Royal Liver Friendly Society.[168] Similarly, Daniel Boyle worked in Manchester as a journalist, and was a member of the Executive Council of the UIL in Britain, and an alderman in Manchester, 1908–17.[169] Dr Charles O'Neill was a doctor at Coatbridge, near Glasgow, and effectively represented the Scottish diaspora in the House of Commons.[170] Thomas Scanlan was a native of Sligo who lived in London

---

[166] In 1881, 8 or 13% of Home Rule MPs were members of the Reform club, and 16 or 26% were members of the National Liberal club. By 1911, the comparable figures were 3 (or 4%), and 16 (or 19%).   [167] Hugh Law was Home Rule MP for west Donegal, 1902–18.
[168] He was Home Rule MP for Dublin College Green, 1900–15.
[169] Boyle was Home Rule MP for north Mayo, 1910–18.
[170] O'Neill had been born in county Armagh in 1849, and emigrated to Scotland in his youth. Initially, he sold tea in the Coatbridge area and eventually saved sufficient money to purchase a

and represented the London Irish in the Irish Parliamentary Party, and later he worked as a Police Magistrate in London, 1924–7.[171]

The members of the Home Rule party in 1911 were recruited from diverse sources and it is clear that while all of them agreed on the necessity of achieving Home Rule for Ireland, they probably agreed on very little else. There were agrarian radicals (John Dillon and Michael Meagher), and agrarian moderates (William Shaw and Wiliam O'Malley). There were pro-labour MPs (Arthur Lynch and D. D. Sheehan stood as Labour candidates for British seats after 1918) and pro-employer MPs (P. J. Brady supported the employers during the 1913 lockout and W. F. Cotton was a director of Wiliam Martin Murphy's Dublin United Tramways Co. in 1913).[172] There were MPs who supported Redmond's pro-recruiting policy during the Great War (Thomas O'Donnell), and those who vehemently opposed it (Michael Meagher). There were those appalled at the alliance between the IPP and Sinn Fein during the conscription crisis of April 1918 (Sir Walter Richard Nugent, for instance) and those who flirted with separatism (Thomas Esmonde and Patrick White) and eventually joined Sinn Fein (Laurence Ginnell).[173] There were also some Home Rule MPs who supported more radical causes: Swift-MacNeill was anti-vivisection, and W. H. K. Redmond was a supporter of women's suffrage.[174] Even so, it is clear that the Irish Parliamentary Party MPs were strongly middle class and that the more radical social groups in Irish society (labourers, artisans, clerks, and small farmers) were beginning to turn their attention to the alternatives to constitutional nationalism that were emerging at the beginning of the twentieth century: Sinn Fein, the Gaelic League, the ITGWU, and the Labour Party.[175] According to John Hutchinson, the young Catholic clerks and professionals in Irish towns and cities felt alienated from the rural and bourgeois nature of the Irish Parliamentary Party, and—during the early years of the twentieth-century—began to look elsewhere for a political and cultural movement to which they could belong.[176]

The Unionist party in 1911 included a broader range of Protestants than the Conservative party of 1881 had done. Whereas twenty-two (or 92 per cent) of the Conservative MPs in 1881 were Episcopalian, and just two (or 8 per cent) were Presbyterian, the Unionist Party in 1911 included twelve MPs (60 per cent of the party) who were Episcopalian, seven MPs (35 per cent of the party) who were

small lodging house and a public house. When he tried to enter politics, he was sneered at for his lack of education, and so he successfully took a medical degree at the University of Glasgow. See Bew, *Ideology and the Irish Question*, 19. He was Home Rule MP for south Armagh, 1909–18.

[171] Scanlan was Home Rule MP for north Sligo, 1909–18.

[172] Cotton was Home Rule MP for south county Dublin, 1910–18.

[173] Patrick White was Home Rule MP for north Meath, 1900–18.

[174] Swift MacNeill was Home Rule MP for south Donegal, 1887–1918.

[175] On the social background of provincial Home Rule and Sinn Fein activists, see Campbell, *Land and Revolution*, Ch. 6.

[176] Hutchinson, *Dynamics of Cultural Nationalism*, 279–83.

Presbyterian, and one Nonconformist. The increased influence of Presbyterians and Dissenters in the Unionist party in 1911 reflected two significant changes since 1881: first, the dissolution of the Irish Liberal party and the defection of some of its members to the Unionist party; and second, the transformation of the Unionist movement from an all-Ireland party to an Ulster party. In 1911, all of the Unionist MPs (with one exception) represented Ulster constituencies, whereas the Conservative party in 1911 had represented Unionists throughout Ireland. It is striking also that neither the Irish Conservative Party in 1881 nor the Unionist Party in 1911 contained any Catholic MPs.

While there is agreement among historians, that Unionism had become an essentially Ulster phenomenon by the third Home Rule crisis of 1912–14, there is disagreement as to when this transformation took place. Gibbons suggests that by the time of the Ulster convention held at Belfast on 17 June 1892, which was the first province-wide demonstration against Home Rule, Unionism had effectively become an Ulster rather than an all-Ireland phenomenon. Jackson, on the other hand, suggests that the critical turning-point came a little later with the formation of the Ulster Unionist council in 1905. Ollerenshaw persuasively suggests, however, that Unionism had become Ulster-based well before 1905 and that the critical transition took place during the 1890s when a divergence between the Belfast and Dublin Chambers of Commerce became apparent, and when many southern Unionist businessmen converted to Home Rule.[177]

In terms of occupation, there was a steep decline in the proportion of landlords in the Unionist party. Whereas the majority of Conservative MPs in 1881 were either landowners (fifteen or 63 per cent) or closely related to landowners (six or 25 per cent), only one-quarter of the Unionist MPs in 1911 were from landed backgrounds. Those landlords that did remain in the Unionist Party tended to own estates of a similar size to their colleagues in the Conservative Party, with more than half of the landed members of both parties owning estates of more than 10,000 acres. Indeed, a number of landed Unionist MPs owned enormous landed estates. The Duke of Abercorn owned 78,662 acres and Captain Arthur Edward O'Neill owned 65,919 acres.[178] However, the declining influence of landlordism in Unionism was also critically important in terms of its gestation from an all-Ireland to an exclusively Ulster phenomenon. Landlords were evenly spread throughout Ireland whereas the newly emerging powerhouse of Unionism—the business elite—was largely based in Ulster, and indeed in Belfast. At one level, then, the rising power of business and the declining power of landlordism within Unionist politics further propelled Unionism into becoming exclusively Ulster-based. Despite the defection of many Liberal voters to Unionism after

---

[177] Ollerenshaw, 'Businessmen and the Development of Ulster Unionism', 42, 49–50.
[178] Abercorn was Unionist MP for Derry city, 1900–13 and O'Neill was Unionist MP for mid-Antrim 1900–14.

1886, and the fact that many of these were Presbyterian farmers, there was no tenant-farmer MP in the Ulster Party in 1911.

The shortfall was taken up by an increase in the proportion of Unionist MPs involved in business (up from four or 17 per cent to six or 30 per cent). The kinds of businessmen who were Conservatives and later Unionists were broadly similar. Indeed, all of the business interests in the Unionist party could be classified as 'big' business. In other words, the small provincial merchants and shopkeepers who dominated the business class of the Home Rule party were not represented in the Ulster party. John Brownlee Lonsdale was a wealthy merchant and banker (he was a director of the Lancashire and Yorkshire bank);[179] the Craig brothers (Charles Curtis and James) were the sons of a self-made millionaire distiller and worked as a solicitor and a stockbroker respectively;[180] William John MacGeagh MacCaw had business interests in the Far East and India;[181] and Robert Thompson was a Belfast linen manufacturer.[182] There was also a certain amount of social mobility within the Unionist Party. Hugh Thom Barrie, for instance, had borrowed £100 from his father when he was a teenager (in the late 1870s) to start a produce business, then emigrated from Glasgow to Ulster, and by the beginning of the twentieth century, had become a successful grain merchant. Indeed, Barrie appears to have been one of the very few 'rags to riches' stories in the annals of Irish business history: 'By dint of perseverance and business aptitude he early attained prosperity.'[183] However, there was—in this admittedly small sample—a shift from manufacturing business interests (Ewart, Chaine, and Corry in 1881 were all manufacturers of different kinds) to more commercial interests (bankers, stockbrokers, investors, and so on). Of the Unionist businessmen in 1911 only Thompson and Barrie were manufacturers. This suggests that there may have been a shift in the nature of the business leadership of the Unionist movement, although Sir Edward Harland and Gustav William Wolff, the Belfast shipbuilders, had both also been Unionist MPs between 1889 and 1910.[184]

[179] Lonsdale was Unionist MP for mid-Armagh, 1900–18.
[180] Charles Curtis Craig was Unionist MP for south Antrim, 1903–22, and Antrim, 1922–9 [in Northern Ireland]. James was Unionist MP for east Down, 1906–18, mid-Down, 1918–21, and he also sat for Down in the Northern Ireland parliament and became Prime Minister of Northern Ireland, 1921–40. The Unionist MPs were one of the elite groups in this study that managed to retain power after the Irish Revolution.
[181] MacCaw had lived for 20 years in India and was a Fellow of the Royal Colonial Institute, and he was Unionist MP for west Down, 1908–18.
[182] Thompson had acted as President of the Ulster Flax Spinners' Association, and as President of Belfast Chamber of Commerce. He was also a director of the Belfast and Co. Down Railway. He was Unionist MP for north Belfast, 1910–18.
[183] Jackson, *Ulster Party*, 61. He later went on to become a senior civil servant (vice president of the Department of Agriculture and Technical Instruction, 1919–21), and later became a senator in the Northern Ireland parliament, 1921–2. Barrie was Unionist MP for north Derry, 1906–18. *Irish Times*, 22 Apr. 1922.
[184] Sir Edward Harland was Unionist MP for north Belfast, 1889–95 and Gustav William Wolff was Unionist MP for east Belfast, 1892–1910. Wolff had represented the constituency of east Belfast, where his shipyards and his workforce were located, for 18 years.

There was also an increase in the proportion of Unionist MPs who were members of the professions, and in particular in the number of lawyer-MPs. Whereas six or 25 per cent of the Conservatives were lawyer-MPs, ten or 50 per cent of the Unionist MPs were legal men. There were many advantages for lawyer-MPs in the Unionist party in 1911 because the positions of Irish Attorney General and Solicitor General in a Conservative government were always selected from one of the lawyers in the Ulster party. William Moore, for instance, 'never made any secret or mystery of why he went into parliament . . . it was the way to get promotion at the bar'.[185] And Moore eventually won the promotion that had first motivated him to enter politics: after acting as private secretary to George Wyndham (1902–4), and serving as an MP for eighteen years, he was appointed a Judge in the High Court in 1917. Similarly, James Henry Mussen Campbell was an 'unrepentant legal careerist' who repeatedly urged his claims on vacant senior positions, and finally became Solicitor General, 1901–5, Attorney General, 1905, and Lord Chancellor of Ireland, 1918–21.[186] Edward Carson was perhaps the more successful Unionist lawyer-MP, rising from QC (in 1889) to Solicitor General (1892, 1900–5), Attorney General (in 1915), 1st Lord of the Admiralty (1916–17), and Lord of Appeal in ordinary (in 1921). He was also the leader of the Unionist Party, 1910–21. Indeed, of twenty Unionist MPs in 1911, four became QCs, two became KCs, three became Irish Solicitor General, two became Irish Attorney General, and two became Judges.

It is also likely that a career in politics enhanced the reputation of lawyers working in the private sector, and many lawyer-politicians were reported to have extensive and prosperous legal practices. Robert James McMordie was a Belfast solicitor with a large and extensive practice,[187] and Andrew Long Horner was a barrister who worked the North-West circuit and acquired a lucrative practice.[188] These were the spoils of a political career for an ambitious young Unionist lawyer.

The proportion of army officers declined from six or 25 per cent of the Conservatives to three or 15 per cent the Unionists. This can be explained by the decline in the number of landed MPs as many landowners tended to be army officers before taking on the reins of an Irish estate. Although there were far more journalists and newspaper proprietors in the Irish Parliamentary Party, the Ulster Party also recruited some wealthy press magnates, including Peter Kerr Kerr-Smiley, the owner of the *Northern Whig*.[189] Although he was not a Unionist MP in 1911 it is noteworthy that Thomas Henry Sloan, a Protestant shipyard worker, had represented the south Belfast constituency as an

---

[185] Quot. Jackson, *Ulster Party*, 59. Moore was Unionist MP for North Antrim, 1899–1906 and Armagh, 1906–17.

[186] Ibid. 110–11. Campbell was Unionist MP for St Stephen's Green, Dublin, 1898–1900 and Dublin University, 1903–16.   [187] *Belfast Newsletter*, 26 Mar. 1914.

[188] *Irish Times*, 27 Jan. 1916. McMordie was Unionist MP for East Belfast, 1910–14 and Horner was Unionist MP for south Tyrone, 1910–16.

[189] Kerr-Smiley was Unionist MP for north Antrim, 1910–22.

independent Unionist between 1902 and 1910. Sloan criticized the Ulster party for neglecting working-class interests, and after his defeat by James Chambers, a barrister who would become Solicitor General for Ireland before his death in 1917, there were no labourers or artisans who were Unionist MPs in 1911.[190]

The proportion of Unionist MPs who had received a secondary education (fifteen or 75 per cent) was slightly higher than that of the Conservative MPs (twelve or 50 per cent). However, the Irish Unionists tended to have received their secondary education in Ireland rather than in England. The majority (eleven or 92 per cent) of Irish Conservatives in 1881 who had received a second level education, had done so in England. However, almost half (seven or 47 per cent) of the Irish Unionists in 1911 were educated (at secondary level) in Ireland. In particular, a significant proportion of them had been educated in Ulster, with three attending Belfast Royal Academical Institution, one attending Wellington Academy, Belfast, and another Foyle College, Londonderry. Only one of the Unionists had attended a Protestant school outside Ulster: James Henry Mussen Campbell had attended Stackpoole's school, Kingstown, in his native Dublin. Fewer of the Unionists had been educated at British public schools than their predecessors in the Conservative party: eight (or 67 per cent) of the Irish Conservatives had attended Eton college, while only seven (or 47 per cent) of the Unionists gained a British public school education (four at Eton, and one each at Winchester, Merchiston, and Clifton College). The declining importance of Eton probably reflects the shift from landlord-MPs in the Conservative party to business and professional men in the Unionist party.

The proportion of Conservatives (thirteen or 54 per cent) and Unionists (ten or 50 per cent) who attended university was almost exactly the same. However, the Unionists were much less likely to have attended Oxbridge than their Conservative predecessors. More than two-thirds (nine or 69 per cent) of the Conservative MPs (who had attended university) gained their degrees from Oxford or Cambridge, while only one-fifth (two or 20 per cent) of the Irish Unionists were graduates of Oxbridge. Once again, this reflects the declining importance of landowners—who tended to send their sons to English public schools and Oxbridge—in the Unionist party by 1911. Instead, the Unionists tended to gain their third-level education in Ireland. The proportion of Unionists who attended Trinity College Dublin (four or 40 per cent) was markedly higher than the proportion of Conservatives (three or 23 per cent) who had done so. Trinity College Dublin was a popular destination for ambitious young men who wanted to forge a successful career at the Irish bar; and all four of the Irish Unionist MPs who had attended Trinity College Dublin (William Moore, Edward Carson, James Henry Mussen Campbell, and Godfrey Fetherstonhaugh) did so *en route* to successful careers as barristers in Dublin. The young Presbyterians who wanted to become successful barristers appear to have

---

[190] Chambers was Unionist MP for south Belfast, 1910–17.

attended The Queen's Colleges rather than Trinity College Dublin: John Gordon attended Queen's College, Galway before becoming a barrister, and Andrew Long Horner graduated from The Queen's College, Belfast before working as a barrister on the North-Western circuit.[191] Another young Presbyterian—Robert James McMordie—attended The Queen's College, Belfast before establishing a successful practice as a solicitor. None of the Conservative MPs in 1881 had attended any of The Queen's Colleges, and the increased importance of this sector reflects the increasingly Northern and Presbyterian character of the Unionist party in 1911.

The proportion of Unionist MPs who were the members of London, Dublin, or Belfast clubs is broadly similar to that of the Conservative MPs in 1881. All of the Conservatives were the members of at least one club, while almost all of the Unionists (nineteen or 95 per cent) held club memberships. In London, the Unionists tended to frequent the same clubs as their predecessors in the Conservative Party: the Carlton, the Constitutional, and St Stephens. In Dublin, on the other hand, the Unionists were much less likely to be members of the Kildare Street Club than the Conservatives: only one (or 5 per cent) of the Unionists was a member of the club as opposed to ten (or 42 per cent) of the Conservatives. This reflects both the declining importance of the Irish landlords among the Unionist MPs in 1911 and the fact that Unionism in 1911 was an essentially Ulster (rather than an all-Ireland) movement. The presence of three of the Unionists (16 per cent) in the Dublin University Club suggests the importance of Dublin Protestant barristers (many of whom were graduates of Trinity) in the Unionist party in 1911. Perhaps the most striking difference between the Unionist MPs' club affiliations and those of the Conservative party is the presence of nine (or 47 per cent) of the Unionist MPs in the Ulster Club (as opposed to only three (or 13 per cent) of the Conservatives). There were also four (or 21 per cent) of the Unionists in the Union Club in Belfast. These affiliations reflect the increasingly Ulster-based nature of Irish Unionism, and also the increased intensity of Unionist feeling in Ulster following the first and second Home Rule crises.

III

On 13 July 1917, the *Irish Times* reported the death of Patrick O'Brien, the Home Rule MP for Kilkenny city, and observed that:

Some twenty years ago Ireland had the distinction of being represented in the House of Commons by the tallest of its members and the smallest, the latter being Mr. Pat O'Brien,

---

[191] Gordon was Unionist MP for south Derry, 1900–16.

and the former being the late Mr. W. H. O'Sullivan, member for one of the divisions of Limerick.[192]

The Irish MPs evidently represented physical extremes in the House of Commons during the 1880s, but to what extent did they represent political or social extremes at Westminster: were they different or similar to the rest of their colleagues in the House of Commons?

Broadly speaking, the Irish MPs—both nationalist and Unionist—were similar to their colleagues in the British Liberal and Conservative parties. Rush's data on the economic interests of the Liberal MPs in 1900 demonstrate that 9 per cent were landed; 57 per cent were in business; 32 per cent were in the professions; and 2 per cent were workers.[193] This is not dissimilar to the Irish Home Rule MPs in 1911, 6 per cent of whom were landowners; 41 per cent of whom were in business (including farming); 54 per cent of whom were in the professions; and 6 per cent of whom were members of the working class (labourers or artisans). Both parties were composed of a similar number of MPs from landed and business backgrounds, although it is likely that the Irish Home Rulers represented smaller business concerns; and both parties contained a significant number of professionals and workers. However, there were more professionals and workers in the Irish Parliamentary Party than in the Liberal party, and more businessmen in the Liberal Party than in the IPP. Furthermore, the Home Rule businessmen were probably less well-off than their Liberal counterparts, and this may explain why as many as 90 per cent of the Liberal MPs were the members of London clubs while the equivalent proportion of Home Rulers was about one-third (33 per cent).[194] But—with this exception—the composition of the two parties was quite similar.

A similar level of congruence can be observed between the Conservative Party in 1900 and the Irish Unionist Party in 1911. According to Rush, the economic interests of the Conservative Party in 1900 included 21 per cent who were landed, 50.5 per cent who were in business, and 28.5 per cent who were professionals.[195] The Irish Unionist party in 1911 was composed of fewer landowners than the Conservative party (10 per cent), and of fewer businessmen (30 per cent), and had a high proportion of professionals (70 per cent). Yet in its broad contours the composition of the Irish Unionist party was not dissimilar to that of the Conservatives, and the majority (95 per cent) of the members of both parties

---

[192] *Irish Times*, 13 July 1917. O'Brien was Home Rule MP for North Monaghan, 1886–92 and for Kilkenny city between 1907 and 1917. William O'Malley also suggests that one of the Irish Home Rule MPs—William Abraham—was 'the handsomest man in the House of Commons' (*Glancing Back*, 189).
[193] Michael Rush, 'The Members of Parliament', in S. A. Walkland (ed.), *The House of Commons in the Twentieth Century* (Oxford, 1979), 103.
[194] Rush estimates that over 80% of all the MPs in the House of Commons during the twentieth century were the members of one or more London clubs, and he suggests that 95% of Conservatives were club-members and more than 90% of Liberals (ibid. 118).   [195] Ibid. 98.

were the members of London clubland. Overall, these data suggest that the Irish political elite was very strongly integrated into the United Kingdom polity.

The most significant change in the composition of the British and Irish political elites between 1881 and 1911 was the enormous decline in the influence of the Irish landlord class. This decline was, however, more marked in Ireland—among both nationalists and Unionists—than it was in Britain. The majority (twenty-one or 88 per cent) of Irish Conservative MPs in 1881 were either landowners or the members of wider landed families, whereas only one-quarter of the Unionist MPs in 1911 (five or 25 per cent) were drawn from landed backgrounds. Similarly, almost half of the Home Rulers in 1881 (thirty or 49 per cent) were from landed families, while only one in ten (nine or 11 per cent) of the Home Rulers in 1911 was either a landowner or closely related to landowners. However, it should be noted that the proportion of landowners was higher in the Unionist Party in 1911 than it was in the Home Rule party. This was—in part—due to the greater level of popularity of Ulster landlords among their tenants than that of landlords in the three southern provinces.

The decline of landlord influence in the Irish political elite as a whole appears to have begun in the 1860s. In 1859, for example, 83 per cent of all of the Irish MPs were landlords. By 1868 this had declined to 51 per cent; and, following the introduction of the Secret Ballot in 1872, this fell still further to 41 per cent in 1874. In 1881, one-third (thirty-six or 35 per cent) of the Irish MPs were landlords, while in 1911 only seven (or 7 per cent) of the Irish political elite were the owners of land. It is also clear that the landed MPs in 1911 tended to own smaller estates than their counterparts in 1881. The proportion of landed MPs who owned estates of more than 10,000 acres declined from about one-quarter (23.5 per cent) to about one in six (15.5 per cent), with the shortfall being taken up by landed MPs who owned estates of between 1,000 and 5,000 acres (who account for 26 per cent of landed MPs in 1881 and 38.5 per cent in 1911). Not only was the influence of landowners in decline, but the influence of the great landowners was in decline as it was the middle-sized landowners (who owned estates of less than 5,000 acres) who were able to maintain their political influence up to 1911. This suggests that those landlords who had a closer relationship with their tenants—which landlords with estates of less than 5,000 acres were reputed to have—were able to retain political influence for a longer period than the 'great' landowners.

The changing composition of Ireland's political elite was also, in part, caused by wider changes taking place in British and Irish society. In the second half of the nineteenth century, landlords were no longer the wealthiest members of British and Irish society. Instead, the new commercial and manufacturing classes were accumulating substantial wealth, and acquiring significant political influence at both the local and the 'national' levels. This process was particularly evident in Ulster where industrial development was creating a class of extremely wealthy and influential businessmen. Of a total of 205 Limited Liability Companies that declared themselves in 1912, 30 per cent were involved in the linen and manufacturing industries. Some members of this new bourgeoisie—the owners and directors of these factories—had by 1911 become leaders of the Irish Unionist movement in Ulster.[196] Ulster business interests were clearly one of the dominant forces in the development of Ulster Unionism at the beginning of the twentieth century.

There was also a clear rise in the proportion of businessmen who were Home Rule MPs between 1881 and 1911. However, what is striking about the Home Rule businessmen-MPs in 1911 is the substantial increase in the numbers of smaller business interests. Only a handful of the Home Rulers in 1911 could be regarded as owning substantial business interests. The remaining Home Rule businessman-MPs in 1911 were generally small provincial shopkeepers, drapers, cattle dealers, millers, and the like. Michael Joseph Flavin had a 'successful general business' in Tralee;[197] Thomas Joseph Condon was a Clonmel cattle dealer and victualler; and John Fitzgibbon was a Castlerea draper and 'one of the largest commercial men in the west of Ireland'.[198] It was these smaller business interests that had made their way into the Home Rule party by 1911. Whereas the increased proportion of businessmen-MPs in the 'Unionist' bloc tended to be big business interests, the new businessmen in the Home Rule party were generally drawn from the small provincial shopkeeping classes. In this respect, the rank and file of the Irish Parliamentary Party in 1911 was generally composed of members of the farming and shopkeeping classes that were becoming the dominant economic power in provincial Ireland in the decades following the Great Famine (1845–9).

Despite the declining political influence of landlords, they remained an important force within Unionism between 1886 and 1914. The first leader of Irish Unionism, Colonel Edward Saunderson, was a landlord who envisaged Irish landlords continuing to play a decisive role in political life. Similarly, Edward Carson, who became the leader of the Irish Unionist party between 1910 and 1921 (although he was a barrister) firmly believed that landlords should continue to be involved in Irish politics and defended their waning position. Indeed, Jackson argues that landlords remained extremely influential in Unionism long after the Ulster convention of 1892 at which he argues the representation of landlords was as significant as it had been in the reaction against Home Rule of 1886. Ollerenshaw, however, points out that only three members (out of a total of twenty) of the organizing committee of the convention were landlords.[199]

[196] Martin Kavanagh, 'The Belfast Business Community and the Unionist Movement, 1885–1926', PhD thesis (University of Ulster, 1995), 36.

[197] *Kerryman*, 6 May 1944; *Kerry Champion*, 6 May 1944. Flavin was Home Rule MP for north Kerry, 1896–1918.

[198] *Roscommon Messenger*, 13 Sept. 1919. Condon was Home Rule MP for east Tipperary, 1885–1918. Fitzgibbon was Home Rule MP for south Mayo, 1910–18.

[199] Ollerenshaw, 'Businessmen and the Development of Ulster Unionism', 42.

Moreover, even if landlords and professionals continued to dominate the political representation of Unionism in the House of Commons, businessmen tended to provide the financial and organizational muscle behind the movement. Thomas Sinclair, the managing director of Kingan and Co., did not put himself forward as a Unionist MP and this gave him more time to spend in Belfast on his business, religious, and political work. Even so, during the 1st and 2nd Home Rule crises contemporaries noted that 'his face was almost as familiar in the lobby [of the House of Commons] as that of a Member of Parliament'.[200] Sinclair was apparently the author of the Solemn League and Covenant in 1912 and when he died his funeral cortege was a mile long and included 200 officers and men of the Belfast battalions of the Ulster Volunteer Force. Indeed, businessmen played a critical role in lobbying influential groups in Britain in favour of Unionism, and also in funding the resistance to Home Rule. Ulster businessmen believed that the termination of the Act of Union would jeopardize their economic interests, and campaigned strongly for the maintenance of the union. The businessmen's committee held an anti-Home Rule demonstration in November 1913 at which they declared that Home Rule would 'deprive us of our cherished rights as citizens of the United Kingdom and degrade our civic status but will bring disaster upon the industries, commerce and credit of Ireland'.[201] And when an indemnity fund was established to raise £1 million to enable the Ulster Volunteer Force (UVF) to purchase 25,000 rifles and 2,000,000 rounds of ammunition from Germany in 1914, the main subscribers to the fund were Ulster businessmen (including Francis Workman and Sir John Milne Barbour). However, other sections of Ulster society also subscribed—albeit lesser amounts—and landlords (including the Duke of Abercorn and the Marquis of Downshire) as well as professionals were at the forefront of Unionism during the 3rd Home Rule crisis.[202] Broadly speaking, by 1912–14, a new upper class had emerged in Ulster which included landlords, professionals, and businessmen; and if Unionism was usually represented in parliament by landlords and professionals, it was the businessmen who played vital organizational and financial roles behind the scenes.[203]

To what extent was there a 'greening' of the Irish political elite between 1881 and 1911? There was certainly a clear 'greening' of the Home Rule party between 1881 and 1911. In 1881, fifty (or 82 per cent) of the Home Rule MPs in 1881 were Catholic while seventy-five (or 90 per cent) of the Home Rulers in 1911 were Catholic. In other words, the Home Rule party became even more 'green' between 1881 and 1911, although it was already dominated by Catholics in 1881. However, the proportion of Catholics who were MPs in the 'Unionist'

---

[200] Ibid. 40.   [201] Ibid. 55.   [202] Ibid. 56.   [203] Ibid. 37, 58–9.

bloc remained unchanged between 1881 and 1911: in both years there were no Catholic 'Unionist' MPs. Clearly, there was no 'greening' whatsoever of Irish Unionism in the late nineteenth and early twentieth centuries. In terms of religious composition, the one striking transformation in the 'Unionist' bloc was the increase in the proportion of Presbyterians and Dissenters from two (or 8 per cent) in 1881 to eight (or 40 per cent) in 1911. This reveals that the Unionist bloc had won the support of many of the Presbyterians from the Irish Liberal Party, and that Irish Unionism was becoming increasingly representative of Protestantism rather than exclusively Episcopalianism. Broadly speaking, however, ethnic bloc politics became more consolidated and distinct in the period between 1881 and 1911: the one party that appealed to both Catholic and Protestant interest groups ceased to exist, and political and social networks or sub-groups became either exclusively Catholic and nationalist (like the 'Bantry band') or Protestant and Unionist (like the Belfast clubs).

Notwithstanding the more populist membership of the Irish Parliamentary Party in comparison with the Irish Unionist Party, the Irish Unionist Party appears to have been better able to win the support of the wider Unionist/Protestant community than the Irish Parliamentary Party was able to win the support of the broad range of political and social interests among the nationalist and Catholic community. During the early years of the new century, a wide range of radical nationalist and socialist organizations began to emerge including Sinn Fein, the Gaelic League, the ITGWU, and the Catholic Association. Each of these organizations represented and promoted the interests of political, social, and cultural groups that were not—by and large—represented in the Home Rule movement as it was constituted in 1911. Although each of these organizations was comparatively minor in terms of membership before the beginning of the Great War, they did constitute a threat to the Home Rule movement and would become a serious challenge to it after 1914. In the pre-War period, however, many of these organizations campaigned on behalf of the interests of young educated Catholic professionals and clerks in urban areas. The Catholic Association, in particular, campaigned on behalf of Catholic professionals and clerks who felt that they were being discriminated against in their attempts to gain promotion in public employment (in the Civil Service and the police, for instance), in the professions, and also in the private sector. The Catholic Association was established in 1902 and quickly gained a voice through the editor and proprietor of the *Leader* newspaper, D. P. Moran, who investigated the Association's claims that there was discrimination against Catholics in each of these areas. According to the Catholic Association, 'there was something working against us', and its members resolved to 'fight with all our might until we have laid our hands on as much of the power, place and position of this country, as our numbers and our ability demand'.[204] The next chapter will investigate the *Leader*'s allegations that Ireland's business elite was dominated by Protestants and discriminatory towards Catholics.

[204] Senia Paseta, *Before the Revolution: Nationalism, Social Change and Ireland's Catholic Elite* (Cork, 1999),103.

5

Business

In the course of 1902 and 1903, the *Leader* newspaper published a series of investigative articles and letters which aimed to expose the alleged sectarian recruiting practices of a number of prominent Irish businesses, notably the major railway companies: the Great Southern and Western, the Great Northern, and the Midland Great Western.[1] On 11 January 1902, for example, a letter from 'MILITANT' regarding 'Religious Intolerance' on the Great Southern and Western Railway explained that:

It is generally recognized that many disabilities—National, Political, Industrial, and otherwise—have been abated since the establishment of the LEADER; and there is every reason to think that your exposure of the religious intolerance on the Great Southern and Western Railway will make it possible for capable and hardworking Catholic officials to expect a share of the sweets of office.

It may be argued that the G. S. and W. Co. is no worse than the other railways. But that does not justify its existence or continuance on any of them, and, as the Great Southern system runs through an almost exclusively Catholic district, and a goodly number of Catholics have money invested in it, it is only natural that the lever aiming at the abolition of sectarian partisanship should be first directed against that Company . . . It is by the asking of questions that the Civil Service, the Post Office, the Customs, the Police, and all the State Departments conceded religious equality to Catholics. Without hurting the feelings of any person the same can be obtained on railways.[2]

According to 'MILITANT', it was 'universally admitted' that the vast majority of employees of the Great Southern and Western Railway Company were Protestant:

the Manager, Secretary, Chief Auditors, the Engineers, the Cashier, the General, and five out of six of the District Superintendents are Protestants . . . all the Chief Clerks, with three-fourths of their staffs in the Dublin Offices, and more than 75 per cent. of the first, second, and third class Station masters are of the same denomination; and . . . Catholics with double their service and equal ability are in less remunerative and more difficult positions.[3]

---

[1] D. P. Moran described the Great Southern and Western Railway as 'the Great Sourface' railway, 'sourface' being his description of what he regarded as a certain type of bigoted Protestant. John J. Horgan, *Parnell to Pearse: Some Recollections and Reflections* (Dublin, 1948), 111.
[2] Letter from 'MILITANT' (n.d.), *Leader*, 11 Jan. 1902.   [3] Ibid.

According to 'X', a similar state of affairs existed on the Midland Great Western Railway. Indeed, such was the alleged level of nepotism within the company—then under the chairmanship of Sir Ralph Cusack—that the article teasingly suggested:

The company may soon be known as Cusack and Family.

The chairman is Sir Ralph Cusack, drawing £1,500 per annum.

Major Cusack, a director, is his son-in-law, and draws £600 per annum.

The accountant, his nephew, was appointed at an initial salary of £500.

The auditor is his nephew.

The locomotive engineer is his son, appointed at an initial salary of £600, and increased to over £700 per annum.

We even have the third generation getting ready to step in. The chief locomotive apprentice is a grand-nephew of the chairman.[4]

In a series of four articles published in the spring of 1903, the *Leader* provided a systematic analysis of the religious composition of a large section of the workforce of the Great Northern Railway Co. (of which all twelve directors were Protestant).[5] The *Leader* claimed in the opening article of this series that they had a full list of the names of all the employees discussed in these articles but that they had decided not to publish this because their quarrel was not with the individuals concerned but with 'the awful state of affairs as regards the exclusion of Catholics'. The newspaper further claimed that their identification of individuals' religious persuasion was 'absolutely correct' and that their data on individuals' salaries were '*substantially* correct'.[6] The fact that no attempt was made to query the data suggests that it was probably an accurate representation of the religious background of the company's employees. Altogether, the religious affiliation of 568 employees is provided and of these 433 (76 per cent) were Protestant and 135 (24 per cent) were Catholic.[7] In the vast majority of cases, the Catholic employees tended to occupy the lower-status positions of clerk and messenger, with a smaller number of Catholic engineers, inspectors, and station masters.

---

[4] Letter from 'X', 'Religious Intolerance on the Midland Great Western Railway', *Leader*, 6 Sept. 1902.

[5] See 'The Great Northern Railway: Its Bigotry Exposed', *Leader*, 7, 14, 21, and 28 Mar. 1903.

[6] *Leader*, 7 Mar. 1903.

[7] The employees discussed in the *Leader* articles included the staff of the general manager's office, the secretary's office, the chief engineer's office, the superintendent of the line's office, the cashier's office, the accountant's office, the audit accountant's office, the parcels office, the booking office, the goods department, the locomotive department, the storekeeper's department, the plant superintendent's office, the stock rail yard, the drawing office, the railway inspectors, and ticket inspectors, district engineers, electricians, canvassers, permanent way inspectors, and finally the stationmasters and clerks on all the main and branch lines.

The *Leader* aimed to expose what it regarded as the sectarian nature of employment practices in the Irish business elite so that more Catholics might be employed in this sector. In particular, the *Leader* appealed to influential Catholics who were directors or shareholders to exert pressure on companies to adopt fairer recruiting practices. In an article on the Midland Great Western Railway, for instance, 'X' argued that both Catholic directors and shareholders needed to do more to influence wider recruiting practices:

What are the Catholic bishops of Ireland doing [about this]? What are the Parish Priests doing? What are the lay Catholic Shareholders doing? Are they . . . all mesmerized into culpable inactivity? . . . It is for those who have the power to use it. I would ask but one question before concluding: Are the clergy and laity of Ireland doing their duty, as Catholics, in the business world? Let their consciences answer.[8]

This chapter will interrogate two central issues raised by the *Leader* newspaper in its series of exposés of alleged sectarianism in the Irish business world at the turn of the century. First, were the Protestant dominated boards of directors of the Irish railway companies typical of the boards of directors of other big businesses in Ireland at this time? And second, did the composition of the Irish business elite change as a result of this and other campaigns for more open recruiting practices to be adopted by big business in Ireland?

I

In order to answer these questions, a detailed study of the social composition of the directors of the biggest Irish businesses in both 1883 and 1911 was undertaken. The biggest Irish businesses were defined as those that had an issued capital (or value) of at least £200,000. The names of the directors of the biggest businesses in Ireland were identified in *Burdett's Official Intelligence for 1883* (London, 1883) and *The Stock Exchange Official Intelligence for 1911* (London, 1911).[9] All of the firms listed in these publications had been incorporated and so an effort was also made to identify privately owned firms of comparable value, and these have also been added to the list of big Irish businesses.[10] Once the names of the chairmen, deputy chairmen, managing directors, directors, secretaries, engineers, general managers, auditors, accountants, solicitors, chief cashiers, debenture stock trustees, and so on were identified in these volumes,

---

[8] Letter from 'X', *Leader*, 6 Sept. 1902.

[9] The year 1883 was selected because the relevant volume for 1881 could not be located.

[10] For instance, Guinness was still privately owned in 1881 (it was not incorporated until 1886) but because it was one of the biggest firms in the world it has been included for both 1881 and 1911. Although two major privately owned companies are not included in this study—Thomas Gallaher's tobacco manufacturing firm and James Mackie's linen-manufacturing machinery firm—both Gallaher and Mackie are included as the directors of other companies.

a search was then made for biographical information about each of these individuals.[11] Altogether, the biographies of 247 members of the Irish business elite were identified: ninety-nine were leading businessmen in 1883, 164 were leading businessmen in 1911, and sixteen were leading businessmen in both 1883 and 1911.

The firms represented in this sample were broadly representative of the Irish economy in this period. Of the thirty-four firms valued at more than £200,000 in 1883, sixteen were Railway companies, eight were Banks (three of which were based in Belfast), one was a major linen manufacturer (the York Street Flax Co. in Belfast), two were major shipbuilding firms based in Belfast (Harland and Wolff and Workman-Clark), one was a brewer based in Dublin (Arthur Guinness), and six were Dublin-based service providers and traders (the Dublin United Tramways Co., the Grand Canal Co., the Dublin Markets Co., the Alliance and Dublin Consumer's Gas Co., the Dublin Steam Packet Co., and Arnott's drapers).

By 1911, the value of many Irish firms had increased considerably and there were at least fifty-one firms valued at more than £200,000 (there may also have been some privately owned firms in this category about which data on capitalization are not available). The majority were railway companies (fourteen), and banks (nine), but there were also a significant number of manufacturers. In Belfast, there were four major linen manufacturers (York Street, Robinson and Cleaver, Richardson and Owden, and the Brookfield Linen Co.), as well as a distiller (Dunville and Co.), and a pork packer (Kingan's). Moreover, by 1911, Harland and Wolff and Workman-Clark had become two of the biggest shipbuilding companies in the world. In Dublin, there was Boland's bakery, Goulding's chemical manufacturers, two distillers (Jameson's and the Dublin distillers), as well as Arthur Guinness (by now the biggest brewer in the world). In addition, there were significant developments in the service sector. In Belfast, there were no fewer than three shipping companies (the Belfast Steamship Co., the Ulster Steamship Co., and the Irish Shipowners Co.), and there was one in Dublin (the Dublin Steam Packet Co.). In general, the Dublin and Cork firms tended to be in the trade and service sectors. There were two tramway companies (the Dublin United Tramways Co. and the Cork Electric Tramways Co.), one bottle exporter (E. and J. Burke), one draper (Pim Brothers), one newspaper (the *Irish Times*), one gas company (the Alliance and Dublin Consumer's Gas Co.), and three other service sector companies (the Artisans' Dwellings Co., the Dublin City Markets Co., and the Grand Canal Co.).[12] Broadly speaking, the Irish economy at the beginning of

---

[11] On the method and sources used to do so, see Appendix.

[12] The remaining two companies included in my sample in 1911 were the Seaham Harbour Dock Co. (the docks were in the north east of England but the Company was based in Belfast) and the Martin Estates Co., a financial company based in Belfast.

the twentieth century was divided into two sections. On the one hand, the major Irish manufacturing companies (notably shipbuilding and linen) based in Belfast, and, on the other, trading and service sector companies that tended to be located in Dublin. In 1907, for instance, Belfast-based manufacturers produced £19.1 million of the total £20.9 million of manufactured goods exported from Ireland.[13]

The companies included in this sample are representative of the five main elements of the Irish economy in this period—excluding agriculture—the banks, the railways, shipbuilding, the brewing and distilling industry, and the linen industry. In 1883, there were eight major banks in Ireland. Three were based in Belfast (the Belfast Banking Co., the Northern Banking Co., and the Ulster Banking Co.); four were based in Dublin (the Royal Bank of Ireland, the Bank of Ireland, the Hibernian Joint Stock Co., and the Munster Bank); and one was Dublin based but had its head office in London (the Provincial Bank of Ireland). By 1911, there were nine major banks in Ireland. Once again there were the three Belfast-based banks (the Belfast Banking Co., the Northern Banking Co., and the Ulster Bank); there were five Dublin-based banks (the Bank of Ireland, the Munster and Leinster Bank, the National Bank, the Royal Bank of Ireland, and the Hibernian Bank); and one Dublin-based bank which had its head office in London (the Provincial Bank of Ireland). There was no shortage of capital in late nineteenth-century Ireland. Bank deposits increased from £16 million in 1859 to £33 million in 1877, and to as much as £60 million in 1913.[14] According to Bielenberg, the increase in Irish bank deposits was even more marked: rising from £8 million in 1850 to £71 million in 1914.[15] Each bank tended to cater for different groups in Irish society. The London-managed Provincial Bank of Ireland tended to have a largely landed and professional clientele, while the Munster Bank (after 1885 the Munster and Leinster Bank) was widely recognized as the farmers' bank. Similarly, the Royal Bank of Ireland tended to cater for Dublin's Protestant business and professional classes while the Hibernian provided banking facilities for Dublin's Catholic businessmen and professionals. Indeed, banks tended to have either a Unionist or a nationalist ethos: the three Ulster-based banks as well as the Bank of Ireland, the Provincial Bank of Ireland, and the Royal Bank of Ireland were broadly Unionist in ethos; while the National Bank, the Hibernian Bank, and the Munster and Leinster were broadly nationalist in outlook.[16] All of the directors of these banks are included in this study.

[13] Martin Kavanagh, 'The Belfast Business Community and the Unionist Movement, 1885–1926', PhD thesis (University of Ulster, 1995), 271. See Michael Farrell, *The Orange State* (London, 1976), 18–19 also.
[14] Joseph Lee, *The Modernisation of Irish Society, 1848–1918* (Dublin, 1973), 11.
[15] Andy Bielenberg, 'Enterprise and Investment in Ireland: 1850–1900', in Andrew E. Burke (ed.), *Enterprise and the Irish Economy* (Dublin, 1995), 25.
[16] Cormac Ó Gráda, *Ireland: A New Economic History, 1780–1939* (Oxford, 1994), 356–7.

The Irish Railway network expanded rapidly during the second half of the nineteenth century. In 1845, Ireland had only sixty-five miles of track whereas by 1914 this had increased to 3,500 miles, at which point Ireland had one of the densest rail networks in the world.[17] Initially, most of the capital investment in Irish railways came from English investors. Only 35 per cent of the capital in the Great Southern and Western Railway (Ireland's largest rail company) was in Irish hands in the 1840s. However, from the 1850s onwards Irish railway stocks became one of the most solid and dependable Irish stocks available, and thereafter native investors provided most of the capital demands of the Irish railways and reaped most of the dividends.[18] By 1914, about 50,000 shareholders—most of whom were Irish—held about £45 million of Irish railway stock that yielded an average dividend of 4 per cent.[19] According to the *Leader*, many of the shareholders of the Great Southern and Western Railway were Catholics: 'The Archbishop of Dublin, and many of the Munster Hierarchy, as well as the clergy, merchants, and farmers in the country, have big financial interests in the Company.'[20] As well as the major Irish railways, there were also substantial tramway companies in Ireland. By 1877, there were three major horse-drawn tram companies in Dublin: the Dublin Tramway Co., the North Dublin Tramway Co., and the Dublin Central Tramway Co. Under the chairmanship of James Fitzgerald Lombard and his son-in-law, William Martin Murphy, the three companies were amalgamated into the Dublin United Tramways Co. in 1880. After 1896, Murphy presided over the electrification of the Dublin tramway system, and within twenty years the company controlled 100 miles of line and was one of the biggest companies in Ireland (worth more than £1.25 million).[21] Murphy was also responsible for introducing an electrical tramway system to Cork and by 1911 the Cork Electrical Tramways Co. was also one of the biggest Irish companies. All of the directors of the major Irish railway and tramway companies are included in this study.

Shipbuilding in Ireland also expanded rapidly in the second half of the nineteenth century. In the 1840s and 1850s, the output of the entire Irish shipbuilding industry, which was then based at Cork, was about 2,000 tons each year. Sixty years later, Harland and Wolff and Workman-Clark produced—between them—more than 150,000 tons annually and accounted for 8 per cent of world output.[22] Workman-Clark alone manufactured 310 ships between 1880 and 1914—most for export to the United Kingdom—and in 1902 the yard turned out more gross tonnage than any other shipyard in the United Kingdom.[23] Similarly, Harland and Wolff had launched more than 430 ships by 1913 with

---

[17] Lee, *Modernisation of Irish Society*, 13.
[18] Bielenberg, 'Enterprise and Investment in Ireland', 23–4.
[19] Ibid. 23.   [20] *Leader*, 11 Jan. 1902.
[21] Thomas Morrissey, *William Martin Murphy* (Dundalk, 1997), 9–10, 31.
[22] Ó Gráda, *Ireland: A New Economic History*, 295.
[23] Kavanagh, 'The Belfast Business Community', 343.

a gross tonnage of 2.2 million gross tons.[24] Indeed, the shipbuilding industry expanded largely due to increased UK demand for ships to service the new markets opened up by the British Empire.[25] The directors of Harland and Wolff and Workman-Clark, as well as the directors of the various shipping companies in Belfast and Dublin, are included in this study.

The brewing and distilling sector also expanded rapidly in post-Famine Ireland. Indeed, the output of the brewing industry trebled between the 1850s and 1914. By 1914, 40 per cent of output was exported, and beer and ale accounted for 3.2 per cent of all exports. This expansion was largely due to the great success of Arthur Guinness which was—by 1914—the largest single brewer in the world, and responsible for two-thirds of all Irish output (from brewing), as well as the bulk of exports. There were also twenty or so other brewers scattered throughout the country, most of which catered only for local markets, although the Cork brewers (especially Murphy, and Beamish and Crawford) were able to hold their own in Munster well into the twentieth century.[26]

The great success of Arthur Guinness during the period when Edward Cecil Guinness (later 1st Earl of Iveagh) was the managing director (1868–1927), was the company's export of stout, porter, and dark beers to the UK market. During this period, the London and other British brewers (notably Bass and Allsopp) stopped making porter and instead focused on ale production, leaving the UK market for dark beers open to Arthur Guinness. Production expanded exponentially as a consequence and increased from an annual average output of 350,000 bulk barrels in 1868, to 725,000 bulk barrels in 1875, 1.2 million bulk barrels in 1886, and an astounding 3 million bulk barrels by the 1920s. In 1886, when the firm was incorporated, it had already become the largest brewery in the world and was valued at £6 million.[27]

Distilling was less successful than brewing. By the early 1900s, whiskey output was only double that of the 1840s. In 1887, there were twenty-eight distilleries in Ireland, and this had declined to twenty-three by 1919 (when eleven were located in the six counties which were about to become Northern Ireland). In 1890, Dunville and Co. in Belfast had an annual output of over 2 million gallons of whiskey.[28] Even so, in 1907, Irish Whiskey accounted for a quarter of the total UK output of whisky/whiskey. In part, the poor fortunes of Irish distillers were related to the decline in population after the Famine, as well as the intensification of temperance campaigns in the second half of the nineteenth century, and this suggests the extraordinary power of the Catholic church in nineteenth-century

[24] Walford Johnson and Frank Geary, 'Gustav Wilhelm Wolff', in David J. Jeremy (ed.), *Dictionary of Business Biography: A Biographical Dictionary of Business Leaders Active in Britain in the Period, 1860–1980*, 5 vols. (London, 1984–6), v. 858.

[25] Kavanagh, 'The Belfast Business Community', 263.

[26] Ó Gráda, *Ireland: A New Economic History*, 304.

[27] Tom Corran, 'Edward Cecil Guinness' in Jeremy, *Dictionary of Business Biography*, ii. 680–1.

[28] Kavanagh, 'The Belfast Business Community', 152.

Ireland, which will be discussed in the next chapter. The combined effect of these factors was a marked decline in whiskey consumption from 1.1 gallons per capita in 1857 (which is very high by modern standards) to 0.63 gallons in 1910.[29] The directors of Arthur Guinness and of the main Irish distillers (Jameson's, the Dublin Distillery Co., and Dunville and Co.) are included in this study.

The linen industry had existed in Ireland since the late eighteenth century. Before the Industrial Revolution, however, it was widely dispersed and largely involved the domestic production of yarn and cloth from home-grown flax. The mechanization of linen manufacturing was introduced in Ireland in the 1820s and 1830s following the introduction of wet-spinning in Leeds in 1824 (a technique that had been invented in France in 1810). As a consequence of this technological innovation, the linen industry in Ireland became increasingly centralized in mills. By the mid-1830s, Belfast had ten substantial steam powered spinning mills, four of which were located on the Falls Road. And by the mid-1840s, nearly £2 million of capital had been invested in the fifty or so mills then in operation. The mechanization of linen weaving caused the price of yarn to drop and centralized linen mills gradually replaced the domestic spinning that had been widespread in north Connacht and Ulster up to the early nineteenth century. According to Bielenberg, the net value of linen output in the early 1840s was £5 million and this accounted for 6 per cent to 7 per cent of national income on the eve of the Famine. The linen industry continued to expand in the second half of the nineteenth century when it also became largely concentrated in Belfast. In 1912, for instance, there were 37,000 power looms for weaving in Ireland, 35,000 of which were in Ulster, and 22,000 of these were in Belfast. The growth of the linen industry was based on the expansion and exploitation of markets abroad, especially those in the United Kingdom and the United States of America.[30] Indeed, from 1870, Ulster became the undisputed centre for the linen trade in the United Kingdom.[31] By 1900, Belfast's York Street Flax Co. had become the largest mill in the world; Barbours of Lisburn was the biggest linen thread company in the world; and the majority of all UK linen workers (65 per cent) were in Ulster.[32] The directors of the four biggest linen manufacturers in Belfast (named above) are included in this study.

Most of the directors included in this study were the directors of more than one company. Almost half of the directors under scrutiny (ninety-six of 247 or 39 per cent) were the directors of more than one firm. Indeed, many of them were the directors of several firms. James W. Murland was the chairman of the Royal Bank of Ireland, the chairman of the Great Northern Railway Co., the deputy chairman of the Great Southern and Western Railway Co., and a

29 Ó Gráda, *Ireland: A New Economic History*, 297–8.　　30 Ibid. 285–9.
31 Kavanagh, 'The Belfast Business Community', 262–3.　　32 Ibid. 338.

director of the Dundalk, Newry, and Greenore Railway Co.[33] Similarly, Joseph Todhunter Pim was the Governor of the Bank of Ireland, the Chairman of the Dublin Artisans Dwellings Co., the chairman of the Dublin City Market Co., as well as a director of Richardson and Owden (a linen manufacturer in Belfast) and a director of Pim brothers, Ltd.[34] Some of the directors under review were also the directors of smaller companies in the provinces. John Francis Smithwick, the auditor of the National Bank and former Home Rule MP for Kilkenny, was a well-known Kilkenny brewer. John Murphy, a director of the Munster and Leinster Bank in 1911, and a Catholic resident of county Cork, was a director of the emerging Cork Distilleries Ltd. And Colonel James Marmaduke Sugrue, a director of the Cork, Bandon, and South Coast Railway company in 1911, was also the Catholic proprietor of the Glen Distillery Co. in county Cork. This study does include, therefore, some of the medium-sized business interests that were emerging in provincial Ireland.

However, the majority of directors included in this study were actually the super-rich of early twentieth-century Ireland, many of whom were probably substantially better off than most of the great landowners in Ireland. To qualify for a directorship of the Ulster Bank in 1911, for instance, a candidate was required to hold 500 shares, and these were on offer at £13 each in 1906, so that only a shareholder who had invested at least £6,500 in the bank was eligible for a directorship.[35] Pirrie, a director of Harland and Wolff, sold his shares in the company for £500,000, and left £175,841 gross in his will (in 1924). Sir John Milne Barbour, managing director of the Linen Thread Co., the largest producer of linen thread in the world, left £177,485 gross in his will when he died on 3 October 1951. When William Martin Murphy died on 25 June 1919, he left a personal estate of £264,005 as well as a range of successful businesses (Clery's, the *Irish Independent*, the Dublin United Tramways Co., and so on). Some less-well-known members of the business elite amassed huge fortunes that exceeded those of many of the 'great landowners' of Ireland. William Findlater, who was a member of the Findlater brewery company, and a director of the Dublin and Meath Railway in 1883, left £128,143 gross in his will in 1906; William Sinclair Kingan, a director of Kingan's pork packers in Belfast in 1911, left £511,143 in his will in 1946; and Sir Thomas Dixon, who was the chairman of his own timber merchant's company in Belfast, a director of the Belfast Shipowners' Co., and a director of the York Street Flax Co. in 1911, left an

---

[33] James W. Murland was born in Co Down in 1814, attended Trinity College Dublin, became a barrister, and was a commissioner of national education, as well as a prominent businessman. He died on 20 May 1890 aged 76 and was described by the *Irish Law Times* as 'one of the most prominent citizens [in Dublin]' (24 May 1890).

[34] Joseph Todhunter Pim was a Quaker born at Kingstown in 1841 and educated at the Friends' School, York. His brothers (Richard Pim and F. W. Pim) were also prominent in the Irish business elite.   [35] Kavanagh, 'The Belfast Business Community', 303.

estate of £917,860 when he died on 10 May 1950.[36] Even these legacies were miniscule, however, when compared with the £13.486 million that Edward Cecil Guinness, who was the second richest man in the United Kingdom, left when he died on 7 October 1927.[37] Directors received large salaries as well as income from their substantial shareholdings. The chairman of the Midland Great Western, for instance, earned £1,500 per annum (in 1902) while his fellow directors each earned £600.[38] During the last quarter of the nineteenth century, the Irish business elite overtook the great landowners as the wealthiest sector of Irish society. This study therefore includes the very top of the business elite in Ireland, as well as some members of the emerging manufacturing and trading interests in provincial Ireland but it does not discuss the thousands of rural shopkeeper-publicans who were—as we have seen—playing a leading role in the emerging Home Rule movement.[39]

A significant proportion of the directors under review were also the chairmen of the companies on whose board of directors they sat. Almost half of the directors under review (104 of the 247 directors or 42 per cent) acted—at some point—as the chairmen of the board of directors of at least one of the companies in which they were involved. This suggests that the businessmen included in this study tended to play a leading role in the decisions reached by the major companies in Irish society during this period, rather than being merely figurehead directors. Joseph Tatlow, the general manager of the Midland Great Western Railway, recalled that the chairman of the board of directors, Sir Ralph Smith Cusack 'attended daily in his office, devoting much time to the company's affairs'.[40] Cusack's obituary also confirmed that:

He is said to have made it a condition of his acceptance of the position of chairman that he was to be given an absolutely free hand, with autocratic power over every department. This power he wielded to the last, but the interest of the shareholders was the test by which every matter was decided. All appointments, from the most important to the humblest position, were made directly by him, and he is said to have known personally every one of the employees. The success of Sir Ralph Cusack's management was largely to be attributed to the good terms which were at all times maintained between him and his subordinates.[41]

[36] For Findlater, see *Irish Times*, 15 June 1906; for Kingan, see *Irish Times*, 29 Nov. 1947; and for Dixon, see *Irish Times*, 31 July 1950.

[37] Bielenberg, 'Enterprise and Investment in Ireland', 31.

[38] 'Religious Intolerance on the Midland Great Western Railway', *Leader*, 6 Sept. 1902.

[39] There were too many small businessmen and shopkeepers in provincial Ireland to be included in this study but, as Ch. 4 has shown, they were gaining substantial power in the decades after the Famine.

[40] Joseph Tatlow, *Fifty Years of Railway Life in England, Scotland and Ireland* (London, 1920), 116.

[41] *Irish Times*, 4 Mar. 1910. The number of strikes and complaints about working conditions on the Midland Great Western suggest that Cusack's obituary probably did not fairly represent his relationship with his employees. For a description of strike activity, see, for instance, *Irish Times*, 17 Mar. 1890.

Indeed, it would seem that all of the directors included in this study were probably responsible for key business decisions and for the day-to-day running of the companies over which they presided. The four directors of the Northern Bank, for instance, were responsible for the efficient day-to-day running of the bank. In addition, an advisory committee was established to ensure that the bank remained financially viable and competitive. Members of the advisory committee of the Northern Bank (not included in my study) had to be either the directors or the owners of a business and to have shares in the bank.[42] Candidates for the advisory committee of the Belfast Bank had to hold at least twenty shares in the bank which were on offer at £45 each in 1901.[43] Indeed, the shareholders elected as members of the advisory committees to banks were charged with ensuring that the directors acted in the shareholders' best interests.[44] Neither were these advisory committees powerless. The members of the advisory committee of the Belfast Bank could impose a fine on a director who was persistently absent from the boardroom.[45] Given that the directors' qualification for the Belfast Bank in 1911 was to hold 400 old or 1,000 new shares, and that shares in the bank in 1901 were on offer at £45 each, it is probably unlikely that a director-shareholder who had invested at least £18,000 in the bank would not turn up for board meetings. Similarly, the directors of the Ulster Bank had an advisory committee to whom all of the directors' decisions were forwarded for approval. If the members of the advisory committee withheld their approval, the directors rarely acted against the committee's wishes.[46] There was good reason for the existence of advisory committees to monitor the decisions of boards of directors. In the 1860s, the directors of the National Bank had engaged in a series of dubious investments that resulted in the bank being left with bad debts of between £300,000 and £400,000.[47] Other banks may have learned a lesson from this episode.

What power did the Irish business elite hold? The directors of the biggest Irish companies were powerful in two critical respects. First, they were the key decision-makers in the businesses over which they presided. And second, they were the employers of a large section of the Irish workforce. In Belfast, Harland and Wolff and Workman-Clark employed—between them—20,000 men in 1914 and 29,000 men in 1919.[48] In 1907, 61,000 people (most of whom were probably women) were employed in the linen industry in Belfast.[49] According to Ó Gráda, at its peak during the Great War the linen industry employed 90,000 people mostly in Belfast.[50] The second-largest railway company in Ireland—the Great Northern—had 5,500 employees in 1907.[51] It is likely

[42] Kavanagh, 'The Belfast Business Community', 293.   [43] Ibid. 303.
[44] Ibid. 300–1.   [45] Ibid. 304.   [46] Ibid. 297.
[47] Ó Gráda, *Ireland: A New Economic History*, 360.
[48] Kavanagh, 'The Belfast Business Community', 348.   [49] Ibid. 336.
[50] Ó Gráda, *Ireland: A New Economic History*, 287.
[51] David J. Jeremy and G. Tweedale, *Dictionary of Twentieth Century British Business Leaders* (London, 1994), 158.

that the other thirteen railway companies in 1911, including the Great Southern and Western—the largest railway company in Ireland—and the two tramway companies in Dublin and Cork, employed perhaps 20–30,000 people. In 1911, the three Ulster banks employed 964 clerks.[52] By 1914, the Bank of Ireland employed 550 officials.[53] It is probably reasonable to assume, therefore, that the other six major banks in Ireland in 1911 each employed about 330 clerks (an estimated 2,000 employees). Overall, it is likely that the major Irish banks employed about 3,000 clerks at any one time. If we take into consideration the number of people employed by Arthur Guinness and Sir John Arnott who has been described as 'the largest employer of labour in Ireland',[54] as well as the other firms included in this study, it is likely that the 247 directors under review were probably responsible for employing at least 200,000 people throughout Ireland on the eve of the Great War.[55] These men would have had enormous power, then, over a large section of the workforce in the three main urban centres of Belfast, Cork, and Dublin.

The boards of directors of these companies had enormous power over their employees, and many of them appear to have adopted discriminatory recruiting practices. Of the 964 clerks employed by the three Ulster banks, only 95 (10 per cent) were Catholic, and Kavanagh suggests that 'Bank staffing up until 1914 [in all three of the Belfast banks] was almost exclusively Protestant'.[56] Ó Gráda confirms that the Bank of Ireland, the Provincial Bank of Ireland, and the Royal Bank of Ireland 'rarely employed Catholics in senior positions'.[57] Oliver MacDonagh examined the notes made by the Bank of Ireland's inspectors during their visits to provincial branches between 1888 and 1903, and found that: 'The returns indicate that at least 80 per cent of the officials were Protestant, the great majority of them members of the Church of Ireland.'[58] This confirms the data contained in a series of articles compiled by 'HP' and published in the *New Ireland Review* in 1908 which suggested that of the twenty-one officials who occupied the chief positions in the Bank of Ireland, only one was Catholic; of sixty-seven agents (or managers) of provincial branches, only ten were Catholic; and of sixty-seven sub-agents (or sub-managers), only twelve were Catholic.[59] It

[52] Kavanagh, 'The Belfast Business Community', 314.

[53] Oliver MacDonagh, 'The Victorian Bank, 1824–1914', in F. S. L. Lyons (ed.), *Bank of Ireland, 1783–1983: Bicentenary Essays* (Dublin, 1983), 41.

[54] Marie-Louise Legg, 'Sir John Arnott', q.v. DNB online <http://www.oxforddnb.com/view/article/55599> (accessed 15 Nov. 2008).

[55] The total workforce employed by Guinness increased from 1,680 in 1886 to 3,457 in 1913. S. R. Dennison and MacDonagh, *Guinness, 1886–1939: From Incorporation to the Second World War* (Cork, 1998), 115.   [56] Kavanagh, 'The Belfast Business Community', 314.

[57] Ó Gráda, *Ireland: A New Economic History*, 357.

[58] MacDonagh, 'The Victorian Bank', 43.

[59] 'HP', 'Catholics and the Bank of Ireland', *New Ireland Review*, 27 (Feb. 1908), 370–2; 'HP', 'Catholics and the Bank of Ireland, II', ibid. 29 (Mar. 1908), 58–63. According to 'HP''s data, 23 (15%) of 155 senior members of staff were Catholic.

is likely, on the other hand, that the directors of those banks that had a nationalist ethos—the National, the Hibernian, and the Munster and Leinster—employed a largely Catholic workforce. Discriminatory employment practices also appear to have been adopted in the Belfast linen industry. One Sandy Row mill owner, John Hughes, drew his workforce entirely from local Orangemen and their families so that his mill became known as the 'Orange Cage'.[60] The data presented above on the recruiting practices of the Great Northern Railway suggest that the railway companies also tended to employ mainly Protestant workers. Similarly, the Protestant- (and Unionist-) dominated boards of directors of Harland and Wolff and Workman-Clark seem to have presided over a largely Protestant workforce in the Belfast shipyards. In 1920, for instance, the workers of Workman-Clark led the movement to expel Catholics from the shipyards and other major factories in the city.[61] Indeed, all of the available evidence points to the conclusion that boards of directors that were Protestant-dominated tended to ensure that their companies favoured the employment of Protestants (and, by the same token, those boards of directors that were dominated by Catholics probably employed a predominantly Catholic workforce). Having said that, the workforce of Thomas Gallaher's tobacco manufacturing firm in Belfast was reputed to be non-sectarian.[62] There were some exceptions to the general rule.

As well as controlling what kinds of people were employed in their businesses, the top directors also wielded great power over the wages, working-conditions, and political activities of their employees. The evidence on wage-levels in Ireland during this period suggests that they were substantially lower than the wages paid to workers in other parts of the United Kingdom. Indeed, the great success of Irish entrepreneurs like William Martin Murphy and Edward Harland has at least partially been attributed to the poor wages that they paid their employees. Despite attempts to rehabilitate William Martin Murphy as the prophet of the Celtic Tiger,[63] it remains the case that his success owed a great deal to the high level of expropriation from unskilled labourers in his employment who worked long hours for low pay.[64] Similarly, the average wage of Harland and Wolff employees was well below that paid to shipyard workers on the Mersey, the Tyne, and the Clyde; and a major cause of Belfast's shipbuilding success was the availability of cheap labour particularly in the case of unskilled men (the wage differential between skilled and unskilled

---

60 Kavanagh, 'The Belfast Business Community', 43–4.

61 David Johnson, 'Sir George Smith Clark', in Jeremy, *Dictionary of Business Biography*, i. 685.

62 David Johnson, 'Thomas Gallaher', ibid. ii. 463. According to his obituary: 'All questions of politics and of religion were excluded rigidly from his works, and neither one nor other weighed in the selection of his workers' (*Irish Times*, 4 May 1927).

63 Morrissey, *William Martin Murphy*, 3.

64 Bielenberg, 'Entrepreneurship, Power and Public Opinion in Ireland: The Career of William Martin Murphy', *Chronicon*, 2 (1998) <http://www.ucc.ie/chronicon/bielen.htm> (accessed 15 Nov. 2008).

workers was much higher in Belfast than in the rest of the United Kingdom).[65] Guinness, on the other hand, appears to have treated its workforce more fairly by paying better wages, introducing welfare and other benefits, and by reducing the number of hours in the working week to 48 in 1897 (when a working week of 54 hours continued to be the general rule for another twenty years).[66]

The Irish business elite—clustered in Belfast, Dublin, and Cork—also believed that they were entitled to control the political activities of their employees. In 1913, as we have seen, William Martin Murphy led the Dublin employers—both Protestant and Catholic—in their crusade to de-unionize the Dublin workers.[67] James Larkin, a native of Liverpool, had founded the Irish Transport and General Workers' Union in Dublin in 1909. By the end of 1911, the Union had gained a membership of 18,000, and campaigned to improve the working conditions and wages of the Dublin working class. The Dublin working class worked in extremely difficult circumstances: workers on the tramways, for example, were paid 25 per cent less than their counterparts in Belfast and Liverpool.[68] Working conditions were also extremely difficult: employees were allowed only one day off in every ten, and a working day could last anything from 9 to 17 hours.[69] Unsurprisingly, the Dublin employers were also vehemently anti-Union. When John Carroll attended a Christmas breakfast organized by Larkin in 1911, he was dismissed by his employer, Jameson's distillery, for having done so.[70]

Larkin led attempts to unionize the Dublin workers and used the policy of the sympathetic strike to enforce union demands on workers. As we have seen, the conflict between the ITGWU and the Dublin employers came to a head in September 1913 when William Martin Murphy, the leader of the newly created Dublin employers' federation, locked out 20,000 workers who refused to sign a declaration renouncing their membership of the union.[71] Murphy refused to meet the union leaders and also ignored the recommendations of a special court of inquiry set up by the Board of Trade which concluded that: 'whatever may have been the intention of the employers, this document imposed upon the signatories conditions which are contrary to individual liberty and which no workman or body of workmen would reasonably be expected to accept.'[72] When the leaders

[65] W. Johnson and F. Geary, 'Sir Edward James Harland', in Jeremy, *Dictionary of Business Biography*, iii. 39–40.   [66] Dennison and MacDonagh, *Guinness, 1886–1939*, Ch. 8.

[67] Murphy may have been allied with Protestant businessmen professionally but he objected to his daughter's relationship with the young Samuel Beckett because he was Church of Ireland and 'separated the young lovers' (Martin Dwyer, 'A Family Skeleton', *Irish Times*, 6 Dec. 2008).

[68] John Newsinger, *Rebel City: Larkin, Connolly, and the Dublin Labour Movement* (London, 2004), 46; Bielenberg, 'Entrepreneurship, Power and Public Opinion in Ireland'.

[69] Newsinger, *Rebel City.*   [70] Ibid. 27–8.

[71] Morrissey, *William Martin Murphy*, 51.

[72] Dermot Keogh, 'William Martin Murphy', in Jeremy, *Dictionary of Business Biography*, iv. 391–2.

of the British unions refused to inaugurate a sympathetic strike in solidarity with their Irish colleagues, the ITGWU was as good as defeated, and after four months without wages during the winter of 1913–14, many workers gradually returned to work and renounced the union in January 1914.[73] Murphy's success in the Dublin Lockout led to his becoming the darling of the Protestant- and Unionist-dominated Dublin Chamber of Commerce, and to his rightful demonization by the *Irish Worker* as 'a soulless, money-grubbing tyrant'.[74] It also demonstrated the extraordinary power that the boards of directors of the major Irish companies had over their employees in the pre-War period. The situation was not dissimilar in Belfast where Thomas Gallaher, the tobacco manufacturer and director of the Belfast Steamship Co., refused to recognize the ITGWU and sent to Liverpool for replacements of striking dock workers in Belfast in 1907. In Gallaher's York Street Factory his opposition to trade Unionism was crystallized into a motto displayed on the factory wall: 'Do not argue'.[75] Indeed, these episodes reveal that Irish Catholic nationalist employers were just as capable of screwing their workers as their Protestant Unionist colleagues.

Finally, it is important to emphasize that the members of the Irish business elite had a great deal of political influence and power. Almost one-fifth (forty-three or 17 per cent) of the 247 businessmen under review were MPs. The majority of these were Conservatives or Unionists (twenty-five or 59 per cent) but there were also a small number of Liberals (three or 6.5 per cent), Liberal Unionists (three or 6.5 per cent), and a substantial minority who were Home Rulers (twelve or 28 per cent). Political influence was useful in two important respects. First, political contacts enabled some of the businessmen in this study to obtain lucrative government contracts. William Martin Murphy, who sat as Home Rule MP for the St Patrick's division of Dublin between 1885 and 1892, was able to take advantage of a series of Acts passed between 1883 and 1891 which provided assistance for the construction of light railways in the west of Ireland. In 1886, Murphy gained a government loan of £54,000 as well as the contract to build the West Clare Railway which he also owned. Of thirteen railway lines constructed under Balfour's Railway Acts of 1889 and 1891, two were built by Murphy and these were later worked by the Cork, Bandon, and South Coast Railway of which Murphy was a director.[76] T. P. O'Connor later recalled that Murphy's presence in parliament was 'useful to him from a commercial point of view' because the building of railways and tramways 'depended largely on the sanction of parliament'.[77] Similarly, the Belfast shipbuilders gained valuable government contracts during the Great War. Workman-Clark, for example, concentrated on Admiralty work during the

[73] Morrissey, *William Martin Murphy*, 56.   [74] Ibid. 38, 47.
[75] Johnson, 'Thomas Gallaher', 463.   [76] Morrissey, *William Martin Murphy*, 11–12.
[77] O'Connor, *Memoirs of an Old Parliamentarian*, ii. 55.

second half of the Great War, and Clark received a baronetcy for his service to the industry during the war.[78]

Second, political influence enabled businessmen to influence the policies pursued by the two main political parties in Ireland after 1886—the Irish Parliamentary Party and the Irish Unionist Party—and thereby to influence government policy towards Ireland during this critical period. A number of prominent businessmen were senior members of the Irish Parliamentary Party from the 1870s onwards. William Shaw, the chairman of the Munster Bank, sat as Home Rule MP for county Cork between 1874 and 1885, and was Charles Stewart Parnell's predecessor as chairman of the IPP.[79] Sir Walter Richard Nugent was a substantial Catholic landowner, the deputy chairman of the Midland Great Western Railway (in 1913), and Home Rule MP for south Westmeath between 1907 and 1918. Similarly, Thomas Henry Grattan Esmonde was a Catholic landowner, a director of the Dublin and South Eastern Railway Co., the chairman of the National Bank, and Home Rule MP for constituencies in Wexford, Kerry, and Dublin between 1885 and 1918 (as well as sometime chief whip of the IPP). Some individuals were Home Rule MPs who later joined or were recruited to the business world. Thomas Sexton, for instance, was a Christian Brothers' School (CBS) educated journalist who sat as MP for constituencies in Sligo, Belfast, and Kerry between 1880 and 1896, and who became chairman of the *Freeman's Journal* (1892–1912) and subsequently chairman of Boland's Dublin bakery. It is possible that some MPs were recruited as directors by companies to provide them with insider knowledge of government policy. Although none of the businessmen who were Home Rule MPs were the leaders of the IPP (with the exception of Shaw), Sexton, Nugent, and Esmonde were all key figures in determining party policy from 1886 onwards. Nationalist entrepreneurs like William Martin Murphy and William Francis Cotton (the managing director of the Alliance and Dublin Consumer's Gas Co., a director of the Dublin United Tramways Co., and Home Rule MP for south Dublin between 1910 and 1917) also ensured that some sections of the IPP adopted a reactionary policy towards trade unionism.[80] Some members of the IPP supported the cause of labour—and there were some vocal critics of the behaviour of the directors of the big railway companies—but the Party tended to take a neutral stance on industrial action.[81]

The leading figures in the Irish Unionist movement were generally prominent Ulster businessmen.[82] The key figures in the Belfast shipbuilding industry, for instance, were all vehement supporters of Unionism. Edward Harland was Unionist MP for North Belfast; Gustav Wolff was Unionist MP for east Belfast,

---

[78] David Johnson, 'Sir George Smith Clark', in Jeremy, *Dictionary of Business Biography*, i. 684.
[79] *Freeman's Journal*, 21 Sept. 1895.
[80] Cotton was firmly on the right of the IPP and even advocated that Dublin Corporation should give loyal addresses to visiting monarchs. See Patrick Maume, *The Long Gestation: Irish Nationalist Life, 1891–1918* (Dublin, 1999), 224–5.   [81] See the discussion of this point in Ch. 4.
[82] This is the central conclusion of Kavanagh's doctoral dissertation.

and he was a patron of the Orange Institution in east Belfast;[83] Francis Workman was not an MP but represented the Victorian ward on the Belfast city council between 1908 and 1925; and Sir George Smith Clark was Unionist MP for Belfast between 1907 and 1910 before becoming a Unionist senator in the Northern Irish parliament between 1925 and 1935. Some of the businessmen who were Unionist MPs played a leading role within the Unionist Party. James Craig, although not one of the directors included in this study, was a major shareholder in Dunville and Co., Unionist MP for various Down constituencies 1906–21, and became the first Prime Minister of Northern Ireland in 1921.[84] The main funders of the UVF were Belfast businessmen. Three-quarters of the UVF Military Council, for instance, were businessmen.[85] William Chaine, a director of the York Street Flax Co., was not untypical, and he donated £5,000 to the UVF Indemnity Fund in 1914.[86] The directors of the Ulster-based banks, however, did not openly express their opposition to Home Rule as they had branches throughout Ulster and in the rest of Ireland, and were concerned that if they were too closely identified with Unionism that this might lead to the withdrawl of deposits by nationalist customers. Banks therefore tried to keep out of public politics and encouraged their staff to do likewise.[87] Even so, it may well be that the strength and influence of Unionism on British government policy 1912–14 was largely due to the financial support which Ulster businessmen gave to the movement.

II

Who were the Irish business elite? The top Irish business people in both 1883 and 1911 were exclusively male: women, it seems, were not eligible to be selected as the directors of the top firms.[88] The top businessmen were also overwhelmingly (81 per cent) Protestant: just over two-thirds (68 per cent) of the top businessmen were Episcopalians, and there were the same proportion of Presbyterians and Nonconformists in the business elite as there were in the general population (they accounted for about 13 per cent of the total population in 1911).[89] The Irish Quakers were, however, significantly over-represented in the Irish business elite.[90]

[83] Walford Johnson and Frank Geary, 'Gustav Wilhelm Wolff', 858.

[84] Craig's father became a clerk with Dunville and Co., distillers, in 1856 (aged 28) and by the age of 50 he was a director of the firm and a self-made millionaire (Kavanagh, 'The Belfast Business Community', 53, 272, 352).

[85] Ibid. 68.   [86] Ibid. 180.

[87] Philip Ollerenshaw, *Banking in Ireland: The Belfast Banks, 1825–1914* (Manchester, 1987), 157–63.

[88] It is likely that this was an informal rather than a formal requirement of eligibility, and that women did play a leading role in some of the smaller companies in Ireland during this period.

[89] The Nonconformists listed here include Quakers, Unitarians, Congregationalists, Methodists, and 'Evangelical Protestants'.

[90] At the yearly Quaker meeting held in Dublin in June 1899, it was reported that the Society of Friends had a total membership throughout Ireland of 2,586 although only about one-fifth of

Quakers accounted for about one-tenth of 1 per cent of the Irish population, and yet they constituted 5.5 per cent of the business elite: some of the Irish Quaker businessmen clearly rose rapidly from 'humble circumstances' at the beginning of the nineteenth century to positions of economic strength by the 1880s due to their careful reinvestment of profits rather than ostentatious spending.[91] Catholics, on the other hand, accounted for about three-quarters of the Irish population in 1911, and yet constituted less than one-fifth (19 per cent) of the business elite in both 1883 and 1911. Catholics were, therefore, enormously under-represented in the Irish business elite.

The vast majority of Irish businessmen were Irish born.[92] Although the data on birthplace are incomplete (we know where 91 of the 247 directors were born or 37 per cent of the total), almost all of these (87 per cent) had been born in Ireland, with a small number born in England (8 per cent), Scotland (2 per cent), Canada (1 per cent), India (1 per cent), and Germany (1 per cent). However, the proportion of non-natives in the Irish business elite (13 per cent) is far higher than their proportion in the Irish population as a whole (1.35 per cent of the Irish population were born outside of Ireland in 1861).[93] Moreover, it is clear that a high proportion of the most successful entrepreneurs in Irish society were immigrants. Sir Edward James Harland, the founder of Harland and Wolff, was a native of Scarborough in England. Gustav Wilhelm Wolff, his partner, was from Hamburg in Germany. Sir George Smith Clark, one of the partners of Workman-Clark, was from Paisley in Scotland. Sir John Arnott, the managing director of Arnott's drapery in Dublin and Belfast, and the owner of both the *Irish Times* and the *Northern Whig*, was a native of Auchtermuchty, Fife, in Scotland. John Cleaver, the managing director of Robinson and Cleaver, a Belfast-based linen manufacturer and silk merchant, was from Sussex.[94]

Furthermore, a number of other prominent Irish-born businessmen inherited businesses from their non-Irish-born parents. Sir John Milne Barbour, for instance, the chairman of William Barbour and sons and the managing director of the Linen Thread Co., inherited the firm that had been initially

these were regular attenders and most of these were in Ulster (Alan Megahey, *The Irish Protestant Churches in the Twentieth Century* (Basingstoke, 2000), 22).

[91] Among the Quaker businessmen were Joseph Todhunter Pim, the chairman of Pim brothers, Dublin and sometime governor of the Bank of Ireland; his brother, Frederick William Pim, a director of various railway companies; Marcus Goodbody, a director of Dublin South City Market Co.; his brother James Perry Goodbody, a director of the Great Southern and Western Railway Co.; and Richard Pim, a stockbroker and chairman of the board of the Dublin and Kingstown Railway Co. and described by his obituarist as 'one of the leading figures in the commerce of his native city' (*Irish Times*, 30 May 1911). On the Irish Quaker population, see D. E. C. Eversley, 'The Demography of the Irish Quakers, 1650–1850', in J. M. Goldstrom and L. A. Clarkson, *Irish Population, Economy and Society* (Oxford, 1981), 59.

[92] This complements MacDonagh's discussion of the directors of the Bank of Ireland whom he describes as 'almost entirely Irish-born' ('The Victorian Bank', 46).

[93] Ó Gráda, *Ireland: A New Economic History*, 328.

[94] See his obituary in the *Irish Times*, 22 Sept. 1926.

Table 5.1. The Religion of the Members of the Business Elite, 1883–1911

Religion	1883–1911	1883	1911
Episcopalian	148 (68%)	61 (71%)	92 (63.5%)
Catholic	41 (19%)	15 (17%)	28 (19%)
Presbyterian	11 (5%)	4 (5%)	10 (7%)
Nonconformist	17 (8%)	6 (7%)	15 (10.5%)
[Quaker	12 (5.5%)	3 (3.5%)	11 (7.5%)]
(Not known	30	13	19)
Number (known)	217	86	145

founded by his Scottish grandfather, John Barbour of Paisley in Scotland, who had first established the linen thread industry at Lisburn in county Antrim.[95] William James Pirrie, whose grandfather was Scottish, was born in Quebec, Canada and went on to become the chairman of Harland and Wolff following the death of Harland in 1895. Although Francis Workman was born in Belfast in 1856, his family had emigrated to Ulster from Scotland at the beginning of the nineteenth century.[96] James Mackie, the managing director of the major linen manufacturing firm, inherited the business from his Scottish-born father, also called James, who migrated to Ireland from Forfar in 1845.

As both Ó Gráda and Lee have emphasized, immigrant businessmen played a critically important role in late nineteenth-century Irish economic development, and a number of foreign born entrepreneurs appear to have been able to capitalize on Irish opportunities in a way that natives—both Protestant and Catholic—could not.[97] Data are available on the place of birth of most of the Irish-born businessmen (seventy-eight out of ninety-one or 86 per cent), and almost half (thirty-eight or 49 per cent) were born in the north-eastern province of Ulster. Most of these (twenty-four out of 38) were born in Belfast or the hinterland of the city in county Antrim. Less than one-third (twenty-four or 30.5 per cent) were born in Leinster, with most of these (twenty-one out of 24) born in Dublin. And about one-fifth (sixteen or 20.5 per cent) were born in the south-western province of Munster, with a large proportion of these (eleven out of 16) born in Cork city. Broadly speaking, these data suggest that the Irish-born businessmen were generally born in one of Ireland's foremost three cities: Belfast, Dublin, or Cork. None of the Irish-born businessmen in this sample was born in the least-industrialized and most agricultural western province of Connacht.[98] The majority of the top businessmen lived in Ireland. Of the 247 members

[95] Kavanagh, 'The Belfast Business Community', 335–6.
[96] David Johnson, 'Francis Workman', in Jeremy, *Dictionary of Business Biography*, v. 892.
[97] Ó Gráda, *Ireland: A New Economic History*, 326–8; Lee, *Modernisation of Irish Society*, 19.
[98] The data on place of birth within Ireland are available for 79.

of the business elite, we know where 232 (94 per cent) resided. More than three-quarters (176 or 76 per cent) lived permanently in Ireland; about one-sixth (thirty-five or 15 per cent) lived permanently in England; and less than one in ten (twenty or 8.5 per cent) oscillated between Ireland and England.[99]

Those who lived in England permanently tended to be those members of English railway companies and banks who appear to have invested in Irish businesses. Sir Richard Moon, for instance, a resident of Coventry, had been chairman of the London and North Western Railway since 1861 before being appointed the chairman of the Dundalk and Greenore Railway Co. Similarly, Charles James Cropper, who lived at Kendal, was a director of the London and North Western before becoming a director of Dundalk, Newry, and Greenore Railway Co.[100] Ernest Haliburton Cunard, a director of the Cunard Steam Ship Co. appears to have invested in the Fishguard and Rosslare Railways and Harbours Co., and was a director of that company. Baron Hillingdon and Lord Revelstoke, both English residents, were investors and directors of Arthur Guinness. As we have seen, the directors of the Provincial Bank of Ireland were based in London. Sir William John Walter Baynes, for instance, was a resident of Putney who was a director of the Provincial Bank as well as chairman of the East and West India Dock Co. and a director of the Atlas Assurance Co.

A number of members of the Irish business elite had business interests in both England and Ireland. Sir David Gamble, for instance, was a director of the United Alkali Co. in St. Helen's (where he lived) and of Parr's bank, as well as a director of the Londonderry and Enniskillen Railway company (in 1883).[101] Maurice Brooks was a director of the Alliance and Dublin Consumer's Gas Co. in Dublin, where he lived, but: 'he had many business establishments [in England]'.[102] Some of the Irish business elite had business experience in other parts of the world before turning their attention to Ireland. Edmund McNeil was born at Cushendun, county Antrim, before becoming a sheep farmer in Victoria in Australia between 1839 and 1847. On his return to Ireland he entered the family land agency business and became a director of the Belfast and Northern Counties Railway. Similarly, William McAndrew, who was probably a native of

[99] One of the top businessmen, Sir Stuart Saunders Hogg, was the chief commissioner of police and the chairman of the municipality in Calcutta.

[100] The London and North Western combined with an Irish railway company to develop the Dundalk and Greenore Railway Co. and that is why these individuals were directors. Because the Dundalk and Greenore Railway Co. had been partially established by the London and North Western it was run as much from London as it was from Dublin.

[101] Gamble was a native of Dublin where his father, who was a native of Fermanagh, was a manufacturer of bleaching powder. However, the family business was relocated to St Helen's in 1828 where Josias C. Gamble and Sons became the basis of the chemical industry of that town, and later amalgamated with the United Alkali Company (*Irish Times*, 7 Feb. 1907).

[102] Ibid. 7 Dec. 1905.

Table 5.2. Location of all Firms in 1883 and 1911

Province	1883	1911
Ulster	10 (29%)	16 (31%)
Leinster	19 (56%)	29 (56%)
Munster	4 (12%)	4 (7.5%)
Connacht	1 (3%)	2 (3.5%)
Other	0	1 (2%)
Number	34	52

Liverpool, had been a merchant in South America (his wife was Peruvian) before becoming a director of the Belfast Central Railway Co. It may be that Ireland was regarded as just one of many international locations where profitable business interests could be developed.

Of those who lived in Ireland, the majority lived in the three major Irish cities. What is striking about the place of residence within Ireland, however, is the large proportion of the business elite who lived in Dublin rather than Belfast. Almost half of the total (ninety-seven or 49.5 per cent) lived in Leinster, with most of these (seventy-one of ninety-seven) living in Dublin. Only about one-third (sixty-seven or 34 per cent) lived in Ulster, and most of these (forty-four of sixty-seven) lived in Belfast and the hinterland of the city. One-sixth (twenty-six or 13.5 per cent) of the business elite lived in Munster, most of whom were residents of Cork city (twenty-three of twenty-six). And a handful (six or 3 per cent) of the top businessmen lived in Connacht, exactly half of these in county Sligo, the Connacht county nearest to Ulster. Broadly speaking, this suggests that Dublin rather than Belfast was the capital of Irish business, if this is determined according to where most businessmen lived. This assertion is confirmed also by the location of most of the businesses in this study which were based in Leinster/Dublin rather than Ulster/Belfast or Munster/Cork (see Table 5.2).

Almost half (103 or 42 per cent) of the members of the Irish business elite were either landowners or the members of landed families. All sections of the Irish landowning class were represented in the business elite (see Table 5.3). About one-third (29 per cent) of the landed businessmen were born on estates of fewer than 1,000 acres; about one-fifth owned medium-sized estates of between 1,000 and 5,000 acres; and half owned estates of more than 5,000 acres (including about one-third who were both members of the business elite and the landed elite who owned estates of more than 10,000 acres). Irish landowners were probably inclined to become businessmen because they had capital to invest, because some of them had business experience from the running of their estates, and because some of the major railway companies built tracks across their estates. It is striking that railway companies whose tracks crossed particular counties tended to have

Table 5.3. The Acreage of Estates Owned by Businessmen who were Born into Landed Families

Acres	1883–1911	1883	1911
0–499	15 (15%)	7 (17%)	8 (12%)
500–999	14 (14%)	6 (14%)	9 (14%)
1,000–4,999	22 (21%)	12 (28.5%)	11 (17%)
5,000–9,999	19 (18%)	5 (12%)	14 (22%)
10,000+	33 (32%)	12 (28.5%)	23 (35%)
Number	103	42 [42% of total]	65 [40% of total]

landowners from those counties on their boards of directors. Philip O'Reilly and Richard Anthony Nugent were both directors of the Midland Great Western, for example, and both were born into estates in county Westmeath that the railway line crossed. However, it is also clear that some of the landowning businessmen were actually entrepreneurs who later bought into land with the profits that they had made from their business careers. Of the thirty-three landowner-businessmen with estates of more than 10,000 acres, thirty owned great estates in Ireland. Of these thirty landowners, twenty can be identified in Ireland in 1848 suggesting that they were old landed families who decided to invest their capital in Irish business during the second half of the nineteenth century.[103] One-third of these top landowner-businessmen, however, were entrepreneurs who made substantial profits from their business ventures and then bought into land in an attempt to buy into the perceived status and respectability of the great Irish landowning class. Two prominent businessmen who bought into land in this manner were Lord Ardilaun and James Bruce. Bruce was a director of Dunville and Co. who purchased the 9,230 acre Benburb estate in Tyrone from Viscount Powerscourt and established a country house there. Similarly, Ardilaun—who was Edward Cecil Guinness's brother—purchased a 31,342 acre estate in counties Galway, Mayo, and Dublin. At a smaller level, Sir Ralph Smith Cusack, who was the son of a surgeon and Professor at the University of Dublin, married Elizabeth Barker 'a lady belonging to an old Meath family', which seems to have provided him with a small estate in the county.[104]

It is often claimed that a successful entrepreneur does not require an education, and particularly a third-level education, in order to be successful. A German

---

[103] I searched for each of these landowners in *Thom's Directory* for 1848 in the county lists of local officers (Lord lieutenants, Deputy lieutenants, High Sheriffs, magistrates, and so on). Those families who were landowners in 1848—before the Encumbered Estates Act was introduced in 1849—were probably old Irish landed families, whereas landowners whose names do not appear in the lists of county officers in 1848 are likely to have bought into land during the second half of the nineteenth century.

[104] *Irish Times*, 4 Mar. 1910. Cusack owned 1,229 acres (valued at £1,062).

Table 5.4. Secondary Education of Businessmen, 1883–1911

Type of school	1883–1911	1883	1911
English Public School	60 (48%)	13 (43%)	47 (47%)
Scottish Public School	1 (1%)	1 (3%)	1 (1%)
English Catholic Public School	15 (12%)	1 (3%)	14 (14%)
English Protestant School	6 (5%)	1 (3%)	5 (5%)
Scottish Protestant School	4 (3%)	2 (7%)	2 (2%)
English Quaker School	8 (6%)	2 (7%)	8 (8%)
English Catholic School	2 (2%)	1 (3%)	2 (2%)
Irish Protestant School	27 (22%)	9 (30%)	21 (21%)
Irish Methodist School	1 (1%)	—	1 (1%)
Irish Catholic School	8 (6%)	2 (7%)	7 (7%)
Privately	1 (1%)	1 (3%)	—
Number	124	30	100

Table 5.5. Tertiary education of Businessmen, 1883–1911

University	1883–1911	1883	1911
Oxbridge	42 (48%)	13 (37%)	29 (51%)
British University	5 (6%)	3 (9%)	2 (4%)
European University	2 (2%)	0	2 (4%)
Trinity College Dublin	34 (39%)	19 (54%)	19 (33%)
Queen's Colleges	6 (7%)	0	6 (11%)
Roman Catholic University	1 (1%)	0	1 (2%)
National University of Ireland	1 (1%)	0	1 (2%)
University College Dublin	1 (1%)	0	1 (2%)
Number	88 [36%]	35 [35%]	57 [35%]

banker, for instance, advised a budding industrialist in 1884 not to bother going to university which he regarded as a mere 'means of enjoyment for times of rest, like the cigar after lunch'. Instead, the banker advised the young man to get into practical business as soon as possible, to look for a financial backer and observe the United States of America.[105] However, a substantial proportion of the Irish business elite did receive both a secondary and a university education (see Tables 5.4 and 5.5). At least half (124 or 50 per cent) of the businessmen in this study had received a secondary education, and it is likely that many others had received some form of private secondary education. Half of these had attended English and Scottish Public Schools—which did not tend to provide an education relevant to the world of business—and it is possible that businessmen sent their sons to these schools in an attempt to ape the manners of

---

[105] Eric Hobsbawm, *The Age of Empire, 1875–1914* (London, 1989), 175.

the landed aristocracy and perhaps to create beneficial networks for their sons.[106] One-eighth of the businessmen had attended English Catholic Public Schools and this suggests that the type of Catholic who was a member of the business elite was extremely well-to-do and probably drawn from a landed background.[107] About one-sixth attended other English and Scottish Protestant schools, and most significant here were the high proportion who had attended the Quaker schools at York, Scarborough, and London, revealing the important role that Quaker businessmen played in the Irish economy.

About one-quarter of the Irish businessmen had been educated at Irish Protestant schools, a significant proportion of whom (twelve) had attended the Belfast Royal Academical Institution (known as 'Inst') which was a Presbyterian school.[108] At a time when the British and Irish education systems did not generally offer a commercial education, this was one of the schools that did provide training in business and science. In the late nineteenth century, the school reorganized its writing department as a commercial department and consequently more entrepreneurs were educated at this school than at any other Belfast school.[109] About one-twentieth of the business elite attended Irish Catholic schools, and these were generally the elite schools of Clongowes and Belvedere, which reflects the fact that Catholic businessmen tended to be drawn from relatively prosperous backgrounds.[110] Overall, it is significant that more than two-thirds of the Irish businessmen had received a secondary education in England and Scotland—rather than in Ireland—which perhaps suggests the importance of immigrants, and the children of immigrant families, to the Irish business elite, as well as the importance that Irish businessmen attached to building networks in other parts of the United Kingdom. The fact that many sectors of the Irish economy were devoted to exporting to the British market meant that cross-channel networks could be enormously beneficial to Irish entrepreneurial endeavour.

More than one-third of the Irish business elite had received a university education. A surprisingly high proportion of these had attended Oxbridge, which did not generally provide an education in commerce or engineering that would have been useful to a business career. It is likely, therefore, that businessmen sent their sons to Oxford or Cambridge in order to gain respectability and status

[106] The English Public Schools attended by the business elite were Eton, Haileybury, Cheltenham, Repton, Westminster, Marlborough, Harrow, Winchester, Charterhouse, Wellington, Rugby, Radley, Clifton College, and Merchiston, Edinburgh.

[107] The English Catholic Public Schools attended by the business elite were Downside, Stoney-hurst, Oscott, Beaumont (Windsor), and the Oratory School, Edgbaston.

[108] Alexander Montgomery Carlisle, R. H. S. Reade, the managing director of the York Street Flax Co., and Pirrie all attended Inst.

[109] Kavanagh, 'The Belfast Business Community', 143–4.

[110] Although one of the Catholic businessmen—Thomas Sexton—had attended a Christian Brothers school.

for their families in a world that did not yet regard business as the new God. A smaller number of businessmen attended other British universities. The chemical industry became increasingly important during the twentieth century and some members of the business elite had gained an education in chemistry that was beneficial to developing their business interests. Sir David Gamble, for instance, the director of the United Alkali Co. and of an Irish railway company, had been educated at University College, London, and at Anderson's college, Glasgow, where his 'attention was specially and designedly directed to chemistry and natural science'.[111] Two members of the Irish business elite had attended universities in Germany—at Bonn and Darmstadt—which undoubtedly provided some training in business and industry. More than two-thirds of the Irish businessmen were graduates of Trinity College Dublin. Once again, this university did not provide a commercial education, and it is likely that status-seeking businessmen who did not have the resources to send their children to Oxbridge, sent them to Trinity instead. Trinity may have also provided the opportunity for young businessmen to make profitable contacts among the sons of Irish Protestant professionals and landowners.

Almost one in ten of the business elite attended The Queen's Colleges (two at Belfast and four at Cork), and it is clear that The Queen's College at Belfast (later The Queen's University, Belfast (QUB)) was beginning to provide a business training in this period. In 1910, QUB opened a Faculty of Commerce that was largely funded by prominent Belfast businessmen like Sir William Crawford (a director of the York Street Flax Co). And from 1912, the university began to offer a degree in mechanical engineering partly thanks to a donation of £7,500 from Pirrie to set up physics and engineering laboratories, 'the Harland laboratories'.[112] However, these developments came too late for the businessmen included in this sample, and—indeed—too late for the golden age of the Ulster economy which fell into decline from the 1920s onwards. Only a handful of Irish businessmen had attended the Catholic universities in Ireland perhaps reflecting both the non-commercial nature of the education on offer, and the small proportion of Catholics who were able to break into the business elite. However, one of the prominent Catholic businessmen in this study, William Francis Cotton, the director of the Alliance and Dublin Consumer's Gas Co., had attended the Dublin Polytechnic Institute which later became the College of Science. Before the development of commercial and industrial education at the Irish universities from about 1910 onwards, the municipal colleges and polytechnics were the only places where a third-level business education was provided in Ireland. Indeed, the Royal College of Science, a foundation of the Department of Science and Art, became the natural centre for education in

---

[111] *Irish Times*, 7 Feb. 1907.
[112] Kavanagh, 'The Belfast Business Community', 114, 127–8, 130–1, 142.

Table 5.6. Occupations of Directors of Irish Businesses, 1883–1911

Occupation	1883–1911	1883	1911
Business only	114 (46%)	45 (45%)	80 (49%)
Business and land	58 (23%)	29 (29%)	32 (20%)
Business and professional	100 (40%)	34 (34%)	70 (43%)
Of professionals			
Barrister	23 (9%)	10	14
Solicitor	10 (4%)	5	6
Engineer	6 (2%)	3	3
Author	1 (0.5%)	0	1
Architect	1 (0.5%)	1	0
Surveyor	1 (0.5%)	0	1
Army officer	38 (15%)	10	28
RAF/Navy officer	3 (1.5%)	0	3
Land agent	7 (3%)	2	6
Accountant	8 (3%)	2	6
Auditor	1 (0.5%)	1	1
Journalist	1 (0.5%)	0	1
Senior administrator	13 (5%)	4	9
Number	247	99	164

Note: Some individuals had more than one occupation.

science in late nineteenth-century Ireland although it tended to recruit students from Britain and its graduates tended to work in Britain and the colonies rather than Ireland.[113]

Ostensibly, the educational experience of the Irish business elite suggests that they were not as well trained in commerce and industry as we might have expected. If we look at the other occupations pursued by members of the Irish business elite (Table 5.6), we can see that very few of them had benefited from specific training in commerce, engineering, or industry. About half (46 per cent) of the businessmen under review had no other occupation and pursued an exclusively business career (I will consider this category in detail below). One-quarter (23 per cent) of the businessmen under review owned landed estates. These individuals probably had substantial capital (especially if they had sold their estates under the Land Acts) as well as a modicum of business experience and these factors are likely to have propelled them into the Irish business world. About one in twenty of the top businessmen were senior administrators in the Irish, British, or Indian Civil Services. These individuals probably also had substantial capital as well as influence over the distribution of

---

[113] Richard Jarrell, 'Differential National Development and Science in the Nineteenth Century: The Problems of Quebec and Ireland', in Nathan Reingold and Marc Rothenberg (eds.), *Scientific Colonialism: A Cross-cultural Comparison* (Washington, DC, 1987), 345.

government contacts, and this would have made senior administrators attractive recruits to any board of directors.

Almost half of the businessmen under review were professionals of some description. A significant number (13 per cent) of the top businessmen were trained in the law as either barristers or solicitors, and these men undoubtedly carried out the essential legal work of their companies. Accountants and auditors (3.5 per cent), surveyors (0.5 per cent), and architects (0.5 per cent) also carried out essential work for the companies which they served. At the inaugural dinner held by the Institute of Chartered Accountants in Ireland at the Shelbourne Hotel in December 1888, accountants, lawyers, and businessmen rubbed shoulders with one another and Maurice Brooks, one of Dublin's most successful businessmen, explained that:

He remembered the time when the presence of an accountant in a place of business was looked upon in much the same light as the visit of an undertaker or a coroner would be. (Laughter.) Now, he was glad to say, that state of opinion had passed away. Accountants were now more or less connected and necessarily connected with every mercantile enterprise of any importance, and with every joint stock company of any magnitude, and on the whole he believed their connection was for the public good . . . he had no doubt it would prosper and be of public benefit.[114]

However, the very low proportion of businessmen who had been trained as engineers (2 per cent) is striking given the key role that engineers played in manufacturing and industry. It may be that some of the key staff of any business were not the members of the boards of directors or the top staff who were listed in *Burdett's Official Intelligence*, and that there was a second tier of skilled staff who played a critically important role in developing new technologies and techniques. This was certainly the case with Guinness's during the last quarter of the nineteenth century when J. T. Purser acted as general manager and was probably responsible for the day-to-day running of the company, and Geoghegan, head brewer, was responsible for the technical and scientific development of the company.[115] It is possible that many of the other companies under review had a second tier of experts who were in a position to advise their boards of directors on scientific and technical developments.

A very high proportion (15 per cent) of the businessmen under review were army officers. Sir Thomas Herbert Cochrane Troubridge, for example, was a Sandhurst educated army officer as well as a director of the Collooney, Ballina, and Belmullet Railways and Piers Co. It may have been the case that some of the skills learned by army officers at places like Sandhurst and Woolwich (knowledge of munitions, for instance, would require knowledge of engineering

---

[114] Brooks's speech, quot. *Accountant*, 1 Dec. 1888, which in turn is quoted in Philip O'Regan, ' "Elevating the Profession": The Institute of Chartered Accountants in Ireland and the Implementation of Social Closure Strategies, 1888–1909', *Accounting, Business and Financial History*, 18 (Mar. 2008), 52.   [115] Corran, 'Edward Cecil Guinness', 681–2.

and physics) were useful in business. However, it is probably more likely that the high proportion of army officers was due to the necessity for the non-inheriting sons of landowners to find alternative occupations; and, having served in the forces as young men, many of them seem to have gone into business later in life. Lastly, it is clear that a significant number of land agents were prominent in the Irish business world; and they account for 3 per cent of my sample. Obviously, land agents were businessmen, responsible for running estates as business concerns, and so the management and business skills learned in that profession were easily transferable to the boardroom. It is noteworthy that Arthur Guinness, the founder of the St James's Gate Brewery, was the son of a land agent. And Fane Vernon, a prominent Irish land agent (he was agent to the Earl of Pembroke and Montgomery's Dublin property), was the chairman of the board of directors of the Great Northern Railway, as well as a director of the Bank of Ireland and of several other railway companies in 1911.[116] William Burton Carson was also a land agent as well as a director of the Royal Bank of Ireland and the Great Northern Railway, and he was also a former apprentice to Fane Vernon.

Perhaps the most important single group within the Irish business elite were the individuals who pursued only a career in business and had not generally benefited from either secondary or tertiary education. In fact, the most successful businessmen in this study tended to have worked their way up from junior positions in their companies to become the managing directors of their companies. Robert Henry Sturrock Reade, the son of a Belfast doctor, attended the Royal Belfast Academical Institution before taking up an apprenticeship with the York Street Flax Co. in 1854 (when he was just 16). As a result of Reade's success in setting up a branch organization of the company in New York in 1856–7, he was rewarded with one of the four managing directorships when the firm was converted into a limited liability company in 1864, a position he retained until his death in 1913. Sir John Arnott began his business career as an apprentice to a Fife draper before going on to establish Arnott's drapery in Dublin and Belfast. Gustav Wolff was educated at the Collegiate Schools, Liverpool, where he learned engineering theory, and began his business career as an apprentice to Whitworth and Co., a Mancunian firm that manufactured tools and machinery. Sir Edward Harland, the son of a Scarborough doctor,

---

[116] Vernon was the grandson (on the mother's side) of John Leslie, Bishop of Kilmore and married the daughter of a Revd (*Irish Times*, 17 Feb. 1923). His wife, and the wives of many other prominent businessmen, were involved in philanthropy in Dublin. See, for instance, the membership list of the Association for promoting the employment of women in the *Irish Times*, 12 Apr. 1902, which included Vernon's wife, Maurice Brooks's wife, Lady Arnott, as well as the landowner—Sir Henry Bellingham—and Mrs Wrench, who was Frederick Wrench's wife and Sir Henry Bellingham's sister. The committees of the various philanthropic societies were a meeting place for the wives of the senior civil servants, businessmen, and landowners.

served a five-year apprenticeship at the engineering works of Robert Stephenson at Newcastle upon Tyne before going on to found Harland and Wolff in 1858. Both Francis Workman and Sir George Smith Clark were apprentices with Harland and Wolff before establishing Workman-Clark in 1880. However, all of these individuals came from families that had sufficient capital to pay for their secondary education or for their apprenticeships, and some of them also had contacts in the business world. This is not to diminish their great success in becoming skilled and effective businessmen, but to emphasize that there were no individuals who came from labouring or small farm backgrounds to become members of the business elite.

A significant number of prominent businessmen were born into a family business or were the sons of the directors of businesses and therefore learned their business skills from their fathers or in the family firm. Almost one-third (30 per cent) of the businessmen in this study were related to other businessmen, and about one in seven (thirty-five or 14 per cent) was the son of a prominent businessman.[117] William Martin Murphy was educated at Belvedere, and studied as a pupil of the Dublin architect, J. J. Lyons, but he learned his entrepreneurial skills when he took over the family building contracting business after his father's death in 1863 (when he was 19 years' old). John Milne Barbour was educated at Harrow, Oxford, and Darmstadt in Germany but he learned the linen trade when he joined his father's firm in the 1890s and later succeeded him as the managing director of the Linen Thread Co. in 1904. Thomas Gallaher, the tobacco manufacturer, learned the rudiments of his business in his father's corn mills as he recalled in the 1920s: 'at twelve and a half I was gaffer in charge of some fifty men. I managed them then without trouble and it has been the same ever since.'[118] Admittedly, he did also serve an apprenticeship with Osborne and Allan, the Derry merchants, where he learned the techniques of tobacco manufacture. James Mackie was born into and joined a successful linen equipment manufacturing firm owned by his father, although he had also received some business education at the Queen Street Working Men's Institute in Belfast (which later became the Belfast College of Technology). Sir William Quartus Ewart, the chairman of William Ewart and Son, flax spinners and linen manufacturers at Belfast, inherited the firm from his father, Sir William Ewart. William Watson junior, the managing director of the City of Dublin Steam Packet Co., took over the running of the firm from his father, William Watson, who oversaw the expansion of the firm in the mid-Victorian period.[119]

---

[117] Altogether, 74 of the 247 (30%) businessmen in this study were related to other businessmen: 35 (14%) had fathers who were businessmen; 7 or 3% had fathers in law who were businessmen; 1 or 0.5% had an uncle who was a businessman; 18 or 7% had brothers who were businessmen; 8 or 3% had brothers in law who were businessmen; and 7 or 3% had sons who were businessmen.

[118] *Northern Whig*, 23 Apr. 1923.

[119] William Watson senior's obituary is in the *Irish Times*, 11 Apr. 1883.

Robert Frederick Steuart Colvill was a director of both the Bank of Ireland and the Great Southern and Western Railway, and his father, James Chaigneau Colvill, had also sat on the board of directors of these two companies.

There were, however, some individuals who became senior members of railway companies after relatively modest beginnings. The senior staff of the Irish railway companies were often English-born men who came from inauspicious backgrounds but who had accumulated extensive experience of how railway companies operated. Joseph Tatlow, a native of Sheffield, whose father worked for the Midland Railway, entered the service of the Midland Railway at Derby in 1867 (aged 16); in 1874 he was appointed chief clerk to the general manager of the Glasgow and South Western Railway; in 1885 he became the general manager of the Belfast and County Down railway; and between 1890 and 1912 he was general manager and traffic manager of the Midland Great Western Railway.[120] Similarly, A. G. Reid, the son of a Congregational Minister at Newcastle upon Tyne, began his career with the London and North Western Railway Co., and later acted as the Superintendent of the Great Northern of Scotland railway for twenty years before becoming the general manager of the Dublin and South-Eastern Railway Co.. Henry Plews began his career with the London and North Western based at Manchester; in 1867, he moved to Ireland to become general manager of the Irish North Western Railway when the INWR worked with the LNWR to build seaworks at Greenore with the intention of linking Greenore with Dundalk and the rest of the INWR. In 1876, the INWR merged with the Northern of Ireland Railway and the Ulster Railway to become the Great Northern Railway; and from 1890 Plews acted as secretary to the company, and between 1896 and 1911 he was the general manager of what was by then the second largest railway company in Ireland. John Kerr graduated from The Queen's College, Belfast before serving an apprenticeship in civil engineering with Mr Bayley, the engineer in chief of the Great Southern and Western, and in 1887 he was appointed the chief engineer of the Cork, Bandon, and South Coast Railway before becoming its general manager in 1903.

A similar pattern is evident in some of the Irish banks. James Taylor Blackwood, a native of Castlenavin, county Down, trained as an accountant and acted as chief accountant for the Ulster Bank for a number of years before becoming secretary in 1870, and finally managing director of the company in 1884. Edwin Darley Hill, was born at Belfast in 1859, educated at the Royal Belfast Academical Institution, joined the Northern Bank in 1874 and managed the Grafton Street

---

[120] Tatlow, *Fifty Years of Railway Life*, 4, 21. Tatlow's father and two of his brothers worked for the Midland Railway so that: 'From pre-natal days I was destined for the railway service, as an oyster to its shell. The possibility of any other vocation for his sons never entered the mind of my father'. By 1912, Tatlow was settled into his success in his house in Dalkey (Kalafat) with his wife, Jane, who was 33 (and 28 years younger than him). When Kalafat was offered for sale in May 2006 it had an advised minimum value of €3.2 million. See <http://archives.tcm.ie/businesspost/2006/05/14/story14079.asp> (accessed 19 Mar. 2009).

Table 5.7. Club Membership of Irish Businessmen, 1883–1911

London clubs	Frequency
Army and Navy	1 (1%)
Downshire	1 (1%)
Atheneum	5 (3%)
Carlton	44 (25%)
Constitutional	9 (5%)
Junior Carlton	14 (8%)
Bachelors	8 (5%)
Reform	24 (14%)
National Liberal	5 (3%)
Travellers	9 (5%)
United Service	7 (4%)
Garrick	9 (5%)
Turf	17 (10%)
St Stephens	3 (2%)
Marlborough	8 (5%)
Royal automobile	3 (2%)
Dublin clubs	
Kildare Street	39 (22%)
Sackville Street	13 (7%)
St Stephen's Green	21 (12%)
Royal St George Yacht, Kingstown	19 (11%)
University	10 (6%)
Friendly Brothers	5 (3%)
Belfast clubs	
Ulster	28 (16%)
Ulster Reform	8 (5%)
Union	9 (5%)
Number	175

branch in Dublin for fourteen years before becoming general manager of the
bank in 1904, and managing director in 1905. Similarly, James Rippingham
Bristow joined the Northern Bank in 1876 as a teenager; became the manager
of the Ballsbridge branch in Dublin between 1888 and 1894, and joined the
board of directors in 1894. Both banks and railway companies clearly required
some members of the senior staff and the boards of directors to have a good
inside knowledge of how their businesses operated, and this was best provided
by individuals who had worked at every level of the firm.

Like the members of the other elite groups considered in this book, the
Irish businessmen were the members of clubs in London, Dublin, Belfast,
and elsewhere (see Table 5.7). More than two-thirds of the Irish businessmen
(71 per cent) included in this study held memberships of at least one club. Most

Table 5.8. The Religion of Businessmen who were the Members of Different Clubs

Religion	Carlton	Kildare St	Reform	Ulster	Sackville
Episcopalian	41 (98%)	31 (80%)	5 (25%)	21 (81%)	10 (77%)
Presbyterian	1 (2%)	1 (2.5%)	2 (10%)	4 (15%)	0
Quaker	0	1 (2.5%)	4 (20%)	1 (4%)	0
Catholic	0	6 (15%)	9 (45%)	0	3 (23%)
(Not known	2	0	4	2	0)
Number (known)	42	39	20	26	13

popular among the London clubs were the Carlton and the Reform, although the Turf, Travellers, Bachelors, Marlborough, Constitutional, and Junior Carlton were also popular haunts for the Irish business elite when in London. In Dublin, the Kildare Street Club was by far the most popular club, and provided a venue where businessmen could socialize with landlords, professionals, and senior government officials. By the eve of the Great War, the membership of the Kildare Street Club was quite different from what it had been in the early 1880s. In 1914, about one-fifth of the members were titled, many of whom were landowners; slightly more than one-third were serving or retired army or naval officers; there was only one serving MP for an Irish constituency—Major Robert McCalmont, the Unionist representative for East Antrim—although there were many prominent former MPs, including Horace Plunkett; and there was only one clerical member (the Revd Beresford Power). What is particularly striking about the membership in 1914, however, is the enormous increase in the number of businessmen who joined the club. About eighty members were connected with the world of business, including the directors of Guinness, bank directors, railway directors, distillers, stockbrokers, and land agents.[121] The St Stephen's Green Club in Dublin was also extremely popular among the business elite as was the Royal St George Yacht Club at Kingstown. In Belfast, the staunchly Unionist Club, the Ulster, was the most popular haunt for the Ulster business elite, although the Liberal Unionist Ulster Reform Club was also popular with a smaller number of Belfast businessmen.

To what extent did Irish Protestant and Catholic businessmen socialize with one another in gentlemen's clubs? Certainly, there were some clubs where businessmen from different ethnic backgrounds could socialize together (see Table 5.8). The Liberal club in London—the Reform—was clearly equally attractive to Irish businessmen from Episcopalian, Nonconformist, and Catholic backgrounds. In Dublin, of twenty-one members of the St Stephen's Green Club, five (25 per cent) were Episcopalians, two (10 per cent were Quakers),

[121] R. B. McDowell, *Land and Learning: Two Irish Clubs* (Dublin, 1993), 84–9.

Table 5.9. The Religious Composition of the Directors of
All Firms, 1883–1911

Religion	1883–1911	1883	1911
Protestant only	51	20	31
Catholic only	6	1	5
Protestant and Catholic	26	11	15
(Not known	3	2	1)
Number (known)	83	32	51

and thirteen (65 per cent) were Catholics.[122] The membership of the club was clearly mixed, although the ethos of the club was predominantly Catholic and pro-Home Rule. Similarly, the Royal St George Yacht Club at Kingstown was reasonably mixed: of the eighteen members who were top businessmen about whom we know their religion, eleven (61 per cent) were Episcopalian, two (11 per cent) were Quaker, and five (28 per cent) were Catholic. However, other clubs tended to have members drawn exclusively from one ethnic group or another. The conservative and Unionist Clubs in London, Dublin, and Belfast, for instance, had an almost exclusively Protestant membership. None of the Catholic businessmen in this study was a member of the Carlton Club in London or the Ulster Club in Belfast, and only a small number of Catholic business-men were members of the Kildare Street Club and the Sackville Street Club in Dublin.

Broadly speaking, the social practices of the Irish business elite suggest that Irish Catholic and Protestant businessmen generally moved in different circles. The degree of separation within the business elite was, however, certainly greater in Belfast and Ulster than it was in Dublin and the three southern provinces. This hypothesis is also suggested by the data on the religious composition of the firms contained in this study. As Table 5.9 demonstrates, two-thirds (66 per cent) of all the firms in 1883 were presided over by a board of directors that—according to my data—was either exclusively Catholic or Protestant (63 per cent were exclusively Protestant and 3 per cent were exclusively Catholic). By 1911, an even greater proportion (71 per cent) of the firms under review were governed by boards of directors that were either exclusively Protestant or exclusively Catholic. Given that the greater level of exclusiveness was accompanied by a significant rise in the proportion of Catholic businessmen, it is clear that where new Catholic businessmen had been recruited to the business elite it tended to be by firms that were already governed exclusively by Catholic directors rather than by Protestant or 'mixed' boards of directors. Indeed, the proportion of businesses that were governed only by Catholic directors increased from 3 per cent of the total in 1883 to 10 per cent of the total in 1911. There

[122] The religious persuasion of one member of the St Stephens Green Club was unknown.

Table 5.10. The Location of
'Mixed' Firms

Province	1883	1911
Ulster	0	0
Munster	3	3
Leinster	8	12
Connacht	0	0
Number	11	15

were clearly significant divisions within the business elite with most businesses in Ireland being governed by either exclusively Protestant or exclusively Catholic directors. However, the division was most emphatic in Ulster where none of the firms under review contained a 'mixed' board of directors whereas there were at least some firms with a 'mixed' board of directors in the other three provinces (Table 5.10).[123]

The differences within the Irish business elite are also evident in the political viewpoints of the businessmen. Data are available on the political outlook of almost half (110 of the 247 or 45 per cent) of the businessmen in this study. About two-thirds (67 per cent) were Conservatives or Unionists; about one in six (15 per cent) was Liberal; about one-twentieth (6 per cent) were Liberal Unionists; and about one in eight (12 per cent) was a Home Ruler. Overall, then, almost three-quarters (73 per cent) of the businessmen in this study were Unionists and just above one-quarter (27 per cent) were either Liberals or Home Rulers, both parties that supported a limited form of self government for Ireland. It is also clear that the majority (89 per cent) of Catholic businessmen was in favour of Home Rule: of the forty-two Catholic businessmen, we know the political viewpoint of nineteen (45 per cent of the total), and of these almost two-thirds were Home Rulers (twelve or 63 per cent), one-quarter (five or 26 per cent) were Liberals, and about one-tenth (two or 11 per cent) were Liberal Unionists. A reasonably clear distinction can therefore be drawn between the political outlook of Catholic and Protestant businessmen with the former generally supporting Home Rule and the latter tending to promote the maintenance of the Act of Union, although—as we have seen—there were some Protestant businessmen who became Home Rule MPs.

Protestant businessmen and particularly those based in Ulster argued that Home Rule would seriously jeopardize Irish economic development. There was a widespread perception among the Irish business elite that Home Rule would be detrimental to Irish economic interests. Following the introduction of the second Home Rule Bill in 1893, for instance, the value of Irish bank shares fell markedly

---

[123] Kavanagh also concludes that Catholic directors in Ulster tended to be in firms exclusively owned or controlled by Catholics. See Kavanagh, 'The Belfast Business Community', 190.

by 8 per cent from £18.47 to £16.94 between May 1892 and May 1893 (during which period the value of Scottish bank shares increased and the value of English bank shares remained the same).[124] Indeed, £983,000 was wiped off the value of the stock of seven Irish Banks, and about £1 million off Irish railway stock following the introduction of the second Home Rule Bill.[125] Harland and Wolff even threatened to move their shipyard to the Clyde if Home Rule was implemented.[126]

Henry Incledon Johns, a director of the Belfast Bank, explained why there was such widespread opposition to Home Rule among the business community at the bank's annual general meeting in 1912:

I will not comment on particular political matters further than to express the hope that the haunting and ever present canker for Home Rule, which like a dark and sombre cloud hangs over us, depressing our commerce adversely, dividing our people and overshadowing our industries, may God's providence soon pass away; for of this I am well assured, that its removal will herald in the dawning of a fairer day for this country and its people than they have ever known.[127]

In 1913, he continued to disregard the bank's stated policy of adopting a non-partisan policy on political issues and explained that:

In every department of trade, of commerce and of agriculture Ireland makes steady progress, but against all this stands the ever-growing menace of approaching disaster. Daily the dreadful consequences of any attempt to force a Home Rule Government upon us begin to take clearer and more definite shape.[128]

Broadly speaking, the Ulster economy—which was largely based on the shipbuilding and linen industries—was dependent on free trade with Britain and on broader imperial trade networks. Belfast depended on the import of raw materials (textiles, steel, coal) from Britain, and relied on the British markets as the main destination for exports (of linen and ships). As the Belfast Chamber of Commerce put it in 1893:

All our progress has been made under the Union. We were a small insignificant town at the end of the last century, deeply disaffected and hostile to the British Empire. Since the Union and under equal laws, we have been welded to the Empire and our progress has been second to none.[129]

If the Union was broken, and the 'equal laws' that had aided Belfast's economic growth in the nineteenth century were changed, Ulster businessmen believed that their businesses would fall into irreversible decline. For this reason, prominent members of the Ulster business community bankrolled the Ulster Volunteer Force to the tune of thousands of pounds. Milne Barbour, for instance, donated £10,000 to the UVF Indemnity Fund in 1914.[130] Three-quarters of the UVF's military council were businessmen, and of thirty members of the Northern

---

[124] Ibid. 330.   [125] Ibid. 259–60.   [126] Ibid. 345.
[127] Ibid. 312.   [128] Ibid.   [129] Ibid. 34.   [130] Ibid. 62.

Bank's Advisory Committee 1900–23, nine were active Unionists who gave substantial donations to the UVF Indemnity Fund.[131] There were, of course, notable exceptions. Pirrie (the chairman of Harland and Wolff after Harland's death in 1895), for instance, never contributed to Unionist funds and even supported Home Rule up to 1916 suggesting that there were sometimes political disagreements among the boards of directors of Irish companies.[132]

The southern Irish economy—which was dominated by the service sector—was less dependent on imports and exports, and this explains why there was a significant number of pro-Home Rule businessmen in Dublin. Most prominent of these was William Martin Murphy. None of his businesses would have been likely to suffer adversely if Home Rule was enacted, although it was the case that Murphy had benefited greatly from gaining government contracts to build railway extensions during the early 1880s.[133] In fact, Murphy made the opposite argument to that put forward by his colleagues in Belfast, and claimed that if the Irish economy was to prosper and develop it would be necessary to create an independent Irish parliament.[134] Murphy also made his views on Home Rule clear at the Irish Convention in 1917 when he argued strongly that the Home Rule Bill would not be worth the paper it was written on if it did not allow Irish control over Customs and Excise.[135] Some British observers felt that Murphy's views were not substantially dissimilar to those of the Ulster Unionists. Cecil Northcliffe told his brother of his discussions with Murphy and explained that 'At times you would think you were discussing the Irish problem with a Black Northerner'. And Murphy himself told the Irish Convention that the union had not restricted his business interests: 'I have never found the existing form of Government in Ireland to hamper or restrict my business interests. I have been able to carry on successfully various enterprises in Ireland and beyond it.'[136] It is also significant that Murphy was the president of the largely Protestant Dublin Chamber of Commerce between 1912 and 1913 when he led both Catholic nationalist and Protestant Unionist employers in the war against the ITGWU. Even so, Murphy and the other pro-Home Rule businessmen's nationalism was genuine, and perhaps emerged from the fact that the southern Irish economy was less dependent on exports; the power of the Fenian argument that the Union had disrupted Irish economic development; and the increasing tendency for Irish nationalism to become the ideology of Irish Catholics.

How old were the Irish business elite? Unsurprisingly, most of them were in their thirties, forties, fifties, and sixties, although the 1911 cohort tended to be older than their predecessors in the 1880s (see Table 5.11). In 1881, for instance,

[131] Ibid. 68, 293–4, 448–9.   [132] Ibid. 158, 347.

[133] Morrissey, *William Martin Murphy*, 10. Of course, Murphy was also likely to benefit from any government building contracts in a future Home Rule Ireland.

[134] See Murphy's lecture on 'The Irish Industrial Question' given at the Wood Quay National Registration Club on 10 Jan. 1887 (and discussed in Morrissey, *William Martin Murphy*, 14–16).

[135] Bielenberg, 'Entrepreneurship, Power and Public Opinion in Ireland'.   [136] Ibid.

Table 5.11. Age of Business Elite in 1881 and 1911

	1881	1911
0–19	0	0
20–9	7 (8.5%)	2 (1.5%)
30–9	17 (21%)	8 (5.5%)
40–9	13 (16%)	32 (22%)
50–9	21 (25.5%)	37 (25.5%)
60–9	16 (19.5%)	40 (27%)
70+	8 (9.5%)	27 (18.5%)
(Not known	17	18)
Number (known)	82	146
Number	99	164

almost one-third of the top businessmen were under the age of 40 (29.5 per cent) whereas in 1911 less than one in ten (7 per cent) was aged under 40. There were also more businessmen aged over 60 in 1911 than there had been in the 1880s. In 1911, almost half were over 60 (45.5 per cent) compared with less than one-third in 1881 (29 per cent). The gradual aging of the business elite cannot be attributed to the fact that the business elite in 1911 was composed of the same people as in 1883 (who were now thirty years older) because only 16 of the 164 businessmen in 1911 (10 per cent) had been members of the business elite at the earlier date. Many of the Irish businessmen enjoyed long lives with most of them living well into their sixties, seventies, and eighties.[137] Indeed, it is remarkable that almost half (45 per cent) of them lived into their seventies during a period when most working men's lives were substantially shorter than this. Undoubtedly, the long life span of these gentlemen can—in part—be attributed to the lives of great privilege and luxury that their enormous wealth provided them with.

The vast majority (97 per cent) of the Irish business elite were married.[138] This may have been partly because marriage was often a critically important step in the creation of a successful business career by extending and consolidating networks of both capital and expertise. About one-twentieth of the businessmen under review were related by marriage to other successful businessmen both as fathers-in-law (seven or 3 per cent) and as brothers-in-law (eight or 3 per cent). William Martin Murphy married the daughter of James Fitzgerald Lombard, who had amassed a fortune in the Dublin drapery business and who later

[137] Data are available on the age at death of 133 of the businessmen under review: 1 (1%) died when aged between 40 and 49; 3 (3%) died when aged between 50 and 59; 24 (18%) died when aged between 60 and 69; 60 (45%) died when aged between 70 and 79; 38 (29%) died when aged between 80 and 89; and 6 (5%) died when aged between 90 and 99.

[138] Data on marriage are available for 207 of the 247 businessmen, and of the 207, 204 (97%) were married and 3 (3%) did not marry.

financially supported many of Murphy's ventures. Murphy married Mary Julia Lombard in 1870 and does not appear to have gone into business partnership with James Fitzgerald until the 1880s—both as founder of Clery's department store and as director of Dublin United Tramways—and it is possible that Murphy's marriage helped him forge a business relationship that was to be of critical importance to his entrepreneurial success. Similarly, William Shaw, the chairman of the Munster Bank, and a former Home Rule MP, was married to the daughter of William Clear, who had been chairman of the bank before him. It was also very often the case that the directors of companies were married to their fellow directors' sisters. Chaworth Joseph Fergusson, a director of the Midland Great Western Railway, was married to Mary Anne Smyth, whose brother, T. J., was also a director of the Midland Great Western. And William Burton Carson, a director of the Great Northern Railway was married to Alice Cairnes, whose brother, W. P., was also a director of the Great Northern. It is likely that marriage ties could initiate or consolidate beneficial business relationships, and that such alliances could play a part in securing promotion to a board of directors.

Most of the Irish business elite were married in their twenties and thirties, although a small number were married later in life in their forties and fifties.[139] And most of those who were married tended to have children. Data are available on the number of children of 102 of those businessmen who were married and this shows that only two (2 per cent) had no children whatsoever, and that most of them had between two and six children.[140] In fact, almost half (47 per cent) of the businessmen under review fathered between one and three children, and most of the Irish businessmen who were married produced at least one heir.

III

To what extent did the composition of the Irish business elite change between 1883 and 1911? As Table 5.1 demonstrates, the proportion of Episcopalian businessmen declined quite significantly from 71 per cent in 1883 to 63.5 per cent in 1911. However, the proportion of Episcopalian businessmen was still substantially higher than their numbers in the total population in 1911. The shortfall was taken up by Presbyterians (up from 5 per cent to 7 per cent)

[139] Data on age at marriage are available for 161 of the 204 businessmen who we know were married, and this reveals that 90 (56%) married in their 20s, 59 (37%) married in their 30s, 8 (5%) married in their 40s, and 4 (2%) married in their 50s.

[140] Of 102 about whom data are available, 2 (2%) had no children; 4 (4%) had 1 child; 15 (15%) had two children; 29 (28%) had three children; 11 (11%) had 4 children; 14 (14%) had 5 children; 12 (12%) had 6 children; 7 (7%) had 7 children; 2 (2%) had 8 children; 1 (1%) had 9 children; 2 (2%) had 10 children; 2 (2%) had 11 children; and 1 (1%) had 12 children.

and Nonconformists (up from 7 per cent to 10.5 per cent) who were—broadly speaking—equally represented in both the Irish business elite and in the total population. Having said that, Presbyterians were slightly under-represented in the business elite given that they accounted for about one-tenth of the Irish population in 1911, while Irish Quakers were very strikingly over-represented (7.5 per cent) in the business elite in 1911 compared to their numbers in the general population (about 0.1 per cent). The proportion of Catholics in the business elite increased very slightly from 17 per cent to 19 per cent. However, the proportion of Catholics remained at only about one-fifth of the total and it is clear that there was no substantial 'greening' of the Irish business elite and that the campaigns of the *Leader* newspaper to improve the representation of Catholics on boards of directors were largely unsuccessful. In other respects (in terms of education and the proportion of landowner-businessmen, for instance), the composition of the Irish business elite in 1911 was very largely the same as it had been in 1883 (see Tables 5.3, 5.4, and 5.5). In other words, the composition of the Irish business elite was largely static in the decades between the Land War (1879–81) and the Great War.

How can the static nature of the Irish business elite be explained? Recruiting to boards of directors was not meritocratic but appears to have been largely based on networks of family, friends, work colleagues, and former classmates. New members of boards of directors were elected by the existing board members who selected candidates known to them, who had relevant business experience, and who held the requisite number of shares in the company. William Martin Murphy, for instance, was elected to the Board of Directors of the Great Southern and Western Railway in 1903 after the death of the deputy chairman—Gerald Dease—who was also a Catholic—as the Irish Railway half yearly Report for 31 December 1903 states: 'the vacancy had been filled by the election of Mr William Martin Murphy, who had had large experience in the construction and management of railways.'[141]

In most cases, candidates for directorships needed to hold a certain amount of stocks and shares in the relevant company. Some companies do not stipulate a directors' qualification in their listings in *Burdett's Official Intelligence* which may mean that none was required, while others demanded that directors hold a certain number of shares (and the value of these shares is not known). However, the directors' qualification for a number of companies is known. In 1883, for instance, a potential director of the Dublin, Wicklow, and Wexford Railway Co. had to hold £2,000 of original stock, and a similar level of stocks or shares were a requirement for directors of the Great Southern and Western, and the Midland Great Western Railway. Smaller railway companies tended to recruit directors who held shares of lesser value: the Dublin and Kingstown Railway,

141 Morrissey, *William Martin Murphy*, 13.

for instance, required its directors to hold £1,000 of stock, while the Dublin United Tramways Co. demanded that its directors hold shares of £500, and the Waterford and Central Ireland Railway Co. stipulated that directors should hold £400 of stock. Banks demanded that their directors held a much higher value of shares in the company. The Provincial Bank of Ireland, for instance, stated that its directors must hold fifty £100 shares (or at least £5,000 in shares in the bank). In 1911, the directors' qualification for railway companies was broadly similar to that in 1883. Directors of the *Irish Times* were required to hold £1,000 worth of shares in the company, and directors of Goulding's chemical manufacturers and the Dublin distillers company, both of which were in Dublin, were expected to hold a similar amount of shares. Arthur Guinness required its directors to hold £2,000 in ordinary shares while smaller Dublin firms like the Alliance and Dublin Consumer's Gas Co. and the Dublin Artisans' Dwellings Co. demanded that their directors held shares to the value of £700 and £300 respectively. In other words, to qualify as even a candidate for a directorship it was necessary for the individual to have a capital investment in the firm in question of between £300 and £5,000 depending on the size and the nature of the firm.

A large section of the Irish population—both Protestant and Catholic—fulfilled this criterion in the early years of the twentieth-century (most of the shareholders in the Great Southern and Western Railway were Catholic according to the *Leader* but they probably did not own enough shares to become directors) so what other criteria were used to recruit new members to boards of directors? Broadly speaking, new directors appear to have been selected from networks of family, friends, work colleagues, and old school and university friends. We have already seen that almost one-third (seventy-four or 30 per cent) of all the businessmen included in this study were closely related to other businessmen, and this demonstrates that many of the recruits to boards of directors were sons, sons in law, brothers, brothers in law, nephews, and even grandchildren of the existing board of directors. This was the case both in family firms (where we would expect this to be the case) but also in banks and railway companies where there are numerous examples of sons taking over on boards of directors from their fathers. R. G. Sharman Crawford, for instance, sat on the Belfast Bank Advisory Committee between 1900 and 1921, while his father, Arthur, had been a director of the bank until his retirement.[142]

Colleagues in the workplace also seem to have provided likely recruits for boards of directors. William Burton Carson, a land agent, served his apprenticeship with Fane Vernon's land agency in Dublin, and by 1911 they were both directors of the Great Northern Railway Co. Similarly, a number of senior figures in the Bengal Civil Service including Sir Stuart Saunders Hogg and Edward Harbord Lushington were directors of the Provincial Bank of Ireland in 1883. Old school and university connections may also have influenced recruitment practices even

---

[142] Kavanagh, 'The Belfast Business Community'.

if individuals had not attended school together as there were ample opportunities to meet and network at alumnus gatherings. Four directors of the Fishguard and Rosslare Railways and Harbours Co. in 1911 were old Etonians which perhaps suggests the power of the old school tie in business recruitment.[143]

The cumulative impact of such recruiting practices was to reinforce the existing profile of the business elite since the Protestant directors of 1883 tended to recruit from networks that were also Protestant dominated. Those Catholics who were recruited to the business elite appear to have been of two main types. First, a significant proportion were Catholics from landed backgrounds who were probably also loyal and would have met with Protestant landowners and businessmen at places like the Kildare Street Club, the Sackville Street Club, and the Royal St George Yacht Club. Indeed, almost half (sixteen of forty-two or 38 per cent) of the Catholic businessmen included in this study were either landowners or had been born into landed families (one other married into a landed family). Richard Anthony Nugent, for instance, was the chairman of the Midland Great Western Railway (in 1911) and was elected Governor of the Bank of Ireland in December 1907. He had been educated at Oscott College, Birmingham, was a member of the Kildare Street Club, and was the son of the 9th Earl of Westmeath who owned a substantial estate.[144] One of his sons—Richard Francis Nugent—later became an officer in the Scots Guards. Nugent was probably typical of a significant number of the Catholic members of the business elite who tended to be landed, loyal, and 'loaded', and to move in the kinds of circles from which all directors were recruited.

Not all of the loyal Catholics were landed but they were often 'loaded'. Luke John McDonnell, a graduate of Trinity, was a barrister, a former Governor of the Bank of Ireland, and a director of the Great Southern and Western Railway. When he died in November 1892, he left £31,047 gross and the *Irish Times* observed that 'His loss will be deeply felt by a large circle of attached friends'.[145] Similarly, James Fitzgerald Lombard, a former chairman of the Dublin United Tramways Co., a director of Arnott's, and William Martin Murphy's father-in-law, sent his son to Clongowes and Trinity, after which he (James William) joined the army and fought in the Boer War. A significant proportion of the Catholic businessmen included in this study were either landed or loyal (or both), and probably tended to be Liberal Unionists.

The second 'type' of Catholic to be recruited to the business elite tended not to be drawn from a landed or a loyal family but to be a genuinely successful entrepreneur who sometimes was also a Home Ruler. These individuals appear to

---

[143] The four directors were 1st Viscount Churchill, Frank Bibby, Ernest Haliburton Cunard, and the 1st Baron Barrymore.
[144] The 9th Earl of Westmeath owned 15,695 acres (valued at £5,486).
[145] *Irish Times*, 7 Nov. 1892.

have been recruited by firms that were already dominated by Catholic directors. The business elite therefore became more segregated between 1883 and 1911. In 1911, for instance, the Dublin Distiller's Co. was exclusively Catholic in terms of the backgrounds of its directors as was the Dublin United Tramways Co. Indeed, in a divided society, the non-dominant section of the community can gain some advantage from segregation by developing its own retail, professional, and personal services; and middle class Catholics appear to have created their own social networks and recruiting practices within the business elite at the end of the nineteenth century.[146] A number of Catholic firms were presided over by Home Rule MPs; and there seem to have been strong social networks binding together the IPP, the Catholic church, and the Catholic businessmen. The chairman of Boland's bakers and millers in Dublin in 1911, for instance, was Thomas Sexton and the managing director of the Alliance and Consumer's Gas Co. in Dublin was William Francis Cotton, who was then Home Rule MP for south Dublin.

A number of the Catholic directors in 1911 had proven themselves to be successful entrepreneurs who ran medium-sized manufacturing and trading firms in Dublin and the provinces. Richard Davoren was the chairman of the board of directors of the Dublin Distillers Co. in 1911 (valued at £650,000); John Murphy of Midleton was a director of the Cork Distilleries Ltd in 1911; and Colonel James Marmaduke Sugrue was the proprietor of the Glen Distillery Co. in county Cork in 1911. In Dublin, Sir Michael Murphy was the managing director of Michael Murphy Ltd, steamship owners, and he was also the governor of the Hibernian Joint Stock Co. in 1883. According to *Who Was Who*, Murphy was 'largely instrumental in reviving the shipbuilding industry in Dublin'. And Sir Richard Martin was a Dublin shipowner and merchant, deputy chairman of the Dublin, Wicklow, and Wexford Railway in 1883, and a former president of Dublin Chamber of Commerce. As these examples demonstrate, there were some slim opportunities for Catholic social mobility into the Irish business elite between 1883 and 1911.[147]

In broad terms, however, the Irish business elite was essentially a 'closed' rather than an 'open' elite group between 1883 and 1911. Indeed, the proportion of the Irish businessmen who were born into 'elite' families actually increased between

---

[146] A. C. Hepburn, *Catholic Belfast and Nationalist Ireland in the Era of Joe Devlin, 1871–1934* (Oxford, 2008), 16.

[147] A significant number of smaller Catholic businesses were emerging in the provinces during the period under review—firms like McDonagh's manure manufacturing business in Galway city—and some of the owners of these smaller firms sat on the boards of the big companies and therefore made their way into the Irish establishment. At Belfast, a number of small Catholic businesses emerged during the nineteenth century including Bernard Hughes' bakery that employed 150 people; Peter Keegan's whiskey distillery; and William Ross's flax mill in west Belfast that employed 600 people (ibid. 13).

1883 and 1911.[148] This was because recruiting practices tended to reinforce pre-existing social, educational, and business networks. Some contemporaries, however, also alleged that Catholics excluded themselves from the Irish business elite by not putting themselves forward for senior positions or directorships, and by not establishing or developing new businesses because they regarded a career in business as lacking respectability. In an address on 'The Irish Industrial Question' to the Wood Quay National Registration Club on 10 January 1887, for instance, William Martin Murphy explained that some Irish manufacturing businesses had failed because of the 'snobbishness and toadyism' of the entrepreneurs who had made money in trade but now regarded it as 'not respectable' and instead aped the 'idle class that lived upon the land'.[149] Presumably—given the pro-Home Rule audience—Murphy was here referring to Irish Catholic nationalist businessmen rather than the Irish Protestant variety.

Similarly, Arthur Clery engaged in a debate with Michael Gill on this question in the pages of the *Leader*. Gill had claimed in an article published in *St Stephens* that Irish industrial decline was partially caused by 'the idea that an industrial career is not respectable' so that there was 'the tendency of clever young Irishmen to rush to the learned professions, leaving the counter and the counting-house to their duller but more prudent brethren'. Clery, writing under his pen-name 'Chanel', made the counter argument that the reluctance of young Catholic Irishmen to go into business was caused not by their perception that an industrial career lacked 'respectability' but because opportunities for Catholic advancement in this business world were limited:

As far as my own experience goes, most clever young men do not enter industrial pursuits, simply because they do not see any way in which to do so. If you are the heir to a business there is no difficulty. But if you are merely the good or the average product of the Intermediate or the University system (let it be either Trinity or the Royal), how are you to start an industrial career. It would be absurd to say that a man who could be a doctor or solicitor should become a factory operative, or a £50-a-year clerk, merely in the hope of one day becoming a manager or partner. Beginning at the foot of the ladder is all right—if you have a ladder. It would be a foolish quest to wander about hoping for someone to drop you a rope. There only remains the method of paying a large fee as an apprentice to learn some business, and then starting for oneself, or buying a partnership; but this method requires a very heavy capital expenditure . . . Most men whom I have known to choose a way of life, have never even considered industrial or commercial pursuits as an alternative, simply because there seemed absolutely no method of adopting them on any reasonable terms.[150]

---

[148] 'Elite' families are defined as those where the father was an MP, JP, landowner, army officer, businessman, reverend, doctor, baronet, bishop, or solicitor. In 1883, 52 of 99 (or 53%) of the top businessmen were born into 'elite' families, whereas in 1911 the comparable figure was 104 of 164 (or 63%). [149] Morrissey, *William Martin Murphy*, 15.
[150] 'Chanel' [Arthur Clery], 'Commercial Openings', *Leader*, 4 Apr. 1903.

In fact, Murphy, Gill, and Clery all suggest that Irish Catholics did exclude themselves from business careers, albeit for different reasons. Murphy and Gill claim that this was because young men regarded a business career as less prestigious than that offered by the professions. Clery, on the other hand, claims that it was because there were few opportunities for Catholic advancement in business.

The process by which a clerkship in the Bank of Ireland was obtained does appear to have favoured the applications of members of the Irish Protestant middle class over those of the members of the rising Catholic middle class. An article in the *Irish Times*' students' column by 'ERASMUS' explains how prospective candidates should go about becoming a clerk in the Bank of Ireland.[151] The first step was to secure a nomination from one of the members of the board of directors, each of whom had a certain number of nominations at his disposal: 'Before being allowed to compete, candidates must secure a nomination from one of the directors. This is not very difficult. A substantial depositor or person of social influence can always do it.' Although at least one of the directors was Catholic, and another was Quaker, gaining such a nomination did, however, require that the individual had access to the social and professional networks of the Irish establishment, and there were very few Catholic members of these networks.[152] Apparently, once the nomination had been obtained, 'The examination is by no means difficult' and it was divided into six parts covering handwriting, arithmetic, orthography/dictation, bookkeeping, 'English History and Geography', and algebra. In order to succeed in the exam, a secondary education was probably required and—given the nature of some of the questions—an education at an English public school or an Irish Protestant school would probably have been the most advantageous form of preparation.[153]

A list of the 'specimen' questions on 'History' is provided in a later article which shows that the examiner—the Revd Thomas Gray of Trinity College—had a preference for the English constitutional variety. All ten history questions pertained to the political and constitutional history of England, although—intriguingly—one question did ask the candidate to 'Give a short account of the treatment of the Jews from time to time during the course of English history'. The questions on 'Geography', on the other hand, asked about the geography of Ireland and particularly the locations of towns, lakes, rivers, and so on.[154] Once the examination had been passed, prospective bank

---

[151] Article on 'Bank of Ireland Clerkships' by 'ERASMUS' in 'Our Students' Column' in the *Irish Times*, 26 May 1900. In that year, there were 90 applicants for 22 clerkships.

[152] See also the later article on Bank of Ireland clerkships in *Irish Times*, 14 Mar. 1903.

[153] Ibid.

[154] It is as if the examiners acknowledge that Ireland had a geography of its own but not a history. The silent assumption appears to be that Irish history, if it did exist, was simply an extension of English history (ibid.). There is a full list of 'specimens of examination papers' here.

clerks were paid only a small salary during their probationary period, which might be of several years' duration, and only then would they be paid a proper salary.[155] At each level then—that of the nomination, the examination, and the probationary period—Catholic candidates who tended to have less access to business networks, less capital, and less knowledge of English history—were discriminated against in their quest to become clerks in the Bank of Ireland. For this reason, the majority of clerks were, as MacDonagh has shown, members of the Irish Protestant middle class whose fathers were the sons of clergy-men—both Church of Ireland and Dissenter—army officers, police inspectors, and gentlemen farmers.[156] Surprisingly, many of these clerks were also bachelors, leading MacDonagh to speculate that the Irish Protestant middle class at the beginning of the twentieth century had a death-wish.[157] It is as if the sense of impending decline of the Irish Protestant establishment hit the bedrooms as well as the pocket books of the aristocracy and some sections of the Protestant middle class.

The existence of a significant number of Freemasons among the Irish business elite was also probably responsible for restricting the access of Irish Catholics (forbidden by their church from becoming Masons) to directorships, middle-management positions, and clerkships in the world of business. 'HP' in her (or his) article for the *New Ireland Review* alleged that twenty of the twenty-one chief officials employed by the Bank of Ireland at its head office on College Green were Protestants, and that at least ten of these, and probably more, were Freemasons. At the end of this article, 'HP' poses the following questions:

There are many Catholics in the employment of the Bank—men of lengthened service, of real ability, of entire trust-worthiness: How is it that not even one in twenty of the chief Dublin officers is chosen from among them? What is it that hinders their promotion? If to their abilities, their length of service, their trust-worthiness, they added the further qualifications—Protestantism and Membership of a Lodge—would not their merits receive more favourable recognition?[158]

I have not systematically researched how many members of the business elite were Masons but a review of the obituaries of some of the leading businessmen reveals that a significant number of them were. At the York Street Flax Co., for instance, the junior managing director in 1911, James Heron Stirling, and a debenture stock trustee, Robert Gordon Sharman-Crawford were both prominent Masons.[159] Frederick Ludwig Heyn, the secretary of the Ulster

[155] MacDonagh, 'The Victorian Bank', 41.
[156] Ibid. 44. The *Irish Times* explained in 1900 that many of the existing Bank of Ireland clerks had volunteered for service in the Boer War which also suggests that they were largely Protestants and Unionists (26 May 1900). [157] MacDonagh, 'The Victorian Bank', 45.
[158] 'HP', 'Catholics and the Bank of Ireland', *New Ireland Review*, 27 (Feb. 1908).
[159] See Sharman-Crawford's obituary in the *Irish Times*, 21 Mar. 1934. Sharman-Crawford was also Unionist MP for east Belfast between 1914 and 1918 and a member of the Carlton, Sackville Street, Ulster, and Cork county clubs. For Stirling's obituary see *Irish Times*, 26 Nov. 1928.

Steamship Co. in Belfast in 1911 was also a Mason.[160] Masons were prominent in the Belfast business elite during the earlier period too: Sir Charles Lanyon, for example, was the deputy chairman of the Belfast and Northern Counties Railway in 1883 and was a Provincial Grand Master of the Freemasons.[161] In Dublin, Maurice Brooks, a director of the Alliance and Dublin Consumer's Gas Co., the Dublin Brick and Tile Co., and a number of other businesses in England was a Mason.[162] In 1911, Andrew Jameson, a director of the Bank of Ireland and the chairman of Jameson's distillery was also a Mason.[163] The presence of Freemasons on the boards of directors of banks, railways, and other businesses meant that they were in a strong position to influence recruiting practices at all levels of their businesses, and that—when they did so—they favoured Protestants rather than Catholics.

Finally, it has been argued that Protestants were culturally and ethnically equipped for business success in a way that Catholics simply were not and therefore we should not be surprised to find comparatively few Catholics in the Irish business elite. This argument was first advanced by Max Weber and was then subsequently taken up and developed by Tawney.[164] Broadly speaking, two arguments were made in favour of this general hypothesis. First, that Protestants worked harder and were more disciplined than Catholics (the so-called Protestant 'work ethic'). And second, that Protestant businessmen (and especially Nonconformists) adopted a paternalistic attitude to their employees which encouraged employees to work harder, to be more productive, and this in turn led to greater business success.

Ostensibly, late nineteenth- and early twentieth-century Ireland appears to provide evidence that supports the Weber–Tawney hypothesis. Only the north-eastern part of Ireland industrialized in this period, and this was the part of Ireland where the Presbyterian and Nonconformist sections of the population were highest and most densely settled. There were almost half a million Presbyterians in Ireland in 1900 (443,276) but of the thirty-six presbyteries into which congregations were grouped, only eleven were outside the six north-eastern counties containing just 14 per cent of the Irish Presbyterian population.[165] Moreover, a significant number of the most successful businessmen in the two key industries of linen and shipbuilding were Presbyterians, Nonconformists, and Quakers. Sir Edward Harland was a Unitarian; Wolff was of Jewish origin, although he became a member of the Church of England; Workman and Clark were both Presbyterians; James Mackie was Presbyterian; and James Nicholson Richardson, a director of Richardson and Owden, Belfast linen manufacturers and bleachers, was a Quaker. Having said

---

[160] *Irish Times*, 5 July 1926.   [161] Ibid. 25 June 1868.
[162] Ibid. 7 Dec. 1905.   [163] Ibid. 17 Feb. 1941.
[164] Weber and Tawney's hypothesis is discussed in Ó Gráda, *Ireland: A New Economic History.*
[165] Megahey, *Irish Protestant Churches*, 12.

that, John Milne Barbour and R. H. S. Reade, chairmen of two of the biggest Ulster linen manufacturing firms, were Episcopalian. Do cultural factors, then, explain the low representation of Catholics in the Irish business elite as some Irish historians have suggested?[166]

A considerable amount of evidence can be marshalled against the Weber–Tawney hypothesis. Recent revisionist accounts have been more critical of Ulster entrepreneurs' performance, and it has been noted (by Lee) that the Protestant work ethic did not save the Ulster economy from the 1920s onwards.[167] Moreover, a considerable proportion of the rest of the island of Ireland (10 per cent) was Nonconformist. Notably, there were 15,000 Nonconformists in county Dublin, and over a quarter of the population of Dublin city and its suburbs were non-Catholic.[168] It is also significant that some Catholics did prove themselves to be extremely successful entrepreneurs. William Martin Murphy is the most well known but other key figures in this study (Cotton, Davoren, Sugrue, Murphy) also prove this point. There were also a considerable number of medium-sized businesses throughout Ireland that were run by Catholics, and the thousands of Catholic shopkeeper-publicans who dominated trade and credit networks in rural Ireland do not appear to have been lacking in business acumen.

The origins of Ulster's industrial success also needs to be interrogated further. Indeed, it is likely that the particular religious or cultural composition of Ulster society had little bearing on the two great economic success stories of fin de siècle Ulster: shipbuilding and linen. It has been argued that the Ulster shipbuilding industry largely developed as a result of Edward Harland's decision to stay in Belfast in 1858 rather than migrating to the Mersey and setting up a shipyard there.[169] Harland joined the Belfast shipbuilders, Hickson and Co., in 1854 and worked for Hickson as general manager for three years. At that point, Harland was considering leaving Belfast to establish his own yard at Birkenhead. However, Hickson had become dependent on Harland and believed that he could not run the shipyard without him. And so Hickson offered to sell his shipyard to Harland for £5,000. Although the details of the transaction are not known, it is likely that Harland obtained the £5,000 to purchase Hickson's yard from Schwabe, a Hamburg-born merchant who was prominent in the shipbuilding industry at Liverpool, and who was related by marriage to the Harland family. Schwabe's nephew was Gustav Wolff, who had been working as Harland's personal assistant at Hickson's yard, and it seems likely that Schwabe gave Harland the capital to purchase Hickson's yard on the condition that Wolff would become Harland's

---

[166] Desmond and Keating's work is discussed in Bielenberg, 'Enterprise and Investment in Ireland', 21.

[167] Ó Gráda, *Ireland: A New Economic History*, 324–5; Lee, *Modernisation of Irish Society*, 16.

[168] Ó Gráda, *Ireland: A New Economic History*, 328.

[169] Lee, *Modernisation of Irish Society*, 14.

partner (and Harland and Wolff became partners from the date of the takeover of Hickson's yard on 1 November 1858).

Schwabe continued to be an important influence on the future success of Harland and Wolff because he was largely responsible for gaining contracts for them from the major Liverpool shipowners (Bibbys and Ismays). In fact, Schwabe was a large shareholder in the Liverpool shipping firm of Bibby and sons, and was largely responsible for Bibbys' placing orders for eighteen ships with Harland and Wolff between 1858 and 1870 (and this accounted for almost half of Harland and Wolff's output tonnage during this period). Schwabe was also instrumental in establishing the White Star Line (with Thomas Henry Ismay) for the transatlantic service, and for ensuring that most of the White Star Line ships be built by Harland and Wolff. Between 1869 and Ismay's death in 1899, for instance, Harland and Wolff built thirty-nine ships for the White Star Line for £7 million, the gross tonnage of which was 22 per cent of Harland and Wolff's total output during this period. Harland and Wolff, therefore, became the largest single shipbuilder in the world by the 1890s. Their closest rival, the Belfast shipbuilding firm of Workman-Clark, was established by two former apprentices of Harland and Wolff, Francis Workman and Sir George Smith Clark. In 1902, for instance, Workman-Clark produced more tonnage than any other shipbuilder in the world.[170] As we have seen, the two Belfast shipyards were responsible for employing 29,000 men in 1919. The Harland-Wolff–Schwabe relationship was, therefore, crucial to the entire development of the Belfast shipbuilding industry, and if Harland had left for Liverpool in 1858 the economic history of Ulster might well have been very different. Indeed, it may well be that Ulster's economic success owed more to accident than culture.

It is also the case that a significant proportion of successful Ulster entrepreneurs were actually immigrants rather than native-born sons. In the linen industry, for instance, which is usually regarded as central to Ulster's economic success story, a significant proportion of the pioneers in the industry were not even from Ulster. William Barbour and Sons, one of Ulster's biggest flax-spinning concerns, had been initially founded by a Scot, John Barbour, in the late eighteenth century.[171] James Mackie's, who manufactured linen machinery, had been established initially by James Scrimgeour, a Scot.[172] And the Linen Thread Co. (established 1898–9) was formed out of three Irish companies, five US companies, and three Scottish firms.[173] Indeed, two of Ireland's most prominent economic

[170] On the history of the shipbuilding firms of Harland and Wolff and Workman-Clark, see Johnson and Geary, 'Gustav Wilhelm Wolff'; Johnson and Geary, 'Sir Edward James Harland'; David Johnson, 'Sir George Smith Clark', in Jeremy, *Dictionary of Business Biography*, i; and David Johnson, 'Francis Workman', ibid. v.

[171] Kavanagh, 'The Belfast Business Community', 335; Ó Gráda, *Ireland: A New Economic History*, 326.

[172] Lee, *Modernisation of Irish Society*, 19.

[173] Kavanagh, 'The Belfast Business Community', 336.

historians have suggested that immigrants played an essential role in Irish economic development generally in the nineteenth and twentieth centuries.[174] The Weber–Tawney attempt to link Catholicism with poor economic performance can—at least on the basis of the Irish evidence—be regarded as unproven.[175]

The business elite discussed in this chapter does not include the thousands of shopkeeper-publicans that dominated the towns and villages of rural Ireland during the post-Famine period. As the nineteenth century progressed, these men and women—most of whom were Catholic—became increasingly powerful in both economic and political terms. They were largely responsible for supplying their localities with all necessary items and services, including credit, and many of them also owned land and benefited from the boom in cattle prices that followed the Famine years. From the late 1870s, they gradually began to penetrate local politics and took many of the seats on Poor Law Unions, and, after the introduction of new democratically elected county councils in 1898, they took most of the seats on these new elected bodies in the three southern provinces. Many of them, as we have seen, were prominent in local nationalist politics—in the Land League, the National League, and the United Irish League—and in the local committees that selected parliamentary candidates; and some of them had become Home Rule MPs by 1911. As individuals, they could not compete with the economic power of the banks and railways, but collectively—as a class of provincial shopkeeper-publicans—they were the most powerful section of Irish society, and ready to take the reins of power in an independent Ireland whenever it emerged.

There were also a large number of medium-sized businesses—many of them run and established by Catholic entrepreneurs—located throughout the towns and cities of provincial Ireland. Men like Martin Mór McDonagh of Galway city—a manufacturer of fertilizer and a substantial employer in the west of Ireland—existed in every Irish town, and although their businesses were not worth anything like £200,000, they possessed great economic and political power in their localities.[176] The driving-force behind these medium-sized businesses was often Catholic Home Rulers, and—surprisingly—very few landowners appear to have invested in these provincial business concerns. In Cork, for instance, Bielenberg found that landlords played only a limited role in providing the capital for local industries and businesses.[177] It is possible that some of these small businesses in provincial Ireland might have developed into very large businesses by the end of the nineteenth-century if Ireland had not been incorporated into a free trade zone with the United Kingdom in 1801.

[174] Lee, *Modernisation of Irish Society*, 19; Ó Gráda, *Ireland: A New Economic History*, 326–8. Kavanagh makes the same point in 'The Belfast Business Community', 341.

[175] Ó Gráda, *Ireland: A New Economic History*, 330.

[176] On McDonagh, see John Cunningham, *'A Town Tormented by the Sea': Galway, 1790–1914* (Dublin, 2004), 187–8.

[177] Andy Bielenberg, *Cork's Industrial Revolution, 1780–1880: Development or Decline?* (Cork, 1991), 128.

Bielenberg's study of business and industry in Cork demonstrates that many of the successful smaller Irish businesses of the late eighteenth and early nineteenth centuries could not compete with the more capital intensive and technically sophisticated industrial production that was in full swing in Britain by the 1840s.[178] For this reason, many small Irish businesses either went to the wall or fell into decline. In the absence of the Act of Union, then, some of the small and promising businesses—that became important employers in the provinces—may have developed into big businesses by the end of the nineteenth century and consequently there would have been more Catholic members of the Irish business elite by the beginning of the twentieth century.

IV

Broadly speaking, this chapter has demonstrated that the directors of the top businesses in Ireland between 1883 and 1911 were largely Protestant; and that the campaigns of newspapers like the *Leader* to change this had not succeeded in changing things before the Great War. There was, however, a widespread perception that the *Leader*'s exposé of sectarian recruiting practices did make a difference to the composition of the workforce of the major Irish companies. Sean T. O'Kelly, for instance, told the Bureau of Military History that 'in many cases Catholics were only a small minority of the total number employed by these bodies [public bodies and institutions]' but that D. P. Moran 'and his forceful pen' was one of 'those who obliged those various public companies and institutions to give Catholics a due share of employment, especially in the higher grades'.[179]

J. J. Horgan, the Cork Home Ruler, also acknowledges that this was the case and explains that:

As a result of Moran's exposure of this state of affairs [the fact that access to clerkships at the Great Southern and Western Railway was closed to Catholics although most of the shareholders were Catholics] a committee of Catholic shareholders, of which I acted as secretary, was formed to demand redress. The directors at first refused to give us any information . . . Finally at the next general meeting of the Company, in February, 1903, the directors acknowledged the justice of our allegations by conceding our demand that the Company's clerical staff should, in future, be recruited entirely by competitive examination. The other railway companies, where similar conditions

---

[178] Ibid. 117, 123. It is also likely that the Irish economy, which had been subordinated to that of Britain during the period when Ireland was a colony during the seventeenth and eighteenth centuries, could do little else but remain subordinate when it became—technically—an integral part of the United Kingdom in 1801. For further discussion of this point, see Terence McDonough (ed.), *Was Ireland a Colony? Economics, Politics and Culture in Nineteenth-century Ireland* (Dublin, 2005).   [179] Sean T. O'Kelly, Bureau of Military History, witness statement 1,765, p. 23.

prevailed, were rapidly forced to follow suit. This event marked a definite step forward in the emancipation of Irish Catholics, a process which was eventually completed when we obtained control of the national government.[180]

The chairman of the Great Southern and Western Railway, William Goulding, told the half-yearly general meeting of the company held at the offices at Kingsbridge Terminus in February 1903 that the recruiting of clerkships had been opened to competitive examination, as the *Irish Times* report noted:

> He was very anxious that any idea of undue preference, however erroneous, should be removed if it was within their power to do so, and, as they might be aware, they had thrown their clerkships open to the public, and arranged that in future the examination of candidates would be competitive, held by two outside examiners, one of whom would be a Protestant and the other a Roman Catholic. (Loud applause.)[181]

Notwithstanding this transformation, the evidence presented in this chapter suggests that the religious affiliation of the 247 directors included in this study was largely Protestant, and that this did not substantially change between 1883 and 1911. Those Catholics who did manage to reach the top positions in the Irish business elite tended to be landed, loyal, and 'loaded', although there was a minority of Catholic entrepreneurs from more modest backgrounds. Even so, it is clear that the Irish business elite was largely a 'closed' elite group, that its composition was largely Protestant and static, and that it was employing discriminatory practices against Catholic candidates for clerkships, apprenticeships, and directorships. Religion was clearly critically important in late nineteenth- and early twentieth-century Ireland not least because it was intertwined with political and ethnic identifications. But who were the religious elite, and how representative of Irish society were they? That is the question to which we will turn in the final chapter of the book.

---

[180] Horgan, *Parnell to Pearse*, 111–12.

[181] *Irish Times*, 16 Feb. 1903. Candidates for the exam were required, however, to have knowledge of 'one foreign language' and this could be French, German, or Latin. However, Goulding explained that a knowledge of Irish could not fulfil this part of the exam because it could not be based on 'sentimental considerations'. German or French would be useful to candidates because they had 'some commerce with those countries, and he hoped some day [that they] would have more'. Clearly, Goulding conveniently ignores the fact that large sections of the Great Southern and Western Railway traversed Irish-speaking areas.

6

Religion

This book has examined the social and religious background of the members of
the Irish establishment, and considered whether this changed to any great extent
between 1879 and 1914. For obvious reasons this question is not applicable
to the members of the religious elite since there could be no 'greening' of the
Irish Catholic Church or of the two main Protestant churches: the Church of
Ireland and the Presbyterian Church. However, what we might call a 'greening'
of religious power did occur in nineteenth-century Ireland with the influence of
the Catholic church over the British state increasing dramatically, and that of
the Church of Ireland declining steeply. This chapter will examine the social
background and characteristics of the individuals who represented and led these
churches in Ireland between 1881 and 1911, and consider how representative
they were of the communities over which they presided, but first I will outline the
nature of the power which the Protestant and Catholic churches held during
the nineteenth century, and consider how this power changed as the nineteenth
century progressed.

The Church of Ireland emerged from the Reformation as a national state
church with the monarch at its head. By the eighteenth century, it was essentially
controlled by the state in that its chief offices were appointed by British politicians,
and its policies were manipulated to serve the needs of the state. Although the
majority of the Irish people remained Catholic after the Reformation, and only
a minority of the population (never more than one-eighth) were members of the
Church of Ireland,[1] it remained the established church after the Act of Union and
had the power to levy a tax, known as a tithe, on the rural population regardless
of their religious persuasion.[2] However, the British state reformed the position
of the Church of Ireland during the 1830s thereby lessening its economic power

---

[1] Donald Harman Akenson, *The Church of Ireland: Ecclesiastical Reform and Revolution,
1800–1885* (New Haven, Conn. and London, 1971), 3–5.

[2] The fifth clause of the Act stated that: 'the Churches of England and Ireland, as now by law
established, be united into one Protestant Episcopal Church, to be called "The United Church of
England and Ireland", and that the doctrine, worship, discipline and government of the said United
Church shall be, and shall remain in full force for ever, as the same are now by law established for
the Church of England.' The Act further asserted that: 'the continuance and preservation of the said
United Church, as the established Church of England and Ireland, shall be deemed and taken to be
an essential and fundamental part of the Union'.

but leaving its privileged position largely intact. Following a serious outbreak of agrarian and anti-tithe protest during the Tithe War of 1830–32, the Irish Church Temporalities Act was introduced in 1833, and this abolished ten sees of the church, reduced the revenue available to Irish bishops, and imposed a tax on the richer benefices. Five years later, the Tithe Reform Act of 1838 converted the tithe into a rent charge on land payable not by the tenant but by the landlord.[3]

The privileged position of the Church of Ireland *vis-à-vis* the British state was further eroded in the late 1860s following the Fenian insurrection of 1867. The British Prime Minister Gladstone believed that reforms were necessary to reconcile Ireland (and particularly Catholic Ireland) to the Act of Union. As part of his subsequent 'mission to pacify Ireland'—and under pressure from the Catholic hierarchy to do so—the Church of Ireland was disestablished on 1 January 1871.[4] This marked a serious depletion in the power of the Church of Ireland, and revealed that its influence over the British state was in irreversible decline. Under the terms of the Irish Church Act, the Church of Ireland ceased to be the established church, its bishops were no longer called to sit in the House of Lords, and it was effectively disendowed by the British state.[5] Bishops and clergy were guaranteed their existing incomes for life but many chose to commute this interest to a capital sum vested in the Representative Church Body which received a total of £7.6 million.[6] After disestablishment, bishops' salaries were substantially reduced and total annual episcopal income declined from £54,319 to £22,424 between 1867 and 1919 and, according to one of the foremost historians of the Church of Ireland: 'The Irish prelates had declined from being ecclesiastical princes and nobility to mere middling gentry.'[7] Notwithstanding these reductions in their power, the Church of Ireland bishops were solidly Unionist after the introduction of the first Home Rule Bill in 1886. However, it is also clear that the main Protestant churches in Ireland experienced an 'evangelical revival' during the first decades of the nineteenth century. This involved a shift away from ritual and towards scripturalism, and an attempt to improve the conduct and religious practice of the Protestant population.[8] This—in turn—resulted in greater separation between the Protestant and Catholic churches since it

---

[3] Kevin B. Nowlan, 'Disestablishment: 1800–1869', in Michael Hurley (ed.), *Irish Anglicanism, 1869–1969: Essays on the Role of Anglicanism in Irish Life Presented to the Church of Ireland on the Occasion of its Centenary of its Disestablishment by a Group of Methodist, Presbyterian, Quaker and Roman Catholic Scholars* (Dublin, 1970), 1–3.

[4] Ibid. 13.   [5] Ibid. 21.

[6] Sean Connolly (ed.), *The Oxford Companion to Irish History* (Oxford, 1998), 149.

[7] Akenson, *Church of Ireland*, 321, 330. In 1867, for example, the Archbishop of Armagh's net income was just under £9,000 while the poorest bishop earned about £2,100. By 1919, the Archbishop Armagh earned £2,500 and the least-well-paid bishop earned slightly more than £1,400.

[8] Sean Connolly, *Religion and Society in Nineteenth-century Ireland* (Dundalk, 1985), 7–17.

emphasized the differences between them; and it also resulted in a large-scale, and largely unsuccessful, attempt to convert Catholics to Protestantism known as the second reformation.[9]

When the Act of Union was implemented, the Catholic church, on the other hand, was still discriminated against under the penal laws. The penal laws were designed to restrict the power of the potentially powerful Catholic landowning class which might threaten the primacy of the new Protestant British state in Ireland. Both Catholics and Presbyterians, who were also regarded as a possible threat to the state, were treated as second-class citizens during the eighteenth century, with the latter being subject to the imposition of a sacramental test and the former being the target of specific legislation. Under an act of 1704, for instance, Catholic priests were obliged to register if they wanted to continue their ministry in Ireland. Moreover, Catholics could not sit in parliament, they could not vote in parliamentary elections (between 1728 and 1793), they could not sit on municipal corporations, and they were excluded from the magistracy and the legal profession.[10] Following Catholic emancipation in 1829—which allowed Catholics to sit in parliament and was the last significant penal law to be abandoned—the influence of the Catholic church over the British state increased markedly. The Maynooth grant of 1845 increased the annual state grant to Maynooth College, the national seminary that had been established in 1795, from £8,928 to £26,360 and this effectively created 500 free places for prospective seminarians at the college.[11] Furthermore, in the post-Famine period the Irish Catholic bishops had reached an accommodation with the British state. Broadly speaking, the state agreed to respect the Church's vested interests especially in the arena of publicly funded education, and in return the Church agreed to use its influence to curb nationalist challenges to the state.[12] On this basis, the Catholic church converted the National education system in Ireland, which had been established in 1831, from its initial non-denominational character to an effectively segregated system. Indeed, by the end of the nineteenth century, the Catholic church had won from the British state an educational system up to third level with which it was satisfied.[13]

The influence of the Catholic church over the British state increased even further when the Catholic bishops entered into an alliance with the Irish

[9] By the 1860s it was clear that the attempt to convert Catholics to Protestantism had largely failed. See Gerard P. Moran, *The Mayo Evictions of 1860* (Westport, 1986), 125.

[10] Nigel Yates, *The Religious Condition of Ireland, 1770–1850* (Oxford, 2006), 18, 24. It does need to be borne in mind, however, that by the third decade of the eighteenth century serious attempts to enforce some aspects of the penal code (particularly those pertaining to the registration of priests) had largely been abandoned.

[11] Connolly, *Oxford Companion to Irish History*, 353; Emmet Larkin, 'The Devotional Revolution in Ireland, 1850–75', *American Historical Review*, 77 (June 1972), 859.

[12] David Miller, *Church, State and Nation in Ireland, 1898–1921* (Dublin, 1973), 4.

[13] Ibid. 4, 5, 29, 31. From 1860 onwards, the seats on the National education board were divided evenly between Catholics and Protestants.

Parliamentary Party. Initially, the bishops had been suspicious of Home Rule but the Irish hierarchy (as a body) changed its views of the national question for two main reasons. First, the leaders of the Irish Parliamentary Party—both Butt and Parnell—supported the Catholic hierarchy's position on the education question, and in return the bishops offered their support to the Home Rule movement. This was first evident during the negotiations of the unsuccessful University Bill in 1877 when Butt accepted almost all of the Catholic bishops' demands and effectively made himself their parliamentary agent in regard to the education question. Butt's position with the hierarchy was further enhanced when it became clear that the Chief Secretary, Sir Michael Hicks Beach, took the bishops' demands regarding the bill seriously.[14] Following this turning-point, the views of the hierarchy began to soften towards Home Rule. However, the critical turning-point came in October 1884 when the clerical–nationalist alliance was first established. At a meeting of the Irish bishops at Maynooth, a resolution was passed stating the following: 'That we call upon the Irish parliamentary party to bring the above resolutions under the notice of the House of Commons, and to urge generally upon the government the hitherto unsatisfied claims of Catholic Ireland in all branches of the education question.'[15] In effect, this statement inaugurated an understanding (rather than a formal agreement) that the IPP would promote the Irish bishops' demands in the sphere of education and in return the Irish Church would support the Home Rule movement as long as it was pursued along constitutional (rather than violent) lines. In addition, the Church established the right to be consulted on the question of the suitability of parliamentary candidates.[16]

The second major reason why the Irish bishops changed their view of Irish nationalism was the increasing power of the Home Rule movement in the 1880s. In particular, when the IPP won eighty-six seats at the 1885 general election and Gladstone converted to Home Rule, it became clear that the 'nation' would at some future point become the 'state'. In this new context, it was essential for the hierarchy to secure its future interests by reaching an accommodation with the 'nation'. Soon after Gladstone's conversion, therefore, the Irish hierarchy endorsed the Home Rule demand (thereby confirming the clerical–nationalist alliance first established eighteen months before in October 1884). For the following thirty years (1886–1916), the clerical–nationalist alliance remained in place (although it ebbed and flowed in terms of the respective power of the church and the party), and the Catholic church was broadly speaking in favour of constitutional Home Rule throughout this period. In other words, the 1884 clerical–nationalist alliance, and the first Home Rule crisis of 1886, resulted in

[14] Emmet Larkin, *The Roman Catholic Church and the Emergence of the Modern Irish Political System, 1874–1878* (Dublin, 1996), 455.

[15] Emmet Larkin, *The Roman Catholic Church and the Creation of the Modern Irish State, 1878–1886* (Philadelphia, Pa., 1975), 244.

[16] Larkin, *1878–1886*, 395; Miller, *Church, State and Nation*, 6.

the Catholic church's alliance with the British state being replaced by an alliance with the Irish Parliamentary Party. By the end of the nineteenth century, then, the Catholic bishops and the Home Rule party were two powerful sections of the Irish establishment that exercised a great deal of influence over the British state on behalf of the new rising Catholic middle class.

The power of the Catholic church in Irish society was also profoundly transformed during the nineteenth century by the increased devotion displayed by the Irish Catholic population. The Catholic church in Ireland experienced a 'devotional revolution' between the 1830s and the 1870s which may have been—in part—a response by the Catholic hierarchy to the evangelical revival and attempts to convert Catholics to Protestantism.[17] Data on church attendance in pre-Famine Ireland suggest that only 33 per cent of the Catholic population went to mass.[18] However, by the 1870s this had increased to over 90 per cent of the Catholic population.[19] There was also a significant increase in the number of priests in Ireland during the nineteenth century. In 1800, there were 1,850 priests; in 1840, there were 2,150 priests; in 1850, there were 2,500 priests; and in 1870, there were 3,200 priests. However, notwithstanding this increase, the ratio of priests to people actually declined in the years before the Famine due to the substantial increase in the Catholic population during this period. In 1800, there was one priest for every 2,100 of the faithful (in a Catholic population of 3.9 million) whereas by 1840 there was only one priest for every 3,000 of the faithful (in a Catholic population of 6.5 million). Following the Famine, the ratio of priests to people increased rapidly due both to an increase in the real number of priests and the substantial population decline brought about by the Famine and its aftermath. In 1850, there was one priest for every 2,100 of the faithful (in a Catholic population of 5 million), and by 1870 this had increased to one priest for every 1,250 of the faithful (in a Catholic population of 4 million).[20]

In addition to these increases in church attendance, the nineteenth century also witnessed a substantial amount of church-building which—as we have seen—greatly benefited Catholic entrepreneurs like William Martin Murphy.

---

[17] See Irene Whelan, *The Bible War in Ireland: The 'Second Reformation' and the Polarization of Protestant–Catholic Relations* (Madison, Wis., 2005).

[18] Larkin, 'Devotional Revolution', 636. In n. 21, Larkin explains that David Miller—the source of the data on church-attendance—has revised his initial estimate and now suggests that about 40% of the Catholic population attended mass in the pre-Famine period. See Miller, 'Mass Attendance in Ireland in 1834', in Stewart J. Brown and Miller, *Piety and Power in Ireland, 1760–1960* (South Bend, Ind., 2000).

[19] Eugene Hynes, 'The Great Hunger and Irish Catholicism', *Societas*, 8 (Spring 1978), 137. For an alternative interpretation of the origins of the devotional revolution to that advanced by Larkin, see Eugene Hynes, *Knock: The Virgin's Apparition in Nineteenth-century Ireland* (Cork, 2008).

[20] Larkin, 'Devotional Revolution', 626, 644. According to James O'Shea, the ratio of priests to people increased from 1:2,700–800 in 1835 to 1:1,500–900 in 1861 and 1:1,100–300 in 1891. See James O'Shea, *Priest, Politics and Society in Post-famine Ireland: A Study of County Tipperary, 1850–1891* (Dublin, 1983), 35.

Between 1800 and 1863, according to Myles O'Reilly, in 944 of the 1,085 Catholic parishes (in twenty-five of the twenty-eight dioceses): 1,805 churches were built, 217 convents, forty colleges or seminaries, and forty-four hospitals, asylums, or orphanages at a total cost of £5,274,368.[21] An impression of the extraordinary power of the Catholic church is gained when we consider that these funds were donated by voluntary payments from the laity during a period of serious poverty in Irish society. Furthermore, the devotional revolution continued well into the final quarter of the nineteenth century. Between 1861 and 1901, the number of clergy, monks, and nuns increased from 5,955 (a ratio of 1 to 1,000 people) to 14,145 (a ratio of 1 to 235 people).[22] The Catholic hierarchy by the beginning of the twentieth century, then, presided over an army of priests, monks, and nuns all of whom exercised—in turn—a great deal of power and influence over the Irish Catholic population as a whole. Moreover, the increased man- and woman-power of the Catholic church in Ireland also had a further 'greening' effect since it greatly increased the number of professional jobs open to young Catholics in convents, monasteries, and the priesthood.[23] An institution with this level of centralized, co-ordinated, and organized power over the political, social, and moral thinking of the majority of the Irish population could not be ignored by the British state in Ireland.

Like Irish Catholics, the members of the Irish Presbyterian church had been discriminated against during the eighteenth century by state-enforced sacramental tests. The Irish Presbyterian community were concentrated in Ulster, and they tended to be the descendants of the Scottish Presbyterians who had colonized the northern province during the seventeenth century. Because Irish Catholics and Ulster Presbyterians felt themselves to be discriminated against during the eighteenth century, both participated in the United Irishmen's insurrection of 1798. However, after the defeat of the insurrection and the introduction of the Act of Union in 1801, Ulster Presbyterians tended to become more allied with the Church of Ireland and with Unionism, rather than with Catholics and Irish nationalism. Even so, tensions between Presbyterians and the Church of Ireland remained significant during the first decades of the nineteenth century particularly because Presbyterians resented having to pay tithes to the 'established' church. Following some years of conflict within Irish Presbyterianism over the question as to whether they should subscribe to the Westminster Confession of Faith, the general assembly of the Presbyterian church in Ireland was established

---

[21] This figure is calculated on the basis that a similar amount of building was carried out in the three dioceses, about which data are unavailable. Myles O'Reilly, *Progress of Catholicity in Ireland in the Nineteenth Century* (Dublin, 1865), quot. Larkin, 'Devotional Revolution', 858.

[22] Ibid. 865, n. 31.

[23] According to Catriona Clear, the number of nuns in Ireland increased from 120 in 11 houses in 1800 to 8,000 in 368 houses in 1900. Quot. John Newsinger, 'The Catholic Church in Nineteenth-century Ireland', *European History Quarterly*, 25 (1995), 257.

in 1840. This newly united Presbyterian church experienced its own kind of devotional revolution during the following decades—both at home and abroad in the form of missionary outreach—partly due to the evangelical revival of 1859 which reinvigorated the church and also made it tend to become more anti-Catholic. The Tithe Reform Act of 1838 and the disestablishment of the Church of Ireland in 1869–71 effectively converted the Irish Presbyterian church into an equal of the Church of Ireland, and just under half of the Protestant population of Ireland at the beginning of the twentieth century were the members of Presbyterian congregations.

The social position of Presbyterians in Irish society was also transformed during the period reviewed in this book. Some Presbyterian Moderators—the Revd Whigham of Ballinasloe among them—made the argument that Presbyterians were inadequately represented in the Irish administration during the 1880s. By 1911, however, there were roughly the same proportions of Presbyterians in the Irish establishment as there were in the Irish population.[24] In many respects, Presbyterians did much better than Catholics at gaining entry to the Irish establishment, and this was partly because the British Liberal Party was keen to appoint Presbyterians and Dissenters to senior administrative positions, but it was probably also a result of the general tendency of the various Protestant churches in Ireland to pull together against Catholicism and Irish nationalism between 1886 and 1914.[25]

Who were the members of the religious elite who presided over and represented the Catholic and Protestant populations in Ireland between 1879 and 1914? The religious elite is defined as the Catholic Bishops in 1881 and 1911; the Church of Ireland Bishops in 1881 and 1911; and a number of individuals who held the position of Presbyterian Moderator in the 1880s and in the 1900s (this position was held by one individual for one year only).[26] The chapter will be divided into three parts. First, I will discuss the Catholic church in Ireland, and examine its structure and organization, the social background of its bishops, and their political and social views. Then, in the second part, I will examine the structure and nature of the Church of Ireland and the Presbyterian church in Ireland, and analyse the social background and political views of the Church of Ireland bishops and the Presbyterian Moderators. And finally, in the third part of the chapter, I will assess the extent to which the religious elite in Ireland was open or closed, consider how representative it was of Irish society, and make some general observations as to the changing relationship between the various churches in Ireland during this period.

---

[24] On Whigham's allegations, see Ch. 2.

[25] For a discussion of the increased representation of Presbyterians and Dissenters in the Irish establishment, see Conclusion.

[26] For the methodology and sources used to compile the data in this chapter, see Appendix. Considerations of time and space have prevented me from examining the social background of the leaders of the other churches—Quakers, Methodists, Congregationalists, Unitarians, Moravians, and so on—whose members were part of the Irish establishment during this period.

I

In 1870, the Catholic population of Ireland was about four million, and these people were ministered to by 3,200 priests.[27] The Catholic population was organized into 1,085 parishes, each of which was presided over by a parish priest who was usually assisted by one or more curates.[28] Catholic parishes in the nineteenth century usually contained two or more churches or chapels because they consisted of two or more of the pre-Reformation parishes which became Protestant civil parishes after the Reformation.[29] For instance, the diocese of Killaloe contained fifty-seven parishes in 1887 which contained 120 churches and twenty-two rural chapels, and were administered by 122 priests.[30] The Catholic parishes were organized into twenty-eight dioceses, each of which was presided over by a bishop; and the dioceses were further organized into the four provinces of Armagh, Cashel, Dublin, and Tuam, each of which was run by an archbishop. Technically, the Irish Catholic church was presided over by the Archbishop of Dublin, the Primate of Ireland, and the Archbishop of Armagh, the Primate of All Ireland, but in reality these were honorific distinctions and the actual distribution of power within the hierarchy was determined more by the individual bishop's personality, ability, standing within the hierarchy, influence at Rome, and capacity for leadership.[31] A very able individual could, therefore, exert a disproportionate influence over the Catholic church in Ireland. The Catholic hierarchy met only twice a year, and much of the business of the church was conducted at more frequent meetings of a standing committee of the four archbishops and five or six of the more prominent suffragans.[32] Of course, the hierarchy in Ireland were also under the authority of the Cardinals of Propaganda and the Pope himself, although, as we shall see, the dictates of Rome were not always implemented by the Irish hierarchy.

The available evidence suggests that the majority of Irish priests were from farming backgrounds. James O'Shea's study of the 575 secular priests in county Tipperary between 1850 and 1891 demonstrates that the vast majority were the sons of farmers.[33] Of these, O'Shea has identified the acreage of farms held by seventy of these families, and the data are presented in Table 6.1. Unfortunately, O'Shea does not give data on the valuation of these farms although it is likely that the land in county Tipperary was almost uniformly of a good quality with the most fertile land concentrated in the south of the county. At any rate, these data suggest that almost one-quarter (seventeen or 24 per cent) of the Tipperary priests

[27] Larkin, 'Devotional Revolution', 644.   [28] O'Reilly, *Progress of Catholicity*, 24.
[29] O'Shea, *Priest, Politics and Society in Post-famine Ireland*, 10–11.
[30] Persico report on diocese of Killaloe, quot. Bernard Canning, *Bishops of Ireland, 1870–1987* (Ballyshannon, 1987), 273.   [31] Miller, *Church, State and Society*, 10–11.
[32] Ibid. 14.   [33] O'Shea, *Priest, Politics and Society in Post-famine Ireland*, 13–14.

Table 6.1. The Size of the
Family Farm of Tipperary
Priests, 1850–1891

Acreage	Frequency
Under 20:	1 (1%)
20–50:	16 (23%)
51–80:	15 (21%)
81–110:	10 (14%)
111–40:	11 (16%)
141–70:	8 (11%)
171–200:	3 (4%)
Over 200:	6 (9%)
Number	70

Source: James O'Shea, *Priest, Politics and Society in Post-famine Ireland: A Study of County Tipperary, 1850–1891* (Dublin, 1983), 312.

from farming backgrounds were born on either small or middle-sized farms of fewer than fifty acres; a further third (35 per cent) were born on large farms of between fifty and 110 acres; and almost half (40 per cent) were substantial tenant farmers who occupied farms of at least 110 acres. Broadly speaking, this suggests that those priests who did come from farming backgrounds tended to be born on farms of more than fifty acres although a substantial minority of about one-quarter (24 per cent) were born on smaller and medium-sized farms of fewer than fifty acres.

The tendency for priests to be drawn from relatively well-off farming backgrounds, rather than labouring or small farm backgrounds, was in part because of the prohibitive cost of a clerical education. Prospective priests usually attended a local diocesan college, where part or all of the training for the priesthood could be attained, before attending a seminary. Most of the Tipperary priests who attended St Patrick's College, Thurles, faced an annual bill of 30 guineas, while the twenty-five priests who attended Carlow college were obliged to pay £25 per year with an additional £25 to cover expenses. Those Tipperary priests who attended St John's College, Waterford, paid annual fees of £26 in the 1820s, and fees of £30 in the 1870s.[34] Given that a labourer's weekly pay in 1900 was between 5 and 15 shillings, and a small farmer's annual income could be as little as £30–£40, neither of these sections of rural Irish society was capable of easily affording the fees for a clerical education at any of the diocesan colleges in Ireland.

[34] O'Shea, *Priest, Politics and Society in Post-famine Ireland*, 15.

Once an education at the diocesan college had been completed, the potential priest had to then go and study at either the national seminary at Maynooth or at one of the continental seminaries in Paris, Rome, or Salamanca. After 1845, when the Maynooth grant increased from £8,928 to £26,360, there were a large number of free places at Maynooth available to individuals from every Irish diocese. Of almost 200 Tipperary priests who attended Maynooth after 1845, for instance, almost all were given a free place and did not have to pay fees although they did have to pay expenses (which stood at about £14 in the 1820s). The continental seminaries were much more expensive, although they also offered a much smaller number of free places. Fees at the Irish College, Rome, for example, were 30 guineas per annum in 1840 plus £25 for expenses, including travel. Bishop James Ryan of Killaloe pointed out that the better-off students were sent to Rome, and the Tipperary priests who were educated there tended to be from substantial farming backgrounds of more than 100 acres. The Irish College at Salamanca was much less popular than that at Rome despite the total cost per annum for each student being slightly less than that at Rome (about £45).[35] Financial considerations were, therefore, a prime consideration when a potential vocation was discussed in a Victorian Irish household. However, financial resources could not automatically purchase a place in the seminaries. The religious convictions of the clerical candidate were scrutinized by the local priests, and the potential priest had to have a reasonable level of intelligence, good health, and a smattering of Latin.[36] Even so, the clerical education was narrow and not comparable to a monastic or university education, being confined to producing a body of professional men capable of carrying out the spiritual and administrative duties of parish life.[37]

Having invested a considerable amount of money in their education, the young man who eventually became a parish priest could look forward to a comfortable standard of living. Evidence of parish revenues in county Tipperary from the 1830s onwards suggests a substantial annual income for priests from parish collections alone. Income for the parish of Kilcommon during the first three months of 1840 alone was £81, while collections in the parish of Ballinahinch between September 1855 to June 1856 yielded £136. In 1852, the parish of Kilmoyler had receipts of £120, whereas in 1882, Sunday and holyday collections in Thurles amounted to £379 per annum. Of course, priests also gained a substantial additional income from conducting baptisms, weddings, and funerals. Individual marriage dues in Tipperary ranged from £1. 5s. 0d. to £7. 18s. 0d., although on one occasion Redmond Burke, the Parish Priest at Newport, told his Archbishop that he had gained as much as £20 for a wedding in 1850. Marriage dues varied according to the individual's social standing in the parish.[38] This is evident in the tariff for clerical dues drawn up by the bishops

---

[35] Ibid. 15–16.   [36] Ibid. 16–17.   [37] Ibid. 20.   [38] Ibid. 20–1.

in the province of Dublin in 1831. Shopkeepers and farmers would be charged 5*s.* for a baptism while labourers could avail of this service for only 2*s.* Similarly, it would cost shopkeepers and farmers £2 to get married while a 'poor labourer' could be married for only £1. A sung mass for dead shopkeepers and farmers would cost as much as 15*s.* while an unsung mass for a dead labourer would cost as little as 5*s.*[39] An English Catholic, T. Chisholme Anstey, told Rome in 1843 that there were few parish priests in Connacht who had incomes of less than £200 per annum, and some who had incomes of more than £500.[40]

Parish priests were assisted by curates, who earned substantially less than their superiors. It would appear that before the late nineteenth century there was no agreed uniform salary for the curate. At Ballyporeen, for instance, Dr Delaney, the parish priest, passed on only £10 of the 1880 Christmas collection of £78 to his curate. However, an annual salary of £20 appears to have been the norm in the mid-Victorian period, with Rome advising as late as 1867 that such a salary was too low. Curates were often understandably dissatisfied with their payment and occasionally requested a raise: in 1854, for instance, John Ryan, a curate at Cashel requested (and appears to have received) an increase to £52. On some occasions, there were separate collections for curates: visitation reports for a number of parishes in county Tipperary, for instance, indicate that there were special curates' collections held each year, usually in September or October (although we do not know how much these collections yielded). It was also customary for curates to share in some of the fees for particular services. Fees that were normally distributed among the various priests in the parish were known as divisible dues, and these probably constituted a substantial part of the curates' income. In the diocese of Cloyne in the 1860s, baptism and marriage dues as well as the Easter and Christmas collections were regarded as divisible dues, and the parish priests tended to pass on one-third of this revenue to their curates.[41]

Most curates tended to be promoted to parish priests when they were aged in their forties, and promotion appears to have been strictly based on length of service rather than individual ability (the average length of service before promotion in county Tipperary was twenty to twenty-four years).[42] However, the bishops controlled all aspects of their priests' careers, including promotions, transfers, and suspension, and if a curate was friendly or related to a bishop or a senior diocesan figure, their promotion might well be accelerated.[43] Indeed, there is suggestive evidence of nepotism in the Church well into the late nineteenth-century. When John MacHale, the Archbishop of Tuam, attempted to appoint his nephew, Thomas, as his Coadjutor (or assistant) Bishop in 1878, the terna (or list of nominated candidates) of the senior clergy who voted for the three episcopal candidates included six senior clergy who were MacHale's 'near relatives'.[44] It is

[39] Larkin, 'Devotional Revolution', 632.   [40] Ibid. 634.
[41] O'Shea, *Priest, Politics and Society in Post-famine Ireland*, 22–3.   [42] Ibid. 22.
[43] Ibid. 22, 240.   [44] Larkin, *1874–1878*, 89.

likely that once families had a son in the priesthood, then he was in a position to assist the recruiting of his nephews and cousins, and so on, to the clergy.

Both parish priests and curates were technically under the authority of the Irish hierarchy. Indeed, as we have seen, because bishops were responsible for the promotion of lower clergy, curates had to be sensitive to the views of their bishops if they did not want to jeopardize their future prospects. However, once a curate had become a parish priest, the bishops' power over his senior clergy was substantially diminished. One observer of episcopal power over senior clergy observed: 'The fact is, his bishop can do very little with a treasonable man when once he has been inducted a parish priest.'[45] There is substantial evidence that bishops' control over their priests was not absolute, and that priests occasionally defied their bishops. In some cases, bishops were regarded as powerless because they were either too old or too infirm to discipline their priests. In 1887, the Pope sent a Papal Legate, Ignazio Persico, to investigate the state of the Church in Ireland.[46] Persico spent about six months in Ireland and wrote reports on every Irish diocese, and in his report on James Walshe, the Bishop of Kildare and Leighlin (who was 84 in 1887), he explained that:

I fear that the clergy in general may be very involved in politics. There are some ardent Nationalists [among the clergy]. Contributing to this is the little or minimum control on the part of the Bishop. There is a bishop [Walshe] and a coadjutor [Lynch] but both of them are old and are not able or firm enough to rule and moderate the clergy.[47]

Similarly, Michael Flannery, the Bishop of Killaloe (who was 69 in 1887) was unable to prevent his priests from delving 'into political questions'. This was, according to Persico, because he was: 'in a decrepit state, habitually ill and has been absent from the diocese for some years. He actually lives in France. In 1872 he handed over to his Coadjutor, Mgr. James Ryan, who is also old and affected by paralysis . . . Thus it can be said that this diocese exists as if it did not have a bishop.'[48]

The Bishop of Derry, Francis Kelly (who was aged 75 in 1887), was, according to Persico, 'physically powerless' and 'leaves the clergy without any supervision and to their own ways'.[49] And Bartholomew Woodlock, the comparatively sprightly 68-year-old Bishop of Ardagh and Clonmacnois, was in Persico's estimation 'a weak and irresolute character who is not respected by the clergy . . . [and] the clergy are without control and under their own power'.[50] However, there were undoubtedly also some bishops (probably the majority of them) who did

---

[45] K. Theodore Hoppen, *Elections, Politics and Society, 1832–1885* (Oxford, 1984), 192; Eugene Hynes, 'Nineteenth-century Irish Catholicism, farmers' ideology, and national religion: explorations in cultural explanation', in Roger O'Toole, *Sociological Studies in Roman Catholicism: Historical and Contemporary Perspectives* (New York, 1989), 59, n. 4.

[46] On Persico, see Canning, *Bishops of Ireland*, 38–9.   [47] Persico report, ibid. 207.

[48] Ibid. 273.   [49] Ibid. 88.   [50] Ibid. 71.

exercise control over their clergy and were, like Abraham Brownrigg, Bishop of Ossory, men 'of sound conscience and moderate in political matters', and capable of 'inspiring calm and moderation in the people'.[51]

There were also a number of other cases where bishops (who were relatively young and comparatively healthy) were incapable of controlling some of their priests. William Delany, the Bishop of Cork, for instance, transferred two curates (John O'Mahony and Denis McCarthy) from the city parish of St Finbarr's to the rural parishes of Kinsale and Bandon, apparently because they had supported Parnell at the Cork city election. This transfer was regarded as a demotion from a higher to a lower curacy (which was usually the punishment for clerical offences like drunkenness), and the two curates appealed to Rome against the bishop's decision. When Rome rejected their appeal, a special petition consisting of almost 4,000 names was presented on behalf of O'Mahony but to no avail. In the event, the two curates were transferred to rustic curacies on the grounds that it was 'best for God' (according to Bishop Delany), but the popular opposition to the Episcopal decision suggests the limits of bishops' power.[52] Similarly, John MacEvilly, the Bishop of Galway, was defied by one of his senior parish priests, Peter Daly, when MacEvilly prohibited him from sitting on a public board in Galway city. Daly openly challenged the bishop and appealed to Rome, and although his appeal was rejected, this case also suggests that Episcopal authority was far from absolute.[53] In the diocese of Ferns, a political priest, Edmond Doyle, who was 'an ardent Nationalist' had defied James Browne, the bishop, and in so doing, according to Persico, undermined the bishop's authority.[54] It is likely that in the vast majority of cases, curates and priests silently accepted the dictates of their bishops. Indeed, a priest 'who had given public scandal in the matter of intemperance' was 'commanded to appear' before John Healy, Archbishop of Tuam, and 'admonished, but encouraged, and told to go and sin no more, and his cure was as complete and enduring as his gratitude'.[55] Even so, these examples suggest that there were at least some limits to Episcopal power.

The five-step process by which the Irish bishops were appointed was established in 1829. First, the senior clergy of the vacant diocese met and commended three names or *terna* to Propaganda, which was the congregation of the Roman Curia administratively responsible for Ireland. Second, the bishops of the province met and reported on the *terna* to Propaganda. Third, a *ponenza* or brief was prepared for the cardinals by Propaganda. Fourth, the cardinals of Propaganda then met and made their recommendation to the Pope for his authoritative approval.

---

[51] Persico report, ibid. 219.   [52] Ibid. 251.
[53] Liam Bane, 'John MacEvilly', q.v. DNB online <http://www.oxforddnb.com/view/article/52705> (accessed 15 Nov. 2008).   [54] Persico report, quot. Canning, *Bishops of Ireland*, 200.
[55] P. J. Joyce, *John Healy: Archbishop of Tuam* (Dublin, 1931), 267. Healy was appointed Coadjutor Bishop of Clonfert in 1884 before ascending to the see in 1896 and becoming Archbishop of Tuam, 1903–18.

And fifth, the Pope finally gave his authoritative approval of the successful candidate.[56]

During the post-Famine period, the most important and decisive aspect of the recruiting process became the report of the provincial bishops on the candidates named in the terna. Indeed, according to Larkin, of the eighteen episcopal appointments made in Ireland between 1860 and 1874, almost all of those appointed had been approved by the provincial bishops in their report. In other words, from the 1850s onward, the Irish bishops became essentially a co-opting body largely responsible for recruiting new members to their body.[57] Although this was the formal method by which Irish episcopal appointments were made, in the post-Famine period it is also necessary to consider an additional factor in determining appointments, that of the influence of Paul Cullen, first as Archbishop of Armagh (1850–2), then as Archbishop of Dublin (1852–78), and finally as Cardinal (1866–78). By 1875, the Irish hierarchy was a largely united body (certainly in comparison to the 1840s and 1850s), and, as Larkin acknowledges, this was partly the achievement of Paul Cullen who used 'his very considerable influence at Rome in the making of Episcopal appointments to structure a like-minded and Roman-oriented Episcopal body in the Irish church'.[58] In cases where Cullen believed that the best candidate had not been put forward by either the terna or the bishops' report, he was prepared to use his extraordinary influence to overturn both, as in 1875 when he successfully promoted the appointment of Thomas William Croke to the vacant see at Cashel.[59] Indeed Whyte has shown that of the forty-four bishops appointed under Cullen's episcopate (including Cullen), three were appointed without the clergy of the diocese being consulted, nine came from outside the terna, eleven had been second or third on the terna, and only twenty-four (or 55 per cent) had been first on the terna. This is in contrast to the period preceding Cullen's arrival in Ireland when three-quarters of the bishops appointed had been first on the terna, and in no case had the terna been ignored completely.[60]

Who was Cullen and what kinds of men did he recruit to the Irish Episcopal bench? Cullen was born at Prospect, near Ballitore, in county Kildare on 29 April 1803. His father was a substantial tenant farmer who occupied 522 acres valued at £628. 10s. (in Griffith's Valuation), and his mother's family (the Mahers) were also substantial tenant farmers in the region.[61] Cullen was, therefore, born into a

---

[56] Larkin, *1874–1878*, pp. xviii, 97. On p. xviii, Larkin describes the process of Episcopal appointments as involving four steps, while on p. 97 he describes it as a five-step process (adding the step at which the brief was prepared by Propaganda for the Cardinals).

[57] Ibid. p. xviii.   [58] Ibid.   [59] Ibid. 56–71.

[60] John H. Whyte, 'The Appointment of Catholic Bishops in Nineteenth-century Ireland', *Catholic Historical Review*, 48 (1962), 27–8.

[61] Emmet Larkin, 'Paul Cullen', q.v. DNB online <http://www.oxforddnb.com/view/article/6872> (accessed 15 Nov. 2008). For acreage of the Cullen farm, see townland of Sherlockstown, civil parish of Sherlockstown, county Kildare (Griffith's Valuation).

relatively wealthy rural family which—according to some commentators—had a tradition of loyalty to the British state in Ireland. According to the testimony of Quaker neighbours, Cullen's father had remained loyal during the bloody rising of 1798 in the south-east part of county Kildare where the Cullens lived.[62] However, it is also widely believed that Cullen's father was himself a United Irishman and that the Quaker neighbours' contrary statements were inspired to prevent harm from coming to him. The considerable wealth of the Cullen family is revealed in some of Paul's correspondence with his brothers. On one occasion in 1837, for example, Thomas Cullen raised £250 for Paul from his brothers and the extended Cullen family.[63] After studying at the local Quaker school at Ballitore, Cullen studied at the Irish College Rome before being ordained at Rome on 19 April 1829. He was then appointed Professor of Scripture at the Irish College, and in 1832 he became the rector of the Irish College Rome at the remarkably young age of 29. During the following eighteen years, Cullen established enduring and influential contacts within the Vatican bureaucracy that would prove enormously helpful to him when he was appointed Archbishop of Armagh and apostolic delegate in Ireland in May 1850.

Cullen has been described as 'the Pope's chief whip in Ireland' and the 'headmaster of the Irish Church', and he was certainly charged by the Papacy with the task of reforming the Catholic church in Ireland which—arguably—led to the devotional revolution.[64] A national synod for the purpose of bringing reform and unity to the Irish Church was convened at Thurles on 22 August 1850 under the presidency of Cullen. The Synod introduced a thoroughgoing Tridentine (or Papal) reform of the Irish Church, tightened ecclesiastical discipline, and introduced greater uniformity in religious practices. Priests were instructed to administer the sacraments more often and only in church, and to lead lives that would serve as an example to their parishioners.[65] It was in the administration of the sacraments, however, that the Synod appears to have had the greatest impact. Before the Famine, the sacraments of baptism, marriage, penance, and the eucharist had generally been celebrated in private houses (the latter two as part of the stations system).[66] However, the new decrees demanded that this tradition be discontinued and that only children in danger of dying or in particularly remote areas could be baptized at home. And, in order to ensure that marriages were celebrated in church rather than in the home, the new decrees stipulated that marriage dues could not be charged by the priest unless the wedding took place

---

[62] Hynes, 'Nineteenth-century Irish Catholicism', 63, n. 6.

[63] Thomas Cullen to Paul Cullen, 8 Sept. 1837, Cullen Papers, quot. Emmet Larkin, 'Church, State, and Nation in Modern Ireland', *American Historical Review*, 80 (1975), 1253, n. 19.

[64] Joseph Lee, *The Modernisation of Irish Society, 1848–1918* (Dublin, 1973), 43.

[65] Samuel Clark, *Social Origins of the Irish Land War* (Princeton, NJ, 1979), 194.

[66] The 'stations', which are still held in Irish parishes, involve mass being said in each parishioner's house for the members of that locality.

within the precincts of a church.[67] The transformation of space, from the home to the church, was a central feature of the new exercise of clerical discipline.[68] The laity were also encouraged to take up new devotional exercises with the aim of shortening the sinners' or the sinners' loved ones' time in purgatory. The new devotions were mainly of Roman origin and included the rosary, forty hours, perpetual adoration, novenas, blessed altars, *Via Crucis*, benediction, vespers, devotion to the Sacred Heart, pilgrimages, shrines, processions, and retreats.[69] In addition, these public exercises of devotion were complemented by the use of devotional tools and aids including rosary beads, scapulars, medals, missals, prayer books, catechisms, holy pictures, and *Agnus Dei*, all of which were blessed by the priests. The liturgy was now extended to the whole world of the senses with singing, music, candles, vestments, and incense.[70]

The combined effect of Cullen's accession to Armagh and the Synod of Thurles was effectively to enforce ultramontanism on Ireland, and this also influenced the kinds of people who were recruited to the Irish Episcopal body after 1850.[71] Cullen believed that priests and bishops should not become involved in popular politics, and that religion and politics should be treated as separate and autonomous spheres. In an interview with Lucas (the editor of the *Tablet*) in Rome on 24 January 1855, Cullen explained that:

On the part to be taken by priests in politics he said the business of a priest was to confine himself to his spiritual duties and in the intervals of these to confine himself to reading and meditation; but if the Church was attacked in such a way that all Catholics must agree upon it, then they should come out; but whenever two Catholics might differ then they should take no part lest by doing so they should get into collision with one part of their flock; that with regard to elections they ought to tell the people their duty to avoid bribery and perjury and to vote for a candidate favourable to the Church; if a candidate avowedly hostile to the Church showed himself they might warn the people against him, though with caution; but if two candidates presented themselves both not professing sentiments hostile to the Church, their business was not to interfere between them but to stick to general principles.[72]

Both the Papacy and Cullen preferred bishops not to engage in political activity, and this is why Persico took such a dim view of bishops who were incapable of controlling politically active priests. Indeed, Cullen told Propaganda in February 1854: 'They [the Irish bishops] should be allied neither with the government nor

---

[67] O'Shea, *Priest, Politics and Society in Post-famine Ireland*, 36.

[68] Tom Inglis, *Moral Monopoly: The Rise and Fall of the Catholic Church in Modern Ireland* (Dublin, 1998), 142.

[69] While he was Archbishop of Tuam, John Healy revived the national pilgrimage to Croagh Patrick which continues today (Joyce, *John Healy*, 254).

[70] Larkin, 'Devotional Revolution', 644–5.

[71] Ultramontanism is the current of opinion in the Catholic church which favours papal over national or diocesan authority. Gallicanism, on the other hand, advocates the restriction of papal power and the enhancement of that of the bishops and the temporal ruler.

[72] Lee, *Modernisation of Irish Society*, 46.

with the popular party, but should be men who occupy themselves with their proper duties as good bishops.'[73] However, Cullen was prepared to intervene in politics if he thought it was in the interest of the Catholic church for him to do so and his dislike of priests' involvement in politics was probably motivated by his concern that this would weaken the overall authority of the church.[74] In fact, a recent account suggests that Cullen was not a 'Castle Catholic' at all as has been alleged but a constitutional nationalist.[75]

A tendency not to be politically active, and not to be an extreme nationalist were, therefore, qualities which Cullen took into consideration when a new bishop was being recruited. This is evident in the process by which a successor to the see of Ferns was selected after the death of Bishop Thomas Furlong in November 1875. There were three main candidates put forward by the terna: James Richards, Vicar Apostolic for Grahamstown, South Africa; Michael Warren, Superior of the House of Missions at Enniscorthy; and William Fortune, the rector of All Hallows College, Dublin. Although Warren was variously described as 'not gifted very highly nor very highly accomplished' and 'a miserable preacher', Cullen supported his appointment as did the provincial bishops. The bishops explained to Propaganda that it had been difficult to find an appropriate person for the South African position, and that they did not want to have to find another candidate so soon after Richards' appointment. Fortune was, on the other hand, a worthy priest but rather too ardent in his politics, particularly for a diocese like Ferns which required a bishop capable of checking the political involvements of the clergy. Cullen and the provincial bishops were both, therefore, in favour of Warren's appointment, but in order to secure the position for him Cullen sent his nephew, Moran, the Bishop of Ossory, to Rome to canvass the cardinals. As a result, the Pope declared that Warren was the new Bishop of Ferns on 13 February 1876.[76]

Cullen was also keen to stamp out nepotism in appointments within the Irish Church.[77] When the claims of a Father MacDermott were advanced to become the new Dean to Bishop Gillooly, for instance, Cullen explained that: 'I know the claims of his family and I would most willingly do anything in my power to oblige the O'Connors but where the interests of the Church at large are at stake we must look to the personal merits of every candidate.'[78] Cullen was determined to appoint men that he regarded as deserving of becoming a bishop, and an

---

[73] Cullen to Propaganda (18 Feb. 1854), quot. Whyte, 'Political Problems, 1850–1860', in Patrick J. Corish (ed.), *A History of Irish Catholicism*, v/ii (Dublin, 1967), 21.

[74] This point is made by Steven Knowlton's *Popular Politics and the Irish Catholic Church* (New York, 1992), quot. Newsinger, 'The Catholic Church in Nineteenth-century Ireland', 263.

[75] Colin Barr, *Paul Cullen, John Henry Newman and the Catholic University of Ireland, 1845–1865* (Notre Dame, Ind., 2003), 138.

[76] On the process by which Warren was appointed, see Larkin, *1874–1878*, 78–82.

[77] Although Cullen had invited his nephew, Patrick Francis Moran, to Ireland to become his secretary in 1866 and this led to his subsequent appointment as Bishop of Ossory in 1872.

[78] Lee, *Modernisation of Irish Society*, 44.

Table 6.2. The Occupations of Catholic Bishops' Fathers, 1881–1911

Occupation	1881–1911	1881	1911
Business	5 (38%)	4 (57%)	1 (17%)
Landowner	2 (15%)	1 (14.33%)	1 (17%)
Tenant farmer	4 (31%)	1 (14.33%)	3 (50%)
Professional	2 (15%)	1 (14.33%)	1 (17%)
Excise officer	1 (8%)	0	1 (17%)
Number	13	7	6

Note: Some individuals had more than one occupation.

indication of Cullen's Episcopal criteria is provided in a letter from Cullen to Kirby at the Irish College Rome regarding the candidature of one Father Kilduff for the see of Ardagh in 1853. According to Cullen, Kilduff was 'a good preacher, a good theologian, full of zeal, and yet courageous enough'.[79] And, according to Larkin, Cullen generally tried to promote men like Kilduff:

who were made in his own image and likeness. They were not only good preachers, adequate theologians, zealous, courageous enough, and young, but they were also generally strangers to the diocese and, therefore, they did not have any of the personal ties or loyalties that might inhibit them in their zeal for reform. If they were not recruited from the regular clergy, moreover, the new bishops were usually rectors or vice-rectors of seminaries—strict, stern, austere men who had both the experience of, and a proven talent for, efficient administration.[80]

Of the twenty-nine Irish bishops in 1881, twenty-four of them (83 per cent) were appointed during the period of Cullen's ascendancy and dominance in Ireland (between 1850 and 1878), while only three had been appointed before Cullen's arrival in Ireland.[81] And all of the bishops in 1911 were appointed after Cullen's death and were essentially co-opted by the Episcopal body that Cullen was largely responsible for creating.

Who were the Irish bishops in 1881 and 1911? Altogether, there are fifty-five individuals included in this study: there were twenty-nine Catholic bishops in 1881, and twenty-seven in 1911, and only one individual was a bishop at both dates (Michael Logue).[82] Of the bishops included in this study, we know something of the social background of a quarter (thirteen or 24 per cent) of them (Table 6.2). More than one-third of the bishops' fathers (about whom

[79] Larkin, 'Devotional Revolution', 646.   [80] Ibid. 648.
[81] Two of the bishops in 1881 (Michael Logue and Bartholomew Woodlock) were appointed after Cullen's death, and three were appointed before Cullen became Archbishop of Armagh in 1850 (John MacHale (appointed in 1825), William Delany (appointed in 1847), and Francis Kelly (appointed in 1849)).
[82] The reason why there were more bishops in 1911 than in 1881 was because there were 2 coadjutor bishops in 1881.

information is available) were involved in some kind of business. In general, these businesses appear to have been rather modest in scale. Michael Logue's father (also called Michael) was an innkeeper and small farmer; John MacHale's father (Patrick) was also an innkeeper, flax dealer, and small farmer; Patrick Dorrian's father (Patrick) was a shopkeeper; Patrick Francis Moran's father (Patrick) was a businessman (and his mother was Paul Cullen's half sister); and William Walsh's father (Ralph) was a watchmaker and jeweller based at Arran Quay in Dublin. We do not know what occupation Thomas Alphonsus O'Callaghan's father held but we do know that 'He was a member of an old Cork family, which in the early portion of the last [nineteenth] century was intimately associated with the commercial life of Cork'.[83] In all cases, except that of Moran and Walsh, these bishops were descended from the smaller provincial Irish business concerns that were about to play a dominant role in the Land League after 1879.[84] It is also clear, however, that the proportion of bishops drawn from business backgrounds was in decline between 1881 and 1911 (from 57 per cent to 17 per cent), and that they were being replaced by bishops from farming backgrounds: farm-born bishops increase from about one in eight (14.3 per cent) to exactly half of the total between 1881 and 1911. This perhaps suggests the rising power of the tenant farmer class in Ireland after the Land War (1879–81), but it is worth bearing in mind that this evidence is impressionistic as we know only the social background of seven bishops in 1881 (24 per cent of the total), and six in 1911 (22 per cent of the total).

Slightly less than one-third (31 per cent) of the bishops under review were drawn from tenant farming backgrounds. We know that four of the bishops contained in this study came from tenant farm backgrounds, but we also know that seven others came from families that occupied a farm and are listed as such in Griffith's Valuation (although we do not know for sure if their fathers worked exclusively as farmers). At least eleven of the fifty-five bishops under review, then, came from some kind of farming background, and the acreage of these eleven family farms is presented in Table 6.3. Given that acreage is not a reliable indicator of the value of a family farm, it is necessary to consider also the valuation of the eleven family farms. Five were valued at under £5; one was valued at between £5 and £10; two were valued at between £10 and £15; one was valued at between £20 and £50; one was valued at between £50 and £100; and one was valued at more than £500. In other words, these data suggest that six of the eleven bishops came from what the government regarded as congested tenant farms or farms that were deemed to be too small and too poor in quality to sustain a reasonable standard of living; a further three were middle-sized farms

---

    [83] *Irish Times*, 24 June 1916. O'Callaghan was Bishop of Cork between 1886 and 1916.
    [84] See data on the Protection of Person and Property Act arrests in Clark, *Social Origins of the Irish Land War*, 249–52.

Table 6.3. Acreage of Tenant Farms Occupied by
Catholic Bishops' Families

Acres	1881–1911	1881	1911
0–9	2 (18%)	1 (25%)	1 (14%)
10–19	1 (9%)	0	1 (14%)
20–29	3 (27%)	1 (25%)	2 (28.5%)
30–49	2 (18%)	0	2 (28.5%)
50–99	0	0	0
100–499	2 (18%)	1 (25%)	1 (14%)
500+	1 (9%)	1 (25%)	0
Number	11	4	7

(valued at between £10 and £50); and only two were in the 'grazier' category, that is farms valued at more than £50. This pattern is confirmed if we then look at the farm-size of the four bishops' fathers who we know were tenant farmers.[85] Three of these were from tenant farm backgrounds defined as congested (at or under £10 valuation) and one was from a 'grazier' background. Broadly speaking, the bishops drawn from farming backgrounds were from small farm households with only a minority from the medium-sized and large farm sectors. If anything, these data suggest that bishops may have been drawn from smaller farms than the clergy more generally (if we compare these data with O'Shea's study of farm-born priests in county Tipperary (see Table 6.1)). However, it is almost certainly the case that priests born on farms in prosperous county Tipperary would have been better off than priests born on farms in other parts of Ireland, and especially the west of Ireland. Even so, this evidence modifies the prevailing assumption that the Irish bishops were usually drawn from the grazier class, and suggests that the social background of the Irish bishops was probably not markedly different from that of the clergy more generally. Some of the confusion regarding this point might arise from the overuse of the term 'respectable farming class' which appears to have meant different things to different people: John MacEvilly's parents—William and Sarah—were described in these terms although they occupied a farm valued at less than £5. However, it is possible that in their locality this was a substantial farm, and that within their community they were

---

[85] John MacEvilly's father, William, was a tenant farmer at Bunowen in Louisburgh, county Mayo who occupied a farm of 112 acres (about 100 acres of which was bogland; valued at £4. 15s. 0d.); Thomas P. Gilmartin's father, John, was a tenant farmer at Knockaphunta, near Castlebar, county Mayo who occupied a farm of 23 acres (valued at £10. 12s. 0d); Patrick O'Donnell's father, Daniel, occupied a farm at Kilrean Upper near Glenties, county Donegal of 38 acres (valued at £4. 5s. 0d.); and Thomas Fennelly's father, Martin, occupied a farm at Moyne, county Tipperary of 214 acres (valued at £88. 11s. 0d.). It should be noted that these farms were held in the home townlands of these bishops' families and that they may have held other farms beyond the home farm. It is also possible that farm-size could have changed over time.

regarded as possessing high status for other reasons. A 'respectable' farmer did not necessarily denote a grazier, as has been often assumed.[86]

Only two of the bishops in this study were born into landowning families. John Power, Bishop of Waterford and Lismore in 1881, was probably a relation of William Power of Affane House, Cappoquin, Waterford, who owned 302 acres (valued at £377). Similarly, Edward Thomas O'Dwyer's father's uncle was General Sir Henry Sheehy-Keatinge who owned 971 acres (valued at £409) in county Tipperary (O'Dwyer was Bishop of Limerick in 1911).[87] When compared with the Church of Ireland bishops, and indeed with the Catholics who were senior members of the Irish administration, however, there were comparatively few Catholic bishops drawn from landowning families. Six of the bishops in 1881 are listed in the *Return of Landowners in Ireland* as owning land in Ireland in 1876 but this was land owned by the Catholic church in their dioceses rather than land owned personally by them or by their families.[88]

Finally, about one in eight of the Irish bishops was drawn from a professional background. Thomas William Croke's father was an estate agent, and John Lyster's father was an architect.[89] And John Keating-O'Dwyer (Edward Thomas's father) was an excise officer (or minor civil servant) in addition to being the member of a Tipperary gentry family. Although we do not know the particular occupation pursued by Edward McCabe's father, we do know that he was the son of poor parents.[90] I have not included the family background of John Healy in the data in Table 6.2 because the complexity of his parents' social background and work-experience cannot be easily reduced to a single occupational category. Healy was a descendant of the O'Helys, Catholic landowners in county Mayo, who had been dispossessed during 'the desolating wars of Elizabeth'. Although Healy felt himself to be the member of a once-great Catholic landowning class, his parents both worked as teachers at Ballinafad during his childhood.[91] However, while Healy was a student at Maynooth, a new priest, Father Quinn, was appointed to his parents' parish at Aghanagh, who dismissed Healy's father from his position—apparently because he was infirm—and Mark and Mary Healy

---

[86] On MacEvilly, see Liam Bane, *The Bishop in Politics: Life and Career of John MacEvilly* (Westport, 1993), 5. For a discussion of the different gradations within the tenant farmer class and how they might have been perceived locally, see Fergus Campbell, *Land and Revolution: Nationalist Politics in the West of Ireland, 1891–1921* (Oxford, 2005), 310–11.

[87] Thomas J. Morrissey, *Bishop Edward Thomas O'Dwyer of Limerick, 1842–1917* (Dublin, 2003), 3–4.

[88] Those bishops listed in the Return as owning land were William Delany, Thomas Nulty, Nicholas Conaty, Patrick Dorrian, James Donnelly, and Francis McCormack.

[89] Mark Tierney, *Croke of Cashel: The Life of Archbishop Thomas William Croke, 1823–1902* (Dublin, 1976), 3–4.

[90] W. A. J. Archbold (rev. David C. Sheehy), 'Edward McCabe', q.v. DNB online <http://www.oxforddnb.com/view/article/17369> (accessed 15 Nov. 2008).

[91] While he was Bishop of Clonfert, Healy 'had the family crest suitably painted on his car' (Joyce, *John Healy*, 4).

Table 6.4. Catholic Bishops' Secondary Education, 1881–1911

School	1881–1911	1881	1911
Clongowes	2 (5%)	2 (14%)	0
Castleknock	1 (2.5%)	0	1 (4%)
CBS	4 (10%)	0	4 (15%)
Diocesan college	34 (85%)	9 (64%)	24 (92%)
Other Catholic school	5 (12.5%)	4 (29%)	2 (8%)
Number	40	14	26

Note: Some individuals attended more than one secondary school.

emigrated to Halifax. In south Yorkshire, Mary worked as a private school teacher until opposition from the local parish priest forced her to give this up to work as a lace maker, while some of her children were sent to work in local factories. Healy's background, then, was that of the declining Catholic aristocracy who had washed up at the end of the nineteenth century as out-of-work teachers, lace makers, and factory workers. Notwithstanding Healy's sense of former familial greatness, this was certainly not a prosperous or a well-to-do family background.[92]

Almost all of the bishops in this study received a secondary education. Table 6.4 demonstrates that forty (73 per cent) of the total number of bishops received a formal secondary education, and that the proportion of bishops who attended secondary school increased from fourteen (48 per cent) in 1881 to twenty-six (96 per cent) in 1911. Most of them attended the diocesan colleges/seminaries where part (or all) of the clerical training could be undertaken, including St Jarlath's, Tuam; St Colman's, Fermoy; St Peter's, Wexford; St Vincent's, Cork; St Flannan's, Ennis; and Carlow College. Some of the bishops from better-off backgrounds went to the elite Catholic schools at Clongowes and Castleknock (but the proportion of bishops who had been to these schools declined markedly between 1881 and 1911). James Lynch, for instance, was educated at Clongowes before taking up medical studies at the College of Surgeons, and then deciding to become a priest instead of a doctor. He went on to become a Vincentian, rector of the Irish College in Paris, and founder of Castleknock College in 1835. An increasing proportion of the bishops attended the new Christian Brothers' Schools that were being established throughout Ireland during the second part of the nineteenth century. And a number of bishops who were from less-well-off backgrounds attended 'other' Catholic schools in the localities from which they came: Michael Logue went to the Robertson School at Kilmacrenan, county Donegal; Patrick Dorrian had attended a classical secondary school at Downpatrick, county Down; and Edward McCabe attended Father Michael Doyle's school on Arran Quay in Dublin. The fees payable at classical or at

[92] Ibid. 3–4; 11–12.

Table 6.5. Catholic Bishops' Tertiary Education, 1881–1911

College	1881–1911	1881	1911
Maynooth	43 (83%)	20 (77%)	23 (88%)
Irish College Paris	4 (8%)	3 (12%)	1 (4%)
St Surplice Paris	1 (2%)	1 (4%)	0
Irish College Rome	2 (4%)	2 (8%)	0
Apollinaire, Rome	1 (2%)	1 (4%)	0
Minerva College, Rome	1 (2%)	0	1 (4%)
London University	1 (2%)	0	1 (4%)
Catholic University of Ireland	2 (4%)	0	3 (12%)
Number	52	26	26

Note: Some individuals attended more than one third level college.

Christian Brothers' Schools were light in comparison to those paid at diocesan colleges: classical school fees, for example, ranged from half a guinea to a guinea per quarter.[93] Given that places at Maynooth were often free after 1845, it probably was possible for a young man from a comparably poor background to become a priest or a bishop. Indeed, the evidence presented above would suggest that some bishops were drawn from small farm backgrounds (although there is no evidence of any bishops or priests being born into labouring families). John MacHale, the influential Archbishop of Tuam (1834–81), for example, appears to have come from relatively humble origins (his father was an innkeeper who bought flax from his neighbours and sold it at the linenhall in Castlebar, as well as a small farmer who occupied a farm valued at less than £5).[94] At the classical school at Castlebar, MacHale distinguished himself as such a promising student that the Bishop of Killala, Dominic Bellew, offered him a free place at the recently opened seminary at Maynooth, and he began his career there in 1807. This does suggest that the Catholic religious elite was not entirely closed to young men from comparatively humble backgrounds.

The vast majority of bishops in this study had also received a third-level education (Table 6.5). Altogether, fifty-two of the fifty-five bishops (95 per cent) had attended either a university or a seminary: in 1881, twenty-six of the twenty-nine bishops (90 per cent) did so, and in 1911, twenty-six of the twenty-seven bishops did so (96 per cent). There was therefore a slight increase in the proportion of bishops who had received a tertiary or seminary education between 1881 and 1911. The majority (83 per cent) of the Irish bishops had attended the national seminary at Maynooth, with a slight increase in those who had done so between 1881 (77 per cent) and 1911 (88 per cent). As we have seen,

93 O'Shea, *Priest, Politics and Society in Post-famine Ireland*, 14.
94 MacHale was the fifth son of Pádraig Mór who Eugene Hynes describes as 'a prosperous merchant/farmer' and who was clearly not 'a poor peasant', but the size of the MacHale farm suggests that they were not wealthy graziers either (Hynes, *Knock*, 77–8).

between 1845 and 1869, there were 525 free places at Maynooth, and during the second half of the nineteenth-century, Maynooth educated the vast majority of priests for the Irish church. By 1850, the great majority of bishops (and by 1875, the great majority of priests) were alumni of the Kildare college.[95] However, some of the late Victorian Irish bishops had been educated elsewhere, notably at the Irish colleges in Paris and Rome (and at other ecclesiastical colleges in those cities). In 1881, for instance, almost one-quarter (24 per cent) of the Irish bishops who had attended a seminary had done so in Paris or Rome, although the proportion who had done so in 1911 had declined to less than one in ten (8 per cent). Cullen, who had been trained in Rome, did not have a high opinion of Maynooth, and the increased number of bishops who had attended the national seminary rather than the Irish colleges in Europe might reflect in a change in recruiting practices after his death.[96]

However, at the beginning of the twentieth century, the Irish bishops were better qualified than their predecessors, and about one in six was a graduate of a university as well as a seminary. One of the bishops in 1911, Patrick Foley, was a graduate of the University of London, and three (John Lyster, Patrick O'Donnell, and William Walsh) had attended the Catholic University in Dublin. Three of the bishops in this study did not attend the seminary at Maynooth or on the continent. John Power, Bishop of Waterford and Lismore, in 1881 did all of his clerical training at the diocesan seminary; John Pius Leahy, Bishop of Dromore in 1881, trained as a Dominican at Lisbon; and Patrick Foley, Bishop of Kildare and Leighlin in 1911, completed all of his clerical training at Carlow college before gaining a BA—presumably by correspondence course—from the University of London.

All of the Irish bishops had been ordained when they were aged in their twenties, and most were appointed bishops when they were aged in their forties or fifties. Data are available on the age at which they were appointed a bishop for all the bishops in this study (Table 6.6). About one in ten (six or 11 per cent) was made bishop in his thirties; almost half (twenty-three or 42 per cent) became bishops in their forties; about one-third (twenty or 36 per cent) became bishops in their fifties; and about one in ten (six or 11 per cent) became a bishop in his sixties. As with the promotion of curates to parish priests, it may be that ascent to a see could be speeded up if the individual had friends or family in senior ecclesiastical positions in the diocese, or even better if they had some influence with the bishops of the province, or with Cullen himself (between 1850 and 1878). Of the fifty-five bishops under review, four were related to another bishop and three were related to a priest, so that at least seven of the fifty-five (13 per cent) were related to other members of the clergy. While this

---

[95] Larkin, 'Church, State, and Nation in Modern Ireland', 1255.

[96] Cullen believed that some of the professors at Maynooth were influenced by Gallicanism in the 1850s and felt that the training at the college did not encourage the development of ecclesiastical virtues. Whyte, 'Appointment of Catholic Bishops', 29, 31.

Table 6.6. Age of Catholic Bishops in 1881 and 1911

Age	1881	1911
40–9	3 (10%)	1 (4%)
50–9	4 (14%)	11 (41%)
60–9	15 (52%)	10 (37%)
70–9	6 (21%)	5 (18%)
80–9	—	—
90–9	1 (3%)	—
Number	29	27

suggests that there were some families that probably included a number of uncles, brothers, cousins, and so on, who were priests, it does not suggest that widespread nepotism was practised within the Catholic church after Cullen's reforms.

In 1881, the majority of the bishops were aged in their sixties and seventies, whereas in 1911 most bishops were in their fifties and sixties. Indeed, the profile of the bishops in 1911 is slightly younger than that in 1881 with only about one-quarter (24 per cent) aged under 60 in 1881, while almost half (45 per cent) were under 60 in 1911. This may reflect a deliberate recruiting policy adopted under Cullen's period of dominance of appointing younger bishops. Persico repeatedly observed that a number of bishops were too old and too infirm properly to run their dioceses, as we have seen. However, it was as late as 1967 before Pope Paul VI decreed that bishops should retire at a certain point (when aged 75), and up to that point (and certainly during the period under review) most bishops appear to have stayed in post until they died, even if they were too ill or too old to carry out their episcopal duties.[97] It would seem that individuals who became bishops were reluctant voluntarily to give up their episcopal powers. According to Persico, Bishop Power of Waterford and Lismore (aged 78 in 1887) 'was unable to act but wanted to govern the diocese up until his death . . . the old Bishop acted under the influence of a few priest confidants'.[98] Similarly, John Pius Leahy, Bishop of Dromore (aged 85 in 1887), was, according to Persico, old and struck down with paralysis but he still 'wants to run everything'.[99]

The majority of priests who were appointed as bishops in Ireland after 1850 were men who had some experience of academic and administrative positions in either diocesan colleges or seminaries. Indeed, a substantial proportion of the Irish bishops had held some sort of academic position (as a professor or rector at a diocesan college or at Maynooth) before becoming a bishop. In fact, more than one-third of the bishops in this study (twenty or 36 per cent) had held an academic post, and had never worked as either a curate or a parish priest.

[97] Canning, *Bishops of Ireland*, 21.   [98] Persico report, ibid. 301.
[99] Persico report, ibid. 131.

A further third (nineteen or 35 per cent) had held both an academic post as well as working for some time as a curate or a parish priest. And less than one-third (sixteeen or 29 per cent) of the Irish bishops had never held an academic post before being appointed to the Episcopal body, and had spent their clerical careers entirely in parish work. This confirms a tendency identified by both Lee and Larkin that Cullen preferred to appoint bishops who were strangers to a diocese and who had administrative and academic experience. This would mean that they would probably pay less attention to local opposition to reforms from above, and that they were the kind of men capable of imposing the devotional revolution on Irish society. It is also clear that at the beginning of the twentieth century, more bishops had had an academic rather than a parish background. In 1911, only four (or 15 per cent) of the bishops had had no academic background (compared with almost half (twelve or 41 per cent)) of the bishops in 1881. In 1911 almost all of the bishops (twenty-three or 85 per cent) had worked as a professor at a diocesan college or at Maynooth before becoming a bishop as opposed to only slightly more than half (seventeen or 59 per cent) of the bishops in 1881. This suggests that the Irish bishops had been successfully Cullenized by the early years of the twentieth-century.[100]

Although there were divisions within the hierarchy, there was a tendency in the post-1850 period for the episcopal body to reach unanimous decisions. In the pre-1850 period, the Irish bishops had been deeply divided and split on critically important questions particularly over the questions of education and support for the Tenant League and the Irish Independent Party.[101] To be sure, divisions and differences remained within the hierarchy after Cullen's arrival in Ireland but most of them tended to be resolved quickly, and there was an emphasis placed on the hierarchy reaching a unanimous decision even on issues which divided the bishops personally (like the Land League and, particularly, the Ladies' Land League).[102] The one exception to this general rule is Cullen's relationship with

[100] This suggests a different pattern from that outlined by John Whyte, who suggests that there was a de-Cullenization process in operation between 1878 and 1900 evident in the increased importance of the terna in Episcopal appointments during that period (27 of the 36 (75%) appointments between 1878 and 1900 had been first on the terna, 4 had been second or third, and only 5 had been appointed from outside the terna). See Whyte, 'Appointment of Catholic Bishops', 31. Although the local clergy and bishops were more involved in appointments after Cullen's death than they had been between 1850 and 1878, it is possible that because many of them had been recruited during his tenure of office they shared his view of what constituted a good bishop.

[101] On these divisions, see Whyte, 'Political Problems, 1850–1860'. The Tenant League was a movement that campaigned on behalf of the interests of Irish tenant farmers between 1850 and 1858. At the 1852 general election, 40 MPs were elected who were committed to the Tenant League and they agreed to act independently of and in opposition to any government that did not offer them the concessions that they demanded. This movement became known as the Irish Independent party and it remained influential until 1866 when it forged an alliance with the Liberal party.

[102] On the division within the hierarchy about the Ladies' Land League between Croke and McCabe, see Larkin, *1878–1886*, 98–103.

MacHale which continued to disrupt the Irish hierarchy throughout Cullen's period of dominance and beyond (up to MacHale's death in 1881). In essence, this was a conflict between the Gallicanism of MacHale and the ultramontanism of Cullen but it was intensified by their personal rivalry, and by MacHale's nationalism and his years of refusal—alone among the Irish bishops—to being dominated and controlled by Cullen. There may have been a greater emphasis on episcopal unity after 1850, then, but it was never absolute. Indeed, during the year after Cullen's death there was serious division among the Catholic hierarchy as to how to respond to the Land War that began in 1879.

At the beginning of the Land War, the Irish bishops were divided as to how they should respond to the conflict.[103] Of twenty-eight bishops in late 1879, five were willing to support the League in public (Croke, Dorrian, Nulty, MacCormack, and Duggan); five others were privately sympathetic (Butler, Fitzgerald, Power, McCarthy (Kerry), and McCarthy (Cloyne)); nine were neutral (McGettigan, Donnelly, Kelly, Leahy, Conaty, Logue, Ryan, Conway, and Lynch), and nine were privately hostile (McCabe, MacHale, MacEvilly, Moran, Warren, Walshe, Delany, Gillooly, and Woodlock).[104] The initial clerical response to the Land League was also divided. In the early months of the Land League it was condemned from many county Mayo altars—where the Land League was first established—but a large number of curates were in favour of the League. Gradually, it became clear that there was widespread clerical involvement in the League both as speakers at meetings and as officers of branches (priests were often appointed the presidents of League branches).[105] However, the bishops did not make a decisive statement as to the hierarchy's view of the Land League. Prominent bishops like MacEvilly, McCabe, and Moran were, at the outset, vehemently opposed to the League, while others like Croke and Dorrian were emphatically in favour.

MacEvilly, however, gradually changed his view of the Land League out of necessity rather than conviction as the following letter to Kirby in December 1879 demonstrates:

The facts are these: a dire famine stares us in the face. The new year will open with a general distress throughout the country. The tenant farmers—the real friends of religion, of the priests, & of the H. See—will be sorely pressed for food. The landlords as a class—there are very many noble exceptions—have no sympathy with the people, with the priests, or the Holy See. They never contribute as a class, to our public charities. Cath. University, Pope, etc. The people alone do so. The Landlords are exceedingly oppressive. As a general rule, the people are oppressed, the rents far too high, and poor tenant robbed of the fruit of the sweat of his brow, obliged to pay double rent for the land his own

---

[103] In effect, the Land War generated a conflict between the Papacy, which was committed to upholding the rights of property, and the Irish farmers who were challenging the property rights of Irish landowners; and this created a serious dilemma for the Irish Catholic hierarchy (Hynes, 'Nineteenth-century Irish Catholicism', 58–9).
[104] Larkin, *1878–1886*, 24.   [105] Ibid. 24–5.

labour reclaimed from utter barren worthlessness. This is but robbing the labourer of his hire on a general scale. The people are very discontented at this state of things. They are now, as a rule, unable to pay rents, shop and bnk. debts. This year the crops have failed. The price of cattle very low, no employment for the labourers. The result is great depression. This state of things is availed of by some dishonest trading Politicians, who, acting on the credulity of our artless people, have managed to gather them together at large meetings, and in many instances, especially throughout the Co. Mayo—a great part of it in the diocese of Tuam—have managed to hold their meetings without reference to the priests of whom they wish to estrange the people, and I am sorry to say, have succeeded to a great extent. At meetings held without reference to the priests or their presence, the most shocking principles have been enunciated. The priests denounced, as unfeeling without any concern for their unfeeling flock, and a dreadful feeling against religion got up. In order to meet this evil and knock the wind out of the sails of these unprincipled ringleaders, it has been deemed prudent for the priests to formulate the restlessness at meetings in the interest of order and religion, to take the lead and keep Godless nobodies in their proper place. In my own opinion, though I have taken no part whatever, this is the wise and proper course.

Whether the priests will it or no, the meetings will be held. Their people will assemble under the pressure of threatened famine to expound their wrongs to landlords and government; if the priests keep aloof, these meetings will be scenes of disorder; if the people attend they will keep the people attached to them . . . It would render the H. See very odious to seem to be influenced by the English against those who sacrificed everything for the Faith, and when the general evictions come, as come they will, in some districts, it would ruin us, if the authorities [in Rome] could be quoted, as against our people . . . Religion in this country would never get over it.[106]

The letter makes it clear that MacEvilly did sympathize with the experiences of the people, if not with the local Land League politicians' attempts to redress the peoples' grievances. The letter also reveals that despite MacEvilly's snobbish hostility to the 'Godless nobodies' who were running the Land League, he acknowledged that the movement would become powerful with or without clerical assistance. In this context, clerical involvement was necessary to, in the first instance, control and moderate the more extreme impulses of the movement and, second, to maintain the power of the Catholic church in Ireland. If the Church opposed the Land League, MacEvilly believed that this would cause a rupture in the Church's alliance with the people, and that this would inaugurate a crisis from which the Irish Catholic Church would not be able to recover. The hierarchy's position on the Land League, then, gradually emerged from the convictions of some bishops and the strategic considerations of others. And the hierarchy's line on the Land League, and indeed on the Irish land question over the following thirty years, was that the Church supported land reform (both land purchase and land redistribution) as

---

[106] MacEvilly to Kirby, 11 Dec. 1879, quot. ibid. 28–9.

long as the agitation for these objectives was conducted in a constitutional and non-violent manner.

The Church did not make a public statement either for or against the Land League but it did not prevent the clergy from being involved in the movement.[107] As a result, there was extensive clerical involvement in both the Land League and its successor, the National League. In county Tipperary, for instance, at least 164 priests (58 per cent of the total) were involved in the Land League or the National League between 1880 and 1890, and 38 per cent of these were parish priests and 62 per cent were curates (which broadly reflected the proportion of parish priests (35 per cent) and curates (65 per cent) in the county more generally).[108] During the land agitation promoted by the United Irish League after 1898, the hierarchy's position was broadly similar: priests were allowed to become involved in the movement, the Church supported the objective of the agitation (land redistribution) but cautioned that all agitation should be kept within constitutional and legal limits.[109]

Even so, it is clear that all of the Irish bishops were not of one mind on the question of land agitation in Ireland. During the later period of agrarian conflict known as the Plan of Campaign (1886–91), when tenants refused to pay their rents to landlords who refused to allow rent reductions, the Papacy issued a rescript (in May 1888) condemning both the Plan and boycotting. In response, the Irish hierarchy—under the leadership of Archbishop Walsh—did not enforce the rescript, realizing that it would jeopardize their standing with the Irish people.[110] However, two bishops, O'Dwyer of Limerick and Healy of Clonfert, who had shared the same classroom during their years at Maynooth, did attempt to enforce the Papacy's policy on the agitation.[111] In a public letter to the mayor of Limerick, O'Dwyer stated that it was a 'grievous sin for any Catholic to disobey it [the rescript]' before preaching that boycotting was 'sinful'.[112] Similarly, Healy who 'detested radicalism' made speeches throughout the diocese of Clonfert (in south Galway)—one of the storm centres of the conflict—denouncing the Plan of Campaign. On one such occasion, 'He stayed overnight with the parish priest of the place, and after he had retired to rest a shot was fired through his bedroom window which smashed in pieces a picture that had been hanging on the wall over his bed'.[113] Walsh was furious with both of his bishops and the hierarchy maintained its initial position on the Plan of Campaign while O'Dwyer and Healy became well known as 'Castle bishops'.

---

[107] According to Bishop Conway of Killala in his report of Nov. 1881, the Land League's argument that the people did not have to pay their unjust obligations meant that some people now refused to meet even their just debts (Canning, *Bishops of Ireland*, 356).

[108] O'Shea, *Priest, Politics and Society in Post-famine Ireland*, 74.

[109] Miller, *Church, State and Nation*, 19–23; 53–4.   [110] Larkin, *1886–1888*, p. xiv.

[111] Joyce, *John Healy*, 138.   [112] Morrissey, *Bishop Edward Thomas O'Dwyer of Limerick*, 81.

[113] Joyce, *John Healy*, 89, 96, 140.

The other major social question of this period to which the Irish bishops had to respond was that of labour and labourers' agitations both in the cities and the countryside. The question of urban labour came to a head with the Dublin lockout of 1913. Archbishop Walsh was on his holidays in France when the lockout began and he had to rely on letters from his secretary, Michael Curran, to keep him informed of the situation in the city. In September 1913, Curran told Walsh that the members of the ITGWU were 'the scum of the slums', and when the conflict persisted he explained that 'The general body of the workers are not yet sufficiently restored to their senses. Though considerably tamed and depressed, they are not sufficiently starved'.[114] Although we do not know how Walsh responded to these smug and pejorative descriptions of the Dublin working class, the fact that Curran felt able to continue his correspondence in the same tone suggests that Walsh did not upbraid him for his condescension. In fact, according to Walsh's most recent biographer, the Archbishop was apparently in sympathy with the workers, although at no point did he make this position publicly clear.[115] It should be noted, however, that Walsh had intervened in an industrial conflict between the Great Southern and Western Railway Co. and its employees at Cork in April 1890 and succeeded in 'arranging the terms of an amicable agreement'.[116]

The 1913 conflict increasingly revolved around the question of whether the children of Dublin workers should be allowed to travel to England to be looked after in the homes of members of the English working class for the duration of the strike. Walsh was quick to castigate those Irish mothers who allowed their children to travel to England under this scheme. They were, he explained, 'no longer held worthy of the name of Catholic mothers if they so far forget that duty as to send away their children to be cared for in a strange land, without security of any kind that those to whom the poor children are to be handed over are Catholics, or, indeed, are persons of any faith at all'.[117] For Walsh, it was preferable that a child should be hungry in an Irish Catholic home rather than well fed in that of an English Protestant or, even worse, an English atheist.[118]

Broadly speaking, the Irish bishops were united in their view of the ITGWU and of Larkinism. While they sympathized with the position of the Irish workers, they were suspicious of what they regarded as the potentially anti-religious objectives of the socialist leadership. According to Cardinal Logue, the ITGWU leadership were 'working not in the interests of the men, but using the unfortunate men for the purpose of propagating and establishing their socialist and syndicalist principles'. The labour movement—with its secularist and socialist ideas—was

[114] T. J. Morrissey, *William J. Walsh: Archbishop of Dublin, 1841–1921* (Dublin, 2000), 245, 246–7. [115] Ibid. 249.
[116] Walsh was granted the freedom of the city of Cork in recognition of his efforts on behalf of the railway workers in Cork (*Irish Times*, 9 Apr. 1921).
[117] Morrissey, *William J. Walsh*, 249. [118] Ibid. 265.

regarded by the Irish hierarchy as a threat to the power and influence of the Church in Ireland, and should therefore be opposed.[119] In this respect, the Catholic hierarchy were of one mind with the leaders of the Irish Parliamentary Party and the emerging Catholic business elite in Dublin and the provinces.[120]

It is possible that individual bishops were influenced by their particular social background to take distinctive positions on the national and social questions that dominated the age. O'Dwyer was the relation of a landed Tipperary gentry family, and the friend of a number of landowners in the south-west; and while Healy's family may have fallen on hard times he still felt himself to be a descendant of the Catholic landed aristocracy.[121] Similarly, Bishop John Joseph Clancy of Elphin was strongly opposed to the United Irish League's agitation to redistribute grazing land, and this position might be explained by the fact that he was born on a reasonably substantial farm of forty-six acres (valued at £28. 5s. 0d. at Ballygrania, Kilross, county Sligo).[122] Healy was also opposed to the later campaign of cattle driving—supported by the United Irish League during 1907 and 1908—and issued an epistle declaring cattle driving to be a criminal act.[123] In contrast, 'During the land struggles . . . Dr. O'Donnell [Bishop of Raphoe] took a keen interest in the welfare of the tenants, especially the poor, struggling farmers, who found it difficult to pay their rents'. Bishop O'Donnell was also a member of the Congested Districts Board and 'his influence and counsel shaped many of its beneficial efforts'.[124] Unlike Clancy, O'Donnell had been born on a comparatively small farm of thirty-eight almost worthless acres (valued at £4. 5s. 0d.) at Kilrean Upper, near Glenties in county Donegal, and this might explain his concern for the well-being of the Irish small farmer class.

As with other elite groups, the particular social background of the individual undoubtedly influenced their political and social views. This probably also explains why the Catholic hierarchy generally supported the campaigns of the tenant farmer class for land reform but that they did not support the agitations of urban and rural labourers for better working and living conditions. Father Walter MacDonald explained that the clergy's greater sympathy with agrarian rather than labour struggles was probably because priests tended to be the sons of farmers rather than the sons of labourers: 'We are all, naturally, disposed to favour the class to which we belong', he observed.[125] Indeed, the Catholic church

---

[119] On this, see Larkin's essays on the Catholic hierarchy's views of socialism discussed in Miller, *Church, State and Nation*.

[120] There is also evidence of the reluctance of priests to support reforms of rural labourers' circumstances. O'Shea, *Priest, Politics and Society in Post-famine Ireland*, 244.

[121] Morrissey, *Bishop Edward Thomas O'Dwyer of Limerick*; Joyce, *John Healy*, 3–4, 11–12.

[122] *The Times*, 21 Oct. 1912, quot. Canning, *Bishops of Ireland*, 342.

[123] Joyce, *John Healy*, 264. On cattle driving, see Campbell, *Land and Revolution*, Ch. 3.

[124] *Irish Times*, 24 Oct. 1927.

[125] Walter MacDonald was the author of *Reminiscences of a Maynooth Professor* (Cork, 1967); Miller, *Church, State and Nation*, 270.

was keen to maintain class and status divisions within the Catholic community as Patrick Shea found when he attended St Peter's Church at Athlone as a child:

It [the church] had three galleries; one was reserved at the late Mass for the soldiers of the garrison, in another the congregation was farmers in their suits of dark cloth and the third . . . was where the more prosperous townspeople came to pray. The galleries were known, respectively, as the Military Gallery, the Bogmen's Gallery and the Grand Gallery.[126]

Broadly speaking, most of the Catholic bishops supported the campaigns for Home Rule and land reform as long as they were conducted in a constitutional and peaceful manner. Even so, these political views meant that Catholic bishops were broadly speaking not welcome in the gentlemen's clubs in London, Dublin, and the provinces, where other members of the Irish establishment socialized and networked with one another. When Healy was invited to dinner with some local landlords in Galway his views on land reform generated some tension between himself and the other guests as his biographer explains:

We have it from one who accompanied him on the occasion that very soon after he became bishop in Clonfert he was still youthful enough to be present at a 'coursing' in south Galway. In the evening of that day, he was invited to dine with a party amongst whom were many landlords, who evidently looked upon him as a 'safe bishop.' In the course of the conversations which ensued—from which the land question could not be excluded—he bluntly gave it as his opinion that the ultimate solution of that problem would require that the landlords as such disappear from Irish life. It was a bombshell, and many of the guests suddenly discovered that they had engagements elsewhere.[127]

With the exception of Archbishop Walsh—who was president of the Catholic Commercial Club in Dublin—none of the bishops was the member of any clubs. Healy was a keen yachtsman but he does not seem to have been a member of any of the yacht clubs that were frequented by other members of the Irish establishment. The bishops' reluctance to join clubs may have also been because some of them took a dim view of sociability. In his Lenten pastoral for 1927, Bishop O'Donnell explained that: 'Amusement has its place and recreation is necessary, but too much pleasure-seeking spoils the young, squanders youthful energies, and puts selfishness in place of service.' Similarly, Thomas Gilmartin who served as Bishop of Clonfert (1910–18) and Archbishop of Tuam (1918–39) looked forward to a time when 'our young people will have patriotism and Catholicity enough to ban forms of dancing which pander to the lower animal instincts'.[128] However, those that were not in favour of strict temperance did enjoy social lives often spent in the company of other bishops and priests. Healy, for instance, purchased a summer residence near Clifden, known as the Priory, where he hosted dinners

---

[126] Patrick Shea, *Voices and the Sound of Drums: An Irish Autobiography* (Belfast, 1981), 18.
[127] Joyce, *John Healy*, 149–50. [128] *Irish Times*, 5 Mar. 1927.

where cigars were smoked and punch was drunk.[129] Many priests and bishops were also keen walkers, and while at Maynooth, Healy, the future Bishop O'Dea and the future Cardinal O'Donnell 'being young and active men, were walking companions'.[130] Archbishop Walsh was a keen cyclist, amateur photographer, and an early patron of the motor car.[131] In the next section of the chapter, I will examine the structure of the Protestant churches in Ireland and the social composition of their leaders.

II

At the turn of the century (as revealed in the 1901 census), about one-quarter of the Irish population of 4.5 million were Protestant. Most of the 1,150,114 Protestants in Ireland (comprising 26 per cent of the Irish population) belonged to the two largest Protestant churches: the Church of Ireland and the Presbyterian church.[132] More than half of the Irish Protestant population were members of the Church of Ireland (581,089) and slightly less than half were Presbyterian (443,276).[133] The members of the Church of Ireland were spread throughout Ireland. In 1871, for example, members of the Church of Ireland composed about one-fifth (21.5 per cent) of the population of Ulster; about one-eighth (12.3 per cent) of the population of Leinster; and only about one-twentieth of the populations of Munster (5.3 per cent) and Connacht (4.2 per cent).[134] The Irish Presbyterian population, on the other hand, tended to be congregated largely in Ulster. Of the twenty-six presbyteries into which the Irish Presbyterian population were organized in 1900, for instance, only eleven (and 14 per cent of Irish Presbyterians) belonged to congregations outside the six north-eastern counties (that would become Northern Ireland in 1920–2).[135] Even so, over half of Irish Episcopalians lived in Ulster, and so the vast majority of the Irish Protestant population was based in the north-east of the country.[136] The Church of Ireland population were better catered for by their ministers with one Irish Anglican priest (*c*.1901) for every 359 Episcopalians, while there was only one Presbyterian minister for every 647 Presbyterians.[137]

Throughout the eighteenth century, the diocesan structure of the Church of Ireland remained constant at four archbishops and eighteen suffragan bishops.

[129] Joyce, *John Healy*, 271.   [130] Ibid. 57.

[131] D. A. Ker and David C. Sheehy, 'William Joseph Walsh', q.v. DNB online <http://www.oxforddnb.com/view/article/38102?docPos=4> (accessed 7 Dec. 2008).

[132] Alan Megahey, *The Irish Protestant Churches in the Twentieth Century* (Basingstoke, 2000), 5.

[133] Ibid. 12.   [134] R. B. McDowell, *The Church of Ireland, 1869–1969* (London, 1975), 3.

[135] Megahey, *Irish Protestant Churches*, 12.   [136] Ibid. 11.

[137] Ibid. 9. This was a much better ratio than that of Catholic priests to the Catholic population at the same time.

Indeed, at the beginning of the nineteenth century, the Church of Ireland technically comprised thirty-five dioceses but had only twenty-two diocesans (four archbishops and eighteen bishops) as some bishops were responsible for running more than one diocese. However, as we have seen, the diocesan structure was transformed by the Irish Ecclesiastical Temporalities Act of 1833 which abolished two archbishoprics and provided that ten dioceses should each be united on the next vacancy to a neighbouring see. By 1850, the Church of Ireland had been reduced to twelve diocesans: the archbishops of Armagh and Dublin, and ten bishops.[138] These bishops presided over their dioceses which were divided up into benefices and parishes.[139]

Although the parish was theoretically the smallest unit of the Church of Ireland, in practice it was the benefice (which was usually composed of one or more parishes) and which was run by a single clergyman. In the late 1780s, there were 1,120 benefices in Ireland; by 1832, this had increased to 1,395; and by 1867 there were 1,518 benefices.[140] At the beginning of the nineteenth century, there were insufficient churches for the Church of Ireland population. In 1787, there were only 1,001 churches in Ireland (which was less than half the number of parishes and 119 less than the total number of benefices). This meant that the Episcopalian laity were poorly supplied with places of worship and some clergymen were appointed to benefices that did not possess even the basic facilities for divine worship. The number of churches did increase, however, as the eighteenth and nineteenth centuries progressed: in 1832, for instance, there were 1,293 parish churches and chapels of ease, and by 1864 the number of churches had risen to 1,579.[141] However, the number of Episcopalians in Ireland declined over the same period. In 1834, there were 853,160 Anglicans in Ireland (10.7 per cent of the total population) and this had declined to 693,357 by 1861 (although this was a higher proportion of the Irish population (11.9 per cent) due to the substantial decline in the Catholic population of Ireland during and after the Great Famine (1845–9)).[142] There was also a decline in the number of clergymen during the last quarter of the nineteenth century: in 1871, there were 2,221 Church of Ireland priests and this had declined to 1,828 just ten years later in 1881.[143] This suggests that—despite the evangelical revival and the increased number of Church of Ireland churches in the nineteenth century—the number of Church of Ireland clergymen did not increase to the same extent as the number of Catholic priests and nuns.

Clerical incomes varied dramatically and were not related to the number of parishioners. An estimate made in 1868 of the net income of incumbents (including the value of the glebe house but deducting the salary to be paid to the curate) suggested that 109 incumbents had incomes of more than £500 per annum; 688 had incomes of between £200 and £500 and 720 had incomes of less

[138] McDowell, *Church of Ireland*, 7.   [139] Akenson, *Church of Ireland*, 6.
[140] Ibid. 322.   [141] Ibid. 323–24; 218.   [142] Ibid. 210.   [143] Ibid. 297.

than £200 (including 300 whose incomes were less than £100 per annum).[144] Curates—who were paid by the incumbents who employed them—were usually paid between £75 and £100 but their stipends were not always punctually paid.[145] There was, however, a steep decline in the number of curates following disestablishment: by 1880 there were only about 350; by 1914 only 290; and by 1925 only about 200. This was probably caused by both declining clerical incomes and the declining Church of Ireland population after disestablishment.

The way in which bishops and incumbents were recruited to the Church of Ireland was changed in the aftermath of disestablishment. Before 1871—and particularly during the eighteenth century—recruiting to an Irish bishopric was essentially a function of factional British party politics. The Crown had the power to appoint to vacant bishoprics, to most deaneries, to certain prebends, and to a number of parish livings. In fact, the monarch did not usually intervene personally in appointments but left this to the Lord Lieutenant who acted in consultation with his English political colleagues. Episcopal appointments were, therefore, part of the British patronage network and were used as payment for English political and social debts.[146] For this reason, many Episcopal appointments in the eighteenth and early nineteenth centuries were of Englishmen. Of 310 appointments made to Irish sees between 1690 and 1840, less than half (153) were of Irishmen. In effect, there were two main routes of recruitment to the Irish Episcopal body before 1871: on the one hand, that of Englishmen, many of whom had previous experience of acting as chaplain to the Irish Lord Lieutenant and, on the other, of Irishmen who had experience of holding decanal rank in an Irish cathedral.[147] During this period, appointments to Irish benefices were usually made by the bishop of the diocese.[148] After 1871, the recruiting mechanisms to the Church of Ireland were transformed. The power of presentation to a benefice was taken from the Bishop and given to a mixed board of clergy and laity. After 1871, then, instead of being dependent on the goodwill of a bishop for a benefice, prospective clergymen were dependent on the decision of a committee most of whose members were laymen.[149] This also suggests the declining power of the Church of Ireland bishops *vis-à-vis* that of the laity following the evangelical revival of the late 1850s in Ireland.

In terms of recruiting bishops a new system was put in place after 1871. When a vacancy occurred, the diocesan synod was convened and the clerical and lay members of the synod were asked to each select three clergymen for nomination (of whom at least one would not belong to the diocese involved) and they were asked to rank each of their nominations first, second, and third. From this process, a select list of the leading candidates was compiled and balloting continued until one candidate had a majority of votes. If one candidate had a two-thirds'

[144] McDowell, *Church of Ireland*, 11.   [145] Ibid. 12.
[146] Akenson, *Church of Ireland*, 10–11.   [147] Ibid. 12–14.
[148] Ibid. 290.   [149] Ibid.

majority of both clerical and lay votes, then that candidate was declared elected as bishop. If, however, the majority was less than two-thirds, then voting was to continue until a second person gained a majority of votes and then the two names were sent to the House of Bishops where the final decision would then be made.[150] In terms of the two senior positions in the Church of Ireland—the archbishoprics of Dublin and Armagh—it was decided that the Archbishop of Dublin would be selected in the same way as the other bishops. When Armagh became vacant, the clerical and lay members of the diocesan synod met and presented four names (who were already bishops) to the Bench of Bishops who selected one candidate to become the effective leader of the Church of Ireland. The vacancy thereby created in the diocese from which the new Primate was recruited was also to be filled by the assembled bishops who were to choose between a clergyman selected by the Armagh diocesan synod and one chosen by the synod of the vacant diocese. In terms of recruiting the leader of the Church of Ireland (and his replacement), then, it is clear that the bishops retained supreme power even if they had lost a great deal power over Episcopal appointments more generally.[151]

This new Episcopal recruiting system introduced after disestablishment appears to have transformed the kinds of men who became Church of Ireland clergymen and bishops. In broad terms, the new recruits to the bench tended to be Irishmen who had some experience of middle-level church administration and had been deans, archdeacons, or cathedral dignitaries before becoming bishops.[152] According to some contemporary commentators, the new recruiting system also had an impact on the social background and education of the men who became incumbents and bishops. J. P. Mahaffy observed:

that by abolishing the glebes and rectories it [the Irish Church Act] tended inevitably to abolish the only resident gentry in the wilder parts of Ireland . . . Now this class has almost disappeared. The present clergy, with all their virtues and their self-denial, cannot hope to replace it socially. Their means are too straitened, their traditions are rarely those of country gentlemen.[153]

Another observer added:

Time was when the sons of noblemen and large landed proprietors worked their way as Fellow-Commoners through Trinity College and when 'Hon. And Rev.' was not a very rare designation of a country parson . . . The cutting off of this class of candidates from the ministry of the Church is to be lamented.[154]

The Bishop of Armagh stated in a visitation charge in 1880 that the education of candidates for ordination was generally lower than the required standard, and that the requirement of a university degree had been dispensed with in many cases.

[150] Akenson, *Church of Ireland*, 292.   [151] Ibid. 292–93.   [152] Ibid. 295.
[153] J. P. Mahaffy, 'The Romanization of Ireland', *Nineteenth Century*, 50 (July 1901), 33, quot. Akenson, *Church of Ireland*, 297.   [154] Ibid. 297–8.

And, in 1881, the Bishop of Derry explained that of forty-six clergy ordained by him during the previous decade only twenty-five had taken university degrees and eleven had not attended university at all.[155] To what extent are changes in social status and educational background evident in the changing composition of the Irish Episcopal bench between 1881 and 1911?

In general terms, the trends noted by these observers are not substantiated by the data on the social composition of the Church of Ireland bishops in 1881 and 1911. It should be noted, however, that the majority of bishops contained in this study were recruited as bishops, if not as priests, after disestablishment. Of the twelve bishops in 1881, only half had been raised to the episcopacy before disestablishment and five others had been recruited after 1871 (with data on one other being unavailable). Of the 1911 cohort, only one of the 13 bishops (William Alexander, who had also been a bishop in 1881) had been recruited before disestablishment. Overall, then, only six of the twenty-four bishops included in this study (25 per cent) were pre-disestablishment recruits to the Episcopal bench. And, if we consider the social background of these six individuals, it is clear that two-thirds of them (four or 66.7 per cent) had been born into landed families as opposed to about one-third (six or 35 per cent) of the bishops recruited after 1871. This does suggest some lessening of social status and landed connection of the Irish bishops after disestablishment. But, if we consider the data on the Church of Ireland bishops in 1881 and 1911 as a whole, there is relatively little change in the social composition of the Irish bench.

It is possible, however, that some of those bishops who were recruited after disestablishment were less intellectually able than their predecessors. Charles Graves, who served as Bishop of Limerick between 1866 and his death in 1899 was an eminent mathematician and a friend of Wordsworth, Mendelsshon, Huxley, Froude, and Matthew Arnold; and his obituary eulogized him as a 'scholar, mathematician, philologist, and a masterful pastoral ruler of a large and important diocese; his attainments, literary eminence, and laborious life cannot easily fade into oblivion'.[156] Richard Chevenix Trench, who was appointed as Archbishop of Dublin in 1863, was also very highly regarded as a theologian, a poet, and a philologist, and famously provided the inspiration for the New (Oxford) English Dictionary.[157] The obituaries of bishops who were recruited later in the nineteenth century emphasized their administrative and pastoral abilities but not their intellectual or rhetorical prowess. 'Other bishops may have been more learned [than John Baptist Crozier who ascended to the see of Ossory in 1897], but, as a practical man, who was a master of business methods, he has had few equals.'[158] Maurice Day, who was appointed as Bishop of Clogher in 1908, had been very highly regarded by his parishioners when he served

---

155 Ibid. 298.   156 *Irish Times*, 22 July 1899.
157 Kenneth Milne, 'Richard Chevenix Trench', q.v. DNB online <http://www.oxforddnb.com/view/article/27702?docPos=10> (accessed 6 Dec. 2008).   158 *Irish Times*, 13 Apr. 1920.

at St Matthias's in Dublin, but his obituary was quick to note that this was 'more, perhaps, on account of his personal worth and kindly manner than for any brilliant pulpit ability'.[159] Similarly, Charles Frederick D'Arcy, who was ordained after disestablishment (in 1885) 'was not what one might call a good orator'.[160] After disestablishment, there was perhaps a tendency to recruit bishops who had pastoral rather than academic experience. When Joseph Ferguson Peacocke became Archbishop of Dublin in 1897, for instance, he was the first person to hold the position for 200 years who had 'held a pastoral charge in the diocese, and was well known as a parish clergyman'.[161]

The Church of Ireland was very much the church of the Irish landlord class and many of the bishops were drawn from landed families. Indeed, ten of the twenty-four (42 per cent) Church of Ireland bishops in this study were either landowners themselves or had been born into landowning families. Moreover, a further six (25 per cent) married into landowning families so that two-thirds of the Church of Ireland bishops in this study (67 per cent) had either been born into or married into landowning families. Many of the Church of Ireland bishops were integral members of the Irish establishment and were at the centre of networks and relationships that encompassed the religious, political, landed, administrative, and business elites. William Conyngham Plunket, who was Bishop of Meath (1876–84) and Archbishop of Dublin (1884–97) married Annie Guinness, the daughter of Sir Benjamin Lee Guinness, the wealthy Dublin brewer, in 1862. He was also a substantial landowner, and the son of a barrister, the nephew of a bishop, and the grandson of a former lord chief justice for Ireland.[162] Similarly, Marcus Gervais Beresford, who served as Archbishop of Armagh between 1862 and 1885, was the son of the Bishop of Kilmore and Ardagh, and succeeded his cousin to the see of Armagh. He was also a substantial landowner who owned more than 8,000 acres in Cavan, and his eldest son by his first marriage, George de la Poer Beresford, was elected the Conservative MP for the borough of Armagh in 1875. According to *The Times*, Archbishop Beresford was 'connected for generations with the highest dignity and power in the civil and ecclesiastical administration of Ireland'.[163] And William Alexander, who served as Bishop of Derry from 1867 and Archbishop of Armagh (1896–1911), was the descendant of a family 'numbering many distinguished members and long honourably connected with the Northern province'.[164] This strongly suggests

[159] Ibid. 29 May 1923.   [160] Ibid. 5 Feb. 1938.   [161] Ibid. 30 May 1916.

[162] William Coyngham, 4th Baron Plunket owned 3,567 acres in Monaghan, Cork, and Dublin; his father, John, was a QC; his uncle, Thomas, Second Baron Plunket was the former Bishop of Tuam; his father-in-law was Benjamin Lee Guinness; and his maternal grandfather was Charles Kendal Bushe, a former lord chief justice of Ireland. Benjamin Lee Guinness funded the major restoration of St Patrick's Cathedral in Dublin in 1864.

[163] Quot. C. L. Falkiner (rev. Kenneth Milne), 'Marcus Gervais Beresford', q.v. DNB online <http://www.oxforddnb.com/view/article/2198?docPos=11> (accessed 6 Dec. 2008).

[164] *Irish Times*, 16 Sept. 1911.

Table 6.7. Acreage of Estates of Landowning Families into which Church of Ireland Bishops were Born

Acreage	Frequency
0–499	4 (40%)
500–999	0
1,000–4,999	2 (20%)
5,000–9,999	1 (10%)
10,000+	3 (30%)
Number	10

the close relationship between the Irish establishment, Irish Anglicanism, Irish land, and Irish Conservatism; and this did not change markedly between 1881 and 1911.

The proportion of bishops who had been born into land or married into land is broadly the same for both 1881 and 1911.[165] Broadly speaking, this evidence suggests a slight decline in the landed connections of Irish bishops but it is clear that the general pattern of a strong relationship between the Church and the landed elite was maintained between 1881 and 1911.[166] The Irish bishops were drawn from the entire range of the Irish landlord class as Table 6.7 suggests. The Church of Ireland bishops who came from landed backgrounds were reared on the smaller estates of less than 500 acres (40 per cent); the middle-sized estates of between 1,000 and 5,000 acres (20 per cent); and the larger estates of more than 5,000 acres (40 per cent), so that the bishops tended to represent most sections of the Protestant landowning class in Ireland. Even so, there were strong relationships between the Church of Ireland bishops and the great landowners. Richard Chevenix Trench, for instance, was a nephew of the first Lord Ashtown who owned estates of more than 40,000 acres in Ireland and England.[167] It is worth bearing in mind, however, that some bishops were recruited from the Protestant middle class. Trench's father was a barrister;[168] John Richard Darley was 'a member of a mercantile family long connected with the city of Dublin';[169] Joseph Ferguson Peacocke, who was elevated to the see of Meath in 1894 and

---

[165] In 1881, 9 (or 75%) had been born into or married into land whereas the comparable figure for 1911 is 8 (62%).

[166] It should be noted that 6 of the bishops in 1881 (50%) had been born into landed families as opposed to 5 out of 13 in 1911 (38%) and so there was some change in the nature of recruits to the Irish bench between 1881 and 1911.

[167] Lord Ashtown owned 43,643 acres (valued at £34,689) in counties Limerick, Galway, Waterford, Tipperary, and in West Yorkshire (Milne, 'Richard Chevenix Trench').   [168] Ibid.

[169] B. H. Blacker (rev. M. C. Curthoys), 'John Richard Darley', q.v. DNB online <http://www.oxforddnb.com/view/article/7152?docPos=3> (accessed 7 Dec. 2008). Darley was bishop of Kilmore, Elphin, and Ardagh, 1874–84. He was aged 74 when he was consecrated as bishop.

Table 6.8. Secondary Education of Church of Ireland Bishops, 1881–1911

	1881–1911	1881	1911
English Public School	2 (18%)	2 (29%)	0
English Protestant School	5 (45%)	4 (57%)	2 (40%)
Irish Protestant School	6 (55%)	3 (43%)	3 (60%)
Number	11	7	5

Note: Some individuals attended more than one secondary school.

became Archbishop of Dublin in 1897, was a doctor's son;[170] and Charles Frederick D'Arcy, who served successively as Bishop of Clogher, Ossory, and Down, and as Archbishop of Dublin and Armagh, was the son of an assistant cashier at the Great Southern and Western Railway Co.[171]

Most of the Church of Ireland bishops under review were Irish born. Information is available on the birthplace of sixteen of the bishops in this study and all of them were born in Ireland. This was the case for both the 1881 and the 1911 cohorts.[172] It would seem that the tendency for more than half of the bishops to have been Englishmen in the eighteenth and the early nineteenth centuries had died out by the 1870s. In terms of education, however, there is some evidence that Church of Ireland bishops were not as well educated in the early twentieth century as they had been in 1881. Whereas almost two-thirds of the bishops in 1881 (58 per cent) had received a secondary education, this had declined to just over one-third (38 per cent) by 1911. Moreover, the bishops in 1911 were much more likely to have attended the lower status (and cheaper) English and Irish Protestant schools rather than the English Public Schools (Harrow and Cheltenham) that their predecessors in 1881 had often attended. This reflects the lower status and lower income of Church of Ireland bishops at the beginning of the twentieth century (Table 6.8). However, more of the bishops in 1911 had received a third-level education than their colleagues in 1881 (100 per cent in 1911 as opposed to 92 per cent in 1881) although there were fewer bishops who had attended Oxford or Cambridge (down from 36 per cent in 1881 to 8 per cent in 1911). The fact that a degree could be obtained more cheaply from Trinity College Dublin and The Queen's Colleges probably explains why more of the bishops in 1911 had taken their degrees at these colleges rather than Oxbridge. Even so, the quality of

[170] J. H. Bernard (rev. David Huddleston), 'Joseph Ferguson Peacocke', q.v. DNB online <http://www.oxforddnb.com/view/article/35426?docPos=3> (accessed 7 Dec. 2008).

[171] A. A. Luce (rev. Kenneth Milne), 'Charles Frederick D'Arcy', q.v. DNB online <http://www.oxforddnb.com/view/article/32713?docPos=5> (accessed 7 Dec. 2008).

[172] Information is available on the birthplace of 11 of the 12 bishops in 1881, and on 5 of the 13 bishops in 1911 and all of these individuals had been born in Ireland.

Table 6.9. Tertiary Education of Church of Ireland Bishops, 1881–1911

	1881–1911	1881	1911
Oxbridge	4 (17%)	4 (36%)	1 (8%)
Trinity College Dublin	20 (87%)	8 (73%)	12 (92%)
Queen's Colleges	1 (4%)	0	1 (8%)
Number	23	11	13

Note: Some individuals attended more than one university.

education at the University of Dublin was extremely high, and most Church of Ireland incumbents and bishops had attended the two-year course at the Divinity School.[173] Indeed, Trinity College Dublin played an important role in binding together the Church of Ireland community in Ireland (Table 6.9). Almost all of the undergraduate population (about 80 per cent) were members of the Church of Ireland, and—in the decades before disestablishment—about one-third of its undergraduates took orders.[174] The University of Dublin also provided a forum for future bishops to meet future senior administrators. While he was at Trinity, John Baptist Crozier counted among his friends 'Sir John Ross and the Right Hon. Richard Cherry, sometime Lord Chief Justice of Ireland'.[175]

Almost two-thirds of the bishops included in this study, fifteen (63 per cent), had been born into elite families and had fathers who were bishops, reverends, professionals, businessmen, landowners, and senior administrators. Many of them also married into elite families, with ten of the bishops under review married into families that were listed in *Walford's County Families*. Like other individuals who were born into elite families, many of the Church of Ireland bishops were the members of clubs in London, Dublin, Belfast, and Cork (see Table 6.10). Undoubtedly, the membership of clubs consolidated the links between bishops and landlords, senior administrators, professionals, and businessmen, and it is striking that the proportion of bishops who were the members of clubland increases over time. Half of all of the Church of Ireland bishops in this study were the members of clubs in London, Dublin, Cork, or Belfast; and the proportion of bishops who were the members of clubs increases from four (33.3 per cent) in 1881 to nine (69 per cent) between 1881 and 1911. Some of the bishops were also prominent members of sports clubs: John Baptist Crozier, for instance, was one of the first members of Wanderers Football Club, and was also vice president of Holywood Cricket Club.[176] Like their Catholic colleagues, the Church of Ireland bishops were

---

[173] On the Divinity School, see McDowell, *Church of Ireland*, 15–17.   [174] Ibid. 14–15.
[175] *Irish Times*, 13 Apr. 1920. Crozier served as Bishop of Ossory, 1897–1907, Bishop of Down, 1907–11, and Archbishop of Armagh, 1911–20.   [176] Ibid.

Table 6.10. Club Membership
of Church of Ireland Bishops

	1881–1911
London	
Athenæum	4 (33%)
Royal Societies	1 (8%)
National	2 (17%)
Dublin	
Kildare St	1 (8%)
Sackville St	1 (8%)
University	8 (67%)
Belfast	
Ulster	2 (17%)
Cork	
County	1 (8%)
Number	12

Note: Some individuals were members of
more than one club.

also keen walkers: Richard Whately, Archbishop of Dublin (1831–63), invited
members of his 'inner circle' to join him on his early morning walks (between
5 and 8 a.m.) to discuss theological and philosophical topics.[177] Membership
of the Protestant religious elite also ran in families, and eighteen of the twenty-
four bishops under review (75 per cent) were related to either a bishop or a
clergyman.[178]

Most of the bishops had been ordained when they were in their twenties.[179]
They then tended to be appointed as bishops when they were aged in their
forties or fifties (see Tables 6.11 and 6.12). The age profile of the bishops in
1911 is slightly higher than that for 1881: 63 per cent of bishops were under
seventy in 1881 compared with only 38 per cent in 1911. Most of the bishops
included in this study were married and—unlike the great landowners and bank
managers—they tended to have fertile marriages.[180] Given their prosperous social

[177] D. H. Akenson, *A Protestant in Purgatory: Richard Whately, Archbishop of Dublin* (Hamden,
Conn., 1981), 19.

[178] Two were the sons of bishops, three were the nephews of bishops, and one was the brother-
in-law of a bishop. Nine others were related to clergymen, with 3 being the sons of clergymen; 2
the grandchildren of clergymen; and 2 the sons-in-laws of clergymen.

[179] Information is available on the date of ordination of 17 of the bishops under review and 15
(88%) were ordained when aged in their 20s and 2 (12%) were ordained in their 30s. Most of them
were ordained when they were aged 24.

[180] Information on their marital status is available for 23 of the 24 and all of these were married.
The age at marriage is known for 21 of the 24 and 9 married when aged between 20 and 29; 9
married when aged between 30 and 39; 1 married when aged between 40 and 49; 1 married when
aged between 50 and 59; and 1 married when aged between 60 and 69. Information is available on

Table 6.11. Age when Appointed Church of Ireland Bishop

40–9	7 (32%)
50–9	9 (41%)
60–9	4 (18%)
70–9	2 (9%)
Number	22

Table 6.12. Age of Church of Ireland Bishops in 1881 and 1911

Age	1881	1911
40–9	1 (9%)	0
50–9	2 (18%)	2 (15%)
60–9	4 (36%)	3 (23%)
70–9	2 (18%)	6 (46%)
80–9	2 (18%)	2 (15%)
Number (known)	11	13

backgrounds and their comparatively high incomes even after disestablishment, many of the bishops under review lived well into their eighties.[181]

In politics, the Church of Ireland bishops were solidly Unionist. John Baptist Crozier 'did not take much part in politics though in his addresses to his clergy he made his adherence to the Union a matter of prominence'.[182] Charles Frederick D'Arcy, whose father was a part of Dublin's business class was 'a strong supporter of Ulster Unionism' as well as an 'ardent associate' of Sir Edward Carson who signed the Solemn League and Covenant in 1912.[183] Alfred George Elliott, Bishop of Kilmore, Elphin, and Ardagh (1897–1915) explained his opposition to Home Rule in much the same terms as the Protestant businessmen discussed in Chapter 5. 'Firmly believing that Ireland's prosperity depended upon her remaining part of the British Empire, he courageously raised his voice against any attempt to divorce this country from the British connection.'[184] As the sons of landlords, professionals, and businessmen, the Church of Ireland bishops were also generally opposed to the Land League during the Land War (1879–81) and to the ITGWU during the 1913 lockout. Broadly speaking, then, the Church of Ireland bishops tended to be drawn from landed backgrounds, and from

the fertility of 11 of the 24 bishops under review and all of these had children. Of 11 bishops about whom information on fertility is available: 3 had 4 children; 4 had 5 children; 1 had 6 children; 1 had 9 children; 1 had 11 children; and 1 had 12 children.

[181] Information on age at death is available for 23 of the 24 bishops under review: 4 died in their 60s; 3 died in their 70s; 15 died in their 80s; and 1 died in his 90s.

[182] *Irish Times*, 13 Apr. 1920.   [183] Ibid. 5 Feb. 1938.   [184] Ibid. 30 Sept. 1915.

the professional and business classes; and so they constituted a vital component of the new Protestant upper class that emerged at the end of the nineteenth century.

The Church of Ireland bishops were, however, not a completely united body particularly during the years after disestablishment. The absence of unanimity was perhaps most evident in the controversy over the revision of the Prayer Book which took place after disestablishment. The conflict was primarily between the evangelical wing of the Church of Ireland—which was largely composed of the laity and a number of evangelical clergy—and the conservative wing of the Church (comprising all of the bishops, about half of the clergy, and a significant proportion of the laity) who wanted to retain the liturgy and doctrine of the United Church of England and Ireland. The evangelicals wanted to remove the Catholic and ritualistic elements from the Irish church while the bishops wanted the Prayer Book to remain as it had been before 1871. In the event, the bishops—who were keen not to create a split in the Church of Ireland—compromised with the evangelicals particularly over the church calendar, the catechism, and the office for visitation of the sick, and this episode reveals the limits of Episcopal power and the rising influence of the laity in the Church of Ireland.[185] This was evident also in the new methods adopted for recruiting bishops and incumbents after disestablishment (discussed above) which put an end to the bishops' sole control of recruitment, and instead vested this power in committees of the laity, the clergy, and the hierarchy.[186] As the nineteenth century progressed, then, 'democracy [and] not hierarchy was established as the dominant principle [in the Church of Ireland]'.[187] In this respect, the Church of Ireland became more like the Presbyterian church as the nineteenth century progressed.

The Presbyterian Moderators were drawn from a rather different section of the Irish population to their contemporaries on the Church of Ireland's Episcopal bench.[188] Presbyterian Moderators were elected by the General Assembly each year, and there is less biographical information available about them, so a sample of twelve Presbyterian Moderators was analysed for both the earlier and the later periods.[189] As we have seen, the Irish Presbyterian population as a whole tended to be more Ulster based than the Church of Ireland population, and to be generally less well off than their Anglican brethren. Indeed, all of the Presbyterian

---

[185] On this conflict, see Akenson, *Church of Ireland*, 302–9.

[186] Ibid. 327.   [187] Ibid. 309.

[188] On Presbyterianism, see Andrew Holmes, *The Shaping of Ulster Presbyterian Belief and Practice, 1770–1840* (Oxford, 2006).

[189] I have identified the 5 Presbyterian Moderators elected: in 1878 (Thomas Witherow), 1879 (Robert Watts), 1881 (William Fleming Stevenson), 1882 (Thomas Young Killen), and 1890 (William Park) as the '1881' cohort. Similarly, I have defined the 7 Presbyterian Moderators elected: in 1900 (J. McCurdy Hamilton), 1901 (James Heron), 1902 (J. Edgar Henry), 1903 (John MacDermott), 1906 (William McKean), 1910 (John Howard Murphy), and 1912 (Henry Montgomery) as the '1911' contingent.

Table 6.13. The Occupations of the Fathers of Presbyterian Moderators

	1881–1911	1881	1911
Landowner	1 (13%)	1 (20%)	0
Tenant farmer	2 (25%)	2 (40%)	0
Minister	2 (25%)	0	2 (67%)
Professional	1 (13%)	0	1 (33%)
Merchant	4 (50%)	3 (60%)	1 (33%)
Number	8	5	3

Note: Some individuals had more than one occupation.

Moderators in this study were born in Ulster.[190] Most of the Presbyterian
Moderators under review also lived in Ulster—seven in Antrim, two in Derry,
two in Dublin, and one in Cork—so that most of them lived near Belfast which
was described by one Moderator as 'the Mecca of Irish Presbyterianism'.[191]

The Presbyterians of Ireland tended to be more middle class that the Irish
Anglicans. This is reflected in the social background of the Presbyterian Moderators included in this study (see Table 6.13). Only one of the Presbyterian
Moderators under review owned a relatively small 'estate' of 608 acres (valued
at £245), and which was probably regarded more as a large grazing farm rather
than as a landed estate. Two of the other Presbyterian Moderators were tenant
farmers and data are available on the acreage of one of these farms—that of
Witherow—whose father owned 566 acres (valued at £36). This was a relatively
comfortable farm and in the middle range of farm sizes in Ireland at that time.
In addition, Robert Watts' father was 'a staunch Presbyterian of the farming
class'.[192] This also reflects the fact that middle-sized farmers composed a substantial section of the Ulster Presbyterian community at the beginning of the
twentieth century, and many of the Presbyterian tenant farmers were involved
in T. W. Russell's campaign for compulsory land purchase in the early years
of the twentieth century.[193] A significant number of Presbyterian Moderators
were also sons of the Manse (or of Presbyterian ministers), and many of them
were from families with long traditions of service to the Presbyterian church.[194]
When McCurdy Hamilton died in 1915, for instance, James Bingham—who
was then Presbyterian Moderator—explained that 'Dr. Hamilton sprang from

[190] Information is available on the birthplace of 11 of the 12 individuals included in this study
and this reveals that 5 had been born in Antrim; 1 in Derry; 3 in Down; and 2 in Tyrone.
[191] A. F. Moody, *Memories and Musings of a Moderator* (London, n.d [1938]), 23. Moody was
Presbyterian Moderator during the 1930s but he is not one of the Moderators included in my
sample.
[192] *Irish Times*, 27 July 1895.   [193] See Campbell, *Land and Revolution*, Ch. 2.
[194] Two of the Presbyterian Moderators were the sons of the Manse and two others were the
sons-in-law of the Manse.

an old and highly respected Presbyterian stock. For generations members of his family have held prominent positions alike in the ministry and machinations of the Presbyterian church'.[195]

Broadly speaking, whereas Church of Ireland bishops tended to be drawn from landed and big business families, the Presbyterian Moderators (like the Presbyterian population as a whole) tended to be drawn from the Ulster Protestant middle class of tenant farmers, merchants, and professionals. Robert Wilson Hamilton who is not included in this study was 'engaged in business' before he became a Presbyterian minister (and—eventually—a Moderator); Thomas Young Killen's father was a merchant at Ballymena; McCurdy Hamilton's father, Hugh, was a merchant at Ballymoney;[196] William Stevenson's father was a merchant at Strabane; and William Park's father at Stewartstown, county Tyrone, was also a merchant. It is striking, however, that although many of the most powerful businessmen in Ireland during this period were Presbyterians, none of these families appears to have produced a Presbyterian Moderator. There was an unsuccessful attempt to appoint a layman and prominent Belfast businessman, Thomas Sinclair, as Presbyterian Moderator in 1905.[197] It is also possible that the big business interests in Belfast had other ways of controlling the statements and actions of Presbyterian Moderators. When A. F. Moody became Presbyterian Moderator he was surprised at the generosity of some Belfast bankers, which may or may not have been freely given, and at the very least, suggests a level of sociability and interaction between the Presbyterian Moderators and the Belfast business elite:

Following my nomination a number of leading citizens, including two Cabinet Ministers, got into communication and, without my knowledge, decided to present me with a luxurious car. It was an act of spontaneous, even quixotic, generosity. The presentation was made privately at the residence of David McKee, Esquire, Chairman of the Belfast Banking Co., in the presence of half a dozen of the principal subscribers.[198]

Presbyterian Moderators were elected annually by the General Assembly. Dr A. F. Moody explained in his memoir that Presbyterian Moderators were elected by the general assembly but that his name was known some months in advance because the thirty-three presbyteries that then composed the Presbyterian church in Ireland met in February and at this meeting each presbytery nominated its preferred candidate for Presbyterian Moderator.[199] The General Assembly, composed of clergy and laymen and meeting for a week each June, wielded enormous power. Local congregations were subjected to official visitations once every seven years and any irregularities were reported to the General Assembly

[195] *Irish Times*, 21 Jan. 1915.   [196] Moody, *Memories and Musings of a Moderator*, 228.
[197] *Irish Times*, 7 Jan. 1905.   [198] Moody, *Memories and Musings of a Moderator*, 15–16.
[199] Ibid. 13–14. According to Moody, the smallest presbytery represents 6 congregations while the biggest represents 60, but both have equal rights to make a nomination.

Table 6.14. Secondary Education of Presbyterian Moderators

	1881–1911	1881	1911
Type of school			
Irish Protestant School	12	6	6
Name of school			
Royal Belfast Academical Institution	8 (73%)	4 (80%)	4 (67%)
Belfast Academy	1 (9%)	1 (10%)	0
Armagh Royal School	1 (9%)	1 (10%)	0
Ballymoney model school	1 (9%)	0	1 (17%)
Bangor	1 (9%)	0	1 (17%)
Number	11	5	6

Note: Some individuals attended more than one secondary school.

Table 6.15. Tertiary Education of Presbyterian Moderators

	1881–1911	1881	1911
Assembly College, Belfast	5 (42%)	1 (20%)	4 (57%)
Queen's College, Belfast	6 (50%)	1 (20%)	5 (71%)
Magee College, Derry	1 (8%)	0	1 (14%)
New College, Edinburgh	7 (58%)	3 (60%)	4 (57%)
Other British university	3 (25%)	1 (20%)	2 (29%)
Other European university	1 (8%)	1 (20%)	0
American/Canadian colleges	3 (25%)	2 (40%)	1 (14%)
Number	12	5	7

Note: Some individuals attended more than one third-level institution.

which was presided over by the Presbyterian Moderator. One late twentieth-century Moderator claimed that this democratic system had its disadvantages since 'People in Ireland know the names of the Catholic Cardinal and the Anglican Archbishop; but few . . . could immediately name any current Moderator'. Even so, within the Presbyterian community he was regarded as a hugely powerful and influential figure 'sustained by a loyalty and treated with a deference which an Archbishop might envy'.[200] According to A. F. Moody, 'The Moderator, like the King, can do no wrong; his ruling is accepted without demur'.[201]

The Presbyterian Moderators included in this study were extremely well educated (see Tables 6.14 and 6.15). All of the Moderators in the earlier period had received a secondary education as had most of those in the later period. Given the fact that all of the Moderators were Ulster-born it is not a surprise to find that all of those who had received a secondary education did

[200] Ibid. 15; Megahey, *Irish Protestant Churches*, 15.
[201] Moody, *Memories and Musings*, 34.

so in Ulster. Most popular was the Royal Belfast Academical Institute (Inst) which two-thirds of the Presbyterian Moderators under review had attended. This was because arrangements had been made for students to receive their training as Presbyterian ministers there and its general certificate was recognized as the equivalent of a university degree.[202] There was very little change in the educational backgrounds of the Moderators between 1881 and 1911 although the importance of Inst declined and there was an increased attendance at Schools outside Belfast (at Ballymoney and Bangor).

All of the Presbyterian Moderators in this study received some form of third-level education. However, there was a decline in the proportion who attended American or Canadian Presbyterian colleges, and an increase in the proportion who attended Assembly's College in Belfast.[203] Some of them were determined to gain their education in the United States: Robert Watts, for instance, 'having early in life decided to enter the Church . . . proceeded to America in 1848 for the purpose of acquiring his theological training'.[204] Attendance at Assembly's College, Belfast, however, increased from one-fifth (20 per cent) in the earlier period to more than half (57 per cent) in the later period, and this reflects the increased importance of the Theological Faculty of the Irish Presbyterian Church in Belfast. The professors at Assembly's college were, according to Moody, 'men of recognized academic distinction and . . . members of the Faculty of Theology in connection with Queen's University'.[205] A much higher proportion of the Presbyterian Moderators in the later period had attended The Queen's College, Belfast (up from 20 per cent to 71 per cent of the total) while New College, Edinburgh remained consistently important throughout: with 60 per cent attending in the earlier period and 57 per cent attending in the later period. Thomas Witherow recalled his student experience at Edinburgh fondly as 'a year which he . . . prized as among the most valuable of his college course'.[206]

Most of the Moderators became ministers when they were aged in their twenties.[207] Like their colleagues on the Irish Anglican bench, most of them were married with only one being unmarried (Hamilton). They tended to marry later than the Church of Ireland bishops: three married in their twenties, and six in their thirties. We have information on the fertility of eight of the married Moderators, and all of these had children.[208] We also know the age at death of nine of them which shows that they tended to die at a younger age than the Church of Ireland

---

[202] Ibid. 73.

[203] The American and Canadian Presbyterian Colleges were: Knox College, Toronto; Washington College, Virginia; and Princeton Theological Seminary.

[204] *Irish Times*, 27 July 1895.   [205] Moody, *Memories and Musings of a Moderator*, 82.

[206] *Irish Times*, 28 Jan. 1890.

[207] Information is available on the age at which 9 of the 12 became Presbyterian ministers which reveals that 7 became ministers in their 20s and 2 became ministers in their 30s.

[208] Information is available on the number of children of 8 of the Presbyterian Moderators: 1 had 1 child; 1 had 2 children; 1 had 4 children; 2 had 5 children; 1 had 7 children; 1 had 10 children; and 1 had 13 children.

bishops.[209] Some of the Moderators appear to have endured a great deal of strain due to overwork. William Stevenson who died in 1886 aged only 53 'was a laborious pastor . . . He has spent all his days and nights in hard work, and his work had left traces upon him'.[210] In part, this may have been caused by the fact that Stevenson devoted his life to the foreign missions and travelled around the world in 1877 visiting mission stations especially in China and India.[211] Thomas Witherow died in 1890 aged 65 from heart disease exacerbated by exhaustion and 'feeling fagged through overwork'.[212] Broadly speaking, the later age at marriage and the earlier age at death reflects the fact that Presbyterian Moderators tended to be drawn from less-well-off backgrounds than the Church of Ireland bishops; and that they appear to have worked harder than some of the other members of the Irish establishment (notably the County Inspectors of the Royal Irish Constabulary). The lower status of the Moderators is also reflected in the fact that very few of them were the members of clubs. In fact, only one Presbyterian Moderator was the member of a club. The Revd William McKean, who was Moderator in 1906–7, was a member of the Royal county Down golf club.

Like the Church of Ireland bishops, the Presbyterian Moderators were stalwart Unionists. During the three Home Rule crises of 1885–6, 1892–3, and 1912–14, Presbyterians made public speeches which emphasized the threat to Protestant liberty that they believed Home Rule posed.[213] J. Edgar Henry, who was a son of the Manse, was: 'A strong Unionist, [and] he was ever ready to support the cause of the Union, and there were few political demonstrations held in the North-West at which he was not one of the speakers'.[214] Similarly, William Park, who was born at Stewartstown, county Tyrone, was a 'Strong Unionist' who articulated an Irish Presbyterian sense of belonging to the wider British Empire: 'It is something to be an Englishman in the widest sense of the word, a citizen of that great Empire on which the sun never sets, and whose flag, wherever it waves, brings justice, liberty and peace.'[215] Even so, the Presbyterian Moderators tended to have a different view of Irish nationalism and land reform from their colleagues in the Church of Ireland. Presbyterians—like the Catholic population—had been discriminated against under the penal laws and before the disestablishment of the Church of Ireland they had been regarded as Nonconformists or Dissenters. Indeed, some of the Presbyterian Moderators

---

[209] Two died in their 50s, 1 in his 60s, 2 in their 70s, 3 in their 80s, and 1 in his 90s.

[210] *Irish Times*, 18 Sept. 1886.

[211] Thomas Hamilton (rev. David Huddleston), 'William Fleming Stevenson', q.v. DNB online <http://www.oxforddnb.com/view/article/26445?docPos=45> (accessed 7 Dec. 2008).

[212] *Irish Times*, 28 Jan. 1890.

[213] Andrew Holmes, 'The Uses and Interpretations of Prophecy in Irish Presbyterianism, 1850–1930' in in Crawford Gribben and Andrew Holmes (eds.), *Protestant Millennialism: Evangelicalism and Irish Society, 1790–2005* (Basingstoke, 2006), 156.

[214] *Irish Times*, 14 Feb. 1911.

[215] Finlay Holmes, 'William Park', q.v. DNB online <http://www.oxforddnb.com/view/article/52715?docPos=1> (accessed 7 Dec. 2008).

under review were keen to campaign on behalf of their co-religionists for fairer treatment in Irish society. McCurdy Hamilton 'was always ready to stand up for fair play and equality of treatment for Presbyterians'.[216] Although they were on the same legal footing as the Church of Ireland after 1870, the Presbyterian Church retained elements of its earlier radical and dissenting tradition. This is evident in the views that some elements of the Presbyterian Church had of landlordism. In 1881, for example, the *Witness* referred to the 'many jolterheads among the Tory landlords of Ulster', and explained that a 'deep, widespread and growing discontent with the system of Irish land tenure pervades the Presbyterian farmers of Ireland'.[217] Indeed, there was sympathy for the land reform if not the nationalist agenda of the Home Rule movement among some sections of the Presbyterian community. One Presbyterian Moderator at the beginning of the twentieth century even declared that the 'web of hate' in Ireland had been 'woven out of three strands—rack-rents, tithes (weighted with religious intolerance) and minority rule'.[218] A. F. Moody added that, 'The landlord as a rule spent no money on his estate'.[219]

III

How open and representative was the religious elite in Ireland between 1879 and 1914? The evidence presented in this chapter suggests that the religious elite was perhaps the most 'open' elite group reviewed in this study. Once an individual had become a priest, a vicar, or a minister, recruitment to the higher levels of the church was apparently based on merit rather than family connections or personal wealth. Of course, the individual first required an appropriate education at both secondary- and tertiary- (or seminary-) levels and this could be costly. However, for prospective Catholic priests the availability of a number of free places at Maynooth meant that if the fees for a secondary school education could be acquired, and if the expenses while at Maynooth could be covered, an individual from a relatively poor background could become a priest and even a bishop. After the disestablishment of the Church of Ireland, the recruiting of bishops became more open as the power of appointment was taken away from the state and the Episcopal bench and placed largely in the hands of the laity. In the Presbyterian church, the laity were also responsible for selecting the Presbyterian Moderator each year. In these respects, the evangelical revival of the nineteenth century was probably responsible for reducing the power of the bishops in the Church of Ireland, and for placing greater power in the hands of the Episcopalian laity.

[216] *Irish Times*, 21 Jan. 1915. The question as to whether the representation of Presbyterians in the Irish establishment had increased between 1881 and 1911 will be discussed in Conclusion.
[217] Quot. Megahey, *Irish Protestant Churches*, 14.   [218] Quot. ibid.
[219] Moody, *Memories and Musings of a Moderator*, 212.

Broadly speaking, the open nature of the religious elites meant that the composition of the leaders of these churches was reasonably representative of their congregations. It is widely believed that Irish priests and—therefore—bishops tended to be drawn from the large farmer or grazier class in nineteenth-century Ireland. Bishop Crotty, President of Maynooth College told the 1826 commission of enquiry that his students were 'generally the sons of farmers, who must be comfortable in order to meet expenses'.[220] Similarly, Emmet Larkin and David Miller explained that they expected most Catholic bishops in late nineteenth-century Ireland to have come from strong farmer backgrounds.[221] The evidence presented in this chapter, however, suggests a more complex pattern of recruitment, with some bishops being recruited from small farm backgrounds. This was probably because the Maynooth grant, by providing a substantial number of free places at the national seminary, enabled some individuals from less-well-off backgrounds to become priests. However, it is largely the case that Catholic bishops were drawn from the ranks of the provincial Catholic middle class—including shopkeeping, professional, and farming backgrounds—but very few (if any) came from rural or urban labouring backgrounds.

Some Catholic bishops were drawn from former Catholic landlord families that had been dispossessed during the colonization of Ireland in the seventeenth century. Cardinal Paul Cullen's predecessors were Catholic landowners who had been dispossessed in the 1650s[222] and Bishops O'Dwyer and Healy also saw themselves as the descendants of a dispossessed Catholic and Gaelic aristocracy. If some Catholic bishops were the descendants of the dispossessed, however, the Church of Ireland bishops were usually the descendants of their dispossessors. The vast majority (67 per cent) of Church of Ireland bishops had either been born into or married into landed families, and the rest tended to be drawn from upper middle-class backgrounds in business or the professions. Notwithstanding disestablishment, the proportion of bishops from landed backgrounds remained high between 1881 and 1911, and the declining influence of the Church of Ireland bishops both reflects and is an aspect of the more general decline of landed influence in Ireland during this period. In fact, the Church of Ireland bishops were an integral part of the new upper class that was emerging in late nineteenth-century Ireland; and some of the Church of Ireland bishops were at the centre of networks of Episcopalian landlords, businessmen, and senior administrators.

---

[220] Quot. Newsinger, 'The Catholic Church in Nineteenth-century Ireland', 259.

[221] Communication from Emmet Larkin with the author (3 Aug. 2007) and communication from David Miller with the author (1 Aug. 2007).

[222] Patrick J. Corish, 'The radical face of Paul Cardinal Cullen', in id. (ed.), *Radicals, Rebels and Establishments* (Belfast, 1985), 174. This fits with Kevin Whelan's argument that elements of the strong farmer class in the nineteenth century were the descendants of Catholic landowners who had been dispossessed during the seventeenth century (Kevin Whelan, 'An Underground Gentry? Catholic Middlemen in Eighteenth-century Ireland', in James Donnelly and Kerby Miller (eds.), *Irish Popular Culture, 1650–1850* (Dublin, 1997)).

The Presbyterian Moderators can be identified as occupying a social identity somewhere between that of the Church of Ireland bishops and the Catholic episcopacy. Many of them were drawn from small business backgrounds in the towns of Ulster—comparable to the small shopkeepers and merchants who were Home Rulers in the other three provinces—but much smaller in scale than the business interests of the families that sent their sons off to become Church of Ireland clergymen and bishops. While many of the Moderators were drawn from tenant farmer backgrounds these were usually relatively large farms; and appear to have been more substantial farms than those on which some of the Catholic bishops were reared. The Presbyterian Moderators, then, represented the Protestant middle class of both urban and rural Ulster and probably saw themselves socially as better-off than many of their Catholic contemporaries in the Catholic clergy and episcopacy but less-well-off than their colleagues on the Church of Ireland bench. It is worth stating that in all of the churches under review there was a tendency for traditions of religious service to develop in some families, and there were, for instance, many Hamiltons, MacHales, and Plunkets who were clerics and bishops in nineteenth-century Ireland. Even so, it was easier for a man from a small farm background to become a Catholic bishop than a Church of Ireland bishop or a Presbyterian Moderator. While there were some individuals from comparatively poor backgrounds who did become Catholic bishops, Church of Ireland bishops were usually the sons of landlords, influential businessmen, and prosperous professionals, while Presbyterian Moderators were often the sons of large farmers or small-town shopkeepers and merchants. There were no labourers who became members of the religious elite.

Finally, it is necessary to return to the question of the 'greening' of religious power and of Irish society more generally during the late nineteenth and early twentieth centuries; and to make some observations on the changing organization and nature of these three churches. Two clear patterns are evident. First, that the Church of Ireland and the Presbyterian church were moving closer to one another. The status and position of Church of Ireland bishops was in decline so that their social profiles were becoming closer to those of the Presbyterian Moderators; the Church of Ireland was increasingly influenced by evangelicalism after disestablishment and this created a greater kinship between the two churches; and sections of both churches were increasingly identifying themselves as supporters of Ulster Unionism rather than Irish Unionism. Tellingly, Charles Frederick D'Arcy who served as Bishop of Clogher, Ossory, Down and Archbishop of Dublin and Armagh, was described in his obituary as 'a strong supporter of Ulster Unionism', and an advocate of a closer relationship between the Church of Ireland and the Presbyterian church. Moreover, when a deputation from the Church of Ireland was sent to call on the Provisional Government after the signing of the Anglo-Irish Treaty—to discuss the treatment of Protestants in the south—D'Arcy as Primate and effective leader of the Church of Ireland sent the Archbishop of Dublin (Gregg) rather than going himself suggesting that the Church of Ireland was in the process of partitioning itself between 1912 and 1922.[223] This transformation was also evident politically with the transformation of the Liberal party (which tended to win the support of Ulster Presbyterians) and the Conservative party (which was the party of the Church of Ireland) into the Unionist party; and into a Unionist party that was increasingly Ulster-centred rather than being all-Ireland. During the late nineteenth century, and following the first Home Rule crisis of 1885–6, there is a sense that the various Protestant congregations in Ireland were moving closer to one another theologically, socially, and politically.

The second clear pattern—which follows on from the first—is that the level of separation, segregation, and sectarianism between the Protestant and Catholic churches in Ireland—and their congregations—intensified and increased during the period under review.[224] As the religious practice and devotion of Catholics, Episcopalians, and Presbyterians increased during the nineteenth century so did the religious elite's obsession with controlling their congregations. The Catholic hierarchy played a significant part in this process by refusing to allow Catholics to be educated in any institution which they did not control.[225] During a period of urbanization—especially in Ulster—the Protestant churches were equally concerned with ensuring that the people who migrated from the Ulster countryside to work in the factories, linen mills, and shipyards in Belfast retained or were converted to the Protestant faith. Henry Montgomery, who was Presbyterian Moderator in 1912–13, worked with the Belfast Town Mission to this end during his student years and devoted his life to missionary work among the burgeoning Belfast working class between the 1870s and his death in 1943. The Mission was interdenominational and aimed at the workers who were migrating to the city from the 1850s, and involved the sending of agents to visit the poor in their homes and invite them to attend church and Sunday school. Montgomery criticized the Belfast businessmen whose shipyards and linen mills were attracting these men and women to come and work in the city, but who often ignored the spiritual and material needs of these migrants, explaining in 1895: 'if we do not reach the masses, the masses will reach us, and in a way some may not like.'[226] The new Belfast working class might have been attracted to socialist politics or even nationalist politics—if they had felt their social mobility to be blocked—in the absence of interventions like that of Montgomery. Indeed, it was the attempts by all of the three main churches in late nineteenth-century

[223] *Irish Times*, 5 Feb. 1938.

[224] Many Belfast Catholics had been prepared to vote for Presbyterian Liberal MPs before 1883 (A. C. Hepburn, *Catholic Belfast and Nationalist Ireland in the Era of Joe Devlin, 1871–1934* (Oxford, 2008), 34).

[225] The papal decree *Ne Temere* of 1908 also reinforced the separation of Protestant and Catholic communities by demanding that the children of a mixed marriage be reared as Catholics.

[226] Elizabeth Malcolm, 'Henry Montgomery', q.v. DNB online <http://www.oxforddnb.com/view/article/52707?docPos=2> (accessed 8 Dec. 2008).

Ireland to consolidate and control the faiths of their congregations that led to the sectarian divide in Irish society becoming even more emphatic than it already was.

There was also a great deal of antipathy between the Catholic and Protestant churches during the nineteenth century. Some Presbyterians appear to have hoped for the extinction of Catholicism. One Presbyterian observed in January 1886, for instance, that 'we confidently look forward to the day when the Man of Sin, with all his superstitions, will vanish away before the light of evangelical Christianity'.[227] Similarly, W. D. Killen, the president of Assembly's College between 1869 and 1902, and therefore responsible for the education of many of the Presbyterian Moderators in this study identified the Antichrist of the Bible with the Papacy.[228] Indeed, in Presbyterian discourse generally, Catholicism was identified as the enemy of intellectual improvement, national prosperity, and the essential well-being of human souls.[229] Some senior members of the Church of Ireland also hoped for the disappearance of the Catholic church, and that Irish Catholics would see the error of their ways and become Protestants.[230] Others—like Charles Frederick D'Arcy—merely regarded Catholics with 'courteous disapproval'.[231]

Catholic bishops spoke of Protestants in much the same way. When John Healy compiled his *Relatio Status* for the diocese of Clonfert in 1885 he described the Protestant school in Ballinasloe in the following terms: 'heretics educate the children of poor Catholics, some of them foundlings, some of them purchased from their parents, some of them kidnapped or in other ways abandoned to the devil.'[232] Some of the Church of Ireland bishops supported the Protestant evangelical movements that attempted to convert Irish and European Catholics to Protestantism during the nineteenth century. In November 1860, for instance, Thomas 2nd Baron Plunket, who was then Church of Ireland Bishop of Tuam as well as a landowner in south Mayo, evicted sixty-eight people from his estate at Tourmakeady allegedly because his tenants would not send their children to the local Protestant school.[233] Similarly, Plunket's nephew William Conyingham Plunket was prominently involved in the Protestant evangelizing movements that attempted to convert poor Catholics in Connemara and Mayo to Protestantism,

---

[227] Andrew Holmes, 'The Uses and Interpretations of Prophecy', 155.

[228] Ibid. 152.   [229] Ibid. 153.

[230] Akenson points out in his biography of Archbishop Whately that he was unusual among his fellow Church of Ireland bishops in not desiring the extinction of Catholicism, in not supporting ultra-Protestant proselytizing societies, and in supporting the Maynooth grant (*A Protestant in Purgatory*, 132, 134, 140).

[231] A. A. Luce (rev. Kenneth Milne), 'Charles Frederick D'Arcy', q.v. DNB online <http://www.oxforddnb.com/view/article/32713?docPos=5> (accessed 8 Dec. 2008).

[232] Joyce, *John Healy*, 87.

[233] These evictions appear to have been conceived as part of the second Reformation which the Second Baron Plunket had strongly supported in the west of Ireland (Moran, *The Mayo Evictions of 1860*, 9, 21, 31, 97, 128).

and with continued attempts to reform Spain, Portugal, and Italy.[234] The Catholic hierarchy strongly resisted these attempts and, in particular, John MacHale earned the respect of the people of Connacht for countering these evangelizing impulses. When Power Le Poer Trench, Archbishop of Tuam (1819–39), and the leader of Irish evangelism, denounced what he called the 'damnable doctrines of the Catholic church' in 1826, for instance, MacHale robustly defended his position by pointing out that the cathedral in which Trench preached had once been Catholic and by objecting to Trench's intolerance and bigotry.[235] For this—among other reasons—MacHale was popularly regarded as what might be termed 'the people's prelate' during the nineteenth century.

The increased polarization between Catholic and Protestant was—in part—the direct result of the British state's attempt to build an alliance with the Catholic middle class. Indeed, the one certain outcome of the 'greening' policy was the alienation of the Protestant aristocracy and middle class with whom the British state had formerly been allied. For these sections of the Irish Protestant community, the British state's attempts to win the support of Catholic bishops, farmers, and civil servants during the second half of the nineteenth century constituted a betrayal of their years of service to the Crown, and made the development of a strident Unionist movement inevitable. Certainly, some members of both communities tried to retain a sense of mutual respect during this period of intensifying sectarianism. When Maurice Day died at Clones his popularity among the wider Protestant and Catholic communities was such that 'when the news of his sudden death became known the bells of the various churches, including the Roman Catholic church, were tolled'.[236] Similarly, when Cardinal O'Donnell, the Archbishop of Armagh, died in 1927 the bells of both cathedrals in Armagh tolled for him in honour of his commitment to the fair treatment of minorities in both the Irish Free State and Northern Ireland.[237] And during the anti-Home Rule riots in Belfast in 1886, Thomas Young Killen, who had been Presbyterian Moderator in 1882, stated that 'we deeply lament the intolerant spirit and fatal riots which have been disturbing the peace and compromising the character of our community', and called on 'all parties connected with our Church to cultivate a sprit of peace and brotherly kindness towards all their neighbours'.[238] But such dignified expressions of goodwill and reconciliation could do little to halt the widening gulf between Irish Protestants and Irish Catholics.

[234] C. L. Falkiner (rev. Kenneth Milne), 'William Conyngham Plunket', q.v. DNB online <http://www.oxforddnb.com/view/article/22416?docPos=2> (accessed 8 Dec. 2008).
[235] Hynes, *Knock*, 73–4.   [236] *Irish Times*, 29 May 1923.
[237] Mary Harris, 'Patrick O'Donnell', q.v. DNB online <http://www.oxforddnb.com/view/article/35291?docPos=15> (accessed 12 Dec. 2008).   [238] *Irish Times*, 4 Aug. 1886.

Conclusion

The question of who ruled Ireland between 1879 and 1914 has recently been publicly debated by the current president of Ireland with a current member of the British House of Lords. In her lecture commemorating the ninetieth anniversary of the Easter Rising delivered at University College, Cork in January 2006, President Mary McAleese claimed that before 1916: 'The administration of Ireland was . . . carried on as a process of continuous conversation around the fire in the Kildare Street Club by past pupils of public schools. It was no way to run a country, even without the glass ceiling for Catholics.'[1] In his response to her remarks, Lord Paul Bew sounded a warning historical note, and suggested that Catholics had been integrated into the Irish establishment well before the Easter Rising:

It is true that even in 1916 there were pockets of anti-Catholic discrimination in Dublin but the fact remains that the peculiarity of the Rising lies in the fact that it is a largely Catholic revolution, one of whose principal targets was the Catholics who had already gone through the glass ceiling.

John Redmond, for example, who had turned down a position in the British cabinet; those dozens of UCD doctors who served in the British army and were highly decorated in the first World War; those Catholic officials who worked at the apex of British administration in Ireland. These were the people who were about to inherit the political leadership of a home rule Ireland, and these were the people who were knocked out of place by the insurgents.[2]

In this conclusion, I will use the data presented in this book to assess which of these views is most correct. The conclusion will be divided into three parts. First, I will consider the extent to which access to the Irish establishment was 'open' or 'closed', and discuss whether there was a 'greening' of the Irish establishment and of Irish society during this period. In part two, I will explain why access to sections of the establishment was open or closed, and why there was only a partial 'greening' process underway in Ireland during this period. Finally, in the third part of this conclusion, I will consider the implications of this study to the origins of the Irish Revolution of 1916–23.

---

[1] *Irish Times*, 28 Jan. 2006.   [2] Ibid. 15 Apr. 2006.

I

To what extent was there a 'greening' of the Irish establishment during the period under review? The composition of the great landowning class was largely static between 1881 and 1918: the majority remained Episcopalian (92 per cent in 1881 and 97 per cent in 1911), the proportion of Presbyterians declined from one to zero, and the proportion of Catholics also declined slightly from 7.5 per cent to 3 per cent between 1881 and 1918. In part, this was because admission to the 'great' landowning class was largely through inheritance and therefore 'closed' to the wider population. However, as many as one-third of the estates of more than 10,000 acres may have been open to purchasers through the Encumbered Estates Court after 1849 and there is evidence that some Irish Catholics did purchase estates through this route.[3] On the other hand, purchase of such estates required considerable capital and this excluded the majority of the Catholic population from purchasing land in this manner. Indeed, it was the series of land acts passed by successive British governments after 1881 that enabled most Catholic tenant farmers to purchase their landholdings from the Irish landlord class. By 1914, 58 per cent of the tenanted land of Ireland had been sold by the Irish landlords to their tenants at a cost of £180 million to the British exchequer.[4] Undoubtedly, this constituted a substantial 'greening' of Irish society since it greatly increased the economic power of the Catholic tenant farmer class who now became owner-occupiers of their land. At the same time, the land acts considerably reduced the economic power of the largely Protestant former landowning class. This decline in economic power was mirrored in the political sphere with the proportion of landed MPs declining from more than one-third (35 per cent) of the total in 1881 to less than one-tenth (7 per cent) by 1911, and this reveals a profound shift in political and economic power in provincial Ireland.[5]

Advancement to the top positions of the state was also largely 'closed' to the wider population. As we have seen, the senior members of the Civil Service were generally recruited from outside the Civil Service and appointed by the Lord Lieutenant, the Chief Secretary, or the departmental heads. Very few of the senior

---

[3] James Daniel Lahiff of Cloon, Gort, county Galway, for instance, who owned 10,927 acres in counties Galway and Clare was a Catholic (email to author from Dermot Lahiff, 4 July 2008).

[4] Fergus Campbell, *Land and Revolution: Nationalist Politics in the West of Ireland, 1891–1921* (Oxford, 2005), 91, 89, n. 21.

[5] The decline of landlord influence among Irish MPs was more marked than in the rest of the United Kingdom, with the proportion of landed economic interests in the House of Commons as a whole declining from 34% in 1868 to 15.5% in 1900 (Michael Rush, 'The Members of Parliament', in S. A. Walkland (ed.), *The House of Commons in the Twentieth Century* (Oxford, 1979), 97.

administrators were recruited by open competition or drawn from the lesser ranks of the service. While there was a 'greening' of the senior membership of the Irish Civil Service from about one-third (33 per cent) who were Catholics in 1891 to slightly more than one-third (37 per cent) in 1911, this does not substantiate the assertion that a systematic 'greening' process was underway or that the administrative elite was 'open' to recruitment from the educated or appropriately qualified population as a whole. Indeed, the fact that most (61 per cent) of the officers and clerks in the Civil Service were Catholic by 1911—following the introduction of competitive examination in 1870—only underlines the extent to which a parallel 'greening' was not taking place at the higher levels of the Civil Service. Similarly, in the Royal Irish Constabulary, the majority of the senior officers of the force were Episcopalians and—in fact—an 'orange-ing' or 'reverse greening' process was taking place during this period. Between 1881 and 1911, the proportion of Irish-born Catholic senior police officers actually declined from slightly more than one-quarter (27.5 per cent) to less than one-tenth (9 per cent). Moreover, this decline took place during a period when about 70 per cent of the rank and file of the Royal Irish Constabulary were Irish-born Catholics. In order to become a police officer, the prospective candidate required a nomination from the Lord Lieutenant, the Chief Secretary, or the Inspector General to allow them to take the examination to qualify as a cadet (although a very small number of police officers were recruited from the ranks). An individual who wanted to become a senior civil servant or a police officer, then, usually had to be known to the senior members of the Irish government and to be a member of the gentlemen's clubs or of the social, political, and professional elite networks in Dublin. Of course, some of these political and social networks were dominated by the leaders of the Irish Parliamentary Party who did play some part in influencing senior appointments to the Civil Service and this partially explains the relatively high proportion of Catholics in this elite group.

The leading businessmen in Ireland were generally Protestants of various kinds and there was only a very slight 'greening' of the business elite during the period under review. Between 1883 and 1911, the proportion of prominent Catholic businessmen increased only very slightly from 17 to 20 per cent of the total. Moreover, these Catholic businessmen tended to congregate in exclusively Catholic firms: in 1883, 66 per cent of all the businesses in this study were presided over exclusively by either Protestants or Catholics, and by 1911 this figure had increased to 71 per cent. It is likely that the new Catholic recruits to the business elite between 1883 and 1911 were recruited to companies that were already dominated by Catholics or that they were the members of newly emerging companies that were run exclusively by Catholics: 3 per cent of the firms in 1883 were presided over only by Catholics and this had increased to one in ten (10 per cent) of all the top businesses by 1911. Catholic-dominated companies were probably more open to Catholic applications for employment, while Protestant-dominated companies were usually open only to Protestant applications for work and closed to applications from Catholics. Indeed, although a significant minority of the top businessmen were Catholics, the business elite as a whole tended to be 'closed' to wider access to the Catholic population. Even at the level of clerkships, there were very few Catholic employees in the world of business.[6] In order to gain employment in business—at all levels—an individual needed to have capital as well as access to the networks of the existing business elite. And because these professional and social networks were dominated by Protestants, most of the recruits to clerkships, middle management, and directorships tended to be drawn from the Protestant middle and landed classes. Of course, there were also a small number of individuals who joined Ireland's business elite by building substantial businesses from small beginnings (Edward Harland, for instance) or who inherited smaller businesses which they transformed into much more successful concerns (William Martin Murphy, for instance) but these were in the minority. In Ireland—as in Britain and elsewhere—there were very few rags to riches stories, which limited the possibilities for Catholic advancement into this group, and most prominent businessmen were from either business families or relatively well-off professional backgrounds.[7]

Recruitment to the political elite was slightly more 'open' than that to the administrative or the business elite. Technically, any man could stand as an MP and, after the introduction of the secret ballot in 1872 and the expansion of the franchise in 1884–5, Irish elections were both free and democratic, at least by the standards of the time. Having said that, local candidates (both nationalist and Unionist) were vetted by local selection panels that were dominated by local power brokers who decided which candidates should be placed before the electorate. In addition, parliamentary candidates usually needed to be extremely wealthy since MPs did not receive a salary until 1911. Prospective parliamentary candidates also needed to have an occupation that enabled them to spend a significant amount of time in the House of Commons. The political elite was reasonably open, then, but access remained limited by the gatekeepers who dominated local conventions and by the significant amount of wealth and time that candidates were required to possess. Even so, there was a certain amount of 'greening' of the political elite: the proportion of Catholic Home Rule MPs increased from 82 per cent to 90 per cent between 1881 and 1911 while the proportion of Catholic Conservative or Unionist MPs remained at zero between 1881 and 1911.

---

[6] The introduction of competitive examination to become a clerk in the Civil Service meant that there were more Catholic clerks in state employment than there were in the private sector by the beginning of the twentieth century (Mary Daly, 'The formation of an Irish Nationalist elite? Recruitment to the Irish Civil Service in the decades prior to independence, 1870–1920', *Paedagogica Historica*, 30 (1994), 297).

[7] As Putnam points out: 'Self-made tycoons risen from humble origins are exceedingly rare' (Robert D. Putnam, *The Comparative Study of Political Elites* (New Jersey, 1976), 25). See also Philip Stanworth and Anthony Giddens, 'An Economic Elite: A Demographic Profile of Company Chairmen', in Philip Stanworth and Anthony Giddens (eds.), *Elites and Power in British Society* (Cambridge, 1974), 86.

Moreover, there was a certain amount of 'greening' of Irish political influence during this period. Following the Irish Parliamentary Party's victory at the 1885 general election, when it won eighty-five of the Irish constituencies and therefore held the balance of power between the Liberals and the Conservatives in the House of Commons, the Liberal Party supported the introduction of Home Rule in Ireland. Later, both Liberal and Conservative governments introduced far-ranging reforms of local government, education, and landlord–tenant relations in Ireland. In other words, after 1886 there was a substantial increase in the influence of the Irish Home Rule MPs over the behaviour of the British state in Ireland, and this amounts to a 'greening' of Irish politics and society. It should be noted, of course, that the increased power of the IPP was largely a consequence of the mass support that the party had gained in the Irish countryside and from the bargaining power that extensive land agitation and attendant disorder in the early 1880s and the early 1900s gave them in their dealings with the government.[8] The influence of Conservative and later Unionist MPs over the actions of the state remained considerable, however, and was able to prevent the implementation of Home Rule for All Ireland and to guarantee the partition of Ireland in 1920–2. The continued influence of Unionism acted as a serious check to the increased influence of Home Rulers after 1886.

It may be that the religious elite was the most 'open' elite group in this study. Catholic Bishops were recruited from the priesthood by committees of priests and bishops, and, technically, any priest could become a bishop. Entry to the priesthood did require a secondary education (which was reasonably expensive) and attendance at a seminary (although most attended St Patrick's College, Maynooth at which there were a number of free places each year). Subsequent recruitment from the clergy to the episcopacy was based more on personal attributes and political viewpoint than on social background and appears to have been genuinely meritocratic. Even so, priests who were the members of prominent bishops' social and kinship networks were probably better placed than their colleagues to become a bishop.[9] Recruitment to the episcopal bench of the Church of Ireland after disestablishment was also reasonably 'open' as bishops were selected by committees of laymen, clergy, and bishops. As with the Catholic bishops, a certain level of secondary education and normally a degree from Trinity College Dublin (both of which were reasonably expensive) was required for an individual to become an incumbent. Once the individual had become a minister, he could—if he won the support of laity, clergy, and episopcacy—put

[8] The Wyndham Land Act of 1903, for instance, was introduced in response to an extensive land agitation organized by the United Irish League that seriously undermined law and order in Ireland (see Campbell, *Land and Revolution*, Ch. 2).

[9] See, for instance, the large number of relations and friends of John MacHale who became prominent priests in the diocese of Tuam during the nineteenth century.

himself forward as a potential bishop. Similarly, Presbyterian Moderators were selected each year by the lay members and the ministers who were the members of the General Assembly. Broadly speaking, then, entry to the religious elite did require a certain amount of wealth that would enable the individual to gain both a secondary- and a third-level education. However, recruitment to the top of the religious elite was generally meritocratic, open, and not determined by family connections or personal wealth. While there could be no 'greening' of the composition of the religious elite, there was certainly a 'greening' or an increase in the influence of the Catholic bishops in Ireland over the behaviour of the British state particularly in the sphere of education. At the same time, the power of the Church of Ireland bishops, who had once been a major influence on the behaviour of the British state, was in steep decline as is obviously evident from the disestablishment of the Church of Ireland in 1869–71.

To what extent were there more Irish Presbyterians and Nonconformists in the Irish establishment in 1911 than in 1881? While one Presbyterian was a great landowner in 1881 (0.5 per cent), this had actually declined to zero by 1911 and reflects the fact that there were very few Presbyterian landowners in Ireland during this period (there were no Nonconformist great landowners in 1881 or 1918). In the political and administrative elites, however, there were a significant number of Presbyterians and Nonconformists. The proportion of Presbyterians and Nonconformists who were MPs remained broadly the same during this period. In 1881, 8 per cent of Conservative MPs and 31.4 per cent of Liberals had been Presbyterians, while in 1911 they constituted more than one-third (35 per cent) of Unionist MPs and 1.5 per cent of Home Rulers. Similarly, Nonconformists constituted 6.2 per cent of Liberal MPs in 1881 and 5 per cent of Unionist MPs and 1.5 per cent of Home Rule MPs in 1911. However, there was a significant increase in the proportion of Presbyterian senior civil servants who increased from zero to 8 per cent between 1891 and 1911, and there was a parallel increase in the proportion of Presbyterian senior police officers from zero in 1881 to 9.5 per cent in 1911. Similarly, Nonconformist civil servants increased from 2 per cent to 4.5 per cent between 1891 and 1911 while Nonconformist senior police officers increased from zero to 2 per cent between 1881 and 1911.

In business, the proportion of Presbyterians also increased from 5 per cent to 7 per cent between 1883 and 1911, while the proportion of Nonconformist businessmen increased from 6 to 10.5 per cent over the same period. Of these Nonconformists, the Quaker businessmen were the most important group who increased from 3.5 per cent to 7.5 per cent of the business elite between 1883 and 1911. Broadly speaking, in a society where Presbyterians constituted 10 per cent of the total population and where less than 3 per cent of Irish society was Nonconformist, these figures suggest that by 1911 Presbyterians and Nonconformists were represented in the Irish establishment in roughly equal proportion to their numbers in Irish society. The increased presence of Presbyterians and Nonconformists in the Irish establishment was caused by the importance of these communities in business but also a consequence of the Liberal party's concern to appoint them to senior positions in the Irish administration and the police.

The same can not be said for the proportion of Catholics who were members of the Irish establishment by 1911. While Catholics were over-represented in the Home Rule party where they constituted 92 per cent of MPs in 1911 and, of course, in the Catholic Episcopal bench, there were far fewer Catholics in the other elite groups under review than in the population as a whole (74 per cent of the Irish population was Catholic in 1911). Almost two-fifths (37 per cent) of senior civil servants were Catholic in 1911 but only one-fifth (19 per cent) of top businessmen, and about one in seven (14 per cent) senior police officers. None of the Unionist MPs was Catholic in 1911 and only one in thirty (3 per cent) of the descendants of the great landowners in 1918 was Catholic. The period between 1881 and 1911 did witness a slight 'greening' of the composition of some sections of the Irish establishment—the Home Rule political elite, the senior civil servants, and the business elite—but it also witnessed a decline of Catholic representation in the landed elite and among the senior police officers. How can this limited greening of the Irish establishment and of Irish society between 1879 and 1914 be explained?

II

The Irish establishment surveyed in this book, it is worth emphasizing, were the very top layer of Irish society. What lay beneath the establishment was a middle-sector of Irish society—of the Civil Service, the police, local government, the lesser professions, smaller businesses, and so on—that had been almost totally colonized by Irish Catholics by the beginning of the twentieth-century.[10] To a very large extent, power had already changed hands—certainly in rural Ireland—before the Irish Revolution took place. Most of the land of Ireland had been sold by the landlord to the tenant by 1914; nationalists had taken control of most of the boards of Poor Law Unions from the 1880s, and of the new county councils in 1899; and most of the rank and file of the Royal Irish Constabulary and of the Irish Civil Service were Catholic by 1914. Most importantly, a seismic shift in power-holding had taken place in provincial Ireland between the end of the Great Famine and the beginning of the new century. Broadly speaking, during this period, the large farmers and provincial shopkeepers replaced the

---

[10] A study of the collective biography of the thousands of Catholic men and women who dominated the middle section of Irish society by 1914—as shopkeepers, large farmers, businessmen, clerks, teachers, poor law guardians, county councillors, and so on—would not have been practicable. None the less, these individuals already held a great deal of power in provincial Ireland before the beginning of the Great War.

landlords as the most wealthy and politically influential classes in Irish society. As individuals, their wealth may have been miniscule compared with the great landowners or the big businessmen, but collectively the thousands of provincial merchants, small businessmen, shopkeepers, and large farmers were the most powerful section of Irish society by 1914. These men and women effectively ran local government in nationalist Ireland; they were extremely influential in nationalist political organizations and in the Irish Parliamentary Party (some of them even became MPs); and together with the Catholic church they effectively controlled political, economic, cultural, and moral life in rural Ireland.

To a certain extent, the Irish establishment was like a head without a body in 1914: it controlled the state, big business, and the professions—most of which were based in Dublin or Belfast—but outside the cities a new alternative establishment-in-waiting was already emerging, gaining influence, and preparing to take power. Even within the cities, there were two establishments vying with one another. On the one hand, the old Protestant, semi-colonial establishment that was still clinging to power and attempting to exclude the rising Catholic middle class from its offices. And on the other, the thousands of Catholics who were effectively running the police force, and who were clerks in the Civil Service, and who had taken control of the middle level of Irish society. One of the impulses behind the revolution undoubtedly came from the large number of Catholics who had risen to the middle ranks of Irish society and were clamouring to reach higher, to gain positions at the top level, and to join the Irish establishment. If they had been allowed to do so in large numbers by the beginning of the twentieth century, the implications of this to the future of Irish society may have been momentous. But as it was, there were almost two different worlds in operation: the Protestant dominated top tier of Irish society and a Catholic-dominated middle level.

Sean O Faolain looked back (from the vantage point of 1943) on the early years of the twentieth century and described the way in which the sons of provincial farmers and shopkeepers were colonizing the middle layers of Irish society:

> By 1898 the farmer had already won real political power on the establishment of the county councils, under the new Local Government Act. By 1905 he was getting solid possession of his land. All the time, his sons were going steadily into business, clerical posts, crafts, trades, and the professions, so that a native town-class had become consolidated by the first decade of this century. By 1914, except for Home Rule, and the economic hand-over of time, the country-folk had retrieved an astonishing amount of ground.[11]

Indeed, it could be argued that in early twentieth-century Ireland, there were two elites vying with one another for control of Irish society: on the one hand, an old elite trying to hold onto power but holding fast to its traditional political

---

[11] Sean O Faolain, 'The Stuffed Shirts', *Bell*, 6 (1943), repr. in Seamus Deane (ed.) *The Field Day Anthology of Irish Writing*, 3 vols. (Derry, 1992), iii. 103–4.

outlook and its network of social and professional ties; and, on the other hand, a new elite attempting to push into the higher reaches of Irish society and prepared to use revolutionary means if necessary to achieve this. It would be 1922, however, before they took the final step up into the Irish establishment, and, as O Faolain put it: '[After 1922] the farmers' sons took a sudden step up. They became, from 1922 on, our new industrialists, business-men, Civil Servants, professionals.'[12] I will now try to explain why the Catholics who had risen into the middle layers of Irish society were prevented from rising further into the Irish establishment.

The first major explanation for the relatively static composition of the Irish establishment between 1879 and 1914 is that Ireland under the Act of Union (of 1801–1921) was governed—by Britain—in a colonial manner. Between the plantations of the seventeenth century and the passage of the Act of Union in 1801, Ireland was governed as a colony of the British state. Technically, under the Act of Union, however, Ireland was incorporated into the United Kingdom and ceased legally and politically to be a separate and colonized nation. Even so, some of the vestiges of colonialism remained in place under the Act of Union. The Lord Lieutenant, for instance, had been responsible for managing the Irish parliament on behalf of the British government before the Act of Union, and after 1801 the position of viceroy was retained, apparently for security reasons. However, in other respects, Ireland was integrated into the wider United Kingdom polity not least by the presence of Irish MPs at Westminster, and the participation of many Irish men and women in British imperial endeavours elsewhere in the world.[13] Broadly speaking, then, Ireland under the Union was a newly post-colonial state which had become an integral part of the United Kingdom. Yet, some elements of colonial rule were retained primarily in order to uphold law and order in Ireland, and the colonial perception of Irish-born Catholics as second-class (and potentially disloyal) citizens appears to have persisted well into the nineteenth century, and beyond. For these reasons, it seems sensible to consider Ireland under the Act of Union as a hybrid colonial and post-colonial state.[14]

S. B. Cook, in his discussion of the affinities between legislation introduced in Ireland and in British India, argues that Ireland's political integration into the United Kingdom under the terms of the Act of Union was:

imperfect at best. Ireland was frequently subject to legislation that was not applied anywhere else in the British Isles . . . At the executive level Ireland retained (unlike Scotland or Wales) a Civil Service and policy administration that was wholly separate from that of England's. As a result, the actual head of the Irish bureaucracy was a

---

[12] Ibid.
[13] See Stephen Howe, *Ireland and Empire: Colonial Legacies in Irish History and Culture* (Oxford, 2000), 230–1.   [14] Ibid. 37.

minister of the crown. Like India, the British administration in Ireland was headed by a viceroy (Lord Lieutenant)... More substantively, the nineteenth century Irish administration was neither structured like nor operated along the lines of its English counterpart.[15]

Consequently, Ireland under the Union was neither a straightforward part of the United Kingdom nor a conventional colony and instead occupied a curious middle place between worlds:

Even though Ireland was not actually considered by policy-makers a colony in its own right, the well-formed habit of analogy and exchange suggests a complicated view by contemporaries of a land whose integration into the rest of the United Kingdom was imperfect and which in some ways occupied what may be described as an anomalous intermediary relationship between Britain and its empire.[16]

The evidence presented in this book corroborates this view that Ireland under the Union was both a colony and a fully integrated part of the United Kingdom, and this context explains the stasis of the Irish establishment during the period under review. If Ireland under the Union had been fully integrated into the United Kingdom, we would expect recruiting practices to the senior positions in the Civil Service and to the Royal Irish Constabulary to be the same as they were in Britain. However, after 1870, senior civil servants in Britain were generally recruited from within the Civil Service by open competition to class I clerkships, whereas in Ireland they were usually appointed from outside the Civil Service by senior officials.[17] Similarly, the senior officers in police forces throughout Britain were recruited from the ranks rather than being recruited through a cadet system outside the force as in Ireland. In both cases, arguments were advanced by the government to explain why those in senior positions were not recruited from the ranks but—as Chapters 2 and 3 demonstrate—these justifications do not stand up to interrogation. By the beginning of the twentieth century, there were a very large number of university-educated Catholics capable of taking up senior positions in the Irish Civil Service, and not a dearth of qualified Catholics as Balfour suggested. Moreover, there were a large number of Head Constables in the Royal Irish Constabulary who were capable of carrying out the duties of police Inspectors, as indeed many of them already were doing. Furthermore, the assertion that the senior officers needed to be men of intellectual distinction who had received a superior education falls short when we consider the fact that most police officers were rather ordinary men (in terms of their intellectual and educational achievements) from the British and Irish Protestant middle classes who tended to leave the serious work of policing to their (predominantly

---

[15] S. B. Cook, *Imperial Affinities: Nineteenth Century Analogies and Exchanges between India and Ireland* (London, 1993), 18–19.   [16] Ibid 136.
[17] R. K. Kelsall, *Higher Civil Servants in Britain: From 1870 to the Present Day* (London, 1955; repr. 1998), 13, 20.

Catholic) Head Constables. The real reason why there were so few Catholics at the top of the Civil Service and the police force was because the British state viewed Irish-born Catholics from non-landed backgrounds as potentially disloyal, and therefore not to be trusted to uphold law and order if there was a rebellion in Ireland.

This concern applied particularly to the Royal Irish Constabulary, for obvious reasons; and the concern became more acute after the Land War which had threatened to become a full-scale rebellion in Ireland. For this reason, there were even fewer Catholics in leading positions in the police force than in the Civil Service, and this also explains why the senior officers of the Royal Irish Constabulary suffered an 'orange-ing' or 'reverse-greening' between 1881 and 1911. Of course, the British state's perception of Irish-born Catholics as second-class citizens and of dubious loyalty constituted an essentially colonial view of the native Irish. After all, if Catholic Ireland was to be integrated into the United Kingdom the first step would be to extend full citizenship rights and respect to individual Catholic Irish men and women. The British state's neurosis that many Irish Catholics might be about to commit a terrorist act or—if in a position of authority—mutiny, was a major obstacle to assimilation and would become a catalyst for revolution.[18] As Chapters 2, 3, and 5 have demonstrated, some Irish-born Catholics were acceptable to the British state and the business elite, but full citizenship appears to have been granted only to those Catholics who were loyal, landed, and 'loaded'.

The decline of landlordism in Ireland can also be usefully considered in this complex colonial context. Historians have argued that the decline of landlord power in Ireland was part of a broader process whereby landowners throughout Britain and Europe also lost power from the 1880s onwards. This decline was largely caused by the collapse of the agricultural base of the European economy due to the arrival of much cheaper foreign goods and produce (especially grain and chilled meat) from the Americas and the Antipodes. Agricultural incomes therefore declined and this had severe consequences for the economic power of the landowning class throughout Europe.[19] At the same time, the members of the new middle class who were making their fortunes in business and industry became the wealthiest and most economically powerful section of European society. The number of millionaire landlords in

---

[18] This preoccupation with the loyalty of Catholics permeated the professions. Joseph Mary Plunkett's uncle, Jack Cranny, was a Fellow of the Royal College of Surgeons who was denied the position of Vice President because while a student at Trinity College Dublin years before he had treated some Fenian prisoners in Mountjoy jail after the uprising of 1867. Honor O Brolchain (ed.), *All in the Blood: A Memoir of the Plunkett Family, the 1916 Rising and the War of Independence by Geraldine Plunkett Dillon* (Dublin, 2006), 76.

[19] David Cannadine, *The Decline and Fall of the British Aristocracy* (New Haven, Conn. and London, 1990), 26.

Britain, for instance, declined from 118 in 1858–79 to thirty-three in 1900–19, while the number of non-landed millionaires in the probate returns increased from twenty-seven in 1860–79 to 101 in 1900–19.[20] The development of industry and the impoverishment of the agricultural economy also increased social tension, and led to the extension of the franchise (with the third Reform Act of 1884–5) which further reduced the political power of the British landlord class.

In Britain, however, the decline of landlord influence was much more gradual than it was in Ireland. In terms of political influence, landlords in Britain retained power for a much longer period than their counterparts in Ireland. As late as 1900, 15.5 per cent of members of the House of Commons represented landed interests whereas in Ireland only 10 per cent of Unionists MPs and 6 per cent of Home Rule MPs were landowners by 1911.[21] In terms of local political power, landlord influence in Ireland was almost completely destroyed by the 1898 local government act which created new democratically elected county councils. This was particularly the case in the three southern provinces of Connacht, Munster, and Leinster where nationalists won 456 (92 per cent) of the available positions on county councils and Unionists won only thirty-nine (8 per cent).[22] Given that landowners were much more likely to be Unionists than nationalists, this suggests that landlord influence in local government in Ireland virtually ceased after 1898. In England, on the other hand, the old landed elite remained the largest single element on the new county councils created in 1888, and even in Scotland (where county councils were introduced in 1889) two-thirds of the convenors of county councils were local landowners in 1892. Only in Wales was the picture similar to that in Ireland where landowner influence declined markedly in all areas except that of Anglicized Brecon.[23]

The Irish experience departs most markedly from the pattern elsewhere in Britain, however, when we consider the decline of economic power and the sale of estates. Whereas in Ireland, most tenanted land had been sold by the landlord to the tenant by 1914 as a result of state intervention, in Britain the sale of estates took place by private sale over a much longer period between the 1890s and the 1930s. In part, the more interventionist response by the British state in Ireland was because the level of landlord–tenant conflict was much more acute and extensive in Ireland than it was in Britain. While there may have been tensions and conflicts between landlord and tenant in Scotland, Wales, and England during the 1880s, there was nothing to compare with the Land War of 1879–81, and for this reason land reform in Britain was a much more minor affair than it was in Ireland.[24] Admittedly, the Crofters Act of 1886 gave the

---

[20] Harold Perkin, *The Rise of Professional Society: England since 1880* (London, 1989), 64.
[21] Rush, 'The Members of Parliament', 97.   [22] Cannadine, *Decline and Fall*, 173.
[23] Ibid. 157–62.   [24] Ibid. 28.

highlanders in Scotland a fair rent but no land reform was passed in Wales and only very minor reforms in England.[25]

Systematic state-controlled rent regulation and land purchase were not introduced in England, Scotland, or Wales. This was because the landlord class in Britain had—to some extent—established a hegemonic relationship over their tenants, and landlord–tenant conflict was moderated by customary vertical ties of local affection. Most of the great landowners in Ireland in 1881, on the other hand, were the descendants of the colonizing planters of the seventeenth century (with a few exceptions who were either recent purchasers or descendants of the Gaelic chieftains or of the Anglo-Normans), and they appear to have run their estates exclusively for profit and without much consideration for their tenants. This is most evident in the fact that Irish landlords did not reinvest in their estates to the same extent as their counterparts in Britain, leading even one of the most sympathetic commentators on Irish landlordism to claim that they did not behave like a real aristocracy.[26] The failure of the Irish landlord class to naturalize their rule in Ireland was, in part, because they were largely the descendants of a colonizing landowner class who viewed their Catholic tenants as second-class citizens who were not deserving of reinvestment in their tenancies or fair treatment.[27] The complex in-between status of Ireland as both old British colony and newly integrated component of the kingdom thus influenced the experience of the Irish administration, the Royal Irish Constabulary, and the landlord class during the period under review; and these colonial and post-colonial contexts enable us to understand some of the dynamics of change, and of stasis, displayed by the Irish establishment between 1879 and 1914.

The second key factor that influenced the static nature and composition of the Irish establishment between 1879 and 1914 is that there was a lag between the political and social emancipation of Irish Catholics. John J. Horgan, the Cork Home Ruler and cultural nationalist, perceptively observed that: 'O'Connell had achieved the political emancipation of the Irish Catholics at the commencement of the nineteenth century but even in 1900 we were still, at least to some extent, socially unemancipated. In commerce and official life the Protestant ascendancy still preserved its prestige, power and position.'[28] We might have expected the state's apparent willingness to appoint Catholics to senior positions in the administration to influence the way in which Catholics were viewed in the society as a whole, and to lead to a gradual 'greening' of the professions and of business. However, there was only a very slight greening

---

[25] Ibid. 67–8.

[26] W. E. Vaughan, *Landlords and Tenants in Mid-Victorian Ireland* (Oxford, 1994), 221.

[27] Cannadine attributes the decline of landed influence in Ireland, Scotland, and Wales to 'the thin soil, the adverse climate, and the peasant mentality, about which owners themselves could do nothing', and he is surely wrong to absolve the Irish landlords from any responsibility for their own decline (*Decline and Fall*, 62).

[28] John J. Horgan, *Parnell to Pearse: Some Recollections and Reflections* (Dublin, 1948), 110–11.

of the business elite and the evidence that is available about the composition of the professions suggests that Catholics were only very gradually being recruited. As Horgan suggested, this was—in part—because the perception that Catholics were second-class citizens—enshrined in the penal laws—did not disappear from Irish society overnight after Catholic emancipation was introduced in 1829. The directors of the top businesses, the members of professional bodies and associations, and the heads of Civil Service departments—all of whom were the gatekeepers of their various elite groups—were largely Protestant, and they probably continued to view Catholics in a negative light for a long time after Catholic emancipation. Some of the members of the Protestant middle class even boasted of their roots in the colonization of Ireland in the seventeenth century. Thomas Sinclair, the managing director of Kingan and Co., told a Liberal Unionist meeting at Carlisle in 1888 that Ulster loyalists were: 'largely the descendants of men whom your forefathers two or three centuries ago sent over to Ireland to plant and develop your idea of progress, and law, and material prosperity.'[29]

Moreover, in order to be recruited to these sections of the elite the individual needed to be a member of elite social circles and gentlemen's clubs in London, Dublin, and Belfast and because there were fewer Catholics in these social circles, there was less Catholic recruitment to these elite groups. This was caused not by a deliberate policy of discrimination against Catholics but by incidental discrimination based on the fact that the kinship, friendship, and social networks from which members of these elite groups were recruited were and had been dominated by Protestants for generations. The process by which Catholics joined these social networks was—necessarily—a slow one.

The third factor that explains the largely unchanging nature of the Irish establishment is the fact that this period witnessed the emergence of a new exclusively Protestant upper class in Ireland. In Victorian Britain, one of the methods adopted by the old landed elite to retain power was to absorb the new rising business and professional classes into a new upper class. Beatrice Webb, the social reformer and daughter of a railway magnate in London, explained how the new upper class broadened itself out to include businessmen, professions, and senior civil servants during this period:

deep down in the unconscious herd instinct of the British governing class there *was* a test of fitness for membership of this most gigantic of social clubs [London society], but a test which was seldom recognized by those who applied it, still less by those to whom it was applied, *the possession of some form of power over people*. The most obvious form of power, and the most easily measurable, was the power of wealth.[30]

---

[29] Philip Ollerenshaw, 'Businessmen and the Development of Ulster Unionism, 1886–1921', *Journal of Imperial and Commonwealth History*, 28 (Jan. 2000), 41.
[30] Quot. Perkin, *Rise of Professional Society*, 65.

Nora Robertson captured a similar shift in the social hierarchy of early twentieth-century Ireland when she observed that: 'Although breeding was essential it still had to be buttressed by money.'[31]

Indeed, a similar process to that in Britain was taking place in Ireland where landed and business interests joined together to form a new Irish upper class. Prominent businessmen bought into land and—perhaps more important-ly—Irish landlords were strongly represented on the boards of directors of the biggest businesses in Ireland. Almost half of the directors of the Irish business elite in both 1883 (42 per cent) and 1911 (40 per cent) were either landowners or had been born into landed families. This alliance between new and old wealth was consolidated by the increased number of businessmen who joined the Kildare Street Club during the first decade of the twentieth century: by 1914, McDowell estimates that eighty members of the club were drawn from the directorates of the banks, railways, breweries, and distilleries.[32] The lines between landed wealth and commercial or industrial wealth were further blurred when landowners began to invest the capital they gained from the sale of their estates in equities, stocks, bonds, and railway shares.[33] The Kildare Street Club was one of the forums where this new upper class met; and it was here that landlords, businessmen, civil servants, army and police officers, professionals, and Church of Ireland bishops gathered together.[34] Undoubtedly this created a new upper-class consciousness or identity among the members of these social groups, most of whom were Protestants.[35]

This new upper class was also held together by private dinners and other social interactions. W. R. Le Fanu, the son of a Church of Ireland clergyman, and an engineer on the Great Southern and Western Railway (and a future Commissioner of Public Works) was a dining companion of Lord Bessborough, one of the great Irish landowners, during the 1860s.[36] Senior civil servants would also have mixed regularly with the business elite in a professional role: John Thomas Mulqueen, for instance, was the Collector of Customs and Excise and in that capacity he became 'well known . . . to the members of the brewing, distilling and allied trades'.[37] In Britain the new alliance of land, business, and the professions was an attempt by the old landed elite to retain power by absorbing those middle-class

---

[31] Nora Robertson, *Crowned Harp: Memories of the Last Years of the Crown in Ireland* (Dublin, 1960), 74.

[32] R. B. McDowell, *Land and Learning: Two Irish Clubs* (Dublin, 1993), 84–9.

[33] Cannadine, *Decline and Fall*, 134.

[34] Of the elite groups under review, 35% of the great landowners in 1881 were members of the Kildare Street Club as were 22% of the businessmen, 25% of the senior civil servants, and 8% of the Church of Ireland bishops.

[35] However, some members of the Protestant business elite had connections with influential figures in the Catholic church: Sir Ralph Cusack, director of the Midland Great Western Railway, for instance, was the Nun of Kenmare's cousin (*Irish Times*, 4 Mar. 1910).

[36] William Richard Le Fanu, *Seventy Years of Irish Life* (London, 1893), 179, 183, 209, 210.

[37] *Irish Times*, 4 Feb. 1933.

elements that threatened to topple it. In Ireland, however, the landowners (and former landowners) formed an alliance only with the Protestant middle class and excluded the rising Catholic middle class, and this probably cost it power.

Paradoxically, the formation of this new Protestant upper class was an inevitable consequence of the 'greening' policy. The policy of 'greening' was doomed to fail because it could not be effective without creating the disaffection of Irish Protestants while simultaneous attempts at retaining the support of Irish Protestants greatly restrained the 'greening' impulse. By the beginning of the twentieth century, the British state was oscillating wildly between attempting to win the support of the Catholic middle class, on the one hand, and trying to placate the Protestant middle class on the other. The Irish middle class was thus split in two by the sectarian policies of the British state; neither Protestant nor Catholic felt that they were getting what they wanted; many disaffected Protestants became Unionists while equally disaffected Catholics became nationalists; and the intensifying enmity between them was such that sectarian war loomed ominously on the horizon. For the British state to have retained its power in Ireland it would have had to encourage the development of a state that was fair to both Protestant and Catholic communities and that facilitated the evolution of a new and plural Irish identity. By the early nineteenth century, the opportunity to create such a state of affairs had already been missed—arguably in the failure to introduce Catholic emancipation alongside the Act of Union—but also because sectarian divisions had already been put in place by British colonization in the early modern period. Even if the British state had wanted to transform ethnic relationships in early nineteenth-century Ireland, it would have taken a lot more than the technical niceties of political integration to do so.[38] And by the end of the nineteenth century, as we have seen, attempts to transform the composition of the Irish establishment had done little to alter the impression of Protestant domination.

III

As outlined in the introduction, the theoretical literature on elites can be broken down into two main schools of thought: that of the classical elite theorists, and that of the democratic elite theorists. Broadly speaking, the classical theorists characterize the elite as all-powerful, 'closed', homogenous, wealthy, and not representative of the society which it dominates. For the democratic

[38] Much has been made of the tendency of Irish revisionist historians to demonize past nationalist movements as a response to the barbarism of the Provisional IRA during the 'troubles' of 1968–98. However, the terrorism practised by the British state in Northern Ireland during the same period has not yet inspired a rigorous interrogation of the—sometimes malevolent—role of the British state in Ireland under the Union (1801–1921).

elite theorists, on the other hand, the composition of the elite is diverse, recruitment is open, and absolute power is restricted by various constraining factors. The evidence presented in this book suggests that the experience of the Irish establishment fits more with the classical elite model than it does with the democratic elite model. The Irish establishment was largely 'closed' to access from all sections of Irish society. Indeed, recruiting to the establishment was generally by personal nomination and through membership of influential social circles rather than through open competition or other meritocratic avenues. Even where meritocratic recruitment strategies were adopted, a second- or third-level education was so expensive as to exclude large sections of Irish society from access to the establishment. Most of the members of the establishment were drawn from wealthy and privileged backgrounds, and there were comparatively few (if any) representatives of the lower social classes.

Admittedly, the Irish establishment does conform—in some respects—to the democratic elite model. The Irish establishment was not homogenous, containing as it did some representatives of marginal ethnic groups and social classes. Moreover, the establishment was not all-powerful or unanimous in its operation. Indeed, one section of the establishment—the state—was responsible for expropriating the economic power of another—the Irish landlord class. Furthermore, the Irish political elite was democratically elected, and these individuals at least were accountable to the electorate, and limited in what they could do by the power of the electorate at periodic general elections. The Irish MPs were also in a position to influence the behaviour of the state at critical points, and both Nationalists and Unionists did so to great effect. Even the state—the leading figures of which were democratically elected (although by the British rather than the Irish electorate)—did not possess unlimited power given their concern with legitimizing state power and winning the consent of the Irish people for British rule in Ireland. In general, the British state was not prepared to rule by coercion alone, and was usually keen to try and win consent for British rule in Ireland. In broad terms, however, the Irish establishment conforms most closely to the classical elite model of a 'closed', unrepresentative and privileged elite. Of course, the classical elite and democratic elite models are—to use Weber's term—ideal types, and suggest general patterns that can be compared across time and space, rather than being prescriptive indicators of the nature of elites in reality.

The classical elite theorists—and notably Gaetano Mosca—suggested that an elite that was largely 'closed' to the educated elements in the society (that had the ability and qualifications necessary to take up positions of power within the elite) would generate political opposition to itself.[39] Given that the Irish establishment fits the general pattern outlined by Mosca, the final section of this conclusion will consider the implications of the data presented in this study to our understanding of the origins and causes of the Irish revolution of 1916–23.

[39] Gaetano Mosca quot. Putnam, *The Comparative Study of Political Elites*, 193.

Some educated young Catholics who felt that their upward social mobility was restricted by discriminatory recruitment practices do appear to have resorted to revolutionary strategies to get what they wanted. Garvin has examined the social composition of the leadership of the republican movement in Ireland between 1913 and 1922 and found that the vast majority of them were young, well-educated, professional men.[40] It is possible that the educated Catholics who were graduating from Irish universities and secondary schools from the 1890s onwards, and who were prevented from joining the professions or the elite of the Irish Civil Service, instead became involved in the separatist politics of Sinn Fein. By doing so, they hoped to force a transfer of power from British to Irish rule, and thereby to benefit from enhanced career opportunities in an independent Irish state. The young educated Catholic professionals and clerks who joined Sinn Fein, then, appear to have viewed a nationalist revolution as a route to upward social mobility. This would explain why so many junior members of staff in the Post Office were Sinn Feiners in 1914, as Matthew Nathan (Under Secretary for Ireland, 1914–16) observed to Charles Hobhouse (Postmaster General, 1914–15) in December 1914: 'for some reason which I am unable to fathom a large proportion of the people treasonable to England (patriotic to Ireland, they would put it) are to be found in the lower ranks of the Government service and in this respect the Post Office has a bad prominence.'[41] William O'Malley also observed that there were a high proportion of Sinn Feiners who were either the sons of members of the Irish Civil Service or graduates of the National University of Ireland.[42] It is possible that the existence of a glass ceiling for Catholics in the Irish Civil Service, among the officers of the Royal Irish Constabulary, in the business world, and in the professions provided them with a powerful motive for revolution.[43]

John Hutchinson has made the argument that blocked mobility in the Irish elite was one of the major causes of the Irish Revolution. The blocked mobility hypothesis originates in Weber's explanation of community formation by the competition for resources of wealth, power, and prestige.[44] According to Hutchinson, the state began to educate Irish Catholics in the nineteenth century so that they could administrate the expanding British state in Ireland and beyond.[45] However, there was overproduction by the state of qualified personnel,

---

[40] Tom Garvin, *Nationalist Revolutionaries in Ireland, 1858–1928* (Oxford, 1987), 48–56.

[41] Matthew Nathan to Charlie Hobhouse, 6 Dec. 1914, Bodleian Library MS Nathan 462, fo. 214ʳ.   [42] William O'Malley, *Glancing Back* (London, 1933), 134, 272.

[43] About 400 officials in the Irish Civil Service (about 1.5% of the total of 26,000 officials) were dismissed for disloyal political activities between 1916 and 1921, the highest-ranking of whom was J. J. MacElligott, a first-division clerk in the Chief Secretary's Office. See M. F. Gallagher, 'The Fateful Week', *Administration*, 14/2 (Summer 1966); Lawrence McBride, *The Greening of Dublin Castle: The Transformation of Bureaucratic and Judicial Personnel in Ireland, 1892–1922* (Washington, DC, 1991), 218–19.

[44] John Hutchinson, *The Dynamics of Cultural Nationalism: The Gaelic Revival and the Creation of the Irish Nation State* (London, 1987), 266.   [45] Ibid. 258–9.

and this led to intense competition for positions in the state administration and in the professions. In order to safeguard their position, the dominant groups in Irish society (notably the British state and the Irish Protestant middle class) excluded new arrivals through a policy of ethnic favouritism.[46] A similar process took place in nineteenth-century British India where the top jobs were reserved for British administrators much to the resentment of qualified Indians from the 1880s onwards.[47] In Ireland, ethnic discrimination created a sense of collective resentment among what Hutchinson describes as the Catholic intelligentsia against the British state in Ireland.[48] As a result, these educated Catholics became cultural nationalists and ultimately Sinn Feiners who were committed to destroying the British state in Ireland and creating a new state where there would be increased opportunities for social mobility.

Senia Paseta, on the other hand, suggests that the university-educated Catholics probably did not experience blocked social mobility and that they tended to become Home Rulers rather than Sinn Feiners. Her work builds on that of Hutchinson but argues instead that the university-educated Catholic elite in the pre-War period were a Home Rule elite in waiting.[49] However, this Catholic-university-educated elite or 'lost generation of leaders'—most of whom were (according to Paseta) Home Rulers—lost power to the rising republican elite that emerged after the 'aberration' of the Easter Rising of 1916:[50] 'Salient issues such as the university question, the growth in women's movements, the expansion of the professions, and even perennial Home Rule, show the Rising of 1916 to be an aberrant rather than logical extension of the social and political battles waged in early twentieth-century Ireland.'[51]

Although she does not explicitly engage with the argument made in Hutchinson's book, Paseta does construct an argument that challenges his blocked mobility hypothesis. According to Paseta, if there was a 'crisis of vocation' among the university elite, it was caused by: 'A perception . . . that Protestants dominated many fields rather than a dearth of employment opportunities.'[52] This 'perception' led university-educated Catholics to establish professional associations—like the Catholic Association—to assist them in 'colonizing' Anglo-Irish institutions like the business elite and the professions. However, Paseta does

---

[46] Ibid. 266.   [47] Ibid. 298, n. 16.

[48] Ibid. 268, 269. According to Hutchinson, the Catholic intelligentsia included both university-educated Catholics from upper-middle-class backgrounds and Catholics who had received only a secondary education or a teaching or Civil Service training and who were usually from small farm, trading, or shopkeeping backgrounds.

[49] Paseta clearly takes her cue from Hutchinson's point that: 'By the late 1890s, however, there were indications of a growing crisis of vocation among the young Catholic intelligentsia, especially the university elite who might expect to become the new governing class, should Home Rule eventuate' (ibid. 166). Paseta is, however, more narrowly concerned with university-educated Catholics (*Before the Revolution*, 1).   [50] Paseta, *Before the Revolution*, 3.

[51] Ibid. 148.

[52] Ibid. 95. Confusingly, Paseta sometimes appears to agree that there was overcrowding in the professions (pp. 82, 96) and on other occasions suggests that this was not the case (p. 95).

not suggest that the perception of blocked social mobility led young Catholic university-educated professionals to become separatist revolutionaries. Broadly speaking, Paseta suggests that the university-educated elite were Home Rulers who perceived that there were obstructions to their upward social mobility, and formed professional associations to assist their career advancement. However, this Home Rule elite in waiting were eventually eclipsed by the new Sinn Fein elite who emerged after the Easter Rising and took the reins of power in independent Ireland.

Hutchinson and Paseta, then, disagree on one fundamental point. Hutchinson argues that the reality of blocked mobility converted the very university-educated elite with which Paseta is concerned into the new Sinn Fein elite of 1916–21. Paseta, on the other hand, suggests that there was a perception of blocked social mobility that encouraged the formation of professional associations but that the university-educated elite remained Home Rulers, and that they were therefore swept away by a new republican elite after 1916. If Hutchinson is right, the rise of Sinn Fein was actually spearheaded by the university-educated elite, rather than '1916' signifying the end of the political road for them. However, neither Paseta nor Hutchinson offer systematic evidence to demonstrate that blocked social mobility—perceived or real—tended to convert educated young Catholics into Home Rulers or Sinn Feiners. Hutchinson does, however, explain that the educated Catholic middle class were inclined to become cultural nationalists (and later Sinn Feiners) because they were excluded from the Irish Parliamentary Party which—he argues—was ageing, oligarchical, preoccupied with rural issues, and therefore not attractive to the generally urban, educated Catholic middle class. Impressionistic evidence suggests that Hutchinson may be correct to assert that the Catholic intelligentsia tended to become Sinn Feiners rather than Home Rulers. Kevin O'Shiel, who was a Sinn Feiner, noted that the way to the top of the Royal Irish Constabulary for Catholics was to become Protestant, and his perception of this block on Catholic social mobility played a part in converting him to republicanism.[53]

Indeed, it is likely that most young educated Catholics at the beginning of the twentieth century were all too aware of the discrimination that they would encounter in the Civil Service, the professions, and the police force. Patrick Shea, whose father was a sergeant in the Royal Irish Constabulary, and who later became a senior civil servant in Northern Ireland, recalled that:

Before 1920, the Catholic boy not of wealthy parents, felt, and indeed was, at a disadvantage compared with the Protestant. His educational opportunities were more

---

[53] Quot. Arthur Mitchell, *Revolutionary Government in Ireland: Dáil Éireann, 1919–1922* (Dublin, 1995), 68. O'Shiel had apparently not experienced blocked social mobility himself—he was a barrister on the north-west circuit from 1913—but he may have shared the general perception that Catholic social mobility was often obstructed by discriminatory practices.

restricted, his employment prospects were at a lower level, he belonged to a community in which a substantial middle class comparable with the Protestant middle class could not have developed. He believed that the social disparity between Protestants and Catholics was the result of deliberate government policy. If he wished to escape from the social conditions of his parents he joined in the competition for a place as a trainee teacher, became a candidate for a minor post in the Civil Service, studied for the priesthood, emigrated or, after years of hard grafting, became the owner of a pub.[54]

It is also significant that the Irish Parliamentary Party worked very closely with Dublin Castle, and that it must have been widely perceived as being as much a part of the British state in Ireland as it was an alternative to it.[55] Members of the IPP took a pledge 'to accept no post of any kind under government', and it was assumed that this self-denying ordinance applied also to their not seeking position for their constituents either. But, as we have seen, most Home Rule MPs did use their influence to get jobs for their friends, families, associates, and constituents in the Irish Civil Service.[56] Indeed, Dublin Castle appears to have operated on the assumption that members of the Irish Party were integral to the recruiting process. Given the close relationship between the IPP and Dublin Castle it was clear that the IPP was part of the existing (and discriminatory) system which Sinn Fein was promising to destroy and replace with a new state in which there would be numerous employment opportunities. This perception tipped the balance for some young nationalists and encouraged them to throw in their lot with the Sinn Feiners rather than the Home Rulers.

The likelihood, however, is that Catholic university students were a diverse group during the early years of the twentieth-century—some were Home Rulers, some were Sinn Feiners, and still others were Home Rulers who became Sinn Feiners—but most of them were united by being Irish nationalists of some kind. C. P. Curran, a student at University College Dublin at the turn of the century recalled that:

the student body . . . was neither cautious nor reticent. No discreet abstinence from politics was evident amongst them. They were eloquently divided between an orthodox majority, readers of the Home Rule Freeman's Journal, many of them sons of members of the Irish Parliamentary Party, and a small minority who read the insurgent United

---

[54] Patrick Shea, *Voices and the Sound of Drums: An Irish Autobiography* (Belfast, 1981), 193. Shea's account of Catholic experience 'before 1920' was written in 1972. Joe Devlin confirmed that the only business in which Catholics could prosper in Belfast under the Union was the drink trade (Hepburn, *Catholic Belfast and Nationalist Ireland,* 12).

[55] Redmond even went as far as to describe Joe Devlin as 'the real Chief Secretary' of Ireland during a speech at Utica, New York in 1910 (Hepburn, *Catholic Belfast and Nationalist Ireland,* 135).

[56] McConnel, 'The View from the Backbench: Irish Nationalist MPs and their Work, 1910–14', PhD thesis (Durham University, 2002), 156.

Irishman and preached the new doctrine of Arthur Griffith and William Rooney . . . The Gaelic League occupied a middle field with general respect.[57]

Curran also provides significant evidence that—far from being a lost generation of Home Rulers swept into oblivion by the storms of Easter 1916—some of the Redmondite students went on to take senior positions in the Irish Free State anyway. Curran himself became the first Chief Justice in the Irish Free State through his association with W.T. Cosgrave and his fellow University College Dublin student, Kevin O'Higgins; and Fitzgerald-Kenney, a Catholic landowner, became a Minister for Justice in independent Ireland.[58]

To return to the question posed at the beginning of this conclusion, it is clear that McAleese clearly overstated her point: the government of Ireland was not conducted only by public school-educated members of the Kildare Street Club, although they certainly played their part. However, Bew also overstated his case: the Irish establishment *was* largely dominated by British and Irish Protestants, drawn from the landed, business, and professional classes. A minority of Catholics had been allowed to join the Irish establishment but many others had been prevented from doing so. The Irish Revolution may have been partially directed against those Catholic Unionists and Home Rulers who had been assimilated into the Irish establishment. But the main target of the Irish Revolution was the British state in Ireland which had presided over a society that continued to regard Irish Catholics as second-class citizens and denied them access to the positions in society to which—by virtue of their qualifications and talents—they were entitled.[59] Mosca's contention, then, that a 'closed' elite that excludes the educated and qualified from the top positions in society will be toppled by revolution does appear to have some application to Ireland. The revolution in Ireland was a consequence of the structural inequalities in Irish society at the beginning of the twentieth century, and of the discontent that some sections of Irish society felt at that time.

IV

In James Joyce's short story 'The Dead', Gabriel Conroy and his wife Gretta attend his aunts' Christmas party at their house in Usher's Island in Dublin.[60]

[57] C. P. Curran, *Under the Receding Wave* (Dublin, 1970), 79.   [58] Ibid. 121, 137.
[59] There has recently been a great deal of debate about whether Irish nationalists of various kinds behaved in a sectarian manner during the Irish Revolution but most commentators have ignored the fact that if there was nationalist sectarianism then it was probably a response to the sectarianism practised by the British state in Ireland throughout the period of the Act of Union (1801–1921).
[60] The events described in 'The Dead' take place—presumably—during the first decade of the twentieth century.

After the dinner, Gabriel makes a speech to the gathered friends and family, and eulogizes the 'tradition of genuine warm-hearted courteous Irish hospitality' that his aunts have perpetuated with their lavish parties:

I feel more strongly with every recurring year that our country has no tradition which does it so much honour and which it should guard so jealously as that of its hospitality. It is a tradition that is unique as far as my experience goes (and I have visited not a few places abroad) among the modern nations. Some would say, perhaps, that with us it is rather a failing than anything to be boasted of. But granted even that, it is, to my mind, a princely failing, and one that I trust will long be cultivated among us.[61]

Before continuing, he remembers a conversation that he had had earlier in the evening with his fellow teacher and Royal University graduate, Molly Ivors. While dancing with her she told him that she had 'a crow to pluck' with him. She had discovered that he wrote a weekly literary column for the *Daily Express*, a Unionist newspaper, and teased him by calling him a 'West Briton'. She then rebuked him further by suggesting that he should spend more time in his own country, keeping in touch with his own language—rather than holidaying in Europe—causing him angrily to tell her: 'I'm sick of my own country, sick of it!' Although Molly had already left the party by the time he stood up to make his speech, Gabriel appears to address the next part of his speech to her:

A new generation is growing up in our midst, a generation actuated by new ideas and new principles. It is serious and enthusiastic, for these new ideas and its enthusiasm, even when it is misdirected, is, I believe, in the main sincere. But we are living in a sceptical and, if I may use the phrase, a thought-tormented age: and sometimes I fear that this new generation, educated or hypereducated as it is, will lack those qualities of humanity, of hospitality, of kindly humour which belonged to an older day.[62]

Finally, Gabriel toasts the hosts of the party, his aunts, Julia and Kate Morkan, and his niece, Mary Jane, all of whom were music teachers, as 'the Three Graces of the Dublin musical world', and drinks to 'their health, wealth, long life, happiness and prosperity'.

Gabriel Conroy and Molly Ivors appear to epitomize the two different varieties of middle-class Catholic that emerged at the beginning of the twentieth-century. Gabriel is probably a moderate Home Ruler, who appears bound to the old-world values of hospitality and neighbourliness, and is nostalgic for the halcyon days of the Irish establishment. Although his brother, Constantine, is a priest, his family are on good terms with their Protestant neighbours (Mr Browne who was 'of the other persuasion' attended the Misses Morkan's party), his father was part of the Dublin business world ('T. J. Conroy of the Port and Docks'), and his grandfather, Patrick Morkan, was sufficiently loyal to attend a military review in the Phoenix Park. Molly Ivors, on the other hand, represents the new generation of university-educated Catholics who rejected the old ways of the Irish

[61] James Joyce, 'The Dead', *Dubliners* (London, 2007 edn).   [62] Ibid.

establishment, and the 'West Briton' ways of the Catholics who had embraced British rule in Ireland. Instead, Molly embraced the culture of 'Irish Ireland': the Irish language, trips to the Aran islands, and a narrow chauvinistic Irish nationalism. Symbolically, Molly leaves the party early, 'telling the Morkans and the Conroys, 'I'm quite well able to take care of myself', before bidding them *"Beannacht libh"* . . . with a laugh'.

Gabriel might regard Molly and the new Catholic middle class as thought-tormented, hyper-educated, and lacking in humanity, but she appears to have looked back on him, and his fellow 'Castle Catholics', as shameful, outdated, and even laughable. Indeed, the increasingly powerful Catholic middle class at the beginning of the twentieth-century was presented with these two choices: that of accepting British rule in Ireland as Gabriel Conroy had apparently done or of supporting Irish nationalism, like Molly Ivors, in the hope of creating a new independent Irish state. The exclusions, prejudices, and snobbery of the old Irish establishment, and its refusal to accept Irish Catholics on equal terms, meant that most middle-class Catholics were forced to follow Molly Ivors and choose the latter course. This choice—taken collectively by large sections of the Catholic middle class—marked the end of the old Irish establishment which, as a consequence, lay buried beneath the cold ground of Ireland well before the time Patrick Pearse pulled on his boots and marched down Sackville street on Easter Monday in 1916.

APPENDIX

Methodology and Sources used to Compile the Biographical Data

This book is largely based on a study of almost 1,200 biographies of prominent men and women in Irish society between the end of the Land War (in 1881) and the eve of the Great War (in 1911). Censal dates were used as the points for snapshots of the composition of the Irish elite to enable the use of manuscript census returns (for 1901 and 1911) in the collection of data and also to facilitate the comparison of my data with the more general data on social structure contained in the census reports for 1881, 1891, 1901, and 1911. Initially, the project aimed to look at the composition of the elite at each of four flashpoints—1881, 1891, 1901, and 1911—but it became obvious early on in the project that an assessment of continuity and change between the earliest and latest dates was the most practicable and sensible way to proceed (because the processes of change and continuity in elite composition usually took place over longer periods than discrete decades).

However, the process of gathering and interpreting the data led to some changes being made to this methodology. Since the landowners of more than 10,000 acres were a very large group (of almost 300 individuals), and because the composition of this elite group was unlikely to have changed significantly between the late nineteenth and the early twentieth centuries, it was decided to examine the composition of this group in 1881 and to then examine a random sample of one in ten of their descendants in 1918 (for which date biographical data was easily available in the 1918 edition of *Walford's County Families*). The available evidence on civil servants was much more widely available for the 1891 cohort than that in 1881 (due to the availability of the relevant directories), and so the composition of the top members of the Irish Civil Service has been examined for 1891 and 1911. Because there were significant changes in the composition of the senior members of the Royal Irish Constabulary from decade to decade, Chapter 3 examines the membership of the top level of the police force in Ireland in 1881, 1891, 1901, and 1911. The Irish MPs have been examined at the two key dates of 1881 and 1911. The data on the membership of the boards of directors of the top Irish companies (defined as those with an issued capital of more than £200,000) were available only for 1883 and 1911 and so the composition of the business elite has been examined for these dates only. Finally, the Roman Catholic and Church of Ireland bishops have been examined in both 1881 and 1911, but since data on Presbyterian Moderators were harder to find (and the position was held by only one person annually), I decided to include a number of Moderators from the 1870s and 1880s in the earlier cohort and a number of Moderators in the first two decades of the twentieth century in the later cohort. Broadly speaking, each chapter examines the composition of the particular elite group at two key dates, and then considers what changes have occurred between these two dates, and finally attempts to explain any evidence of change or continuity. I will now discuss the sources used to compile the biographical data on each of the individuals examined in this study.

The names of most of the members of the Irish elite were first identified in *Thom's Official Directory* for the relevant year. The names of the landlords who owned estates of more than 10,000 acres were listed in *Thom's Official Directory* for 1881; the names of the senior civil servants were listed in the 1891 and 1911 editions of *Thom's*; the names of the senior police officers were listed in *Thom's* in 1881, 1891, 1901, and 1911; and the names of the Roman Catholic and Church of Ireland Bishops were also listed in *Thom's* in 1881 and 1911. The names of the Irish MPs, on the other hand, were listed in Brian Walker, *Parliamentary Election Results in Ireland, 1801–1922* (Dublin, 1978); the names of the directors of the top Irish businesses were identified in *Burdett's Official Intelligence for 1883* (London, 1883) and *The Stock Exchange Official Intelligence for 1911* (London, 1911); and the names of Presbyterian Moderators were identified in Alan Megahey, *The Irish Protestant Churches in the Twentieth Century* (Basingstoke, 2000).

Once the list of names of members of the elite was completed I then searched for all of these individuals in a number of directories including the *Oxford Dictionary of National Biography* (online, 2004), *Who Was Who* (1897–1998), *Thom's Irish Who's Who* (Dublin, 1922), E. M. Cosgrave, *Dublin and County Dublin in the Twentieth century: Contemporary Biographies* (Brighton and London, 1908), R. M. Young, *Belfast and the Province of Ulster in the Twentieth Century* (Brighton and London, 1909), R. J. Hodges, *Cork and County Cork in the Twentieth Century* (Brighton and London, 1911), John Bateman, *Great Landowners of Great Britain and Ireland* (1883, 4th edn, Leicester, 1971), *Return of Owners of Land of One Acre and Upwards* (Dublin, 1876), Henry Boylan, *A Dictionary of Irish biography* (Dublin, 1978), G. D. Burtchaell, *Alumni Dublinenses* (London, 1924), Joseph Foster (ed.), *Alumni Oxonienses* (London, 1887–8), John Venn and J. A. Venn, *Alumni Cantabrigienses* (Cambridge, 1922–54), and *Walford's County Families* (1879, 1898, and 1918).

Using this wide range of sources I was able to compile a good deal of general information about the lives of each of the individuals examined in this study. However, I then examined more specific sources which contained information about particular elite groups. For members of parliament, I examined Michael Stenton and Stephen Lee's *Who's Who of British Members of Parliament, 1832–1885* (Brighton, 1976) and *Who's Who of British Members of Parliament, 1886–1918* (Brighton, 1978). I also found obituaries for most of the Irish MPs in provincial Irish newspapers and in the *Irish Times*, the *Belfast Newsletter*, and the *Freeman's Journal*. For businessmen, I used David J. Jeremy's *Dictionary of Business Biography: A Biographical Dictionary of Business Leaders Active in Britain in the Period 1860–1980* (London, 1984–6) and also his *Dictionary of Twentieth-century British Business Leaders* (London, 1994). For Irish police officers I made use of the Royal Irish Constabulary Officers' Register held at the National Archives at Kew and Jim Herlihy's *Royal Irish Constabulary Officers: A Biographical Dictionary and Genealogical Guide, 1816–1922* (Dublin, 2005). On the Irish civil servants, Lawrence McBride gave me access to his copies of the obituaries of senior members of the Irish administration that he had found in the *Irish Times*, *The Times*, and the *Belfast Newsletter* during his research for *The Greening of Dublin Castle* in the mid-1970s. Further biographical information on them was also obtained in the *Royal Commission on the Civil Service* (1913), and in the various parliamentary papers on recruiting to the Irish Civil Service. On the Catholic bishops, Bernard J. Canning's *Bishops of Ireland, 1870–1987* (Ballyshannon, 1987) was extremely useful. A valuable source for identifying Catholics who were members of the Irish elite is a letter to Monsignor Persico signed by all the prominent Irish Catholics and published in *The Times* on 25 April 1889. On the Presbyterian Moderators, the *Fasti of the General Assembly of the Presbyterian Church, 1871–1890* (Belfast, 1987) was a valuable source. For all of the elite groups under review I have also read the extensive secondary literature on them (which includes a large number of biographies which are cited in the footnotes) and in this way I found numerous further pieces of biographical information that I then added to the database.

One of the central questions of this book has been to investigate the extent to which there was a 'greening' of the Irish elite between 1881 and 1911 and so the identification of each individual's religious persuasion has been of vital importance. However, the vast majority of directories, dictionaries, and obituaries do not provide information on the religious persuasion of the individual (in some cases, however, this information is provided). Given the absence of manuscript census returns for 1881 and 1891 (this material was burned in the Four Courts during the Irish Civil War in 1922), and the great difficulty in finding baptismal and marriage records (not all of which are extant) that would confirm an individual's religious affiliation, I have had to deduce each individual's religion from a very wide range of sources and information. The main strategy that I have used to determine the religious outlook of an individual is his or her secondary education. I have presumed—unless there is evidence to the contrary—that individuals who attended Protestant secondary schools were Protestant and that individuals who attended Catholic secondary schools were Catholic. While it is undoubtedly true that there were some exceptions to this general rule, broadly speaking this is a reliable method for deducing religious background. It is also worth emphasizing that where there were exceptions to this rule, they were usually pointed out in the kinds of sources that I have been investigating in my research for this book (obituaries, directories, and so on). The *Dictionary of National Biography* entry for Lord Thomas O'Hagan, Lord Chancellor of Ireland in 1881, for instance, explains that while he was a student at the Royal Belfast Academical Institution in the 1820s he was the only Catholic pupil there at that time. I have also presumed—in the absence of contrary evidence—that individuals who attended Trinity College Dublin were generally Episcopalian. Flanagan has demonstrated that about 80 per cent of the annual intake of students at the University of Dublin were Episcopalian, between 7 per cent and 9 per cent were Catholic, and between 3 per cent and 6 per cent were Presbyterian, and so the vast majority of students who attended the university were Episcopalians.[1] In addition, I have searched for every person included in my database in the *Alumni Dublinenses* and these listings generally indicate if a student at Dublin university was Catholic. In cases where I have been unable to ascertain an individual's religion and I have found that they attended Trinity College Dublin, I have assumed—when there was no other evidence available to the contrary—that they were Episcopalians. Of course, a very significant number of Catholics did attend Trinity College Dublin and I have been able to identify them

---

[1] Kieran Flanagan, 'The Rise and Fall of the Celtic Ineligible: Competitive Examinations for the Irish and Indian Civil Services in Relation to the Educational and Occupational Structure of Ireland, 1853–1921', DPhil (University of Sussex, 1978), 150.

from other information contained in their biographies as well as from the *Alumni Dublinenses*.

In cases where it was obvious that an individual was Protestant, there was then the further question of deciding what kind of Protestant they were. In the absence of contradictory evidence, I have presumed that individuals who attended the top English Protestant public schools (Eton, Rugby, Harrow, Charterhouse, Westminster, Marlborough, Radley, Bradfield, and so on), Oxbridge, and Trinity College Dublin were Episcopalian. This assumption is supported by the general data on attendance at these schools and universities in the nineteenth century which suggest that very few Presbyterians or Dissenters attended them. It is more difficult to identify if the individuals who attended Irish Protestant schools were Episcopalian, Presbyterian, or Nonconformists. Most Irish Protestant secondary schools were Episcopalian but some Presbyterians were educated at them, and—by the same token—some Episcopalians attended Presbyterian schools like the Royal Belfast Academical Institute. In cases where I have been unable to prove that an individual was a Presbyterian or a Dissenter through a systematic search for other available evidence about them I have presumed that they were Episcopalian (because the proportion of Irish Protestants who were Episcopalian was higher than that which was Presbyterian or Dissenter). I think that it is possible—given these problems with the data—that I slightly exaggerate the importance of Episcopalians and underplay the importance of Presbyterians and Nonconformists in the Irish elite.

In cases where the individual did not attend a secondary school or university or where that information is not available, I have investigated their wider family background (including that of the family into which they married) and if I have found evidence that a member of their family was Protestant or Catholic, then I have presumed that the individual shared this religious affiliation. There are two obvious problems with this approach. First, that some individuals experienced religious conversion during their lives. Among the Irish elite under review, William Edward Forster (Irish Chief Secretary in 1881), for instance, converted from Quakerism to Anglicanism and Joseph Gillis Biggar (Home Rule MP for Cavan, 1874–90) converted from Presbyterianism to Catholicism. However, the widely held view that religious conversion was relatively unusual in Ireland between 1879 and 1914 meant that when it did occur it tended to be reported and remarked upon especially if the individual in question held a high-profile position in Irish society (like Forster or Biggar). Having said that, among the less-well-known members of the Irish elite included in this study, it is possible that my assumption that individuals usually shared the same religious affiliations as their families (and wider families) has caused me to overlook some individuals who may have converted to a different faith to that of their families. The second main objection to my assumption that individuals usually shared the same faith as their wider families is that some individuals married outside their faith. John Redmond, the Catholic leader of the Irish Parliamentary Party, for example, married a Protestant, as did Arthur Lynch (Catholic Home Rule MP for Galway city, 1901–3, and west Clare, 1909–18) whose wife was a Methodist. However, censal evidence suggests that 'mixed' marriages between Protestants and Catholics were comparatively rare in early twentieth-century Ireland. Of forty-two Dublin-based senior civil servants in 1911 about whom information on their spouse is available, for instance, only two (less than 5 per cent) were the members of 'mixed' marriages, and—if this evidence is broadly similar to that of the rest of the Irish elite—almost all the members of the Irish elite (at least 95 per cent) were probably married to people of the same religious belief as themselves. Despite these two objections, then, it is probably fair to say that in a large group of almost 1,200 people the relatively few cases of conversion and mixed marriage probably do not dramatically contradict the assumption that most individuals shared the same religious beliefs as their spouses, families, and extended families.

The recent online provision of the 1911 census for Dublin (easily searchable by name) has enabled me precisely to identify the religious persuasion of a large number of individuals and particularly those who were civil servants and businessmen in 1911 (since many of them lived in Dublin city or county). Problematic cases—where I could not identify an individual's religious affiliation using the methods outlined above—have also been thoroughly checked in the *Irish Times* and *The Times* (online editions where it is possible to search for all the mentions of an individual in the *Irish Times* between 1859 and 2008 and in *The Times* between 1785 and 1985). These sources provide a wealth of information some of which can be used to identify an individual's religious persuasion. Even so, I was unable satisfactorily to identify the religious persuasion of some of the members of the Irish elite who are included in this study, and in such cases I have entered a 'Don't know' in the database. I should also explain that the identification of religious affiliation was not a problem for the religious elite discussed in Chapter 6 or for the senior members of the police force (discussed in Chapter 3) since the Royal Irish Constabulary officers' register contains precise data on the religious composition of the Royal Irish Constabulary. The only elite groups whose religion was more difficult to identify, then, were the landlords, MPs, businessmen, and civil servants. Given that I have systematically searched for each individual included in this database in all of the general sources outlined above at least twice, as well as searched for biographical information about all of them in the secondary literature, I think that it is likely that the data on which this study is based are extremely accurate. I have also consulted experts in particular fields as to the religious affiliation of individuals included in this study and I would like to thank Andrew Bielenberg, Stephen Lee, Patrick Maume, Andrew Shields, and Kathleen Villiers-Tuthill for providing me with specific information about individuals.

General Index

Butt, Isaac 155, 156, 245
Byrne, John Peter 106
Byrne, Dr Joseph 107
Byrne, Sir Joseph Aloysius 106–7

Cadogan, George 55, 56, 88, 92
Cahill, Michael 157
Cairns, Alice 228
Cairns, W. P. 228
Caledon, Earl of 27
Cameron, Charles Ewen 117
Campbell, Henry James Mussen 182, 183
Campbell, John 63, 72
Canada 8, 30, 65, 208, 209
Cannadine, David 2, 309 n. 27
Canning, Bernard J. 323
Cape Frontier War 27
Carden, Andrew 117
Carden, Arnold Philip 117
Carlisle 310
Carlisle, Earl of 105
Carlton club 32, 34, 37, 60, 70, 147, 184, 222, 223
Carroll, John 204
Carson, Sir Edward 163, 182, 183, 187, 284
Carson, William Burton 228, 230
Cashel 249, 252, 255
Castlebar 264
Castlerea 187
Castlereagh, Viscount 145
Castlestuart, Earl of 44
Castletown, Lord 47
Catholic Association 189, 315
Catholic Association (of Daniel O'Connell) 156
Catholic Commercial Club 35
Catholic Church, Irish 3, 5, 143, 164, 168, 170, 197, 232, 242, 244, 249–74, 295, 304, 321
  bishops of the 8, 248, 257–9, 292, 293, 296, 322
    and academic experience 266–7
    age profile of 265–6
    education of 263–5
    and gentlemen's clubs 273
    and labourers' agitations 271–2
    and the Land League 267–70
    power of 252–4
    provenance of 259–63, 292
    recruitment of 254–5, 258–9, 291, 301
  and the Catholic population 249
  and church-building 246–7
  'devotional revolution' in the 246–7, 256, 267
  hierarchy of the 243, 245, 246, 247, 249, 267, 268, 270, 272, 294, 296

influence over the British state 242, 244–6, 302
  and the Irish Parliamentary Party (IPP) 245, 246
  and the National education system 244
  nepotism within the 252, 258, 265–6
  number of clergy in the 246–7
  and politics 257–8, 267, 268, 273, 294
  and the Pope 249, 253, 254, 255, 258, 266, 268
  power of the 242, 246–7, 272
  priests of the 249
    education of 250–1
    income of 251–2
    provenance of 249–50
    recruitment of 251, 291
  Propaganda 249, 254, 257, 258
  reform of the 256–8, 266
  structure of the 248–9
  see also Catholicism; Catholics
Catholicism 46–7, 56, 248
Catholics 10, 53, 54, 60, 61, 62, 63, 65, 72, 75, 81–3, 88, 89, 97, 98, 314
  and access to education 76–9, 138
  see also discrimination, 'anti-Catholic'; Ireland, 'Catholic middle class in'
Cavan (county) 117, 279, 324
Cavendish, Frederick 58
Chaine, James 146, 153, 181, 207
Chamberlain, Neville 104, 106, 118, 124, 133
Chambers, James 183
Chatterton, Sinclair Dickson Smith 115
Cherry, Rt. Hon. Richard 282
China 290
Church of England 144, 164, 285
Church of Ireland 4, 5, 7, 33, 39, 46, 64, 82, 86, 97, 109, 144, 164, 202, 235, 242, 247, 274–85, 291, 294, 295, 321
  bishops of the 248, 262, 274–5, 290, 292, 293, 322
    age profile of 283–4
    and gentlemen's clubs 282–3
    nationality of 281
    social and educational background of 278–82, 284–5, 293
  and the British state 242–3
  diocesan structure of the 274–5
  disestablishment of the 243, 248, 276, 277, 278, 279, 284, 285, 290, 291, 292, 293, 301, 302
  income of clerics of the 275–6
  and the Irish landlord elite 279–80
  'openness' of the 301
  and politics 284, 293, 294
  power of the 242–3, 276, 291, 292
  recruitment practices within 276–7, 285, 301–2